BATTLES ON SCREEN

COLIN M. BARRON

Other Books by Colin M. Barron

Running Your Own Private Residential or Nursing Home

The Craft of Public Speaking

Planes on Film: Ten Favourite Aviation Films

Dying Harder: Action Movies of the 1980s

BATTLES ON SCREEN

World War II Action Movies

Colin M. Barron

Battles on Screen: World War II Action Movies by Colin M. Barron.

First published in Great Britain in 2017 by Extremis Publishing Ltd.,
Suite 218, Castle House, 1 Baker Street, Stirling, FK8 1AL, United Kingdom.
www.extremispublishing.com

Extremis Publishing is a Private Limited Company registered in Scotland (SC509983) whose Registered Office is Suite 218, Castle House, 1 Baker Street, Stirling, FK8 1AL, United Kingdom.

A CIP catalogue record for this book is available from the British Library.

ISBN: 978-0-9955897-0-4

Typeset in Goudy Bookletter 1911, designed by The League of Moveable Type.

Printed and bound in Great Britain by IngramSpark, Chapter House, Pitfield, Kiln Farm, Milton Keynes, MK11 3LW, United Kingdom.

CONTENTS

BATTLES ON SCREEN

World War II Action Movies

Colin M. Barron

INTRODUCTION

MORE than 70 years have passed since the end of the Second World War, but it remains a source of fascination to both the general public and military enthusiasts alike. Here in the UK we have countless military museums, including the Imperial War Museum which itself has three branches at Lambeth, Duxford and Manchester, plus the preserved cruiser *HMS Belfast*. In addition there is great interest in the preservation and operation of WW2 military vehicles, tanks and aircraft.

In 1967 the producers of the film *Battle of Britain* could only find three airworthy Hawker Hurricanes despite a worldwide search. In 2017 there are 15 flyable Hurricanes in the world with more in the pipeline, plus about 55 airworthy Spitfires. Numerous WW2 tanks and military vehicles have been restored to running order, including some rare German types.

Almost every week there are news items in the press or TV about WW2 and there is even a magazine – *Britain at War* – specifically dedicated to the UK's military past, while there are several others covering wartime aviation and the restoration of military vehicles.

All this has had an effect on the film industry which continues to produce films about the Second World War. The critical and financial success of Christopher Nolan's *Dunkirk* (2017) in both the UK and the USA shows that there is still money to be made from war pictures. Less war films are being made, though, than in the 'golden era' of the genre which was between the early fifties and the late seventies. There are a number of reasons for this, one being that war films are extraordinarily expensive to make because of the cost of hiring period equipment, particularly tanks and aircraft. In one of my previous books, *Planes on Film* (2016), I mentioned how Group Captain Hamish Mahaddie purchased five airworthy De Havilland Mosquitos for use in the film *633 Squadron* (1964) for just £75 each, including a full tank of fuel. In 2017 there just three airworthy Mosquitos in the world – one in Canada, and two in the USA – and each must be worth about £5 million.

The late film critic Barry Norman once recalled a conversation he had had with respected film director Stanley Kubrick. Norman asked Kubrick why he had never considered making a film about the French Resistance's successful efforts to delay a German armoured division's transfer to Normandy in June 1944, following the Allied invasion. Kubrick agreed that it would indeed make a great film, but the cost of hiring a sufficient number of German tanks would be prohibitive.

It is this cost factor that has probably led to several projected war films being either delayed or cancelled outright. Examples might include Peter Jackson's remake of *The Dambusters*, various proposed films about the Battle of Britain, a movie about the early days of the SAS, and *Destroyer* – a feature about *HMS Coventry's* exploits during the 1982 Falklands War. Cost wasn't such an issue in the 1950s, as much of the equipment used during WW2 was still in service. For example, the Austin K2 Ambulances, M3 halftracks, Bedford

QL trucks and other vehicles which appear in *Ice Cold in Alex* (1958) were still in service with the British Army at the time the film was made.

The ten war films which I have reviewed in detail in this book were made between 1959 and 1998, and reflect changing public attitudes towards the war. War movies made in the 1940s and 1950s tended to be patriotic flag wavers in which Allied troops were clean-cut heroes with the Germans and Japanese being dastardly villains. Admiral Lutgens in *Sink the Bismarck!* (1960), for example, is a stereotypical Nazi.

A year later *The Guns of Navarone* (1961) was one of the first movies to have a clear anti-war message. Alistair MacLean's original novel was a straightforward thriller but screenwriter Carl Foreman made many changes, in line with his own pacifist, left-wing views. Mallory's commando team are tired, war-weary and cynical about the war. Despite Foreman's efforts, the movie was hugely popular as an action thriller with most cinemagoers not noticing the anti-war slant.

By the late sixties though, the conflict in Vietnam and the rise of flower power, hippies, and various peace and anti-nuclear movements had lead to public distaste for any movie glorifying military action. Thus *The Bridge at Remagen* (1969) contains many subtle references to Vietnam. The US soldiers in the movie are depicted as being tired of the war and sceptical about decisions made by their commanders.

Kelly's Heroes (1970) takes things a stage further. Like the troops in *The Bridge at Remagen,* the US soldiers are more interested in food, drink, booze, women and money than in wartime combat, but they are capable of fighting courageously when they are presented with a large financial incentive. In this venture they are joined by a hippy tank commander, Oddball (Donald Sutherland), who represents what was actually happening in the USA at the time the film was made.

The last film considered in detail in the book, *Saving Private Ryan* (1998), is without a doubt a technical masterpiece. Yet it attracted some criticism at the time from British veterans of the Normandy campaign who complained that the film never mentioned the role of America's Allies in the D-Day invasion. This is a recurrent complaint about Hollywood's depiction of the war. When the Errol Flynn movie *Objective Burma* (1945) was first shown in British cinemas, it lead to riots involving British veterans who complained (quite correctly) that the majority of Allied troops in the Burma theatre were from the UK.

There have been similar complaints about more recent movies such as *Patton* (1970), *U-571* (2000) and *Pearl Harbor* (2001), with the latter suggesting that Ben Affleck's character – Rafe McCawley – won the Battle of Britain for the RAF (though in 1941 not 1940!). It should also be noted that screenings of the American TV series *The Rat Patrol* (1966) on BBC 1 were abruptly stopped after complaints from British Eighth Army veterans who pointed out that the series suggested that the war in North Africa was won solely by the Americans.

I hope you enjoy my choice of movies, which I consider to represent a cross-section of the genre. In case you are wondering why no aviation movies (such as *Battle of Britain*) are included, it is because they are covered in my earlier volume *Planes on Film* (2016) which is available from the usual outlets.

Colin M. Barron
August 2017

NAVAL EPIC
KENNETH MORE · DANA WYNTER
in JOHN BRABOURNE'S Production of
SINK THE BISMARCK!
U
LEWIS GILBERT
CINEMASCOPE

1

SINK THE BISMARCK!

(1960)

Twentieth Century Fox Film Corporation

Director: Lewis Gilbert
Producer: John Brabourne
Screenwriter: Edmund H. North,
from a book by C.S. Forester

S*INK the Bismarck!* is probably the best film ever made about British naval operations in WW2. It was one of several Second World War movies directed by Lewis Gilbert, who had served in the RAF Film Unit during WW2 and went on to direct several classic British war movies including *Albert RN* (1953), *The Sea Shall Not Have Them* (1954), *Reach for the Sky* (1956), and *Carve Her Name with Pride* (1958). He subsequently helmed three very spectacular James Bond movies: *You Only Live Twice* (1967), *The Spy Who Loved Me* (1977), and *Moonraker* (1979). Gilbert also directed the original version of *Alfie* (1966) starring Michael Caine, and two very successful eighties movies: *Educating Rita* (1983) and *Shirley Valentine* (1989).

The film deals with the first mission of the *Bismarck* in May 1941, its battle with *HMS Hood* and *HMS Prince of Wales*, and its eventual sinking by the Royal Navy three days later. The screenplay by Edmund H. North was based on the

1958 book *The Last Nine Days of the Bismarck* by C.S. Forester, a prolific British novelist who was also responsible for the series of twelve *Hornblower* books published from 1937 onwards which formed the basis of both the 1951 movie *Captain Horatio Hornblower* starring Gregory Peck and the ITV series *Hornblower* (1998-2003) featuring Ioan Gruffudd.

In the early part of the 20th century battleships were regarded as 'super-weapons', something that is often forgotten today. There were even attempts to limit the number, tonnage and firepower of battleships operated by different nations, resulting in the infamous Washington Treaty of 1922 and the London Treaty of 1930. The provisions of these agreements were scrupulously observed by the British but not by other nations, particularly the Germans and Japanese who by the mid 1930s seemed determined to build the biggest battleships that were possible, mounting the largest guns that could be manufactured. As things happened, the Second World War proved to be the swansong of the battleship as even the largest warships with the thickest of armour mounting huge numbers of anti-aircraft guns proved vulnerable to air attack.

One problem facing the makers of *Sink the Bismarck!* was how to realistically depict vessels which no longer existed, as most of the ships which took part in the various sea battles in the film had either been sunk or scrapped many years before. One exception was *HMS Victorious*, which was a brand new aircraft carrier in May 1941 and remained in service until the late 1960s. In the film *Victorious* plays herself and also doubles for *HMS Ark Royal* in some scenes.

The producers were also fortunate that Britain's last battleship, *HMS Vanguard*, was still in service in 1959. Although she couldn't double for the *Bismarck* (or any of the

British warships) in long shot as she looked so different from them, many deck scenes and shots of gun turrets (both interior and exterior) were filmed on this vessel. In fact, taking part in this film was probably the most important thing this ship did in her entire service career as, by the time she was launched, the era of the battleship was already over.

The filmmakers also shot some scenes aboard *HMS Belfast*, a *Town*-class cruiser which was in active service in 1959 and is now preserved (as a tourist attraction) close to Tower Bridge, London by the Imperial War Museum. Curiously, the interior of the *Belfast* was also used to depict the inside of a spaceship in the 1994 independent video production *Shakedown*, which featured the return of the Sontarans – aliens who had previously appeared in four *Doctor Who* stories in the 70s and 80s. Director Lewis Gilbert also had access to some decommissioned Royal Navy ships which were laid up at Portsmouth awaiting scrapping, and scenes of fires and explosions were shot on these vessels.

Although as much footage as possible was shot aboard real warships, it was clear that extensive miniature work would be required to recreate various sea battles. At that time it was thought that the world's greatest experts in miniature work were to be found in the USA (rather than the UK), so the first person the producers contacted was L.B. Abbott (who later created the excellent model ship scenes in *Tora, Tora, Tora* in 1970). In the end Abbott didn't take part in the production, so the job was given to Howard 'Babe' Lydecker, a Hollywood special effects expert. Along with his brother Theodore, Lydecker had created many very realistic model shots for various Republic Serials in the 1940s and had worked on a huge number of movies.

The Lydecker brothers invented a system for flying model aircraft on invisible wires which involved three filaments – two along which the model would fly and a third to pull it along. They also realised the importance of making miniatures as large as possible and of using forced perspective and natural lighting to achieve realism. A few years later Howard Lydecker collaborated with L.B. Abbott on the miniature effects for two Irwin Allen TV series, *Voyage to the Bottom of the Sea* (1964-68) and *Lost in Space* (1965-68). Though these two productions are nowadays regarded as somewhat cheesy, their miniature effects are top notch.

The miniatures themselves – consisting of several warships and a number of Fairey Swordfish torpedo bombers – were built by John Stears of Shawcraft Models in Uxbridge. Stears was a keen aeromodeller, and built numerous miniature aircraft for *Reach for the Sky* (1956). He later achieved fame for creating the models and special effects for the first five James Bond films and some of the special effects for the first *Star Wars* film in 1977.

Up to that point, the usual way of depicting moving ship models in British films involved using bottomless craft which ran along railway lines on the floor of the studio water tank, but the ships in *Sink the Bismarck!* were cast in fibreglass and actually floated, being pulled along by underwater cables. A huge water tank at Pinewood Studios, the size of a football pitch, was used and incorporated an enormous painted backdrop.

The film was shot in Cinemascope using an anamorphic lens, but this was not ideal for model shots where a large depth of field was required so these were filmed on standard 35mm stock which was then 'cropped' top and bottom to achieve the correct picture ratio. As a result the miniature shots have a somewhat lower resolution than the rest of the movie and are slightly grainy, something which actually adds to their realism.

Edmund North's screenplay was fairly accurate, though one oddity was that in many cases the actual names of individuals were not mentioned. For example the character played by Laurence Naismith was described as 'The First Sea Lord' and never as 'Dudley Pound'. Similarly, the real names of the Captains of various British vessels never appear in the screenplay. At the time this was common practice in film scripts to avoid litigation, but it is hard to see why this always necessary as many of the characters depicted were dead. Kenneth More played the part of a 'Captain Shepard' who was in charge of the hunt for the *Bismarck*. In reality this would have been Captain R.A.B. Edwards, Chief of Naval Operations, but More's character was made fictional so that various additional elements such as his grief over his wife's death, his fears for his son's safety and his implied future romance with Wren officer Anne Davies could be added for dramatic effect.

The film opens with authentic newsreel footage – complete with the original German commentary – taken on 14 February 1939, which depicts the *Bismarck* being launched by Adolf Hitler. The action then shifts to Trafalgar Square. A caption reads 'London May 1941' as an air-raid siren sounds and Captain Jonathan Shepard walks briskly to the British Naval Intelligence HQ at the Admiralty Arch off Trafalgar Square.

Meanwhile, the American journalist Ed Murrow (himself) is making a radio broadcast from a studio in London. He describes how the British public has remained steadfast and unflinching despite grim news on every front. The British are being defeated in the desert, and the Battle of the Atlantic is going badly with 600,000 tons of merchant shipping sunk.

As Murrow continues with his broadcast, Shepard arrives at his new place of work: a War Room, 200 feet underground. He is introduced to his staff including his predecessor Captain Banister (Michael Goodliffe), WRNS Second Officer Anne Davis (Dana Wynter), and Commander Richards (Maurice Denham) who is munching a sandwich. Banister is relieved to be leaving his post – which he found 'a strain', and hated – for a command at sea.

Shepard is shown into his office. A small room can be seen next to it with a desk and chair. Richards and Davis enter, and Shepard immediately complains about the informality and lack of discipline in the Department. Richards was eating a sandwich when he was first introduced, a naval rating wasn't wearing a jumper, and a Wren was addressed by her forename which he considered 'irregular'. From now on he wants proper discipline to be maintained and people to dress correctly while on duty. (Shepard's speech in this scene is very similar to Douglas Bader's address to the scruffy pilots of 242 Squadron in *Reach for the Sky*, made four years earlier with Kenneth More playing Bader, which was also directed by Lewis Gilbert.)

Suddenly an RNVR Signals Officer (Jack Watling) arrives with a priority signal, which Shepard then discusses with the Assistant Chief of Naval Staff (Geoffrey Keen) and the First Sea Lord (Laurence Naismith). As noted earlier, in 1941 the First Sea Lord was actually Admiral Sir Dudley Pound who was to achieve notoriety the following year when he made the highly questionable decision to order the Arctic convoy PQ17 to scatter in the face of a supposed (but in fact non-existent) threat from the *Tirpitz*, resulting in the convoy's near-annihilation. Pound's poor judgement on that occasion may have been due to the fact that he was suffering from a brain tumour from which he died the following year.

Shepard reads the signal with great excitement. Two large German warships are sailing through the Kattegat for three months of training in the Baltic. Could it be the *Bismarck* and *Prinz Eugen*? The battleship *Scharnhorst* and heavy cruiser *Prinz Eugen* had already accounted for 22 Allied merchantmen, and they had inferior firepower to the *Bismarck*. Pound gives instructions that the Commander in Chief of the Home Fleet is to be given every scrap of information they have.

As Shepard leaves to get on with his work, Pound and the Assistant Chief of Naval Staff discuss the change that seems to have come over Shepard in recent months, which they believe is due to events of a 'personal nature'. They then mention the spy they have in southern Norway, and the ACNS says they must get in touch with him despite the risks.

The next shot shows two ships – the *Bismarck* and *Prinz Eugen* – travelling from right to left through the mist. The two vessels are observed by a spy on the shore who narrowly escapes detection by a German guard with an Alsatian dog. The agent returns to his hideout in a hut, where he sends an urgent radio message to England by Morse code. Suddenly two German soldiers arrive and silence him with a burst of fire. But the agent is not dead, and resumes his signalling before being killed by a further bullet.

The next scene shows the *Bismarck* and *Prinz Eugen* heading out to sea and then the action shifts to the Royal Navy base at Scapa Flow in the Orkneys where *HMS King George V*, *HMS Prince of Wales*, *HMS Hood* and assorted cruisers and destroyers are at anchor.

Meanwhile Shepard is reading a signal from Admiral Andrew Cunningham who is in charge of the Royal Navy's Mediterranean fleet. The situation in Crete is deteriorating as German paratroops have captured Maleme airfield. Cunningham's signal refers to what the Germans called 'Operation Mercury', the invasion of Crete by German airborne troops in late May 1941. Although the operation was ultimately successful, the Germans suffered heavy losses in both men and equipment, as did the Royal Navy.

It is agreed that Admiral Cunningham's Force 'H' will have to remain in the Mediterranean, based at Gibraltar, to guard the convoys supplying Malta. Meanwhile the German capital ships *Gneisenau* and *Scharnhorst* are berthed in Brest on the French Atlantic coast, maintaining a threat to Allied convoys. The Royal Navy is thus overstretched, and even if it had 100 more ships it still wouldn't be enough. He then reads an incomplete signal from the agent in Kristiansand, Norway, which mentions two enemy ships including the *Prinz Eugen* heading seaward at 0335. Pound doesn't know the identity of the second ship but assumes (correctly) that it is the *Bismarck*.

The next scene is set at Scapa Flow, where Admiral Sir John Tovey (Michael Hordern) is on board his flagship, the *King George V*. Tovey answers a 'phone call from the First Sea Lord and agrees that it is safe to assume that the two German ships that are heading to the Atlantic are the *Bismarck* and the *Prinz Eugen*. Tovey consults a chart and sees that there are four possible routes the German ships could take to reach the Atlantic, including the Denmark Strait between Iceland and Greenland.

The next shot shows a Photo Reconnaissance (PR) Spitfire flying high above the two German warships. Flak bursts around the aircraft as it banks to get a closer look. This sequence was achieved using footage from various sources. First there is a shot of Spitfire Mk.IIa P8074 taken from the film *The First of the Few* (1942). A studio cockpit shot then follows using Spitfire Mk.XVIe TE341 which had been acquired by Pinewood Studios in 1955 for use in the film *Reach for the Sky*. Some footage of Spitfire Mk.IIa P8441, supplied by the Crown Film Unit, then appears followed by shots of an unidentified Spitfire.

A few hours later the Spitfire's film is developed in the UK and confirms that the two ships spotted by the pilot are indeed the *Bismarck* and *Prinz Eugen*. The RAF is keen to bomb the ships but unfortunately the weather is too bad for a successful air attack as visibility would be nil.

Back at the Underground Control Room at the Admiralty in London, Captain Shepard thinks that a number of Royal Navy vessels will have to be transferred to the Home Fleet if it is to have a chance of defeating the *Bismarck* and *Prinz Eugen*. He suggests moving the cruiser *HMS Arethusa* to Scapa Flow along with the new carrier *HMS Victorious* and the battlecruiser *HMS Repulse*. *Victorious* is due to escort a troop convoy with 20,000 soldiers on board around the Cape of Good Hope to the Middle East, so her departure will put the convoy at risk. However, Shepard discusses this with the First Sea Lord and points out that there is a difference between a gamble and a calculated risk.

At Scapa Flow Admiral Tovey announces that the *Victorious* and *Repulse* will be joining the Home Fleet along with the new battleship *HMS Prince of Wales*, which is still working up. As it has only been commissioned recently it still has a lot of teething troubles. In particular, there are problems with the gun turrets and a squad of civilian workers is still aboard.

The next shot shows the *Bismarck* lying offshore in foggy conditions. In the foreground are some snow-covered rocks. Many of the miniature shots in the movie used fog, mist and smoke, which added greatly to their realism. Aboard the battleship Admiral Lutgens (Karel Stepanek) tells Captain Lindemann (Carl Mohner) that there are to be two days of bad weather which will greatly help them to break out into the Atlantic. He says that there will be 'Glory in the voyage, glory for the Third Reich, and glory for us'. Karel Stepanek plays Lutjens as a stereotypical Nazi, but in fact he was cynical about the Nazi regime and refused to give a Hitler salute.

The Admiral then goes on to say that he got no recognition in the previous war. 'The world only remembers winners, and we must make sure it is us.' Lindemann listens to his rant and confirms that they can make steam in 30 minutes. Soon the *Bismarck* weighs anchor and moves out of the fjord.

Back at the Admiralty in London, Shepard learns the news about the RAF PR Spitfire's photos which confirm that two enemy vessels – presumed to be the *Prinz Eugen* and *Bismarck* – have sailed from Norway. Shepard puts two markers on the plotting table.

The next shot shows British ships leaving Scapa Flow. Messages are flashed by Aldis lamp as three vessels (depicted with miniatures) sail past the camera consisting of *HMS Suffolk*, *HMS Dorsetshire*, and (in the background) *HMS Rodney.* The *Rodney* was one of two *Nelson*-class battleships built in the 1920s, and was commissioned in 1927. Her size was limited to 35,000 tons by the 1922 Washington Treaty and, as a result, she was 'cut down' in size. This gave her an odd appearance as her main armament was concentrated in three triple turrets forward of the superstructure, which was itself mounted well aft, making her look a bit like an oil tanker.

In addition, the shortening of the hull gave these vessels a slower speed of only 23 knots. (In naval architecture it is widely known that one way to make ships go faster is to make them longer, and that is the reason that the 'stretched' Type 42 destroyers of the 1980s were faster than the original, shorter vessels.) Nonetheless she and her sister ship *HMS Nelson* had a devastating armament of nine 16-inch guns, the heaviest weapons ever fitted to British warships. Winston Churchill, who had considerable knowledge of naval matters, considered that at least one *Nelson*-class battleship would be required to sink the Bismarck and subsequent events would prove him to be correct.

At the Admiralty, Shepard chats with the ACNS about his son, who is an air gunner on a Fairey Swordfish torpedo bomber based on *HMS Ark Royal*. 'You must be glad he's not mixed up in all this,' says the ACNS, but Shepard replies that he will have to take his chances just like everyone else.

Meanwhile on the *Bismarck* Admiral Lutjens asks Captain Lindemann for permission to address his crew using the ship's tannoy. Some of the crew are lined up in front of a pair of 15-inch guns (a shot filmed on *HMS Vanguard*) as the Admiral speaks. He gives a fanatical address reminding them that their ship is 'unsinkable' and faster than anything the British have. 'Never forget you are Nazis,' he says. One of the anti-aircraft gun crews in this sequence is manning a twin 40mm Bofors, a weapon which was never fitted to the *Bismarck*.

Back in London, Captain Shepard shows the Air Vice Marshal the plotting table with various markers depicting ships. He mentions the problems the *Prince of Wales* is having with its turrets and then goes to his office to write a letter to his son, Tom. At this moment Davis enters with some tea, mentioning that Simpson is off with flu and that an air raid is in progress above their heads. Shepard asks Davis if she is concerned about her family and she explains that her family is in Canada. He then asks why she is not married and she explains that she was engaged but her fiancée went missing in action at Dunkirk a year ago. She believes it helps to talk about such things, but Shepard disagrees as he thinks that getting emotional about things is a peacetime luxury.

Suddenly the 'phone rings. The ACNS is on the line explaining that Able Seaman Dexter has been placed on duty for the next three nights. Dexter subsequently sees Shepard, asking for some time off as his nurse girlfriend is sailing for overseas duties the following night. Shepard is unwilling to accede to his request though, particularly during the current crisis.

Having dismissed Dexter, Shepard learns that Admiral Lutjens is on board the *Bismarck*. He feels that he has a very personal score to settle with the man, as one of his cruisers sunk his ship. Meanwhile, Richards report that a bed has now been made up next to Shepard's office.

The next scene is a miniature shot of the three-funnelled British cruiser *HMS Suffolk* travelling from left to right. The Captain (Ernest Clark) surveys the scene as an Able Seaman (Michael Ripper) moans about the fact that the *Bismarck* carries armour a foot thick. Suddenly a lookout reports two ships on a bearing of 45 degrees, and the Captain orders a turn to port to escape from the German ships. On board *Bismarck* Captain Lindemann asks Lutjens if they should follow the cruisers and destroy them, but the Admiral says they have more important jobs to do.

The Captain of the *Suffolk* sets a new course of 130 degrees to shadow the two German ships from a distance using radar and signals the Admiralty, who in turn instruct *HMS Hood* and *HMS Prince of Wales* to intercept the enemy vessels.

Vice Admiral Holland, on board *Hood*, asks for a course that will result in contact being made at first light as he does not want to fight a night action. The instructions are also relayed to *HMS Prince of Wales*, where two civilian workers (played by Sam Kydd and Sydney Tafler) are complaining about having to sleep in hammocks. Tafler was Lewis Gilbert's brother-in-law, and appeared in small roles in many of his films.

The ship's Captain (Esmond Knight) speaks to the crew on the tannoy, telling them that they will see action at first light. One of the seamen in this scene is played by Johnny Briggs, who also appeared in *633 Squadron* (1964) and had a long-running role as Mike Baldwin in *Coronation Street*.

Esmond Knight was an established actor before the Second World War and then enlisted in the Royal Navy after the conflict broke out. In May 1941 he was a serving officer aboard *HMS Prince of Wales* (though not the Captain), and was blinded by shrapnel during the Battle of the Denmark Strait (q.v.). Despite his blindness he continued to work as an actor, and in 1943 some vision was restored to his right eye by ophthalmological surgery. Nothing could be done about his left eye, which had been completely destroyed and then removed in 1941. Though having only partial sight, Knight had a long career in acting, with his last film being *Robin and Marian* in 1976.

Back at the Admiralty in London, the ACNS is telling Davis about Shepard's past and advises her not to judge him too harshly. His ship had been sunk in the Norway campaign a year earlier, and it had affected him greatly. He also has a son, Tom, who is serving as an air-gunner aboard *HMS Ark Royal*.

Nearby, Shepard orders a signal to be set to the *Hood* and *Prince of Wales* telling them that they should make contact with the *Bismarck* and *Prinz Eugen* at 0510 hours and wishing them good luck. On board the *Prince of Wales* a bugler is playing to signify that they are going to action stations. Meanwhile, the civilian workers continue to grumble about being on board.

The next shot (filmed with miniatures) depicts the two British capital ships closing on their quarry. There is then a cut to some footage filmed inside a turret on *HMS Vanguard* (Britain's last battleship) showing 15-inch shells being brought up on hoists and rammed into the breeches, along with separate bagged propellant charges. An exterior shot then shows a British 15-inch gun turret rotating (*HMS Vanguard* again), accompanied by a sound effect which rather curiously is the same one used for the cable car operating mechanism in *Where Eagles Dare* (1968).

The sea battle which follows has since become known as 'The Battle of the Denmark Strait', and has been studied by naval tacticians ever since. When the film was made in 1959 some details of the action were still classified, so the movie presents a shortened and simplified version of the battle.

On board the *Bismarck,* Captain Lindemann sees the two British ships approaching. He is reluctant to open fire as destruction of British warships is not his primary mission, but

Admiral Lutjens insists he engages them. In reality it was the other way around.

Although at first glance the British and German ships involved in the battle might seem evenly matched, this was anything but the case. *HMS Hood* and the *Bismarck* had the same main armament of eight 15-inch guns, but the German vessel was brand new and had the latest optics and fire-control directors while the British ship was 21 years old and had much thinner armour than her German counterpart. In particular, her deck armour was only three inches thick and was vulnerable to plunging fire (the very weakness which led to her demise). *Hood* was actually classed as a battlecruiser rather than a battleship (the difference between the two types of vessel is that a battlecruiser has the same heavy gun armament as a battleship, but has much thinner armour to make it lighter and faster). The *Prince of Wales* was a new ship with good armour but it only had 14-inch guns and was suffering from a number of teething troubles during the action, in particular problems with its gun turrets.

Thus the decision to put these two vessels up against the *Bismarck* and *Prinz Eugen* may have been a mistake. It might have been better simply to shadow the vessels at long range and wait for reinforcements to arrive, particularly *HMS Rodney* which, with its devastating main armament of nine 16-inch weapons, comfortably out-gunned the *Bismarck*. Thus a much larger British force could have surrounded the German vessels and attacked from multiple directions simultaneously, reducing the amount of firepower the Germans could bring to bear on any one ship.

However, that is not what happened on that fateful day on 25 May 1941. Vice Admiral Holland's plan was to steam straight for the German ships as fast as possible with

Hood in front (during which time it was only possible to fire from the two forward turrets) to close the range as quickly as possible, and then do a 90 degree turn in order to bring all *Hood's* guns to bear at relatively close range. This manoeuvre was considered necessary in order to minimise the time that *Hood* was exposed to plunging fire. At shorter ranges, shells from *Bismarck* and *Prinz Eugen* would have a flatter trajectory and would have had to penetrate the thicker side armour of the British vessel.

In the world of battleship tactics there is a technique called 'closing the T', in which the Captain presents the side of his warship directly in front of the bow of the enemy in order to fire with all his guns while his opponent can only return fire with his forward guns. In carrying out his chosen manoeuvre Holland actually 'closed his own T', with disastrous consequences.

Holland also put *Hood* in front when it would have made more sense to have the thickly-armoured *Prince of Wales* leading with the *Hood* following behind. In addition, the British assumed that the leading ship was *Bismarck* when it was actually *Prinz Eugen.* They had swopped places because the *Bismarck's* forward radar had broken down. This meant that when the shooting started the Royal Navy ships initially concentrated their fire on the *Prinz Eugen*, assuming it was the *Bismarck.*

The *Hood* comes under fire from *Bismarck* as it attempts to turn to starboard. The first two salvoes straddle the vessel, but the third strikes home. One shell strikes the deck amidships and sets off a catastrophic explosion in the magazine. Within seconds there is an enormous explosion, the vessel breaks in two and sinks.

The *Prince of Wales* signals to the Admiralty that the *Hood* has been lost and the news is received in London with great shock. Meanwhile the *Prince of Wales* continues to exchange fire with the German battleship even though her bridge has been destroyed. On board the British vessel the navigating officer (Edward Judd) in the compartment below the bridge discovers blood dripping from his speaking tube.

The *Prince of Wales* puts up a smokescreen and retreats, heavily damaged, while under fire. Captain Lindemann wants to pursue the enemy vessel but the Admiral overrules him. Churchill later criticised the decision made by the *Prince of Wales'* captain to withdraw, stating that he should have continued fighting, but in this particular case I am in no doubt he was wrong. If the *Prince of Wales* had tried to stay in the battle she would have been sunk as she was both outgunned and outnumbered.

The next scene is a montage of international newspaper and radio reports about the sinking of the *Hood*, which came as a great psychological blow to the British as she was a popular ship. In another of his radio broadcasts from London, Ed Murrow mentions that about 1,500 sailors were lost in the battle, with just three survivors.

On board the *Bismarck*, Captain Lindemann and Admiral Lutjens discuss the recent action over drinks. The *Bismarck* sustained one hit on the port side, causing some loss of fuel oil. (In fact she took three hits from the *Prince of Wales'* 14-inch guns.) Although the damage was not serious, the Captain suggests returning home for repair. Admiral Lutjens is aghast at the suggestion and insists they must continue with their mission of seeking out and destroying Allied convoys.

At the Admiralty in London the First Sea Lord takes a 'phone call from Churchill. The British Prime Minister emphasises that he can have whatever ships he needs to sink the Bismarck. Her destruction is now top priority. Shepard elects to transfer some vessels from Force H which is based at Gibraltar, consisting of the cruiser *HMS Sheffield*, the battlecruiser *HMS Repulse*, and the aircraft carrier *HMS Ark Royal*.

The next scene supposedly showing the *Ark Royal* at Gibraltar is actually a shot of *HMS Victorious*. This particular carrier was commissioned early in WW2 and was still in service in 1959 when the film was made. She was eventually modernised with an angled flight deck and steam catapults to operate jets, and remained in operation till the late 1960s. In the film she portrayed both herself and the *Ark Royal*, and can be easily identified as she has what looks like a huge searchlight (but is in fact a type of radar) in front of her funnel. On board the *Ark Royal* Captain Shepard's son Tom receives a letter from his father.

The force hunting the *Bismarck* now includes two aircraft carriers, the *Victorious* and *Ark Royal*, the battleship *King George V* (sister ship to the *Prince of Wales*), the battle cruiser *HMS Renown*, the 16-inch battleship *HMS Rodney*, plus various cruisers and destroyers. The *Rodney* is hardly mentioned in the film but she played a pivotal part in the eventual sinking of the *Bismarck* (as I shall reveal later), as she was the only vessel in the hunting force which carried 16-inch guns. The *Rodney* and her sister ship *HMS Nelson* were the only Royal Navy battleships ever to carry 16-inch guns, giving them unparalleled firepower.

On board the *Ark Royal* the Captain speaks to his crew over the tannoy. The ship is to sail to the North Atlantic to hunt down the *Bismarck*. In the meantime the crews of the Fairey Swordfish torpedo bombers aboard *HMS Victorious* are ordered to prepare for an airstrike.

Meanwhile, on the bridge of the *Bismarck*, the crew realise that they are being followed by two British cruisers (*HMS Suffolk* and *HMS Norfolk*). The *Bismarck* turns and fires a volley at the British vessels. In the resulting confusion, and in foggy conditions, the *Prinz Eugen* escapes.

On board *HMS Victorious*, Fairey Swordfish torpedo planes start their engines and take off. Only two airworthy Swordfish were available to the producers in 1959, Mk II LF326 (at that time owned by Fairey Aviation) and Mk III NF389 which was based with 781 Squadron, Fleet Air Arm at Lee-on-Solent in Hampshire. Although some shots of the real *HMS Victorious* were employed in the production, all scenes showing Swordfish taking off were filmed in the English Channel using the small carrier *HMS Centaur*.

The next shot showing twelve Swordfish flying through clouds in formation was achieved using some very convincing miniatures built by John Stears and flown on wires. After flying for some time, the Swordfish crews see the *Bismarck* through a gap in the clouds and dive to attack.

The *Bismarck* opens up on the attacking planes with its anti-aircraft guns, but these are depicted by footage of twin 40mm Bofors cannon firing and wartime newsreel footage of a British eight-barrelled 2-pounder QF 'pom-pom' weapon mounted on top of a gun turret, neither of which were mounted on the real *Bismarck*.

Three of the Swordfish drop their torpedoes, but Captain Lindemann orders his helmsman to make a hard turn to starboard which enables him to 'comb' the torpedoes (a manoeuvre in which, by careful positioning, the weapons pass parallel to the side of the ship without exploding). Later in the war the US Navy developed a technique to counter this tactic, known as a 'hammer-and-anvil' attack, in which two formations of aircraft would attack a ship from different sides simultaneously and at a ninety degree angle to each other. Manouevring to avoid one formation's torpedoes would result in the ship presenting a perfect target to the weapons being launched from the other side.

Despite Captain Lindemann's expert handling of his ship, one torpedo strikes on the bow on the port side resulting in slight damage, while one of the attacking Swordfish is shot down. Admiral Lutjens then orders him to zig-zag and get out of radar range before the British realise what has happened. Back at the Admiralty in London, the ACNS wonders if another airstrike can be mounted that night but Shepard suggests it is now too dark. Suddenly an RNVR signals officer reports that *HMS Norfolk* has now lost contact with the Bismarck.

Early the next morning Ed Murrow makes another broadcast from his London studio. It is now 24 hours since the *Hood* was sunk. She has shaken off all pursuing surface ships and an air attack. He wonders if she can be stopped?

At the Admiralty, Shepard draws a large circle on a chart. He has no idea where the *Bismarck* is, but knowing her speed he is certain she must be within the circle. The two main possibilities are that she is heading for a French port to refuel and have her battle damage repaired, or else she must be returning to Germany.

At that point the RNVR Signals Officer arrives and reports that the Flagship of the hunting force *HMS King George V* is short of fuel. Shepard feels that they must proceed on the assumption that the *Bismarck* is heading for a French port, possibly Brest. As an aside, throughout the film

Shepard is portrayed as making decisions on the basis of hunches and intuition, when in reality he was guided by Bletchley Park's decrypts of German coded messages sent on Enigma code machines ('Ultra' decrypts). At the time the film was made (1959) this information was still classified, and details of the Bletchley Park codebreakers' work were not released until 1975.

As Shepard is pondering over what to do, a naval rating collapses with a high temperature, having been on duty for many hours. Shepard asks the time and is told that it is 6.30 a.m. (this is an error throughout the film, as both the Royal Navy and the Admiralty used the 24 hour clock).

Meanwhile Force H hunts for the *Bismarck* on the assumption she is heading for Brest. A pair of Swordfish is launched from the *Ark Royal* and proceeds to search the ocean. Later Davis tells the ACNS that the aircraft have found nothing. More worryingly, a pair of Swordfish have run out of fuel and gone down in the ocean.

Shepard asks Davis to stay on late. She explains that it is now 7.00 p.m. and she has a dinner date at 9.00 p.m., but is quite happy to stay on a bit longer. Eventually Davis gets so engrossed in her work that before she knows it, it is 1.30 a.m. Shepard is impressed by her dedication and asks her to stay on in the long term as his full-time assistant

Just then the 'phone rings. It is Captain Farnham from the casualty section, and he wants to speak to Shepard. He has some bad news. Two Swordfish have gone down and his son is missing. A distraught Shepard immediately tells Davis, who reassures him that there is a good chance he will be picked up. Shepard then mentions that he had lost his wife the previous year when their house in Wellbeck Place was bombed. Davis reminds him that she has been through a similar trauma as she lost her fiancée at Dunkirk.

Suddenly the ACNS bursts into the room. He has some good news. An RAF Consolidated PBY Catalina flying boat has spotted the *Bismarck* and she is heading for Brest. Shepard is pleased to hear the news but is clearly distracted. At that point there is some archive footage of a Catalina, with some added special effects flak bursts.

On the bridge of the *Bismarck*, Captain Lindemann announces that they only have 35% of their fuel left. But the Admiral is in an ebullient mood. By the morning they will have Luftwaffe air cover and, after repairs and refuelling, they might go on a mission with the *Scharnhorst* and *Gneisenau*. It will be the most powerful fleet ever.

At the Admiralty, Shepard asks for data on the fuel reserves of the *Rodney* and the *King George V*, the two battleships involved in the pursuit of the *Bismarck*. The German ship only has another 140 miles to go before it reaches Brest. The ACNS realises that the only chance they have of getting the *Bismarck* is if they can slow her down with an air strike.

In the briefing room of the *Ark Royal* the Swordfish crews are told the importance of their mission. Their torpedoes have been fitted with the new magnetic exploders which should give very good results against the *Bismarck*, which is only 24 miles away. The Swordfish take off and head towards the *Bismarck*. But just then the Royal Navy learn that the cruiser *HMS Sheffield* is between the *Ark Royal* and the German battleship. There is the possibility of a 'friendly fire' incident.

Meanwhile the Swordfish formation has spotted the *Sheffield*. As feared, they mistake it for the *Bismarck* and commence their attack. But the new magnetic exploders are faulty and most of the torpedoes explode as soon as they hit the water. Malfunctioning torpedoes were a common problem in the early years of WW2. The US Navy was particularly affected, and there were many instances in the first 18 months of the Pacific War when US submarines launched torpedoes at Japanese ships which then failed to detonate.

One of the torpedoes launched by the Swordfish works as advertised and heads for the *Sheffield.* Fortunately the cruiser is able to 'comb' the torpedo. Just then the aircrew hear a radio message which confirms that the ship they are attacking is the *Sheffield.* They peel off and head back to their carrier.

Once they get back to the *Ark Royal* the crews are briefed again. After the failure of the magnetic exploders, they will go back to using contact detonators with take-off at 1830 hours. The crews get on board their planes and depart. Soon they are attacking the *Bismarck* and achieve two hits, one on the port side amidships and a second on the port rudder, affecting the steering. From the German perspective this was the worst place the *Bismarck* could be struck, because it made her impossible to steer and compelled her to travel in a large circle.

Two of the attacking Swordfish are seen to be shot down but this is pure fiction, as no Royal Navy torpedo bombers were lost during any of the attacks on the *Bismarck*, possibly because the predictors on the ship's anti-aircraft fire control directors were set for a minimum target speed of 100mph and in a strong wind the Swordfish didn't fly that fast!

The Admiralty receives reports from *HMS Sheffield* which indicates that the *Bismarck* is heading north – away from Brest. Shepard speculates (correctly) that the battleship has taken a torpedo hit on her rudder which has jammed it. That night the destroyer *HMS Solent* launches a torpedo attack from 4,000 yards, resulting in a single torpedo hit. The *Bismarck* retaliates by blowing the *Solent's* bow off with her big guns, and the British warship sinks. This incident was entirely fictitious and was added for dramatic reasons.

On board the German battleship a diver has been lowered into the flooded steering compartment, but soon finds that repairs are impossible. Other British destroyers attack the *Bismarck* and achieve three torpedo hits, but they don't even slow her down.

Back at the Admiralty Shepherd receives news that three airmen have been picked up in a rubber boat, but he doesn't yet know if his son is amongst them. A little later Shepard gets a message that he is to phone the ACNS. He makes the call rather nervously and is told that his son has been picked up alive and well. The ACNS is expecting the Captain to be over the moon, but he just puts the 'phone down without saying anything. A few minutes later, Davis goes into Shepard's room and sees him crying in his makeshift bedroom.

Suddenly the RNVR Signals Officer arrives with some exciting news. The *King George V* has sighted the *Bismarck* and is preparing to engage her. An excellent miniature shot then follows, showing the British ships moving from left to right intercut with footage of the interior of battleship turrets, large guns being loaded, and turrets rotating.

Captain Lindemann is pessimistic about the *Bismarck's* chances of success in the forthcoming engagement. They are out-numbered two to one, and they can't do more than 10 knots. The *King George V* opens fire with her 14-inch guns and scores telling hits with her first salvo. Soon the *Bismarck* is being pounded by British shells. Interestingly, the film makes little mention of *HMS Rodney* whose barrage of 16-inch shells contributed greatly to *Bismarck's* demise. In the real battle *Rodney* fired 340 x 16-inch shells, some 9-inch gun broadsides and 716 x 6-inch shells at the *Bismarck*, scoring many hits from a range of less than 3,000 yards and blowing the *Bismarck's* stern off. The reason for this may have been purely financial, as only a small miniature of *HMS Rodney* was created for background scenes. By comparison a single large, detailed miniature of a *King George V* class battleship (used to represent both the *King George V* and *HMS Prince of Wales*) was made for the production, and this is probably the reason that the film gives the (incorrect) impression that it was the *King George V* (and not the *Rodney*) which sank the *Bismarck*.

The *King George V* gets closer and continues to pound *Bismarck* with all her guns. Soon the German battleship is ablaze from stem to stern. The order is given to abandon ship as *HMS Dorsetshire* finishes her off with six torpedoes launched from close range. As the German vessel sinks, *Dorsetshire* is ordered to pick up survivors. In fact the British cruiser had to curtail this activity after only a small number of survivors had been rescued, because it was feared that there were German U-boats in the area.

At the Admiralty, the ACNS tells Shepard that the Prime Minister wants to see him tomorrow at 11.00 a.m. Davis offers her congratulations and Shephard asks her to join him for dinner. She accepts and, as Shepard leaves, he puts the small model of the *Bismarck* from the plotting table in his pocket. As the two go outside the building Shepard realises it is 9.00 a.m., not 9.00 p.m., and suggests they go for breakfast instead. An Able Seaman (Victor Maddern) witnesses Shepard's confusion and remarks that naval officers don't even seem to know what time of day it is. Maddern appeared in similar roles in a lot of British war movies in the 60s and 70s.

Sink the Bismarck! was released on 11 February 1960 and was a great success – even making $3m in the USA and Canada – set against a budget of $1.3m. This is all the more remarkable when you consider that most British war movies do badly at the US box office. The film also revived interest in the *Bismarck* and lead to several plastic kit manufacturers releasing models of the vessel. The classic 1:600 scale Airfix kit was first issued in 1961, and other manufacturers such as Tamiya and Trumpeter have released larger and more detailed models in recent years. The success of the movie even led to a pop record *Sink the Bismarck!* being released by singer Johnny Horton in 1961. It can be viewed on YouTube.

Sink the Bismarck! (1960)
Production Credits

Production Credits
Director: Lewis Gilbert
Screenplay: Edmund H. North
Original Book: C.S. Forester

Cast
Captain Shepard: Kenneth More
Anne Davis: Dana Wynter
Captain Lindemann: Carl Mohner
First Sea Lord: Laurence Naismith
A.C.N.S.: Geoffrey Keen
Admiral Lutjens: Karel Stepanek
Commander in Chief (*King George V*): Michael Hordern
Commander Richards: Maurice Denham
Captain Banister: Michael Goodliffe
Captain (*Prince of Wales*): Esmond Knight
Signals Officer: Jack Watling
Captain (*King George V*): Jack Gwillim
Captain (*Ark Royal*): Mark Dignam
Captain (*Suffolk*): Ernest Clark
Captain (*Sheffield*): John Horsley
Captain (*First Destroyer*): Peter Burton
First Workman: Sydney Tafler
Captain (*Hood*): John Stuart
Admiral (*Hood*): Walter Hudd
Edward Murrow: Himself
Spitfire Pilot: Robert Arnold
Able Seaman (*HMS Suffolk*): Michael Balfour
Officer P.R.O.: John Barron
Petty Officer: Richard Beale
Officer on *Bismarck*: Victor Beaumont
Signal Officer (*Ark Royal*): Brandon Brady
Seaman (*Prince of Wales*): Johnny Briggs
Gunnery Officer (*King George V*): Robert Brown
Naval Rating: Mark Burns
Seaman (*Prince of Wales*): Roy Castle
First Lieutenant (Destroyers): Peter Cellier
Seaman (*Ark Royal*): Donald Churchill
Dexter: Robert Desmond
Airman: Harold Goodwin
Signals Officer (*Bismarck*): Walter Gotell
Civilian Worker (*Prince of Wales*): Cameron Hall
Lt Becker (*Bismarck*): John G. Heller
Seaman (*Ark Royal*): David Hemmings
Officer (*King George V*): Ian Hendry
Officer (Prince of Wales): Ronald Hines

Adolf Hitler: Himself (archive footage)
Seaman (*Prince of Wales*): Glyn Houston
Agent in Norway: Patrick Jordan
Navigating Officer (*Prince of Wales*): Edward Judd
Civilian Worker (*Prince of Wales*): Sam Kydd
Firing Officer: Bernard Lee
Somers (*King George V*): Ronald Leigh-Hunt
Mail Clerk (*Ark Royal*): Sean Lynch
Able Seaman (final scene): Victor Maddern
Air Vice Marshall: Russell Napier
Operations Officer (*Ark Royal*): Anthony Oliver
Officer of the Watch (*Sheffield*): Olaf Pooley
Damage Control Officer (Bismarck): George Pravda
Bridge Officer: Edwin Richfield
Captain Lindemann (voice): Robert Rietty
Able Seaman/lookout (Suffolk): Michael Ripper
Extra: Michael Sarne
Damage Control Officer: Frederick Schiller
Petty Officer Williams: Graham Stark
German Officer: Gordon Sterne
Tom Shepard: John Stride
Air Commodore (phone montage): Donald Tandy
Extra: Jack Taylor
Able Seaman (final scene): Ian Whittaker
Torpedo Control Officer (First Destroyer): Brian Worth

Production
Producer: John Brabourne

Cinematography
Director of Photography: Christopher Challis

Film Editing
Editor: Peter Hunt

Casting
Casting: Nora Roberts
Art Director: Arthur Lawson

Makeup Department
Hairdresser: Ivy Emmerton
Make-up Artist: W.T. Parleton

Production Management
Production Manager: Edward Joseph

Second Unit Director/Assistant Director
Assistant Director: Jack Causey
Second Assistant Director: Claude Watson
Third Assistant Director: Anthony Waye

Art Department
Set Dresser: Arthur Taksen
Draughtsman: Bill Bennison

Draughtsman: Maurice Pelling
Assistant Art Director: Don Picton
Draughtsman: Tony Rimmington
Draughtsman: John Siddall

Sound Department
Sound Mixers: Red Law, Dudley Messenger
Dubbing Editor: Win Ryder
Sound Camera Operator: Ron Butcher
Boom Operator: Danny Daniel
Assistant Dubbing Editor: Archie Ludski
Assistant Boom Operator: Vivian Temple-Smith

Special Effects
Unit Manager (special effects): Richard Goodwin
Supervisors (special effects unit): Howard Lydecker, Bill Warrington
Special Effects Assistants: Freddie Cooper, Cliff Culley, Martin Shortall
Visual Effects Cameramen (special effects unit): Skeets Kelly, Jack Welch

Model Ships Construction: John Stears

Camera and Electrical Department
Camera Operator: Austin Dempster
Focus Puller: Steve Claydon
Clapper Loaders: Roy Ford, Mike Fox
Second Camera Operator: John Harris
Still Photographer: Ian Jeayes

Editorial Department
Assistant Editors: John Gilbert, Norman Wanstall
Assembly Cutter: Jeremy Saunders

Music Department
Conductor: Muir Mathieson

Other Crew
Continuity: Shirley Barnes
Technical Advisor: Lt Cdr Peter Peake, R.N. (Retd.)
Publicist: Bob Herrington
Production Secretary: Phyl Russell (uncredited)

STILL!..THE GREATEST HIGH ADVENTURE EVER FILMED!
COLUMBIA PICTURES presents
GREGORY PECK
DAVID NIVEN
ANTHONY QUINN
in CARL FOREMAN'S
THE GUNS OF NAVARONE
co-starring
STANLEY BAKER · ANTHONY QUAYLE · IRENE PAPAS · GIA SCALA and JAMES DARREN
Written & Produced by CARL FOREMAN
Based on the novel by ALISTAIR MacLEAN
Music Composed & Conducted by DIMITRI TIOMKIN
Directed by J. LEE THOMPSON
A HIGHROAD PRESENTATION
COLOR and CINEMASCOPE

2

THE GUNS OF NAVARONE

(1961)

Columbia Pictures Corporation/ Highroad Productions

Director: J. Lee Thompson
Producer: Carl Foreman
Screenwriter: Carl Foreman, from a novel by Alistair MacLean

ALISTAIR MacLean, who was born in Glasgow in 1922, wrote popular thrillers and adventure novels. He joined the Royal Navy in 1941 and eventually ended up as a Leading Torpedo Operator on *HMS Royalist*, a *Dido*-class light cruiser. MacLean saw action in various theatres of war including the Arctic, Mediterranean, Atlantic and Pacific. In 1946 MacLean was discharged from the Royal Navy and went on to study English at Glasgow University, graduating in 1953. While he was a student, MacLean earned extra money from writing and, after winning a short story competition in 1954, he wrote his first novel *HMS Ulysses*, based on his experiences on Arctic convoys in WW2. The book was published in 1955 and was a great success. MacLean followed this up with another wartime adventure story, *The Guns of Navarone*, which was released in 1957.

Like *HMS Ulysses*, *The Guns of Navarone* was based on factual events. In the autumn of 1943 – following the Italian capitulation – Churchill ordered British Forces to occupy a number of Greek islands including Kos and Leros. The resulting military disaster was one of Churchill's few follies in WW2 and reflected the Prime Minister's obsession with the Balkans and what he called 'the soft underbelly of Europe'. Eventually the Germans sent sufficient forces to recapture most of the islands, and the British were forced to make a humiliating withdrawal at a time when the tide had turned against the Axis on almost every front. The main problem was that the Allies couldn't spare a sufficient number of long-range fighters (USAAF P-38s and RAF Beaufighters) to provide adequate air cover for the operation. Two squadrons of RAF Spitfires were based on Kos but were rapidly eliminated.

In MacLean's book, the island of Leros became the fictional 'Kheros', and the plot centred around an Allied commando mission to destroy a huge coastal gun battery on the fictional island of Navarone. Like *HMS Ulysses*, the novel *The Guns of Navarone* proved very popular and within months of its publication Columbia Pictures announced plans to make a film version, to be shot in 1959 with interiors to be filmed at Shepperton Studios in London and Associated British Studios in Elstree.

Originally it was intended to make the entire film in the UK. When no suitable locations could be found the producers considered shooting the movie in Cyprus, which at that time was under control of the British who maintained a large garrison on the island. It was hoped that the Royal Navy, Royal Air Force and British Army could supply all the troops and equipment required for the production, particularly as British forces had previously helped out with a number of war pictures which had been filmed in North Africa and the Mediterranean, such as *Sailor of the King* (1953), *They Who Dare* (1954), *Sea of Sand*, and *Ice Cold in Alex* (both 1958).

Unfortunately there was a problem with Cyprus, as it was undergoing a period of great instability. In the late 1950s many of the islanders desired independence from the UK and a union with Greece (*enosis*), and there was even a terrorist group (Ethniki Organosis Kyprion Agoniston , or EOKA) which was attacking British forces on the island. The situation was complicated by the fact that the majority of the population were Greek while a sizeable minority were Turks, thus creating tensions between these two groups similar to those which exist in Northern Ireland.

Cyprus did eventually gain independence from Britain in 1960 (although it never achieved 'enosis' with Greece, and the northern part of the island was invaded and occupied by Turkey in August 1974), but in 1959 the situation was tense and producer Carl Foreman was concerned that British troops might be taken away from duties on the film to restore order. For that reason he chose instead to make the film in Greece, with most of the location work being filmed on the island of Rhodes (which became Navarone) with a few scenes also being shot near Athens and on the island of Gozo near Turkey and in the Liquarian Sea.

The Greek government co-operated fully with the producers and made available 1,000 troops (to play German soldiers) plus twelve destroyers, a harbour defence launch, a Piper Cub spotter plane, M24 Chaffee light tanks, M5 halftracks, M3 Scout Cars, M8 armoured cars, howitzers, and assorted vehicles. All of this was provided free of charge. As Rhodes was only 12 miles from Turkey, and considered a demilitarized zone, agreement had to be reached with the Turkish Government to allow troops and equipment to be based on the island for the duration of filming.

The producer and screenwriter was Carl Foreman, an American who at that point was best-known for scripting *High Noon* (1952) and *Bridge Over the River Kwai* (1957). In 1951 Foreman had been summoned to appear before the House Committee on Un-American Activities (HUAC). Foreman admitted that he had once been a member of the American Communist Party a decade earlier but had quit. However, as a result of his refusal to give the names of fellow Party members, he was labelled an 'uncooperative witness' and was blacklisted by all the studio bosses. Foreman responded to these dramatic developments by moving to the UK, where he continued to write screenplays using pseudonyms and he was thus perfectly placed to write and produce *The Guns of Navarone* when pre-production started in 1959. The original screenwriter had been Eric Ambler (who had penned the screenplay for *The Cruel Sea* in 1953), but he subsequently dropped out.

The Guns of Navarone can thus be considered a 'British' war movie made with American money, as would be the case with other blockbusters such as *633 Squadron* (1964), *Operation Crossbow* (1965), *The Dirty Dozen* (1967), *Where Eagles Dare* (1968) and *Battle of Britain* (1969). Between 1950 and 1985 British studios benefitted from the 'Eady Levy', which provided financial incentives for Hollywood producers to make films in the UK with the main condition being that 80% of the cast and crew had to be British.

Foreman made extensive changes to Alistair MacLean's story in his screenplay. MacLean's original book does not feature any female characters, but Foreman changed the gender of two Greek resistance fighters. Thus Louki became Maria and Papayanis was changed to Anna. The character of Major Roy Franklin was introduced, and there were any other amendments – in particular a series of speeches in which various characters question the morality of war and the difficult decisions that have to be made.

For the key role of Captain Keith Mallory, Foreman hoped to cast William Holden who he had previously worked with on *Bridge Over the River Kwai* (1957) and *The Key* (1958). At the time Holden was considered a great box-office draw and was offered a fee of $50,000 plus 10% of the takings (coincidentally the same deal that was offered to Richard Burton for *Where Eagles Dare* eight years later), but he turned down the role as he felt it was too similar to his part in *Bridge Over the River Kwai.* Cary Grant was also considered for the role – as a British citizen he would have met the Eady Levy conditions – as were Richard Burton, Louis Jourdan, John Mills, Dean Martin, Peter Finch, Jack Palance and Hugh O'Brian, but in the end the part went to 44 year-old Gregory Peck. Although Peck is now considered a Hollywood icon, at the time his career was in the doldrums as his recent films had all done poorly at the box office.

Corporal Miller was originally to be played by Kenneth More but unfortunately the actor had a row with Rank Chief Sir John Davis at a public function which resulted in him being refused permission to do a film for another studio. Eventually the part was given to 50 year-old David Niven, while 45 year-old Anthony Quinn played Andrea Stavrou and Franklin was played by Anthony Quayle, who was 46. One legitimate criticism of the film (which was even made at the time of its original release) was that the lead roles were played by relatively old actors whereas in reality the members of a WW2 commando team would be young, fit men in their twenties.

The youngest cast member was James Darren, 23, who played Spiro Pappadimos, while 32 year-old Welsh actor Stanley Baker (who had already appeared in several war movies) played the part of Brown.

Greek opera singer Maria Callas, 35, was originally earmarked to play the resistance fighter Maria but she eventually dropped out and was replaced by Irene Papas, 33, who at that time was a very famous Greek actress. The other resistance fighter, Anna, was portrayed by Liverpool-born actress Gia Scala who had a Sicilian father and an Irish mother.

A number of directors were considered including Michael Anderson, Ken Annakin and Guy Hamilton, and Foreman even considered directing the film himself but in January 1960 filming commenced with Foreman and Second Unit Director Peter Yates shooting various scenes which employed doubles as the cast members had not yet arrived on set. The plan was for all the Second Unit work to be done first and then the cast would join the production with director Alexander MacKendrick at the helm. MacKendrick was born in Boston, Massachusetts but subsequently went to live in Scotland. His most famous films up to that point were *Whisky Galore* (1949), *The Man in the White Suit* (1951), and *The Ladykillers* (1955). He had also directed *The Maggie* (1954) about a Scottish puffer (a small, steam-powered coastal vessel), and it was this experience filming with boats which may have endeared him to the producers.

However, a few weeks into filming MacKendrick suffered a back injury and had to be flown home, and on 21

March 1960 he was replaced by the diminutive British director J. Lee Thompson who at that point was best known for directing *Ice Cold in Alex* (1959), *North West Frontier* and *Tiger Bay* (both 1959). Known as the 'Mighty Mouse', Thompson believed in doing a lot of rehearsals which were then followed by a single take, in contrast to the majority of directors who believed in a large number of takes in the hope that one of them would give them what they required.

The film begins with a view of some Ancient Greek ruins which are in fact the famous Parthenon in Athens. The ancient building, first completed in 433 BC, had been clad in scaffolding since 1833 as part of ongoing restoration work (which shows that Greek builders must be even slower than their British counterparts), and this was removed for the film and then replaced afterwards. The credits then start in yellow 'Ancient Greek' lettering and begin by giving thanks to the Greek Army, Navy and Air Force for their help in the production. The British Admiralty and War Office are also credited (as they would have given assistance during pre-production of the feature when it was planned to make the film in Cyprus), as are the Greek people for their hospitality during the filming.

A prologue then begins which sets the scene for the action that follows. Originally Carl Foreman had intended this to last 10 minutes, but it was condensed down to just four minutes by using monochrome archive footage inset into coloured artwork of a map of the Aegean sea with the fictional islands of Navarone and Kheros added. The animated maps and Greek lettering which are used throughout the film – and took six months to make – were largely produced by UPA (who were famous for the *Mr Magoo* cartoons), but were credited to Halas and Batchelor. The voiceover at this point is by actor James Robertson Justice (who also played Commander Jensen in the film) and briefly explains the plot: the Allies had attempted to occupy several Greek islands in the Dodecanese but had been defeated by stronger Axis Forces. Now 2,000 Allied soldiers awaited rescue on the island of Kheros. There was a problem though, as the Germans held the island of Navarone and its defences included a pair of powerful radar-controlled large-calibre guns inside a cave which was topped by a huge overhanging rock, making air attack difficult.

However, an air attack had to be attempted and this prologue ends with monochrome archive footage showing various RAF bomber types taking off to attack Navarone comprising Vickers Wellingtons, Armstrong-Whitworth Whitleys, Bristol Beauforts, and Short Stirlings. Of these types only the Wellington was actually used in the Middle East.

The credits then follow (in the same yellow 'Ancient Greek' lettering used earlier) accompanied by Dimitri Tiomkin's famous theme music. Even at that time veteran Russian-born composer Tiomkin was considered a legend in Hollywood as he had scored a huge number of Hollywood movies. Tiomkin is also credited with inventing what we now know as the film soundtrack album. Prior to the 1950s film companies had never realised there were profits to be made from releasing all of a film's incidental music on an album. Tiomkin also pioneered the idea of featuring a song in a movie which then became a hit single in its own right. For *High Noon* (1952) he wrote the song *Do Not Forsake Me* which was covered by 27 different artists and even included a version in Yiddish.

After the titles, a caption reveals that it is 'The First Day at 0200' at 'An Allied Airfield Somewhere in the Middle East'. A four-engined Avro Lancaster bomber comes in for a crash landing, flames and smoke pouring from its port inner engine. Seconds later the aircraft pancakes on the runway, throwing dirt everywhere.

Originally it had been intended to use a genuine airworthy Lancaster (PA474) for the scene showing the aircraft aloft with an engine on fire, but this proved too difficult to achieve so a studio miniature flown on wires was used instead. The realism of this scene is somewhat marred by the fact that a second Lancaster model is suspended in mid-air in a stationary position behind the crashing bomber, though this is partly concealed by the 'day for night' effect (which in the 2002 DVD release has been a bit overdone, meaning that you can't really see what is going on). In any case, the use of an Avro Lancaster is totally inaccurate anyway, as this type of bomber was never used in the Middle East. A Handley-Page Halifax or Vickers Wellington would have been more likely. MacLean's book describes the attacking bombers as 'Liberators', i.e. Consolidated B-24 Liberators, and this is a rare piece of historical accuracy from that author as the RAF did have a single unit of Liberator IIIs (178 Squadron) in Egypt in 1943.

A sand-coloured Jeep with its headlights on draws up outside a briefing room at the RAF base. Like all the supposedly night-time scenes in the movie, this was filmed 'day-for-night' as was usual in the 1960s. Nowadays such scenes are usually filmed during the hours of darkness for greater realism.

Captain Keith Mallory (Gregory Peck) jumps out of the Jeep and enters a building on the airfield where he meets Commander Jensen (James Robertson Justice). Jensen has noticed that Mallory is late and is told that the aircraft which took him out of Crete was hit in one engine and was late getting in to Alexandria.

In Alistair MacLean's book, Mallory is a New Zealander, but in the film his exact nationality is never revealed. Peck was unable to master a convincing British accent for the role and spoke in his usual way. He also couldn't speak believably in German or Greek, and these sections of dialogue were overdubbed by actor and voice specialist Robert Rietty (who also dubbed many male character voices in the first few Bond movies).

Mallory is introduced to the leader of the forthcoming operation, Major Roy Franklin (Anthony Quayle) and all three of them, plus Cohn (Bryan Forbes), go next door to the crew briefing room where Squadron Leader Barnsford (Richard Harris) is ranting about the failure of the bombing mission. Barnsford's tirade, in a not-very-convincing Australian accent, includes several uses of the world 'bloody', which in 1960 was considered a very bad swear word. For that reason, in British cinema releases of the film and TV versions the word was changed to 'ruddy'. Incidentally, the same change had to be made to some of John Mills' dialogue in *Ice Cold in Alex* (1958) – also directed by J. Lee Thompson – and that is the reason he talks about the beer in a bar in Alexandria being 'so ruddy cold'.

Barnsford concludes his diatribe by suggesting that the 'joker who thought this one up' should be taken along on the next mission and thrown out at 10,000 feet. Jensen smiles and admits that he was the 'joker' in question, but is appreciative of the squadron's courage and determination. The main obstacle to a successful air attack was the cliff overhang above the gun battery, and one airman stands up and suggests a solution – packing an aircraft with explosives and then flying it into the cave. The only problem would be finding a volunteer pilot for such a suicidal mission.

In reality, towards the end of the war both the Americans and Germans experimented with unmanned aircraft packed with explosives which could be aimed and directed at a target using a radio-control unit in another aeroplane. The German version called *Mistel* involved an unmanned Junkers Ju-88 with either a Messerchmitt Bf109 or Focke-Wulf Fw190 fighter sitting on top of it. Both aircraft took off together as a composite airframe and then the fighter detached near the target and guided the explosive-packed bomber to its destination using radio control. The Americans had a similar system using old USAAF B-17s (Operation Aphrodite) or US Navy PB-4Ys (Operation Anvil), which were filled with explosives and flown to the target area by a pilot who subsequently bailed out, with the final steering of the craft being carried out from another aircraft using radio control.

In practice, none of these systems worked well owing to the limitations of contemporary radio control technology. Many of these aircraft detonated prematurely, and the *Mistel* combinations were appallingly vulnerable to attack by Allied fighters. Nonetheless, despite their lack of success the aircraft were the predecessors of today's 'Smart' weapons systems.

After hearing this rather disappointing report, Mallory goes next door where he is given a briefcase by Jensen (which is locked to his right wrist), and they both travel to another HQ in a Ford WOA2 4 x 2 military vehicle. During the journey, Mallory looks at the papers which include some photographs. The plan is to land a force on the south coast of the island of Navarone and then climb the near-vertical 400 foot cliff. As the cliff is considered unclimbable, the top is not guarded.

Once they reach their HQ, Mallory examines the photos of the cliff with a magnifying glass. Although he was a climber before the war, he declares that it would indeed be impossible to scale that particular escarpment. 'It can't be done', he says.

Major Franklin then offers to 'have a go' at climbing the cliff as the situation is so desperate. If nothing is done, 2,000 men on Kheros will be killed or captured. Mallory reluctantly agrees to take part as he realises Franklin won't be able to manage the climb and no-one else is available.

In the next scene Jensen introduces Mallory to the other members of his team by means of large monochrome photos (a bit like the 'dossier' scene at the start of each episode of the TV series *Mission Impossible*). First there is Andrea Stavrous (Anthony Quinn), a former Major in the Greek Army who has been working as a partisan on Crete with Mallory. Then there is Corporal Miller (David Niven), a former Professor of Chemistry who is a genius with explosives and once blew up Rommel's HQ in North Africa without causing any collateral damage. In Alistair MacLean's novel, Miller was American and a former silver miner who was similar to Shaffer in the book *Where Eagles Dare* as he kept addressing the mission leader as 'Boss'.

The radio operator for the team is Brown (Stanley Baker), who is also an excellent engineer and very proficient with a knife. During the Spanish Civil War he was known as the 'Butcher of Barcelona' owing to his skill at killing Germans with a blade. Lastly there is Spiro Pappadimos (James Darren), a young Greek who had spent much of his life in the USA and was good at killing whether with a gun or a knife. At the time Darren was a teen idol and pop star, and was glad to be cast against type as a ruthless killer.

Jensen emphasises that the team must destroy the guns on Navarone before six Royal Navy destroyers can evacuate the 2,000 troops on Kheros. At that point a car arrives to take Mallory to a nearby hotel where Stavrou is waiting, lying on top of the bed smoking a pipe, reading a newspaper and wearing a shoulder holster.

Once Mallory has departed, Cohn gives Jensen a coffee. As he sips it, he expresses doubts about the chance of the mission succeeding but concedes that war can sometimes bring out the best in people as they discover qualities of ingenuity, courage and self-sacrifice that they never knew they had.

The next scene uses a double-exposure technique (a method repeated throughout the film) to show footage of a white RAF Consolidated PBY Catalina flying boat on its way to the Greek island of Castelrosso as a moving map shows their route. The Catalina is correct for the period, although they weren't usually operated by the RAF in the Middle East. In MacLean's book the aircraft is a Short Sunderland, a type which had only recently been retired by the RAF at the time the film was made. The Greek Armed Forces did not operate this type, so a civilian example had to be borrowed for this scene and RAF roundels applied.

The caption 'The First Day 1800 hrs' is overlaid on the screen as the aircraft taxies into the harbour and a launch comes alongside. The commando team, now wearing standard British Army woollen battledress and berets, check their equipment as they wait for transport to take them to the local Army HQ. Brown practices with his knife while Pappadimos checks his pistol and silencer. Corporal Miller, though, looks bored as he lies on his kit bag and smokes. Niven was a lifelong non-smoker but took up the habit especially for the film. Eventually an officer, Major Baker (Allan Cuthbertson), arrives with Sergeant Grogan (Percy Herbert) with transport to take the team to room in a local Army base. Stavrou immediately gets to work checking for hidden microphones while revealing that he is a Colonel in the Greek 19th motorized regiment, a military unit which no longer exists.

Major Franklin spreads out a map on the table and starts to reveal details of the mission, but Stavrou says he has an alternative route and asks for a pencil. On a piece of paper he writes a few words to tell everyone to keep talking and holds it up. While the others appear to discuss this alternative plan he tiptoes to the door and pulls it open suddenly causing the laundry boy Nicolai (Tutte Lenkow) to fall into the room. Stavrou realises he has been listening for some time and starts to slap the boy on the face while questioning him in Greek. The boy refuses to talk so Major Baker is summoned.

Baker refuses to listen to the team's concerns. As far he is concerned, Nicolai is just the laundry boy and doesn't speak English so is no threat. Franklin gets angry, pointing out that he was discovered listening at the door and was carrying a knife. He demands that Major Baker arrest him and lock him up at least until the mission is over. Baker refuses so Franklin tells Pappadimos to shoot Nicolai and kill Baker as well if he tries to stop him. Baker is outraged, but Mallory backs up Franklin and points out that it would only take one 'phone call from him to get Baker sent back to the UK on the next troopship and a demotion to the rank of private. Eventually Baker agrees to do as Franklin suggests, and Sergeant Grogan marches Nicolai to the cells.

The next scene shows the Catalina flying to its next destination (indicated by a superimposed map display) with the team on board. A caption reveals that it is 'The Second Day at 0730 hrs'.

Mallory inspects the boat they have been offered – an old 55 foot caique (Greek fishing boat) which has clearly seen better days. Major Weaver (Michael Trubshawe) explains that if he was prepared to wait he could have the use of a German E-Boat which is currently in Rhodes, but Mallory says he doesn't have time. Brown uses his mechanical skills to sort the engine while Miller tells Mallory he can't swim.

The caique leaves the secluded cove in perfect weather as Brown checks in on the radio and learns that a storm is expected that night. Soon after this, a German spotter plane appears and circles the boat. The aircraft used for this scene was a Piper L-21B Cub with its Greek markings removed. Oddly, no German insignia were applied.

The commandos (who are now dressed as Greek fishermen) wave at the plane as it circles. A little while later another boat appears on the horizon. In MacLean's original novel this was another caique manned by Germans and armed with a 2-pounder (40mm) gun and two 'Spandau' machine guns. The 'Spandau' was actually the name given to a number of machine guns manufactured by the Germans during WW1, but during the Second World War the term was often used (incorrectly) by British forces to describe any type of German machine gun.

In the film though, the enemy vessel is actually a British-made Harbour Defence Launch (HDL) with the pennant number P274 supplied by the Greek Navy and armed with two 20mm Oerlikon cannon. The German vessel comes alongside the caique and the captain (Nicholas Papakonstantinou) orders the crew to take down their sail and prepare to be boarded.

Mallory continues with the pretence of being Greek and appears not to understand the German Captain. The Allied commando team sew nets and tarpaulins and peel potatoes as the German sailors board the vessel and start searching. Suddenly Pappadimos fires his Sten gun through a tarpaulin which is sitting on his knees. The other commandos attack the German sailors, spraying the decks of the launch with bullets and preventing the crew from using their powerful 20mm guns. Stavrou throws one German into the sea after grabbing his MP40 machine pistol. The commandos chuck two grenades at the enemy vessel, causing another German sailor to jump into the ocean, his tunic ablaze.

Miller delivers the *coup de grace* by tossing a powerful satchel charge into one of the patrol boat's engine room vents. The bomb falls into the bowels of the ship and explodes, causing a massive explosion and orange fireball which blows out the bottom of the craft, causing it to sink. One obvious 'goof' in this scene is that the Allied soldiers' caique is apparently undamaged by the huge explosion occurring next to it, even though it is carrying large amounts of ammunition, explosives and petrol! This scene was done for real, with just a small amount of studio miniature work showing the boat sinking. It was even more spectacular than originally intended, as director J. Lee Thompson insisted on using a bigger explosive charge than first planned. As a result the launch was completely destroyed and really did sink, much to the annoyance of the Greek Navy who immediately withdrew from all further involvement with the film. Fortunately all the other sea scenes were already 'in the can', including the climactic scenes involving six destroyers.

As the enemy boat sinks beneath the waves, one of the apparently-dead German sailors recovers consciousness and attempts to attack Brown, who is cleaning his knife. But Brown appears to have lost his nerve and hesitates for a moment. Suddenly Pappadimos appears with a Bren gun and kills the German with a short burst.

The next scene shows another map as the vessel heads toward the formidable South Cliff on the island of Navarone. By now the threatened storm has arrived and Franklin takes the wheel from Mallory as the pair discuss recent developments. Franklin is aware that the German Captain spoke to them in English and wonders if their cover had been blown. Mallory agrees with him but the reason for this is never explained, though Mallory says that 'our friend (Major) Baker may have some explaining to do', suggesting that he had eventually let Nicolai go. In the book Mallory suspects that Nicolai may not have been imprisoned after all and was therefore responsible for the leak. This particular plot thread – which is never fully explained in either the book or film – would be taken up again in the sequel *Force 10 from Navarone* (1978).

Miller arrives in the wheel house with some hot coffee as Mallory explains his difficult relationship with Stavrou. 18 months earlier, while fighting with the partisans on Crete, Mallory had allowed safe passage to a German patrol to allow them to get their wounded to hospital. But the Germans took advantage of this chivalrous act, shot their own wounded men and attacked Stavrou's house, resulting in the death of his wife and three children. Stavrou held Mallory responsible for their murder and had said he would kill him once the war was over. In the meantime Stavrou would allow Mallory to live as long as he could help him kill Germans. Mallory finishes his discourse with the following observation: 'The only way to win the war is to be as nasty as the Germans. What worries me is that one day I'll wake up and discover I have become nastier than the Germans.'

The storm worsens and eventually the boat crashes on the rocks. These sequences were filmed using a full-sized mock-up of the caique in a studio water tank, intercut with some miniature work by Bill Warrington. Gregory Peck gashed his head badly during the making of these scenes, while David Niven and Anthony Quayle opened up old war wounds. Niven also cut his lip and this later became infected from the stagnant water in a sequence set in the gun cave towards the end of the movie. Niven then developed septicaemia and spent weeks in hospital. There were concerns that he might die and large portions of the film might have to be reshot, but he eventually recovered in time to finish the gun-cave sequence.

The commandos rescue as many stores as they can from the boat's hold while Mallory starts to climb the 400-foot cliff – in the dark with heavy rain falling – by driving in pitons. Some of these shots were achieved for real by the Second Unit using a stuntman, but most of the climbing sequences were filmed on a soundstage at Shepperton Studios and were not nearly as dangerous as they looked. The cliff face was created on the floor of the studio with the view looking down behind Gregory Peck added using a blue screen matte technique. Thus Peck only had to crawl along the floor to achieve the effect of climbing a cliff. This is a familiar camera trick going back to the early days of cinema, which was often used to produce shots of people hanging off the top of a high building.

Mallory continues to climb up the escarpment, closely followed by Stavrou. At one point Mallory is in trouble and has difficulty grabbing a rope but he succeeds at the third attempt, thus obeying 'The Rule of Three' in action movies. Eventually the two soldiers reach the cliff top where a guard is patrolling. Mallory distracts him by throwing a piton.

When the guard investigates, Stavrou pounces on him and throws him over the edge. The rest of the commando team climb up a rope that has been carried up by Mallory but Franklin, temporarily blinded by blood running into his left eye from a gash on his forehead, falls on the slippy rock near the top of the cliff and breaks a leg.

Mallory takes stock of the situation. They have salvaged all the guns, ammunition and explosives but the food and medical supplies have been lost in the shipwreck. However, they should be able to get them from the Greek Resistance in St Alexis. Mallory elects to take over command of the mission, something that is noted by the cynical Miller. They will have to build a makeshift stretcher and splints for Franklin. Mallory then berates Brown for hesitating with his knife on the boat and the soldier tries to justify his actions, saying he is tired and fed up as he has been killing Germans since 1937. But Mallory is unimpressed, telling him that his job is to kill enemy soldiers.

Suddenly a field telephone by the clifftop buzzes. Stavrou wonders if they should pick it up, as there may be a codeword. Eventually Mallory lifts the receiver and answers in perfect German, saying 'alles in ordnung' (everything in order). But the German soldier on the other end of the line is suspicious and sounds an alarm. A platoon of German soldiers runs out of a command post and heads for the clifftop in two trucks.

Back on the clifftop, Mallory orders his men to move out as quickly as possible, while Brown comments that Franklin really needs sulphonamide drugs to prevent gangrene from setting in. Mallory realises that they have three options as far as Franklin is concerned – they can leave him behind, in which case he will receive medical attention from the Germans though he may talk and reveal details of the mission. Mallory suggests he may do this without realising it as he may be given scopolamine as a pre-medication (which will supposedly work as a truth serum, though the drug was never used for this purpose until after WW2 and nowadays is regarded as useless in this role). The second option is that they take him with them in the hope they can find a doctor. The third option is that they shoot him. Eventually Mallory decides to take the Major with them and Brown is given the job of looking after him. The team wade through a river and climb through the hills which are covered in snow.

At this point there is a matte painting of Mount Kostos and the caption informs us that it is the 'Third Day at 0930 hrs'. Franklin lies on his stretcher in a cave, obviously drowsy, while Miller smokes a cigarette and then gives it to him.

Brown contacts Jensen on the radio and receives bad news. The Germans are going to land on Kheros a day early, which means midnight the day after tomorrow is the new deadline for completing the mission. Brown goes back to the cave and discovers Franklin is gone. He is soon found a short distance away, holding a pistol to his head. He is rapidly disarmed and then Mallory asks to be left alone with the Major. He then tells Franklin that the mission has now been scrubbed and the Allies are going for an amphibious landing on the east coast the day after tomorrow. The commando team does not need to spike the guns; instead they have to make as much trouble as possible to distract the defenders.

Suddenly a large formation of German troops is spotted advancing up the hill. Stavrou elects to stay behind and delay the troops while the others escape. The Greek soldier proves highly proficient with his rifle (wrapped in fabric as camouflage) and telescopic sight, hitting several Germans and changing his position between each 'kill' to avoid counter-fire. Eventually the Greek retreats, having delayed his pursuers considerably.

The next scene is captioned 'The Third Day at 2000 hrs' and is set in some ancient ruins in 'St Alexis', plus some studio recreations. Suddenly someone arrives and is knocked unconscious by the suspicious commandos, who subsequently discover that the 'boy' is actually a young woman named Anna (Gia Scala), working for the resistance, who has brought them food. Gia Scala was a young, beautiful actress with long hair. Director J. Lee Thompson insisted that her hair be cut very short for this scene (so that she would initially be mistaken for a boy) and the actress later got her revenge by pretending to be a trained hairdresser and giving Thompson an 'extreme' haircut!

As the soldiers examine the concussed Anna, another woman, Maria (Irene Papas) arrives and holds them all at gunpoint, using a Sten Gun with a silencer (suppressor) fitted. She relaxes when she realises who they are. She asks for Major Franklin, then reveals her father is a Mr Pappadimos and she has a brother Spiro who lives in the USA. Mallory points out that her brother is closer to hand than she thinks and she is introduced to him. Immediately she slaps him for not writing to her.

She then tells everyone a bit more about Anna, who was held prisoner in the Germans' fortress for six months and beaten until 'her bones showed through her flesh' and her back was covered with scars. She was left mute by her ordeal but is a good fighter. Later a squad of German troops arrive at the ruins, but they are too late as the soldiers and resistance fighters have left.

The next scene starts with a caption 'The Fourth Day at 0800 hrs'. Again, a double exposure technique is used to combine images of a map of Navarone with shots of the fortress next to the gun cave and of German troops on the move. One of the 'German' vehicles seen in this shot is an American-made White M3 Scout Car with a direction-finding radio aerial. The same spotter plane we saw earlier in the movie overflies the countryside looking for the Allied team.

In the village of Mandrakos a Greek wedding is in progress in the village square as a number of German troops arrive. In a nearby olive grove overlooking the village, the Allied commandos observe the village unseen. Brown removes a poultice from Franklin's leg. It smells bad, showing that he has developed gas gangrene which will require the leg to be amputated to save his life. Brown uses the opportunity to speak to Mallory about his role in the group: 'I don't want to be left out; I want to be part of the team.'

The commandos intend to move into the village once the Germans leave, but things don't go to plan. A spotter plane flies overhead, observed by Anna who is hiding up a tree. Then several German military vehicles arrive. Soldiers spill out and set up mortars which they use to fire on the Allied soldiers. The team is forced to retreat up a gully leading to a tunnel in the mountainside. Suddenly two Junkers Ju-87 Stuka dive bombers appear overhead and start to dive on the soldiers, dropping bombs and firing their twin wing-mounted 7.9mm machine guns.

To film this sequence, several methods were used. Long shots of the Stukas flying and then diving were achieved using two North American AT-6 Harvards of the Royal Hellenic Air Force with their undercarriage lowered to simulate the fixed, spatted undercarriage of the German aircraft. This was intercut with footage of studio miniatures of the Stukas with flashing lightbulbs in the wings to simulate firing machine guns. Two-dimensional cut outs of photos of these miniatures were animated by special effects maestro Wally Veevers for some shots. This was one of his trademark techniques, and was also used to produce the shots of Heinkel 111s flying over London in *Battle of Britain* (1969) and the large formations of flying Airspeed Horsa gliders in *A Bridge Too Far* (1977). Some shots were 'reversed' in the cutting room to depict Stukas climbing away after an attack, and a single Sikorsky UH-19D helicopter was also used for shots of a distant aircraft departing the scene.

Eventually the commandos reach the sanctuary of the tunnel, with a limping Anna bringing up the rear. None of them are injured by the attack, though Brown is forced to leave his radio behind.

The next scene (according to the onscreen caption) is set on the fourth day at 1500 hrs where the wedding in the town of Mandrakos is continuing. The commandos finally arrive, with Stavrou, Brown, Maria and the injured Franklin travelling on a cart. The four go into a building, where they are expecting to be met by a local doctor. Instead they are confronted by a German Officer, Oberleutnant Muesel (Walter Gotell), and a large contingent of armed German soldiers. Gotell was born in Bonn, Germany but fled to Britain after the rise of Nazism. He appeared as a German soldier in a huge number of British war films and also played the role of the KGB chief General Gogol in several James Bond films in the 70s and 80s.

The rest of the team (Mallory, Miller, Pappadimos and Maria) go into an adjacent building and narrowly avoid being captured by an arriving German force, escaping through a high window. They make their way to the town square where the wedding continues with dancing and singing. Pappadimos even sings the second verse of a traditional Greek folk song. A small group of off-duty German soldiers arrive, but they are sent elsewhere by a waiter.

Suddenly a platoon of German soldiers marches into the square led by Oberleutnant Muesel, who goes straight up to Mallory and demands his surrender. In the original 'roadshow' cinema release of the film there is an intermission at this point, complete with specially-composed music.

After the intermission, an onscreen caption informs us that it is now 'The Fourth Day at 2100 hrs', and the action is now set in the local German HQ where Oberleutnant Muesel addresses Captain Mallory. He starts off by congratulating the Captain on the success of his mission so far, but points out that his position is grim as his team have been captured wearing civilian clothes and could therefore be shot as spies. However, if he would tell him where the explosives are hidden then he and his team will be treated leniently. A Captain in the SS is coming and his methods are 'most severe'. As a historical note, in 1942 Hitler issued a notorious order that all captured Allied commandos were to be shot, even if they were wearing uniforms.

Suddenly Stavrou moves forward and claims to be a simple Greek peasant, a fisherman from Cyprus who was taken prisoner by the team two days previously and had been forced to help them. But Muesel doubts his story. Why then was he wearing a shoulder holster when he was caught?

Things get even worse for Stavrou as the sadistic SS Officer Hauptmann Sessler (George Mikell) arrives and is even more suspicious than Muesel. But Stavrou sticks to his story and is slapped by Muesel. The Germans have a file on

Stavrou (which includes his photo), and thus know his true identity.

Sessler now tries to find the location of the explosives by threatening to torture Franklin and takes out his Luger pistol. He holds it above Franklin's broken leg and prepares to press it into one of his infected compound fractures. By this time Stavrou is crawling about the floor, pretending to be sick. As two German soldiers try to pick him up, he overpowers them. Within seconds the highly skilled Allied saboteurs have turned the tables on their captors and have grabbed their weapons.

Using a captured MP40 machine pistol, Mallory threatens Sessler and forces him to ask his sentry to come into the room so he can be overpowered. He then tells Sessler to use his 'phone to say that he is not to be disturbed until further notice, while reminding him that he speaks perfect German. Mallory then speaks to Franklin, reminding him that an amphibious landing is to take place the following night.

The sabotage team steal the Germans' uniforms and tie them up. Mallory tells Sessler that he is going to leave behind a wounded British officer (Franklin) and expects him to receive medical treatment. Sessler emphasises that the Wehrmacht does not make war on wounded men. However, he also refuses to tell Mallory where the radio room is. He is then gagged by Brown.

Before the commandos depart Miller speaks to Franklin, saying that after the war they can look forward to going to a restaurant for delicacies like roast beef, Yorkshire pudding and steak and kidney pie.

The team then move into the square and steal a German truck (actually an American-made Dodge M-601 weapons carrier). Stavrou, Mallory and Maria sit in the front while the rest climb in the back. Using the truck, they charge into a German checkpoint while the soldiers in the back shoot the guards as they crash through. As the vehicle travels into the Greek countryside, Maria talks to Stavrou while she drives. She asks him if he is married and he explains that his wife and children are dead. After asking him if he has killed many people, she announces that she likes him and he confirms that he has similar feelings for her. This scene never featured in MacLean's book, in which the two Greek partisans were male, but Carl Foreman changed the gender of the two resistance fighters to introduce an element of romance into the story. Alistair MacLean tended to avoid having sexual or romantic scenes in his stories, as he felt they slowed up the action.

The team take shelter in a monastery for the evening. Stavrou gives himself a clean shave and removes his moustache while Brown also shaves, so that they can pass for German soldiers. As the commandos eat and drink, Mallory tells them that they will put the lights out in five minutes as they will need to get as much rest as possible before the mission. The next morning they will have to get a different vehicle (as the Germans will be looking for the stolen truck). Mallory is gambling that Franklin, under the influence of scopolamine, will reveal details of the non-existent amphibious assault on the island while he and Miller attack the guns. Stavrou, Pappadimos and Brown are to create diversions to keep the Germans occupied while the two women steal a fast boat from the harbour.

Miller, though, is angry, wondering what will happen if the Germans don't use scopolamine. Will they resort to more 'traditional' methods – in other words, torture?

'You've used up an important human being. You're a ruthless human being,' he screams. Miller then rants for a few minutes about the futility of war, saying that he has been on a hundred missions that never achieved anything. He is then asked about the frightening prospect of Turkey joining the war on the side of the Germans and he says he doesn't care.

'What about the 2,000 men on Kheros?' asks Mallory.

Stavrou then joins the debate, pointing out that Major Franklin was already finished when he broke his leg on the cliff. Miller then finishes his diatribe by saying that he hopes he gets the chance to use Mallory in the same way he has used Franklin. This whole sequence doesn't appear in MacLean's novel, and is one of a few 'anti-war' speeches inserted into the screenplay by Foreman in accordance with his own pacifist views.

Mallory takes the first watch outside the door, and after a few minutes he is joined by Anna. Mallory asks her if she felt he has made the right decision, but the mute Anna doesn't respond. Then Mallory put his arm round her and they kiss. This is the nearest Mallory gets to a love scene in the story.

The next scene shows a bare-chested Franklin strapped to a chair while being tortured by the SS. Suddenly a German General arrives and orders the interrogation to be stopped – instead scopolamine is to be used.

The action then shifts to the Greek countryside. The caption reads 'The Last Day at 0630 hrs' as a church bell rings. The sabotage team's Dodge truck is lying at the side of the road, apparently broken down as they flag down a passing German military vehicle which curiously is of British manufacture – a 1941 Morris Heavy Utility truck with right-hand drive. This is not necessarily inaccurate, as the Germans made great use of captured British vehicles – particularly in North Africa – and it is entirely possible that the vehicle in this scene was one of the many left behind by British forces when they were forced to withdraw from Greece in 1941.

Maria and Anna are hiding behind a large rock overlooking the road. Two Germans get out of the Morris and are quickly disarmed by the commandos, but a third occupant of the vehicle – who has remained unseen – prepares to shoot the Allied soldiers. Suddenly Pappadimos opens the canvas flap at the rear of the Morris and kills the German with a burst from his Sten gun. The team commandeers the Morris and pushes the Dodge truck off the edge of the road. It falls into a ravine and explodes.

As the team set off towards the Navarone fortress, the village of Mandrakos can be seen burning in the background. The Germans have torched it in reprisal for the occupants helping the Allies.

As the Morris approaches the ancient gates of the town, the team kill the German sentries. There is a goof at this point, as the studio shots of Maria driving the vehicle show it to have left-hand drive and the Morris has right-hand drive. It is likely that this came about because they re-used the interior of the American Dodge truck seen earlier in the film for these shots. As the Morris makes its way through the streets of Navarone, Maria points out that this part of the town has been evacuated because the vibration from the guns' firing has damaged the foundations of the buildings. Maria parks the vehicle, and Mallory looks up at the gun fortress which is depicted by an excellent miniature shot.

A caption appears on the screen which reads 'The Last Day at 2100 hrs', indicating that the team has just three hours left to spike the guns.

Meanwhile, Franklin is being prepared for surgery and has been given scopolamine as his pre-med. As expected, he spills the beans about the (non-existent) Allied amphibious assault on the island just before he is given an anaesthetic.

Shortly afterwards an alarm sounds within the Navarone fortress and large numbers of troops and armoured vehicles leave the castle. The German tank formations are depicted by a squadron of American M24 Chaffee tanks while M5 halftracks, M3 White Scout Cars, Ford M8 six-wheeled armoured cars and genuine VW Kubelwagens also appear in these scenes.

In a building inside the gates of the city, the sabotage team prepare for action. But an angry Miller drops a bombshell as he discovers his equipment has been sabotaged.

'The party's over; someone's stood on the cake.'

Miller then produces the evidence: Exhibit A, a clockwork fuse (based on an alarm clock) which has had its contact arm broken; Exhibit B: all his slow-burning fuses are missing, and finally Exhibit C: all his time pencils have been damaged.

Miller makes his point – this is the work of a traitor who must be in the room. He is certain the culprit must be Anna, who had been left alone in the back of the truck with the explosives. He also suggests she had been signalling the spotter plane with a mirror when she was up a tree and at one point lagged behind with a limp which she no longer has. He suspects she has been leaving messages for the Germans, which explains why the team seems to have been almost captured on several occasions.

Maria is aghast at these revelations but refuses to believe them. 'You are an insane man,' she says. But Miller suggests a way of proving that he is correct. Anna has previously claimed to have been whipped, resulting in a badly scarred back. 'Let's see these scars,' he says. He goes to grab Anna but she runs away, only to be caught by Stavrou who rips open the back of her dress. The skin on her back is unblemished. 'QED,' says Miller (QED stands for 'Qed Qod Erat Demonstrandum', which is Latin for 'That Which Was to Be Demonstrated'). This dress-ripping scene was considered very daring in 1961, and was lucky to escape trimming by the censors.

Her cover blown, Anna talks for the first time in the film, claiming that she had been tortured and couldn't stand pain. The Germans were going to put her into their brothels.

'You never had any chance. You'll never get out of here,' she blurts out.

Miller then explains the team's dilemma. They can leave Anna behind, take her with them or kill her. Eventually Mallory realises he will have to kill her and takes out his pistol. He points it at Anna.

There is then a close-up of the muzzle of a pistol. A single shot is fired and as the camera tracks up from the smoking gun, the audience realises that it is Maria – not Mallory – who has fired the fatal shot. Nowadays this is a cliché, but in 1961 it was a fresh idea and had quite an impact.

Mallory tells everyone to get on with their tasks, and he is left alone with Miller. The necessary death of Anna has made him angry, and he vents his feelings on the corporal. 'You're in it now, up to your neck. You told me you're a genius with explosives... start proving it. You got me in the mood to use this thing,' he says, waving around his pistol. 'If you don't come up with something, I'll use it on you. I mean it!' The two depart on their mission, leaving behind Anna's dead body.

The next scene is set in the fortress of Navarone, where German armour is streaming out as Mallory and Miller attempt to drive in. As they sit in the Morris they look at a rough map of the area which shows the location of the gun cave.

Meanwhile Stavrou and Pappadimos are creating mayhem with the occupying German forces. Enemy vehicles are sprayed with Sten gun fire while German motorcyclists are brought down by nets stretched across the road.

As the diversions continue, Mallory and Miller drive into the courtyard of the fortress and park the Morris as a German song plays on the radio in the background. (Many people think this song is 'Lilli Marleen' as sung by Lale Andersen, but it is actually 'Treu Sein' – a track specially composed for the movie by Dimitri Tiomkin and sung by Elga Andersen. It can be heard on YouTube.) They notice some rails on the ground which wind their way into a corridor leading to the gun cave. There are a pair of open, metal, vault-style doors at the entrance to the corridor. Mallory puts a silencer on his pistol, enters a concrete pillbox in the courtyard and kills a German guard. A second guard enters and is also shot by Mallory.

Mallory and Miller, in German uniforms, walk from the Morris to the entrance to the gun cave while carrying their equipment. Their journey is noticed by the gun crews who are relaxing in their barracks within the courtyard, but they take no action as so far they have seen nothing suspicious. The two British saboteurs enter the corridor leading to the guns and then close and lock the heavy metal doors behind them. Immediately alarms sound and the gun crews and guards rush to the doors, but they are too late as the saboteurs have got inside.

Once inside the gun cave, Mallory and Miller take the lift to the lower level and see the huge guns in their entirety for the first time. Side views of the guns showing the surrounding countryside were achieved using matte paintings while others depicting the sparkling ocean in the evening light were effected by the simple method of placing thousands of strips of aluminium foil on the fields immediately in front of the set on the backlot at Shepperton Studios. When these moved with the wind and reflected sunlight, and were then treated to the 'day for night' process, the impression was given of a moving seascape.

The huge guns built for the movie were 60 foot long, cast from fibreglass and built by the British aircraft manufacturer Handley-Page. 30 foot and 15 foot versions were also created for some scenes. All these guns were based on the German 280mm 'Big Bertha' siege guns which were used in both World Wars. The huge gun cave set, three storeys high, was designed by production designer Geoffrey Drake and was created on the back lot at Shepperton, taking several months to build.

The Germans start to attack the main doors with sledgehammers as Mallory attaches a rope to a railing overlooking the sea in order to enable the commandos to make a quick getaway.

Meanwhile, a large force of German tanks, armoured vehicles and 105mm field guns have assembled on the coast to repel the expected attack, while in Navarone harbour Brown and Maria steal a motor boat. Unfortunately things don't quite go to plan and, in a struggle with a German soldier on the boat, Brown has to knife his assailant who in turns stabs him back. Both men die.

As this is happening, Stavrou and Pappadimos are continuing with their diversions. Stavrou throws a grenade under an M8 armoured car, disabling it, while Pappadimos engages in a submachine gun duel with a German officer, which results in him dying. The German officer in this sequence was played by Bob Simmons, who later became the stunt arranger on several James Bond films. Rather oddly, his character carries a British Sten Gun in this scene rather than a German MP40. Stavrou throws a few more grenades at the Germans and then retreats.

Back at the fortress the Germans, having failed with sledgehammers, are now trying to cut through the door with an oxy-acetylene torch as Miller installs charges of plastic explosive on the guns. Out at sea, six Royal Navy destroyers are approaching the Navarone channel as the Germans bring up a pneumatic drill to break through the door.

In the gun cave, Miller is now installing another bomb at the base of the gun hoist. Standing in chest-high water, Miller explains his plan to Mallory. He expects the Germans to find and disarm the first set of bombs on the guns themselves, so he has set up a second charge at the base of the gun hoist. To trigger the bomb he has attached two vertically-orientated bare wires to an upright metal post and then smeared them with black grease. His plan is that when the gun hoist comes down, its metal wheels will complete an electrical circuit and trigger the bomb. (In Alistair MacLean's novel, the two commandos steal a lead/acid battery from a German truck to provide some electric current for the circuit, but this detail is omitted from the film.) The bomb that will be detonated consists of some plastic explosive combined with a charge from one of the main guns. (Large-calibre guns of this era didn't use an all-in-one shell containing a propellant. Instead a cylindrical, bagged propellant charge had to be loaded separately from the shell that was fired. Even the relatively small British 25-pounder field gun used this system.)

To cause further confusion, Miller leaves another 'red herring' – an explosive rat – and then departs with Mallory. The two abseil down the cliff below the gun cave as the Germans arrive and then dive into the water where they are picked up by Maria in the captured motorboat. A German searchlight soon picks them out and they come under fire from the shore. Fortunately Stavrou sees what has happened and destroys the searchlight with his Sten gun.

After smashing the searchlight, Stavrou swims out to the motorboat where he is rescued by Mallory who offers him a boat hook. 'Grab it', he says. Interestingly, Anthony Quinn wore a red undershirt throughout the filming and a little bit of it (such as a cuff) can be seen in some sequences. In this scene towards the end, the undershirt can be seen in its entirety (as it can in the earlier monastery sequence). Apparently Quinn had planned this all along so he would stand out in these shots.

Back at the gun cave, the Germans are preparing for action. They have found and disarmed Miller's first bomb and removed the explosive rat, which bursts into flames while being held in a pair of tongs. Suddenly their radar picks up the six British destroyers. The two giant guns are loaded as the hoist make its first journey downwards. Unfortunately its wheels stop just short of the two concealed wires.

Out at sea Stavrous explains that Pappadimos is now dead as 'he forgot why we came to Navarone'. Mallory signals one of the destroyers by Aldis lamp, requesting that they be picked up.

Back at the gun fortress, the giant weapons traverse slightly and then fire at the leading destroyers. The gun crews are all wearing anti-flash hoods and cover their ears with their hands in unison as the huge guns fire. Two mighty tongues of flame belch out from the muzzles of the weapons and a few seconds later the two shells land either side of the leading destroyer. They have missed.

The gun hoist makes its second journey downwards and again stops just short of the wires. The main guns are reloaded and fire a second time. Again the two shells miss.

The gun hoist makes its third trip downwards but this time the metal wheels make contact with the hidden wires. There is a flash of an electrical spark and then Miller's bomb goes off, followed within seconds by a series of secondary explosions as all the ammunition in the gun cave blows up. An enormous fireball reaches up into the night sky as the two massive guns are blown out the cave by the blast and tumble into the sea.

This scene illustrates perfectly the 'Rule of Three' in action movies, which can also be found in the cliff climbing sequence. As former *Doctor Who* producer Russell T. Davies once said in an episode of *Doctor Who Confidential*, it is an unwritten rule in writing that when the hero is trying to grab and pull an important lever he should only succeed at the *third* attempt.

From his hospital bed, where he recovering from the amputation of his leg, Franklin sees the Navarone Fortress blowing up and smiles with satisfaction. All the British destroyers sound their sirens to celebrate the destruction of the guns while in the small motorboat Stavrou persuades Maria to come back with him to Crete as there is a lot of work to be done. It is implied that they are going to start a new life together.

On board one of the British destroyers Mallory and Miller view the burning fortress. Miller offers Mallory his apologies and also his congratulations. At times he has wondered if they were ever going to succeed, and Mallory agrees he felt the same.

Filming wrapped on *The Guns of Navarone* in October 1960, but the Royal World Premiere was not held in London until 27 April 1961. For the next year the film was shown as a 'roadshow' presentation at selected cinemas (normal practice in the 1960s), in which there would be a prologue slide (with special music) plus an intermission and pre-booking. The film didn't go on general release until Easter 1962.

Despite concerns about the film's final budget of $6million, it went on to make $28.9 million at the box office and even proved popular in the USA, breaking the usual rule that British war movies do badly in America. It was also a critical success, though most audiences perceived it as an action/adventure movie rather than an outright anti-war film. It was nominated for six Oscars though only won one (for Best Special Effects).

Carl Foreman followed up *The Guns of Navarone* with *The Victors* (1962), an outright anti-war film which – like his earlier production – was filmed in European locations and at Shepperton Studios. However, this rather depressing movie did poorly at the box-office and wasn't helped by being made in black-and-white. By this time most major productions were being shot in colour.

Force 10 From Navarone

The success of *The Guns of Navarone* lead Carl Foreman to consider a sequel which was originally to be filmed soon after the original and feature many of the original cast, including Gregory Peck and David Niven. At one point the film was to be called *After Navarone* and would have featured a screenplay by Carl Foreman. Eventually the film was titled *Force 10 From Navarone* (after Alistair MacLean's 1968 novel of the same name) and went before the cameras in 1977. The screenplay was by George MacDonald Fraser and Robin Chapman, based on an original story by Carl Foreman. By this time Gregory Peck and David Niven were far too old to play Mallory and Miller, so their parts were played by Robert Shaw and Edward Fox. The director was Guy Hamilton, who had previously been considered to helm the first Navarone film. Hamilton had some previous experience of directing war movies including *Battle of Britain* (1969), arguably the greatest aviation picture ever made, and had also directed four James Bond movies. This time most of the location work was carried out in Yugoslavia in late 1977, with some scenes shot in Jersey in January 1978.

The film begins with some excerpts from the ending of the original movie with Mallory and Miller sabotaging the giant guns on Navarone and concludes with a shot of the two saboteurs (this time played by Shaw and Fox) on the deck of a British destroyer.

The rest of the movie has two distinct plot threads. Colonel Barnsby (Harrison Ford), leading a commando unit (the 'Force 10' of the title), helps Mallory and Miller to steal an RAF Lancaster bomber from Termoli air base in Italy (a serious inaccuracy, since Lancasters never operated from Italian bases). The Allied soldiers are then forced to parachute into German-occupied Yugoslavia after their aircraft is attacked by night fighters.

Mallory and Miller are determined to find out the true identity of 'Nicolai', the traitor who betrayed them during the Navarone mission. Eventually they discover he is posing as Captain Lescovar (Franco Nero) a Yugoslavian partisan, and he is subsequently shot by Barnsby. Mallory and Miller then help Barnsby to destroy a crucial bridge across a ravine by blowing up a nearby dam and releasing a vast quantity of water.

The film premiered in December 1978 but was not as financially successful or popular as *The Guns of Navarone*. Things weren't helped by the fact that its main star, Robert Shaw, had died from a heart attack some months before and so wasn't available to publicise the movie. Nonetheless, the movie is of great interest to film historians as it features the very last score written by Ron Goodwin. In 2016 there were even rumours that a remake of this film was in the pipeline, but we shall have to wait and see if this comes to pass.

The Guns of Navarone (1961) Production Credits

Director: J. Lee Thompson
Original Novel: Alistair MacLean
Screenplay: Carl Foreman

Cast
Captain Mallory: Gregory Peck
Corporal Miller: David Niven
Andrea Stavrou: Anthony Quinn
Brown: Stanley Baker
Major Roy Franklin: Anthony Quayle
Spiro Pappadimos: James Darren
Maria Pappadimos: Irene Papas
Anna: Gia Scala
Squadron Leader Barnsby: Richard Harris
Cohn: Bryan Forbes
Major Baker: Allan Cuthbertson
Weaver: Michael Trubshawe
Sergeant Grogan: Percy Herbert
Sessler: George Mikell
Muesel: Walter Gotell
Nicolai: Tutte Lemkow
Commandant: Albert Lieven
Group Captain: Norman Wooland
Bride: Kleo Skouloudi
Patrol Boat Captain: Nicholas Papakonstantinou
German Gunnery Officer: Christopher Rhodes
German Officer in Gun Cave: Victor Beaumont
German Soldier on Patrol Boat: Jack Cooper
German Soldier at Wedding: Maxwell Craig
German Radar Operator: Carl Duering
Radio Operator: Wolf Frees
British Commando: Peter Grant
Mallory (German voice): Robert Rietty
Extra: Michael Sarne
German Soldier: Bob Simmons
General's Aide: John Tatum

Producers
Associate Producers: Leon Becker, Cecil F. Ford
Producer: Carl Foreman

Production Crew
Music: Dimitri Tiomkin
Cinematography: Oswald Morris
Film Editor: Alan Osbiston
Production Designer: Geoffrey Drake

Makeup Department
Makeup Artists: George Frost, Wally Scheiderman
Production Manager: Harold Buck

Second Unit Director or Assistant Director

Assistant Director: Peter Yates
Second Assistant Director: Joe Marks
Second Assistant Director: Roy Millichip

Art Department
Draughtsman: Robert Cartwright
Props: Chuck Ferrigno
Set Dresser: Maurice Fowler
Set Designer: John Graysmark
Assistant Art Director: Frank Wilson

Sound Department
Sound Recordists: John Cox, George Stephenson
Sound Editor: Chris Greenham
Boom Operator: Jack Davies
Sound Effects: Chris Greenham
Sound Camera Operator: Ernest Webb

Special Effects
Special Effects: Wally Veevers, Bill Warrington, Brian Gamby, Jimmy Harris, Fred Heather, Garth Inns, Jimmy Ward
Visual Effects: Bob Cuff
Stunts: Bob Anderson, Peter Brayham, Jack Cooper, Philip Crawford, Bill Cummings, Joe Dunne, Jock Easton, Arthur Howell, George Leech, Rick Lester, Eddie Powell, Joe Powell, Nosher Powell, Jack Silk, Bob Simmons, Doug Smith, Terry Yorke
Stunt Double (Anthony Quayle): Peter Grant
Stunt Double (David Niven): Jimmy Lodge
Stunt Double (Anthony Quinn): Joe Powell
Stunt Double (Gregory Peck): Bob Simmons

Camera and Electrical Department
Camera Operator: Denys N. Coop
Additional Photography: John Wilcox
Still Photographer: Kenneth Danvers
Focus Puller (Model Unit): Geoff Glover
Director of Photography (Second Unit): Anthony Heller
Electrician: 'Bumble' Lloyd
Camera Operator (Second Unit): Dudley Lovell
Focus Puller: Ronnie Maasz
Clapper Loader (Second Unit): Douglas Milsome
Key Grip: Martin O'Connor
Clapper Loader: Mike Rutter
Apprentice Cinematographer: Abdus Samad
Chief Electrician: Jack Sullivan
First Assistant Camera (Second Unit): Jimmy Turrell
Key Grip: Michael Walter

Costume and Wardrobe Department
Wardrobe: Monty Berman

Wardrobe Designer: Olga Lehman

Editorial Department
Associate Editor: Oswald Hafenrichter
First Assistant Editor: Joan Morduch
Associate Editors: Raymond Poulton, John Victor-Smith
Colourist: Sati Tooray

Music Department
Songs: Elga Anderson
Lyrics: Alfred Perry, Paul Francis Webster
Conductor: Dimitri Tiomkin
Music Arranger (German songs): Benny Carter
Orchestrators: Michael Heindorf, Charles Maxwell, George Parrish, Leonid Raab
Lyricist (German songs): Alfred Perry
Orchestra Leader: Lucie Svehlova
Music Arranger (German songs): Herbert Taylor
Music Arranger (exit music): John Williams

Other Crew
Technical Advisors: Lt General Fritz Bayerlein, Lt Col P.J. Hands, Lt Col. P.F. Kertemilidis, Major N. Lazaridis, Major W.D. Mangham, Cmr John Theologitis, Brig. Gen. D.S.T. Turnbull
Publicist: Jean Osborne
Continuity (Second Unit): Lee Turner
Continuity: Pamela Davies

"The first twenty-four
hours of the invasion....
for the Allies as well as
Germany, it will be
the longest day..."
DARRYL F. ZANUCK'S
THE
LONGEST
DAY
FROM THE BOOK BY CORNELIUS RYAN
Released by 20th Century-Fox

3

THE LONGEST DAY

(1962)

Twentieth Century Fox Film Corporation/ Darryl F. Zanuck Productions

Directors: Ken Annakin, Andrew Marton, Bernhard Wicki and Gerd Oswald
Producer: Darryl F. Zanuck
Screenwriters: Cornelius Ryan, from a book by Cornelius Ryan, with additional scenes written by Romain Gary, James Jones, David Pursall and Jack Seddon

T*HE Longest Day* tells the story of Operation Overlord, the Allied invasion of Normandy on 6 June 1944, and the events immediately preceding it. It was not the first film to be made about D-Day, though. An earlier production, *D-Day: The Sixth of June* (1956), had dealt with the invasion but – in my opinion – was not a true war film. There was little action, and the storyline centred around a love triangle involving Captain Brad Parker (Robert Taylor), Lt. Col. John Wynter (Richard Todd) and Valerie Russell (Dana Wynter). At the end of the film, Lt. Col. Wynter solves his personal crisis by deliberately stepping on a landmine. Love triangles have featured in a number of war movies, including *Mosquito Squadron* (1970) and *Pearl Har-*

bor (2001). *The Longest Day* was a completely different type of film though, as it was a documentary account of the Normandy landings, based on a 1959 book by Cornelius Ryan who was a war correspondent in WW2 and later wrote *A Bridge Too Far*, which was also turned into a film in 1976 and is covered elsewhere in this book.

Work on bringing *The Longest Day* to the big screen started in 1960, when French producer Raoul Levy signed a deal with Simon & Schuster to purchase the filming rights to Cornelius Ryan's book. At this point the film was to be made at the Associated British Picture Corporation's studios at Elstree, with Michael Anderson directing. Unfortunately it proved impossible to raise the required $6 million budget, and the rights were eventually purchased from Levy by former 20th Century Fox mogul Darryl F. Zanuck for $175,000. The screenplay was written by Cornelius Ryan but, as is often the case in the world of moviemaking, other writers were brought in to polish the script including James Jones and Romain Gary with some input from Zanuck himself.

Bearing in mind the scale of the production and the number of battle scenes that would be required, Zanuck considered that four directors would be needed, so Ken Annakin, Andrew Marton, Gerd Oswald and Bernhard Wicki were all employed on the production. Annakin directed the British scenes, Marton helmed the shots involving Americans, while Oswald and Wicki directed the German segments of the film. In addition Darryl F. Zanuck is rumoured to have directed a few scenes on an uncredited basis. At any one time, between two and four units were filming simultaneously to ensure the film was completed within a reasonable time span.

One of the biggest problems facing the filmmakers was that of acquiring a sufficient number of period vehicles, equipment and weapons. Fortunately the armed forces of Britain, France, the United States and Germany were able to help out. One thing that kept costs down was the fact that in 1961, just sixteen years after the war had ended, much WW2 equipment was still being used by the armed forces of many nations. The French Army, for example, still owned a number of Sherman tanks, M3 halftracks, DUKWs, Dodge weapons carriers and Jeeps. Furthermore, the French Hotchkiss company was still producing its own version of the wartime American Jeep called the M201 and, incredibly, this remained in service with the French Army until the early 2000s. The British War Office (now called the Ministry of Defence) also helped out with the provision of British vehicles and equipment.

One scene that might have been very expensive to shoot was that involving the US landings at Omaha Beach, but Zanuck solved the problem by obtaining permission to film 1,600 US Marines landing on Corsica as part of a US Sixth Fleet exercise between 21-30 June 1961. With the addition of some special effects explosions and beach obstacles, this became Omaha Beach in 1944. Zanuck also shot footage of 22 US Navy ships of the Sixth Fleet at sea though the aircraft carriers had to be kept out of shot as there were none at D-Day. Some footage of 1,000 British paratroopers dropping over Cyprus was also shot for use in the film, though this ended up on the cutting room floor.

Many period weapons were still required though, and the Imperial War Museum in London supplied a PIAT (Projector Infantry Anti Tank). No ammunition could be found for the PIAT, so replica shells had to be cast in plastic. Several German guns of various calibres were obtained from French sources and used as part of the beach defences in various scenes.

Six aircraft were acquired for use in the production, comprising four Supermarine Spitfire Mark LF IXs (MH434, MH415, MK297 and MK923) and two French Nord 1002 Pingouin IIs (F- BFYX and F-BGVU), licence-built versions of the wartime Messerschmitt Bf108. The Spitfires were all supplied by COGEA, a Belgian target-towing firm based in Ostend, and were fitted with new Rolls-Royce Merlin engines and painted in Free French markings. No genuine wartime gliders could be found, so wooden replicas of an RAF Airspeed Horsa and a US Army CG4A Waco glider were built for ground sequences. Rather oddly, no effort was made to obtain C-47 Skytrain aircraft for the parachuting scenes, and the finished film has no shots showing paratroopers boarding their aircraft. This can only have been done to keep costs down, as in 1961 the C-47 (and its civil counterpart, the DC-3) was still in use with many of the world's air forces and airlines. British European Airlines (BEA), for example, only retired its last DC-3s in 1962.

50 international stars took part in the film, although some (such as Sean Connery and Richard Burton) only had cameo roles with these two actors only doing one day's filming each. Many of the actors were much older than the characters they played. For example John Wayne, 55, played the 27 year-old Lt. Colonel Benjamin Vandervoort, while Robert Ryan, 51, portrayed the 37 year-old General James Gavin. Even Richard Todd at 42 was really too old to portray the 31 year-old Major John Howard. Todd, incidentally, was a paratrooper in WW2 and took part in the real-life assault on Pegasus Bridge, and at one point consideration was given to the idea of letting Todd play himself in the film. In the end Todd was cast as Howard, who led the initial glider-borne attack which preceded the attack by paratroopers.

To portray the huge number of soldiers in various scenes, 2,000 extras were used, all of whom were serving soldiers in the French and US Armies. 60 Frenchmen were also used to portray German soldiers, and these received three weeks of training by Johnny Jendrich, a former German paratrooper.

Music plays an important part in most war films, but *The Longest Day* was quite unusual in that there was very little of it. The striking theme tune was composed by singer Paul Anka (who also appears in the film as a US Army Ranger as does Fabian, another contemporary pop star) and is reused at the end of the film and in a couple of scenes where it is played on a harmonica and a piano. But apart from this there is very little incidental music.

Unlike in most war films, the Germans speak German and the French speak French with subtitles used so that English audiences can understand what is going on. However, all scenes were also shot a second time in English to enable the film to be screened without subtitles.

The film was made entirely in mainland France and Corsica. The original locations were used wherever possible, but in some cases filming had to be conducted elsewhere. For example, it was not possible to film on the actual Omaha Beach because of the huge memorial on the site. Thus the Omaha Beach sequences were filmed in Corsica and at Ile De Re (an island off the west coast of France), while the Ouistreham casino segment was lensed at Port-en-Bessin.

The Longest Day was one of the first films to make extensive use of helicopter shots, which were made possible by the flying skills of Gilbert Chomat, who many regarded as the best helicopter pilot in the world. Chomat's usual mount was the Sud-Aviation SA318 Alouette II helicopter which proved ideal as a camera ship. Chomat worked on a number of 1960s productions with aerial camera work including *The Blue Max* (1966) and *You Only Live Twice* (1967), but was killed when his Alouette collided with a replica SE.5A during the filming of *Zeppelin* in Ireland in 1970.

At an early stage the decision was made to make the film in black-and-white, for three reasons – to give it a documentary feel, to enable archive film to be used, and to make the relatively old stars look younger. Thus *The Longest Day* became one of the last major features to be shot in monochrome and was the most expensive black-and-white film to be made until *Schindler's List* (1993).

Personally I think this was a mistake, as very little newsreel footage was used in the production (which could have been easily omitted) and the film would have been much more spectacular in colour. The fact that a colourized version was made in 1994 would support my contention.

Rather oddly, the film begins with a black screen rather than the familiar 20th Century Fox logo. Four drumbeats are heard – three short and one long, which are Morse Code for the letter 'V' which is three dots followed by one dash (...-). This 'V' for Victory – which can also be represented by the first few bars of Beethoven's Fifth Symphony, three short notes followed by one long – is a musical motif which recurs repeatedly throughout the first third of the film. (Incidentally, Beethoven's Fifth Symphony also provided the first few bars of the pop classic *Roll Over Beethoven* which was first performed by Chuck Berry and subsequently covered by both The Beatles and The Electric Light Orchestra. The symphony was also used as the main theme for the 1970 ITV series *Manhunt*, which was set in WW2 France.)

The black screen is then replaced by the striking asymmetrical image of a GI helmet lying inverted on a beach as waves lap on the shore. Then a caption (in military-style white stencil lettering) informs the viewer that the film is set in 'Occupied France in the Fifth Year of World War II'.

The action then shifts to a scene of a man – presumably a member of the French Resistance or a Special Operations Executive agent – running through the countryside pursued by a Mercedes staff car. A German officer standing in the vehicle shoots the fleeing Frenchman with a burst from an MP40 machine pistol, retrieves his briefcase, and examines the papers inside. The screenplay never reveals what information is in these documents, but it can be safely assumed that they are false papers implying that the invasion is to take place at the Pas De Calais.

Meanwhile, the German Sergeant Kaffekanne (Gert Frobe) is making his way to the bunkers on a French beach on a horse which is laden with cans and flasks containing the troops' breakfast. The surname 'Kaffekanne' may be a joke by the scriptwriters, as it means 'coffee pot' in German. It is good, though, that the writers recognised the role of horses in the German Army, something that is not usually depicted in war movies. Contrary to popular belief, the German Army was never fully mechanized in WW2 and used 1.1 million horses to pull carts and artillery. This meant that 80% of their towing requirements were provided by horses. The only theatre in which they were not used was North Africa.

A Frenchman looks out the window of his farmhouse at the German Sergeant with disdain, obviously dismayed at the continuing German occupation.

Some stock footage of German troops marching is followed by a brief scene in which Major General Gunther Blumentritt (Curt Jurgens) and Field Marshal Gerd von Runstedt (Paul Hartmann) discuss the deteriorating war situation.

In the meantime, Janice Boitard (Irina Demick) – a very attractive member of the French Resistance in the Caen era – is riding a bicycle when she is stopped by German troops at a checkpoint. Fortunately her papers are in order and she is allowed to proceed. Demick was Darryl F. Zanuck's girlfriend at the time the film was made.

In the nearby town of St Mere Eglise, German troops are preparing their defences while a local priest – Father Louis Rolland (Jean-Louis Barrault) – is telling the local population to be strong in these difficult times. On the beach on the Normandy coast which we saw earlier (and which the Allies codenamed 'Omaha'), Major Pluskat (Hans Christian Blech) is reviewing the defences with Field Marshal Rommel (Werner Hinz). Rommel stresses the need for mines and beach obstacles to hinder any attackers, as the key to repelling any invasion will be pinning down Allied troops on the beach and then throwing them into the sea.

There is a technical 'goof' at this point. The shot of Rommel against a sea background was achieved by optically combining an image of Rommel (filmed in the Studio de Boulogne in Paris) against a black backcloth, with footage of the sea shot on location. Unfortunately in the final cut, Rommel disappears at one point leaving only a view of the sea. It is extraordinary that this error was never picked up and corrected, bearing in mind the number of cinema and home entertainment releases there have been of this movie. My 2001 DVD release contains this mistake, and that was issued nearly 40 years after the film was first shown!

A brief title, *The Longest Day*, then follows, accompanied by a few bars of Beethoven's Fifth Symphony which – as I explained earlier – is linked to the concept of the liberation of France.

Immediately the action moves to a German HQ in France where General Gunther Blumentritt has arrived in a Mercedes Staff Car. Oberst Hellmuth Meyer (Heinz Spitzner), the Abwehr (Military Intelligence) Chief of the 15th Army, is very interested in several 'Personal Messages' which have been broadcast on BBC radio in recent days. These include 'the long sobs of the violins of autumn' and 'wounds my heart with a monotonous langour'. He listens to recordings of these messages, and concludes that they are instructions to various Resistance groups to attack certain targets, indicating that invasion is imminent. Perhaps Von Rundstedt should be informed; but all the same, he doubts if an invasion can happen at the moment as the weather is so bad. A German officer looks out the window at the driving rain as a junior officer arrives to announce that Allied fighter-bombers had struck the Pas De Calais area the previous day. Currently there are five-foot waves in the English Channel with 30-40 mph winds.

The next scene is set in the UK. A large caption reads 'ENGLAND', with the sub-heading 'One of 1,108 Allied Camps' as the camera tracks down from a leaden sky to reveal a rain-sodden US Army camp. In the background are a group of parked M4 Sherman tanks. All carry correct US Army markings, but have the later 76mm long-barrelled M1 guns with large muzzle brakes in T23 turrets indicating that they are late-war versions and not the 75mm M3 gun variants that took part in the invasion. In the foreground several Willys MB Jeeps and 'Deuce-and-a-half' GMC trucks are driving about as soaked troops queue up for their lunch. One soldier complains about the quality of the food, while another moans about the fact he hasn't slept since he arrived in the camp. A further GI claims he has heard the mission is on for that night.

In a British Army camp in another part of southern England, two squaddies – Private Watney (Michael Medwin) and the Camp Cook (Victor Maddern) – are trying to avoid the torrential rain as they eat lunch. Watney wants to write a letter to his wife as she is having a baby.

At a dock on the south coast of England, three DUKWS are being loaded onto an LST (Landing Ship Tank). The DUKW (known simply as the 'Duck') was an amphibious version of the GMC CCKW six-wheeled truck, and first saw action during the landings on Sicily in July 1943. The LST was one of the vessels which made the Normandy invasion possible. 1,000 were built in the USA and 80 in the UK. With a displacement of 4,800 tons the vessels were powered by two reciprocating steam engines and could carry 18 Sherman tanks or 33 three-ton trucks.

As they were fitted with flat bottoms they could be driven right up onto the shore to discharge tanks and heavy vehicles directly onto a beach. The main snag of the LST was that its flat bottom made it roll heavily, making its crews and passengers prone to seasickness.

On board the LST, the bespectacled US Private Morris (Roddy McDowall) slumps in a Jeep as a colleague moans about the stench of fuel and blocked-up toilets on the vessel. Morris is despondent about the awful weather and remembers how his father used to take him camping in June when he was in the USA. McDowall took this role in the film during a break in filming of the troubled *Cleopatra* (1963), as did Richard Burton.

At a US Army camp elsewhere in southern England, Lt. Colonel Benjamin Vandervoort (John Wayne) is champing at the bit, pointing out that three million men are waiting to go. He discusses his concerns with Captain Harding (Steve Forrest) and Lt. Sheen (Stuart Whitman). Forrest later became well-known for playing John Mannering in the ITC TV series *The Baron* (1966-67), which was very similar to the Roger Moore TV series *The Saint* (1962-69). Vandervoort points out that the British have been enduring the war for five years.

In another US Army Camp in England, General Norman Quota (Robert Mitchum) of the US 29th Division shelters from the rain in a Quonset hut and examines a lifebelt. Suddenly Colonel Thompson (Eddie Albert) arrives with the news that the operation is on for that night.

Cota is relieved and points out that 4,000 ships are loaded and ready to go, backed up by thousands of planes. His own view is that they must proceed with the operation, regardless of the weather. The troops have been aboard the ships for three days and must be suffering from seasickness. The longer they stay aboard, the worse their condition will become.

In a huge US Army barracks, soldiers are lying on their bunks while others are gambling with dice. Private Dutch Schultz (Richard Beymer) has won 2,500 dollars and his colleagues wonder what he is going to spend it on. As he opens a letter, Schultz recalls that he once fractured a leg while training at Fort Bragg and spent two months in traction.

In another part of southern England, Flight Officer David Campbell (Richard Burton), an RAF Spitfire pilot, is resting in the mess as he discusses the events of the last few years with his (unnamed) colleague, played by Donald Houston. As Campbell talks, a piano in the background plays a slow, sombre version of *The Longest Day* theme. 'Flight Officer' is actually an incorrect designation, it should be 'Flying Officer'.

As mentioned earlier, Burton took on the role of David Campbell during a break in the filming of *Cleopatra.* It was the only time he ever played an RAF pilot, though he was the first choice to play Douglas Bader in *Reach for the Sky* (1956). Donald Houston actually served in the RAF during the war and later gave a memorable performance as Group Captain Don Barrett in *633 Squadron* (1964).

Campbell's colleague asks if he has seen 'Johnnie', as he had borrowed his boots and is told that he is now lying dead at the bottom of the English Channel as he was hit by ack-ack over Calais. Campbell is saddened to hear this news and remarks that 'the Few seem to be getting fewer': a reference to Winston Churchill's famous speech in 1940 in which he said that 'Never in the field of human conflict has so much been owed by so many to so few'.

At another US Army barracks in southern England, General Gavin (Robert Ryan) of the 82nd Airborne meets Lt. Colonel Vandervoort to discuss the forthcoming operation. Vandervoort uses a blackboard to explain the problem. His unit (the 2nd battalion of the 504th Parachute Infantry Regiment) has been assigned to capture the town of Saint Mere Eglise. If his men undershoot the drop zone they will end up in a swamp, and if they overshoot they will land bang in the middle of the town and be shot up by the defending Germans. To lessen the chance of this happening, Vandervoort asks for new drop zones.

The next scene is set in London, where the RAF Meteorologist Group Captain J.N. Stagg (Patrick Barr) is explaining the current problem. An intense low pressure area is causing strong winds, high waves and heavy rain in the English Channel. It is the worst Channel storm for decades and highly unusual weather for June. However, there are signs that there will be an improvement in conditions on 6 June which will allow the invasion to proceed. Barr was a well-known character actor at the time, with two of his best-known roles being the Vickers test pilot 'Mutt' Summers in *The Dambusters* (1955) and Hobson in *The Moonbase* (1967), a classic *Doctor Who* story which featured the second appearance of the Cybermen.

In Paris, General Wolfgang Hager (Karl John) is on the 'phone to Colonel Josef 'Pips' Priller (Heinz Reincke), a top Luftwaffe ace who has been assigned to an airbase in Northern France. Priller is despondent at his situation, as he has only two serviceable aircraft which he describes as 'two stinking crates'. As he speaks on the phone, the two aircraft can be seen outside the window, though these appear to be painted representations on a canvas backdrop. One thing that gives the game away is that real Bf108s and Nord 1002s have two-bladed propellors, whereas these painted fighters appear to have three-bladed units (with the lower blade apparently missing).

In reality the two planes in question were highly capable Focke-Wulf Fw-190A-8s of Luftwaffe squadron JG.26, but as no airworthy Fw-190s or Messerschmitt Me-109s were available in 1961, the producers acquired two Nord 1002 Pingouin IIs which were French-built versions of the Messerschmitt Bf108 Taifun, a light four-seat liaison aircraft which had a superficial resemblance to the later Bf109 fighter. The two Nords were ex-military machines formerly operated by La

Marine Nationale and supplied by French aircraft dealer Alexandre Renault.

Nord 1002s were used to represent Luftwaffe fighters in a number of 1960s war films. In 1963 the same two aircraft that were used in *The Longest Day* were employed in a similar capacity in *633 Squadron* (1964). Nords also appeared in *Von Ryan's Express* (1965) and *Weekend in Dunkirk* (1964), while the footage of the two Nords in action from *633 Squadron* was re-used in *Mosquito Squadron* (1970).

In Paris a Luftwaffe officer asks for updates on the weather in the English Channel, while Field Marshal Rommel elects to return to Germany for his wife's birthday (which is on 6 June). He has bought her a new pair of shoes and is confident that no invasion can take place at the moment because the weather is so bad. 'Why didn't they attack in May when the weather was perfect?' he wonders.

Meanwhile General Erich Marcks (Richard Munch) is studying a large wall map. Up to now the German High Command have assumed that the Allies will land at the Pas De Calais (where the Channel is narrowest) in good weather. But perhaps they will do the opposite and attack Normandy, where the Channel is widest, and in bad weather? Marcks was actually one of the few German officers to correctly predict the landings in Normandy. Allied deception plans (Operation Bodyguard) were so effective that most of the German High Command (including Hitler) thought the main attack would come at the Pas De Calais and continued to believe this even after the Normandy landings had taken place.

Back in England, Group Captain Stagg addresses senior officers and explains the situation. The weather will improve on 6 June but will still not be perfect, as there will be overcast skies and moderate winds. The Supreme Commander, General

Dwight D. Eisenhower (Henry Grace), says they can either go now in marginal conditions or postpone again in the hope of getting perfect weather. He asks Field Marshal Montgomery (Trevor Reid) for his opinion, and the British Commander says they should proceed with the operation.

Henry Grace was a movie set decorator, not a professional actor, and was only given the role because he looked like Eisenhower. At one point the producers considered asking Eisenhower to play himself, but this idea was eventually dropped when it was realised that no amount of make-up could make the former Allied Commander look seventeen years younger than his real age.

Eisenhower then points out that the troop convoys assigned to Omaha and Utah Beaches have the furthest to travel, and will have to be given the order to sail in the next half-hour if the mission is to proceed. The next available slot when the tides and moon will be right for a landing will be sometime in July. Such a postponement would be too bitter to contemplate.

Back in France, General Marcks looks at the sky and the rain and thinks an imminent invasion is unlikely, while in England Eisenhower decides to proceed with the operation. The invasion is 'on', come what may.

In a huge hangar with scores of trestle tables which are being used to pack parachutes, Lt. Colonel Vandervoort receives a 'phone call which informs him that the invasion is on. General Cota and Colonel Thompson also receive similar calls, as does Lord Lovat (Peter Lawford) of the Special Service Brigade and General Raymond D. Barton (Edmond O'Brien).

As the invasion starts to get underway, various commanders address their men. General Gavin speaks to his Pathfinders, specialised parachute troops who will land on the drop zones, hold them and mark them with flares and smoke for the following troops. 'You will have one friend: God. And this', he says, holding up an M1 rifle.

At a British airbase, an RAF Briefing Officer (Jack Hedley) shows his aircrews an invention known as 'Rupert', which is a dummy dropped in large numbers using small parachutes to simulate a mass attack and create a diversion. The real 'Rupert' was nothing more than a bag of sackcloth, but the cinematic version was an accurate representation of an Allied paratrooper about a metre high, rather like an oversized 'Action Man' doll. The RAF officer describes Rupert as a 'one man army', and asks for the lights to be dimmed to demonstrate what Rupert can do. Immediately the room reverberates to the sound of exploding firecrackers, simulating a gun battle. Actor Jack Hedley later became well-known for playing Colonel Preston in the popular BBC TV series *Colditz* (1972-74).

In an aircraft hangar, Captain Harding briefs his men on the forthcoming mission. In the background is a British Airspeed Horsa glider, or – to be more precise – the sole replica of this type built for the film. The mock-up is fairly accurate, though it lacks a serial number and has the wrong type of RAF roundels for the period on the upper wings. In 1944 the roundels on the upper wings of RAF aircraft consisted of a red dot surrounded by a thick blue ring, whereas those on the film replica had a white ring between the red and blue sections plus a yellow outer band. Additionally, the replica had green and grey camouflage instead of the green and dark earth of the genuine article. (In case you are wondering how I can possibly know the colours used when the film was made in black-and-white, I would point out that colour Pathé newsreel film of the Horsa replica in the Pegasus Bridge sequence can be viewed on YouTube). British-made Horsa gliders were indeed used by US airborne forces, as they were larger than the American WACO gliders but in such instances American markings were usually applied.

Lt. Col. Vandervoort then addresses his men and shows them the clicker which they can use to communicate with friendly forces at night. One click should be answered with two clicks. The actual device used by the 101st Airborne was known as the 'Acme type 470 Cricket Clicker', was made of brass and was manufactured by J. Hudson & Co Ltd of Barr St, Hickley in Birmingham. The version used in the film was larger and louder than a real 470 clicker, with the sound probably added in post-production. I suspect it was a 'toy' version, which was very popular with children in the 1960s and was eventually banned in the UK for inexplicable reasons. Real ACME clickers look like brass clothes pegs whereas the cinematic versions were shaped like sea shells.

Over in France, a Frenchman is reading a newspaper as he listens to the wireless. The BBC is continuing to broadcast personal messages such as 'John has a long moustache'. He realises this is a call for action and rushes out of the house, leaving his wife to drink his soup.

In another part of Normandy a group of downed RAF airmen, who are being hidden by the French Resistance, are also listening to the radio as Janine Boitard bandages the arm of one of them. The message 'wounds my heart with a monotonous langour' is a call for action, and a group of them head off to the Caen Bridge. A Luftwaffe radio monitoring post also hears the messages but does not know what they mean. However General Von Salmuth (Ernst Schroder), who is playing cards, decides to put the 15th Army on full alert.

Some archive footage of the invasion fleet at sea is followed by a shot of four radial-engined fighters flying over the ships. The aircraft are actually US Navy Douglas AD-4 Skyraider attack bombers of the US Sixth fleet. The Skyraider was a highly successful strike aircraft which took part in the Korean and Vietnam Wars and first flew in 1946. Though it arrived too late to see action in WW2, it makes a passable stand-in for the Republic P-47 Thunderbolt fighter-bomber which were used in huge numbers by the USAAF during the Normandy invasion.

On board a US Navy destroyer, its commander (Rod Steiger) looks at the huge number of ships around him and on his radar screen and comments that this is the largest fleet the world has ever seen. On board one of the vessels a large group of GIs look in awe as thousands of Allied planes pass overhead (an excellent matte shot by Wally Veevers).

On another vessel, Lt. John H. Fuller (Jeffrey Hunter) is discussing problems with his marriage as he had received a 'Dear John' letter two weeks previously. Hunter was a well-known movie star at the time and and had appeared in an earlier war film, *Sailor of the King* (1953). Hunter later played Captain Christopher Pike of the *USS Enterprise* in the first pilot episode of *Star Trek*, entitled *The Cage* (1964). He would have continued in this role were it not for objections from his wife, who considered him a film star rather than a TV star. As a result, a second pilot – *Where No Man Has Gone Before* (1966) – was made with William Shatner playing Captain James T. Kirk. Hunter later died of a brain haemorrhage in 1969 following an accident on a film set.

As the clock on the church tower at St Mere Eglise shows midnight, the Germans scan the sky. A minute later a group of German officers congratulate General Marcks on his birthday and cut a cake.

Meanwhile, a squadron of RAF Avro Lancasters is towing Airspeed Horsa gliders towards Pegasus Bridge on the river Orne. The Lancaster was the best British four-engined bomber of the war, but was never used to tow gliders as it was considered too valuable to be used for other tasks. Since this sequence was achieved using miniatures rather than real aircraft, one wonders why the actual type of towing aircraft used in the operation – Handley-Page Halifaxes – was not created in miniature for these scenes, since it is surely no more difficult or expensive to make a model Halifax than a miniature Lancaster? And as some versions of the Halifax had the same engines as the Lancaster – namely four Rolls-Royce Merlins – the same sound effects could have been used. Some writers who don't know much about WW2 aircraft seem to have a fixation on the Avro Lancaster as it is the only RAF bomber they seem to recognise, hence its appearance in this film plus *The Guns of Navarone* (1961) and *Force 10 from Navarone* (1978), and the novelization of *Where Eagles Dare*.

Inside one of the Horsas a group of British paras are singing the popular song *The Lambeth Walk* as their glider is released from its towing plane. Their leader, Major John Howard (Richard Todd) of the 6th Airborne, thinks of his recent briefing (which is presented to the viewer as a voiceover representing his inner thoughts). His orders are to 'Capture the Orne bridge and "hold until relieved... hold until relieved".'

There is very effective point-of-view shot taken from a camera helicopter, combined with some model footage, as the gliders descend towards the bridge. The paras link arms, brace themselves and raise their feet to minimize the chance of injury as the Horsa lands with a thump and slides along the ground for some distance before coming to a halt (an effect that was achieved very simply by towing the replica with a rope). The troops quickly jump out and charge the bridge. Some attack the small German garrison with grenades and Sten gun fire while others go under the bridge to remove German demolition charges. The German garrison tries to 'phone for help but are quickly thwarted as the French Resistance blows up the telegraph poles. Major Howard wonders where the unit's medical officer is, and is told that he was on the third glider which came down in the river.

A moment later the 'Doc' (Howard Marion-Crawford) turns up, having crossed the bridge from the German side, while another soldier reports that all the demolition charges have been removed. They have achieved all their aims in just 15 minutes... but how long can they hold out?

General Max Pemsel (Wolfgang Preiss) of the 7th Army is informed of the airborne assaults and is dismayed that so many officers are away on leave.

The next shot shows a number of RAF Avro Lancasters in formation. Inside them are American paratroopers of the 2nd Battalion of the 505th Parachute Infantry Regiment lead by Lt. Col. Vandervoort. This is another serious error in the film. American paratroopers only used USAAF Douglas C-47 Skytrains, and the Lancaster was never employed as a paratroop-dropping aircraft. Even if it had been, the paratroopers would have had to exit from a hatch cut in the floor as the rear fuselage door on the starboard side of the Lancaster was just in front of the tailplane, which meant that jumping parachutists were at high risk of being blown against the starboard tailplane by the slipstream. RAF aircrew did sometimes leap from this door to escape a blazing bomber but were normally advised to lie on the floor and roll out to lessen the risk of injuring themselves on the tailplane. This was not such an issue with the C-47, as there was a reasonable distance between the cargo door on the port side and the tailplane. In addition, the C-47 flew much slower than the Lancaster so the slipstream was less intense.

During WW2, American airborne troops only jumped from C-47s, while their British counterparts used the C-47 (which the British called the Dakota) plus various converted bombers including the Armstrong-Whitworth Whitley, the Short Stirling, the Handley-Page Halifax and the Armstrong-Whitworth Albemarle.

At a German HQ, soldiers are frantically trying to get hold of Rommel while at Caen the time is now 0107 hrs as German soldiers sound klaxons, switch on searchlights and man anti-aircraft guns which in this scene include American quad fifty-calibre machine-guns in an electrically-driven M45 Maxson turret. The M45 turret was never used by the Germans in WW2, but it has appeared in many war films where it has been used as a stand-in for the German quad 20mm *Flakvierling* weapon.

There is then a cut to a studio shot showing an RAF dispatcher throwing 'Ruperts' out the rectangular doorway on the starboard side of the rear fuselage of a Lancaster. This obvious studio mock-up features an error, as an RAF roundel can be seen to the left of the doorway. In a real Lancaster the roundel was forward of the doorway with the aircraft's serial number between the door and the starboard tailplane. The Ruperts' parachutes open and the dummies float to earth. The attached firecrackers ignite and panic the defending German troops, who call for reinforcements. The 'Ruperts' have worked.

Near Caen, Resistance worker Janine Boitard is involved in a scheme to blow up the main railway line with the assistance of a Resistance worker and two paratroopers who have an airdropped container full of supplies. In the dark, Janine tries to slip past two German soldiers standing on the line while pushing her bicycle, but she is seen and ordered to stop. When she is asked where she is going, she tells them she is heading to a nearby farm. 'No-one lives in that farm', says one of the guards. He asks to see her papers. She is led away to be questioned as another German soldier discovers explosives on the track. Eventually Janine ends up in the river fighting a German soldier who tries to drown her by pushing her head underwater. In the nick of time a British paratrooper arrives and kills the German with a single round from his Sten gun. By now a train is hurtling towards the sabotaged section of the track. The bomb explodes and the train quickly derails (thanks to some excellent miniature work) and crashes.

At General Marcks' HQ, reports are coming in that 'rubber dummies' have been dropped by parachute. One soldier shows the General one of the 'Ruperts'. Marcks realises that the diversion must have been created for a reason. They are still waiting to hear from Field Marshal Rommel who is in Germany.

By now Allied paratroopers are landing all over Normandy, though many are dispersed by the wind. One lands in a river and is shot by a German sentry. Another drops into a well. One German officer is in such a hurry to get outside and see what is happening that he puts his right boot on his left foot (and vice versa). Other paratroopers end up in the courtyard of a German HQ.

Meanwhile, the Padre of a British Airborne unit (John Gregson) has landed in a large pond and is upset to discover he has lost the case containing his communion set. After ducking underwater a few times he eventually finds it.

In a house near the coast, Major Werner Pluskat is woken by a ringing telephone. His men in a bunker on Omaha Beach are concerned that something is about to happen. Pluskat looks out the window and sees flares. He agrees to get dressed and go to the bunkers. In Saint Mere Eglise the local Fire Brigade have been called out to deal with a blazing house while a local woman tells the Mayor about parachutes that have been spotted descending from the sky.

Above the French town a large contingent of American paratroopers are preparing to jump. Private John Steele (Red Buttons) is repeating the phrase 'Je Suis Americane' ('I am American'). The green light comes on by the exit door and the Americans leap out. Unfortunately many of them miss the designated drop zone next to the town and land in the square itself. As they descend towards the town they are fired on by German troops and some are killed. One para uses his Thompson submachine gun to fire at the Germans as he descends, while Private Steele's parachute gets caught on the spire of the bell tower meaning that he is stuck next to the clock and almost deafened by the noise of the bells.

To achieve this scene, a contingent of French stuntmen wearing parachutes actually jumped from helicopters, but they kept landing in the wrong places so eventually the desired shot was achieved by attaching a few parachutists to cranes which could drop them on an exact spot.

The shot of a mass of parachutists descending on the St Mere Eglise area at night was achieved using the rubber 'Rupert' dummies dropped from a helicopter which explains why the filmmakers used accurate representations of human figures when creating these mannequins.

On Omaha Beach on the coast of Normandy, Major Pluskat drives up to a bunker in his VW Kubelwagen and goes inside. His men have reported some bombing raids but nothing else. Pluskat picks up a pair of binoculars and scans the horizon. There is nothing to be seen, but he agrees to stay for the night and sits down to drink coffee with his men.

Some miles away in the hedgerows of Normandy, an American paratrooper of the 101st Airborne hears a noise. As instructed, he takes his ACME clicker and makes a single click. After a few seconds this is answered by a clearly audible double click. He steps forwards and is promptly shot by a German with a rifle. As he lies dying, he mutters that he definitely heard a double click. A German soldier then steps into view carrying his rifle. He works the bolt to eject a spent cartridge, in the process making a sound very like the double click of the ACME clicker.

Nearby another group of American paratroopers of the 101st Airborne Division are using their clickers to join up. After forming into a group they walk to their destination while passing a low stone wall. Another group of soldiers pass in the opposite direction. They are actually Germans, but in the dark no-one notices.

Having finished his coffee, Major Pluskat is becoming increasingly anxious as hundreds of Allied aircraft are flying over his bunker heading inland. He 'phones Lt. Col. Ocker (Peter Van Eyck) to report his concerns, particularly as the sea is now much calmer.

Lt. Col. Vandervoort has landed in Normandy but has broken his right ankle during the parachute drop. An army paramedic examines his foot and declares he has a 'compound fracture'. (A 'compound fracture' is one in which there is also a skin wound which exposes the broken bone to the air. As

Vandervoort's skin is unbroken, the medic's assertion is incorrect.)

Vandervoort is unwilling to be evacuated as a casualty and simply asks the paramedic to put on his boot and lace it tight. Vandervoort is facing another problem, as his men have landed in a swamp five miles from the designated drop zone.

At the German HQ, Major General Max Pemsel (Wolfgang Preiss) briefs his fellow officers on the situation. It is clear that an Allied invasion has taken place, but not everyone agrees that this is the main attack. General Von Rundstedt still believes the main attack will be at the Pas De Calais, as does Hitler. An assault against Normandy defies all logic, and the German High Command are reluctant to send Panzers to Normandy in case there is an even larger attack elsewhere.

On board a ship heading for Normandy, Lord Lovat is briefing his commandos while on a US Navy vessel, Brigadier General Theodore Roosevelt Jr. (Henry Fonda) is pleading to be allowed to go ashore and see action. Roosevelt thinks he is being barred from action as his father was the former US President Theodore Roosevelt (not to be confused with the then-current American President Franklin D. Roosevelt), but it is pointed out that a more genuine reason for this decision is that he suffers from arthritis. Roosevelt says he hasn't had any problems with this ailment for months, but as he leaves the cabin he picks up a walking stick.

On another ship a group of French commandos lead by Phillipe Kieffer (Christian Marquand) are being briefed on their planned attack on a French casino which is being used as a command centre, while over in France General Oberst Alfred Jodl (Wolfgang Lukschy) is unable to contact Hitler as he has taken a sleeping pill and has given orders that he is not to be disturbed. Major General Blumentritt is incensed that they cannot get an order to send Panzers to Normandy.

At the Omaha Beach bunker a sentry stands guard outside with Pluskat's dog. Inside, the Major takes another look at the horizon with his binoculars. There is nothing to be seen. 'Where's my dog?' he mutters before gazing through his binoculars again.

As the mist clears, he sees a huge fleet on the horizon. Hundreds of vessels are heading for Normandy. Quickly Pluskat gets on the 'phone to his superior Lt. Col. Ocher, but his claims are not believed. 'The enemy don't have that many ships,' says Ocher. 'Where are they heading?'

'To me!' blurts out Pluskat.

The next shot shows a huge fleet at sea as the four Skyraiders we saw earlier fly overhead. US General Omar Bradley (Nicholas Stuart) views the scene with some satisfaction and is informed that in two minutes the fleet will open fire. Admiral Jaujards of the Free French contingent addresses his sailors by tannoy as the naval vessels rotate their turrets until they are pointing towards the Normandy coastline.

As the fleet prepares to open fire, Sergeant Kaffekanne is occupied with his usual morning ritual of taking breakfast to the troops manning the bunkers on Omaha Beach. The French farmer we saw at the beginning of the movie looks out his window and sees the vast armada assembled a few miles offshore (a shot achieved with an excellent matte painting). Suddenly flashes appear on the horizon and naval shells start falling on and around the bunkers. Kaffekanne's horse bolts while the farmer waves a French Tricolour from his window. The day of liberation has arrived!

The shots of US Navy ships firing their triple 6-inch turrets at the beach defences were filmed on the two cruisers

USS Little Rock and *USS Springfield*. These were both WW2 vintage *Cleveland*-class cruisers which had been upgraded to carry guided missiles in the 1950s.

Inside one of the bunkers, which has already been damaged by a naval shell, Pluskat is on the telephone frantically trying to convince his superiors that an invasion is underway. 'Can't you hear?' he says as shells burst around him.

On his airbase near the Normandy coastline, 'Pips' Priller is finally ordered to take off and attack the invading troops. Priller and his wingman Sergeant Heinz Wodarczyk (uncredited) don their flying jackets. By now it is 0632 hrs and thousands of US troops are boarding landing craft which will take them to Omaha beach, where an alert has now been sounded. Hundreds of German soldiers run to take up defensive positions and a PAK 38, 50mm anti-tank gun is wheeled into position.

The landing craft head towards the beach – ignoring the shells that are now bursting around them – and drop their ramps, discharging their human cargoes. 36 landing craft were used in the film, all supplied by the US Navy, but these were all LCM-8s which didn't see service until 1954.

Other troops arrive by DUKW. The defensive fire is ferocious, far greater than the Americans had anticipated, and many troops are killed and injured but enough make it through the withering fire to pose a threat to the Germans. Sheltering in a hollow, General Cota tells a soldier to go back and retrieve his rifle which he had dropped. Miraculously the soldier achieves this feat without getting hit.

On a US Navy ship, General Bradley receives news that the initial assault on Omaha beach has run into unexpectedly fierce resistance and the third wave of attacking troops has floundered. On Utah Beach, more landing craft have arrived and drop their ramps. Brigadier General Theodore Roosevelt gets off carrying his stick. Private Morris sees a German soldier and has to put on his glasses before he can shoot him. But the Sergeant to his left has been killed.

Brigadier General Roosevelt realises that his men have been dropped on the wrong beach as they are a mile and a quarter south of where they were supposed to be. This could be a problem if their reinforcements are landed on the correct beach, but Roosevelt insists that these reinforcements will have to follow them wherever they are, and they will move inland.

At that point Priller's two Messerschmitt fighters arrive over Gold and Juno beaches (in reality it was Sword Beach). Initially we don't see the planes, only a point-of-view shot which can only have been taken by a camera helicopter as it is far too slow-moving for an aircraft-mounted camera. To begin with, the shot is looking down on the beach from an almost stationary aerial viewpoint. Then the camera dives and moves along the beach, though still moving far too slowly to represent a strafing fighter which would have carried out its attack at about 300mph. The footage is then intercut with that taken from a camera mounted on the front starboard seat of one of the Nord 1002s, but again the low-powered aircraft moves much more slowly than a real WW2 fighter.

Priller and his colleague rake the ground troops with machine gun fire, but it is a pointless exercise and – after using up all their ammunition – the two planes head for home. Laughing to himself, Priller says that 'The Luftwaffe has had its greatest moment!' These cockpit shots were filmed in the studio using the fuselage of a scrapped SIPA S.12 aircraft.

The action then shifts to Sword Beach at 0653 hrs, where British landing craft are about to drop their ramps.

Lord Lovat tells his men that they are going to 'Give it back for Dunkirk', while Privates Flanagan (Sean Connery) and Clough (Norman Rossington) prepare to disembark. This was the last film Sean Connery made before appearing as James Bond in *Dr No* (1962). His portrayal of the gormless Private Flanagan – complete with cod Irish accent – is worlds away from the way he played the suave James Bond. Only seconds after his first appearance in the film, Flanagan falls into the sea for comic effect as Lord Lovat wades through the surf to the accompaniment of bagpipes.

Royal Navy Beachmaster Colin Maud (Kenneth More) waves a shillelagh (an Irish walking stick that can double as a club) as he directs traffic on his beach, accompanied by his faithful dog (who in real life was called Winnie). He is most anxious that everyone should get off the beach as quickly as possible and move inland.

As Maud continues with his work, two Sherman tanks with 76mm guns in T23 turrets (incorrect, as only 75mm gun Shermans took part in the initial landings) trundle past in the background. One with the number '15' painted on the turret has a large metal deep wading snorkel attached to the engine deck while the other, marked '33', has a mock flotation screen fitted to the hull to make it look like a DD (Duplex Drive) Sherman. The DD Sherman was a British invention which involved fitting a collapsible flotation screen to a specially modified Sherman tank. This enabled the tank to swim ashore using a propeller with was powered by the tank's engine. DD tanks had specially sealed hulls and were usually fitted with a deep wading snorkel to keep the engine exhaust and air intake well above the water level. They were not designed to swim great distances. Nor were they intended to be used in rough weather, as a single large wave could flood them. Nonetheless, they proved very useful at D-Day, although some were lost due to the sea conditions. A DD version of the British Valentine tank was also created, but was never used in action.

A newsman attached to the invading troops asks if a newsflash can be sent by military radio. His request is refused, so the journalist tries to send a message by carrier pigeon which promptly flies east towards the German lines.

Private Watney is having trouble with his Universal Carrier, which is broken down and won't start. He thinks the engine is full of seawater. But Maud has the answer as he recalls the advice given to him by his grandmother: 'Anything mechanical... give it a good bash'. He promptly thumps the engine compartment of the vehicle with his shillelagh and Watkins is able to start the Carrier.

The Universal Carrier (also known as the Bren Gun Carrier) was the standard Armoured Personnel Carrier (APC) used by British and Commonwealth forces during WW2. Powered by a Ford V8 engine delivering 85hp, it remained in production until 1960 and was produced in greater numbers than any armoured vehicle in history with 113,000 being manufactured. It could be fitted with a variety of weapons including a Bren gun, various mortars and the 2-pounder anti-tank gun, and could also tow the 6-pounder anti-tank gun.

As Watkins moves off, a Frenchman wearing a WW1 helmet and clutching a bottle of champagne arrives on a bicycle to welcome Lovat. As the two converse briefly, a Churchill tank trundles past in the background. Manufactured by Vauxhall Motors, the Churchill was not actually named after the British Prime Minister (it was named after one of his ancestors) and was one of the most underrated tanks of WW2. Fitted with thick armour plate (in the Mark VII version the front glacis plate was 150mm thick, which was 50% more than a Tiger I and the same as a German Tiger II), it was the best-protected Allied tank of the war. It also had phenomenal hill-climbing abilities, which meant it could defeat many anti-tank ditches.

The main snags of the Churchill were that it was slow (16mph top speed) and under-powered, and also under-armed as the largest gun it could be fitted with was the 75mm due to its narrow hull and small turret ring. A widened version with the powerful 17-pounder gun known as the Black Prince (aka Super Churchill) was developed towards the end of the war, but never went into production because an even better tank – the Centurion – was about to enter service.

As Lovat's men move off towards Pegasus Bridge, Pluskat is driving through the French countryside in a VW Type 82 Kubelwagen. Suddenly two fighters – British Spitfire Mark LF IXs flown by Free French pilots – appear overhead and strafe the vehicle with their 20mm cannon and 0.303 in machine guns. The VW is hit and overturns, and Pluskat is lucky to escape with his life though he is wounded in his left arm. This sequence was filmed at La Ferte Alais, 30 miles south of Paris, with former Free French Spitfire pilot Pierre Laureys at the controls of one of the aircraft.

Back in Germany, Rommel is presenting a pair of shoes to his wife when he receives a telephone call informing him that the Allies have landed in Normandy. Rommel is angry at his own stupidity and makes plans to return to Normandy urgently.

The action then shifts to Point Du Hoc at 0711 hrs where a force of US Troops (actually Rangers, the American equivalent of the British commandos, though this is not explained in the film) is approaching the shore in landing craft and DUKWs. The contingent of Rangers are played by various actors and stuntmen including Robert Wagner, Paul Anka, Fabian, and George Segal.

The Rangers land on the beach and quickly set up special mortars to fire grappling irons attached to ropes to help them climb the steep cliffs. Many of the grappling irons secure themselves in the barbed wire defences at the top of the cliff. Other Rangers scale the heights using extra-long extending ladders. Some of the soldiers are shot by the Germans and fall to their deaths but enough make it to the top to secure the objective, helped by naval gunfire support (NGS) from ships lying offshore. Finally the Rangers take the bunkers only to find them empty. Their intelligence was wrong, as the guns had not yet been installed. They had come all this way and taken heavy casualties for nothing!

Back at the German HQ, Von Rundstedt is furious at Hitler's refusal to send the Panzer divisions to Normandy as he is still convinced the main attack will be at the Pas De Calais. At Pegasus Bridge sporadic fighting is still continuing as Private Watney hears the sound of bagpipes. Reinforcements have finally arrived in the form of Lord Lovat's commandos, who begin to cross the bridge.

Some miles away Lt. Col. Vandervoort and Captain Harding are near St Mere Eglise, where the commander is resting in a two-wheeled trailer which is being pulled by his men. A smashed WACO glider with US markings (a replica specially created for the film) can be seen in the background. Lt. Sheen arrives from St Mere Eglise and explains that many of the paratroopers overshot their drop zones. He recommends that the paras withdraw from St Mere Eglise and regroup, but the American commander is adamant that they should take the town. In the operations room for the invasion, Brigadier General Edwin P. Parker Jr (Leo Genn) is reviewing progress and is astonished that the Germans have still not committed their Panzers.

On the French coast a contingent of French commandos led by Commander Phillipe Kieffer are preparing to capture the Ouistrehan Casino, which is being used as a German strongpoint. There is a spectacular helicopter shot as the soldiers race along the quayside and cross a bridge as shells explode in the water. But the German defences include a 20mm Oerlikon cannon and a 50mm Pak 38 anti-tank gun (probably the very same one we saw earlier as part of the Omaha Beach defences). The PAK 38 is proving a particularly hard nut to crack, as it is firing out the narrow slit of a concrete bunker in the lowest floor of the casino.

Kieffer realizes that tank support will be required and – after his radioman has failed to get a message out – decides he will have to fetch a tank. Kieffer runs across the bridge, which is hit by a shell. He falls into the water as he is crossing, but the Frenchman manages to clamber up the other side. The remaining French commandos are in trouble, as the building they are sheltering in is hit by a 50mm shell. They attempt to take out the PAK 38 with a British PIAT (Projector Infantry Anti Tank) weapon, but the operators are hit by enemy fire after missing with their first round. At this desperate moment eight nuns arrive at the building held by the commandos, led by a Mother Superior. They are all qualified nurses and have come to tend to the wounded.

Suddenly there is the noise of a tank engine and an armoured vehicle (the mock DD Sherman we saw earlier) appears at the quayside. The Sherman fires a round from its main gun which damages the building but misses the PAK 38. The gunner rotates the turret slightly and fires again. This time a large part of the building collapses, taking the German gun with it. The French commandos run out screaming and storm the casino.

Back at the German HQ, Major General Pemsel is wondering what has happened to the Luftwaffe. The Americans appear to be bogged down and vulnerable to counterattack. He remembers the words of Rommel, who had always said that if they could hold the Allies on the beach the invasion would collapse.

At Omaha Beach the Americans are indeed bogged down, and Colonel Thompson suggests the only option is to re-embark on landing craft and withdraw before everyone is wiped out as they have already taken 1,000 casualties. Brigadier General Cota does not agree, and is adamant they must advance. He mentions that there is a gulley leading off the beach which is blocked by barbed wire, beyond which is a concrete sea wall. Previous attempts to breach these defences have failed, but they must try again... or die. 'Only two kinds of people are going to stay on this beach. Those that are dead and those that are going to die', he says.

Back at the 'Operation Overlord' control room, Brigadier General Parker reports that the situation at Omaha Beach is a 'bloody shambles... Ike is hanging on by his fingernails'. At the German HQ, Major General Pemsel is on the 'phone, urging his defending troops to regroup. He is desperate to get to Normandy to see for himself how things are going.

At St Mere Eglise, Private Steele has now been rescued from the clock tower and is resting in a building as Lt. Sheen arrives. Sheen tries to talk to him, but Steele can't hear as the ringing bells have made him temporarily deaf. Lt. Col. Vandervoort finally arrives in the town and orders his men to take down the bodies of some dead American paratroopers who are hanging from the trees.

In the Overlord Operations Room, Brigadier Parker learns that Lord Lovat's unit has captured Pegasus Bridge, the American 82nd Airborne have taken St Mere Eglise, and the 101st Airborne is moving towards Utah Beach.

At Omaha Beach, Brigadier General Cota speaks to Lt. Fuller and orders him to advance to the gulley where he is to attempt to blow up the barbed wire with a Bangalore Torpedo. Fuller bravely agrees to the mission and, under heavy fire, crawls up the gulley, fits the tubes of the weapon together, goes back down the gulley while carrying the reel of electrical cable which will detonate the device, and attaches it to an electrical plunger. Fuller presses down on the plunger and destroys the barbed wire. The first stage of his mission has been a success, although two soldiers have been killed in the process. The Bangalore Torpedo was a British invention and was created by Captain McClintock of the British Army in 1912. The US version used on D-Day was known as the M1A1.

Now Fuller makes his way up the gulley again and, with the assistance of some soldiers, places some cases of explosives in a gap underneath the concrete sea wall. He attaches the electrical cable to the detonator and makes his way down the gulley, but before he can reach the plunger he is hit. Another brave soldier takes his place, retrieves the cable reel, attaches the wires to the detonator and pushes the plunger. There is a large explosion and the sea wall is breached, allowing all the troops on the beach to race up the gulley and storm the pillboxes from behind. The assault is successful, though Colonel Thompson is killed by enemy fire. The battle for

Omaha Beach has been won by the Americans, albeit with heavy casualties.

At the German HQ the occupiers are burning papers as they realise the battle has been lost. In the penultimate scene of the film, Flight Officer Johnnie Campbell is lying wounded in a barn as an American soldier, Private Dutch Schultz, enters and offers him a cigarette. Campbell explains that he was shot down by ack-ack during the night and sustained a wound to his right leg, which a medical orderly closed with safety pins as he had no sutures left. A German officer lies dead in another part of the barn and Campbell points out that he has his boots on the wrong way round.

On Omaha Beach, Cota gets into his Jeep and drives up the hill as thousands of American reinforcements are landed. *The Longest Day* theme plays, this time with a few lyrics, as the end titles play.

The Longest Day premiered in France on 25 September 1962, followed by the USA premiere on 4 October and the UK premiere on 23 October. The film made $30 million in worldwide rentals against a final budget of $10 million, and effectively saved 20th Century Fox after the financially disastrous *Cleopatra*. The film attracted favourable reviews and won five Academy Awards for Art Direction, Cinematography, Editing, Special Effects and Best Picture. It has had several cinema releases up to the early seventies, including a 70mm version in 1969. Despite a number of historical and technical errors it remains one of the great action war movies.

The Longest Day (1962) Production Credits

Directors: Ken Annakin (British exterior episodes), Andrew Marton (American exterior episodes), Bernhard Wicki (German Episodes), Gerd Oswald (parachuting scenes), Darryl F. Zanuck (uncredited).

Screenplay Credits
Original Book: Cornelius Ryan
Screenplay: Cornelius Ryan, Romain Gary, James Jones, David Pursall, Jack Seddon

Cast
Col. Thompson: Eddie Albert
US Army Ranger: Paul Anka
Madame Barrault: Arietty
Father Louis Rolland: Jean-Louis Barrault
Private Dutch Schultz: Richard Beymer
Major Werner Pluskat: Hans Christian Blech
Mayor of Colleville: Bourvil
Flying Officer David Campbell: Richard Burton
Major General Dr Hans Speidel: Wolfgang Buttner
Private John Steele: Red Buttons
Maid: Pauline Carton
Private Flanagan: Sean Connery
Captain Frank: Ray Danton
Janine Boitard: Irina Demich
US Army Ranger Major: Fred Dur
US Army Ranger: Fabian
Major General Robert Haines: Mel Ferrer
Brigadier General Theodore Roosevelt Jr: Henry Fonda
Captain Harding: Steve Forrest
Sergeant Kaffekanne: Gert Frobe
Brigadier General Edwin Parker Jr: Leo Genn
British Padre: John Gregson
Field Marshal Gerd Von Rundstedt: Paul Hartmann
Young GI: Peter Helm
Field Marshal Erwin Rommel : Werner Hinz
RAF Pilot: Donald Houston
Lt. John F. Fuller: Jeffrey Hunter
General Wolfgang Hager: Karl John
Major General Gunther Blumentritt: Curt Jurgens
Major General Walter Bedell Smith: Alexander Knox
Lord Lovat: Peter Lawford
Louis: Fernard Ledoux
Commander Phillipe Kiefer: Christian Marquand
Sergeant Wilder: Dewey Martin
Private Morris: Roddy McDowall

Private Watney: Michael Medwin
Private Martini: Sal Mineo
Brigadier General Norman Cota: Robert Mitchum
Captain Colin Maud: Kenneth More
General Erich Marcks: Richard Munch
General Raymond Barton: Edmond O'Brien
RAF Officer: Leslie Philips
Major General Max Pemsel: Wolfgang Preiss
Joe Williams: Ron Randell
Mother Superior: Madeleine Renaud
Sgt Guy de Montiaur: Georges Riviere
Private Clough: Norman Rossington
Brigadier General James Gavin: Robert Ryan
US Army Ranger: Tommy Sands
US Army Ranger: George Segal
Rear Admiral Janjard: Jean Servais
Destroyer Commander: Rod Steiger
Major John Howard: Richard Todd
Lt. Wilson: Tom Tryon
Lieutenant Colonel Ocker: Peter Van Eyck
US Army Ranger: Robert Wagner
British Paratrooper: Richard Wattis
Lieutenant Sheen: Stuart Whitman
Alexandre Renaud: Georges Wilson
Lieutenant Colonel Benjamin Vandervoort: John Wayne
Group Captain J.N. Stagg: Patrick Barr
Man at Resistance HQ: Yves Barsacq
Officer at Eisenhower Briefing: Geoffrey Bayldon
Lieutenant Walsh: Lyndon Brook
French Resistance Fighter: Jean Champion
Paratrooper: Yvan Chiffre
Ronald Callen: Bryan Coleman
Officer on Destroyer Bridge: Gary Collins
Colonel Caffey: John Crawford
French Navy Captain: Jo D'Avra
Blumentritt's Adjutant: Armin Dahlen
Private Harris: Mark Damon
British Soldier: Richard Dawson
Bill Millin-Piper: Leslie De Laspee
German Soldier: Eugene Deckers
French Commando: Gil Delamare
Zanuck: Colin Drake
Private Coke: Frank Finlay
British Paratrooper: Harry Fowler
Private Hutchinson: Bernard Fox
Meyer's Aide: Robert Freitag

French Commando: Bernard Fresson
German Guard on Train Track: Arnold Gelderman
British Soldier: Harold Goodwin
German Soldier: Walter Gotell
General Dwight D. Eisenhower: Henry Grace
Frau Maria Rommel: Ruth Hausmeister
RAF Briefing Officer: Jack Hedley
Manfred Rommel: Michael Hinz
Admiral Creasey: Walter Horsbrugh
Paratrooper: Jean Pierre Janic
British Soldier: Patrick Jordan
Captain Helmuth Lang: Til Kiwe
US Airman: Mickey Knox
Air Chief Marshall Leigh Mallory: Simon Lack
British Soldier: Harry Landis
German Soldier: Rudy Lenoir
US Army Ranger Sparrow: Joseph Lowe
Colonel General Alfred Jodl: Wolfgang Lukschy
Camp Cook: Victor Maddern
Glider Doctor: Howard Marion-Crawford
Canadian Doctor: Neil McCallum
US Army Soldier: Edward Meeks
Rear Admiral Alan Kirk: John Meillon
Captain Ernst During: Kurt Meisel
Paratrooper: Gerard Moisan
Cook: Tony Mordente
Air Marshall Tedder: Louis Mounier
Mayor,St Mere-Eglise: Bill Nagy
German Commander: Kurt Pecher
Lt Fritz Theen: Rainer Penkert
German Officer with Rupert: Maltze Petzel
Roosevelt's Aide: John Philips
WREN: Sian Philips
Jean: Maurice Poli
Sergeant Bernhard Bergsdorf: Harmut Reck
General Montgomery: Trevor Reid
Joseph 'Pips' Priller: Heinz Reincke
Admiral Sir Bertram Ramsay: John Robinson
Colonel Schiller: Paul Edwin Roth
General Hans Von Salmuth: Ernst Schroder
Luftwaffe Major: Dietmar Schonherr
Lt. Col. Helmuth Meyer: Heinz Spitzner
Lt. Gen. Omar N. Bradley: Nicholas Stuart
German Officer: Hans Sohnker
Housekeeper: Alice Tissot
German Officer: Serge Tolstoy
French Commando: Michael Tureau
Para in Garden: Lionel Vitrant
Pemsel's Adjutant: Vicco Von Bulow

US Army Medic: Joe Warfield
French Spitfire Pilot: Dominique Zardi

Producers
Producer: Darryl F. Zanuck
Associate Producer: Elmo Williams

Production Crew
Cinematographers: Jean Bourgoin, Walter Wottiz
Film Editor: Samuel E. Beetley
Art Directors: Leon Barsacq, Ted Haworth, Vincent Korda
Production Managers: Julien Derode, Christina Ferry, Lee Katz, Louis Wipf

Second Unit Director or Assistant Director
Assistant Directors: Bernard Farrel, Tom Pevsner, Louis Pitzele, Gerard Renateau, Jean Herman, Henry Sokal Jr
Second Assistant Director: Henry Wise
Second Unit Director: Elmo Williams

Art Department
Set Designer: Gabriel Bechir
Property Master: Sam Gordon
Production Illustrator: Mentor Huebner

Sound Department
Sound: Joseph De Bretagne, Jacques Maumont, William Sivell

Special Effects
Special Effects: Karl Baumgartner, Johnny Borgese, Joseph De Bretagne, Karl Helmer, Augie Lohman, R.A. McDonald, Alex Weldon

Visual Effects
Optical Effects: Jean Fouchet
Matte Painter: Bob Cuff
Additional Visual Effects: David Horsley
Visual Effects: Wally Veevers

Stunts
Stunts: Ken Buckle, Yvan Chiffre, Jack Cooper, Gil Delamare, Joe Powell, Nosher Powell, Alexandre Renault, John Sullivan, Ian Yule
Aerial Photography: Guy Tabary

Casting Department
Casting UK: Maude Spector

Costume and Wardrobe Department
Wardrobe: John Mc Corry

Music Department
Conductor: Maurice Jarre
Theme Music Composer: Paul Anka

Music Arranger: Mitch Miller

Transportation Department
Driver: Frank Khoury

Technical & Military Advisors
Technical and Military Advisors: Jean Barral, Roger Bligh, Gunther Blumentritt, Willard H. Bushy, Maurice Chauvet, Hubert Deschard, The Earl of Lovat, Lt. General James Gavin, A.J. Hillebrand, Major John Howard, James R. Johnson, Capitaine Phillipe Kieffer, General Pierre Koenig, Captain Helmut Lang, General Sir Frederick Morgan, Lt. Commander E.C Peake, Lt. General Max Pemsel, Major Werner Pluskat, Captaine Ferdinand Prevost, Colonel Josef Priller, Frau Lucie Maria Rommel, Friedrich Ruge, Colonel Albert Saby, Colin Maud, Joseph B Seay
Battle Coordinator: Elmo Williams
Helicopter Pilot: Gilbert Chomat
Script Consultant: Romain Gary
Publicist: Fred Hift
Script Consultants: James Jones, Jack Seddon, David Pursall, Erich Maria
Dialogue Coach: Mickey Knox
Continuity: Lucie Lichtig

DIRECT FROM ITS RESERVED SEAT ENGAGEMENTS!
FIRST TIME AT POPULAR PRICES!
Warner Bros.' super action show of shows!
BATTLE OF THE BULGE
The most intensely personal drama of men ever told.
HENRY FONDA · ROBERT SHAW · ROBERT RYAN · DANA ANDREWS · PIER ANGELI
BARBARA WERLE · GEORGE MONTGOMERY · TY HARDIN · CHARLES BRONSON · HANS CHRISTIAN BLECH
WERNER PETERS · JAMES MacARTHUR and TELLY SAVALAS
ORIGINAL SOUND TRACK ALBUM ON WARNER BROS. RECORDS.
TECHNICOLOR · ULTRA-PANAVISION

4

BATTLE OF THE BULGE

(1965)

United States Pictures/Cinerama Productions

Director: Ken Annakin
Producers: Milton Sperling and Philip Yordan
Screenwriters: Philip Yordan, Milton Sperling and John Melson

B*ATTLE of the Bulge* tells the story of the Germans' last offensive of WW2, when an armoured spearhead of 1,214 tanks backed by 406,000 infantrymen attacked through the Ardennes forest in the hope of reaching Antwerp and splitting the Allied armies in two. It is, though, a very controversial film which divides critics. Historians and military vehicle enthusiasts have slammed the movie for its gross over-simplification of the Ardennes battle, its out-of-period tanks and vehicles, and its use of Spanish locations which look nothing like Belgium in winter.

However, I would defend the film for a number of reasons. It is no more historically inaccurate than many other war films made in the sixties and seventies, particularly the critically-acclaimed *Patton* (1970) which was also shot in Spain with Korean War-era tanks and vehicles, some of which were the very same ones employed in *Battle of the Bulge*. It also suffered from locations which didn't look much like the originals, and featured a number of historical and technical errors. In the 1970 film, Patton is shown as hating General Bernard Montgomery – who is depicted as a complete twit – and the British Army and RAF are portrayed as incompetent. Patton and General Omar Bradley are also close friends in the film, something which was not the case. When I first saw *Patton* in late 1970 I was very disappointed. There was very little action. All the tanks were wrong for the period, British officers were portrayed as idiots and there was an odd strafing scene when two large, slow Heinkel He-111s machine gun American troops (the incident *did* happen, but the aircraft involved were fast Focke Wulf Fw-190s – not Heinkel He-111s in European theatre camouflage).

Battle of the Bulge, on the other hand, has plenty of action, excellent photography, sparkling dialogue, good miniature work and a magnificent score by Benjamin Frankel, and features one of Robert Shaw's finest performances as the fanatical Panzer commander, Colonel Martin Hessler. It also happens to be the only WW2 film to have been made in Cinerama, an ultra-wide screen process.

In the early fifties, film-makers became concerned at the growth of television which meant that people were becoming less inclined to visit their local cinemas. As a result, a number of technical innovations were introduced to make movies more competitive. These included stereo and multi-track sound, greater use of colour stock, 3-D films, and several widescreen formats such as VistaVision, Panavision and Todd A-O.

The ultimate widescreen technique though, was Cinerama, which premiered in 1952 and employed an ultra-wide curved screen which was actually made of individual vertical strips of reflective material. In its original form, the process involved three separate cameras and a trio of projectors. The middle camera filmed the centre portion of the scene, the left-hand camera was angled to film the right-hand part and the right-hand camera filmed the left-hand section of the action. When the resulting three films (which were shot with a single shutter) were screened using three projectors, an ultra-wide image resulted.

The results could be very impressive, but the original Cinerama system had a number of snags such as distortion of perspective. Also, the joins between the three different films could sometimes be seen and this lead to some directors placing an object such as a fence pole or a tree at these positions to make the seam less apparent.

The three camera set-up was also very unwieldy, so by the early sixties a simpler version of Cinerama involving a single 70mm Ultra-Panavision camera was devised. The first film to utilize this method was *How the West Was Won* (1962), which employed traditional Cinerama for most scenes and the newer single camera version for the raft sequences. This new version of Cinerama was the one employed in *Battle of the Bulge*.

The film was produced by Philip Yordan and Milton Sperling. Yordan was a prolific screenwriter and producer who, at this point in his career, was based in Spain where he made a number of pictures which were funded by American studios. Two examples would be his earlier production *El Cid* (1961) and his later film *Custer of the West* (1967), which was also made in Cinerama.

Milton Sperling had served with the US Marines in WW2 and became a combat cameraman in the Pacific theatre. His combat experience came in handy when he came to write the script for *Battle of the Bulge*, along with co-producer Philip Yordan and writer John Melson.

At around the time Warner Brothers were planning to make the film, Columbia Pictures were preparing their own rival production – *The Battle of the Bulge* – to be directed by Michael Anderson, which featured David Niven as Field Marshal Montgomery, John Wayne as General Patton and Laurence Olivier as Adolf Hitler. Columbia Pictures took out a lawsuit against Warner Brothers, and one consequence was that no real-life historical figures appeared in the Warner Brothers film. As things transpired, the Columbia Pictures film of the battle was eventually cancelled.

The director of *Battle of the Bulge* was British-born Ken Annakin, who had made a large number of films from 1942 onwards. In recent years he had tended to make large-budget films such as *The Longest Day* (1962), in which he directed the British segments, and *Those Magnificent Men in Their Flying Machines* (1965) about an air race prior to WW1. Richard Fleischer – who later directed *Tora, Tora, Tora* (1970) – was also approached about directing the film, but declined.

As mentioned earlier, the completed script grossly simplified the entire Ardennes counter-offensive. In reality, the battle lasted from 16 December 1944 to 25 January 1945 and ended with the Germans being shoved back to the start line with heavy losses, whereas the film implies that the battle only lasted a few days. No mention is made of the British role in the battle, the role of Allied tactical airpower in smashing the offensive, or the massive German air attack on Allied airfields on New Year's Day 1945 which was known as Operation Bodenplatte. The siege of Bastogne and its subsequent lifting is barely mentioned.

The film also suggests that the sole reason that the Germans lost the battle was that they were short of fuel and some American soldiers set fire to a single petrol dump. Again this is an oversimplification. By this point in the war the Germans were very short of oil for a number of reasons. Key oilfields were in Allied hands and oil targets such as fuel synthesising plants, refineries and storage tanks were being bombed round the clock.

The Germans intended to capture Allied fuel supplies (as had often happened in North Africa), but the Americans burned fuel dumps as they retreated. Poor weather from 16 December onwards had prevented the Allies from employing their massive tactical airpower to smash the advancing Germans, but on 23 December the weather cleared, allowing USAAF P-47 Thunderbolt and P-38 Lightning fighters and RAF Typhoons to attack the Panzers with rockets, bombs and machine gun fire. The same clear skies also meant that besieged Allied troops at Bastogne could be re-supplied by parachute drops. Eventually Bastogne was relieved by General Patton's 3rd Army and the Allies won the battle of attrition. The Germans also failed to capture key roads which were essential to the success of the offensive, and Montgomery's forces took up blocking positions on the Meuse to prevent the Germans from advancing further.

For the key role of German tank commander Martin Hessler the producers chose British actor Robert Shaw, who had made a great impact as 'Red' Grant in the James Bond movie *From Russia with Love* (1963). Shaw received a record $350,000 paycheck for his role in *Battle of the Bulge*, a sum that is worth nearly $3 million in today's money.

As well as being an actor, Shaw was a novelist and playwright and was married to the Scottish actress Mary Ure.

Shaw was originally earmarked to play the part of SS Standartenfuhrer Joachim Peiper, who had led a column of German tanks during the Ardennes counter-offensive. Peiper was implicated in the 'Malmedy Massacre' when 84 American prisoners were executed on 17 December 1944 and was tried, found guilty and sentenced to death by the Allies after the war. Following a series of appeals his sentence was commuted to life imprisonment and then time served. He was eventually released from prison in 1956. Rather unwisely, he later moved to France and was murdered by former members of the French Resistance in 1976.

In 1965 though, Peiper was still very much alive and in a position to object to the way he was portrayed in the film. For this reason the real-life character of Peiper was replaced by the fictional Colonel Martin Hessler. Though a fanatical and ruthless German soldier, Hessler is not a member of the SS and is shown to be critical of the Malmedy Massacre. It is odd that the producers could be fearful of legal action from a man who had been a serving member of the SS, had been found guilty of war crimes and originally sentenced to death, but sometimes fact is stranger than fiction.

The hero of the film though, was Lieutenant Colonel Daniel Kiley, played by Henry Fonda. Kiley's character was fictional but was based on a number of US Army intelligence officers. Other distinguished actors who took part in the production included Robert Ryan, Dana Andrews, Charles Bronson and Telly Savalas.

Filming started in Madrid and the Sierra de Guadarrama mountain range in Spain in February 1965 and continued over the spring and summer. This meant though, that some scenes which were supposed to be taking place in Belgium in December were actually lensed during the blazing Spanish summer, something that is rather apparent from the bright sunlight and short shadows. This is a common problem in film-making, as scenes set in mid-winter are sometimes filmed in summer and vice-versa. *The Wicker Man* (1973), for example, was set in mid-summer but was filmed in October and November which meant that fake leaves had to be stuck on trees.

Filming snow scenes in the summer is not usually a problem as there are a number of types of artificial snow that can be employed, including foam from fire tenders, fragmented Styrofoam, Epsom salts, domestic salt and shredded paper. For *Battle of the Bulge* very little effort was expended on the creation of snow-covered landscapes, though some scenes incorporated genuine snow which happened to be on the ground at the time – for example during the initial Panzer attack, and the Malmedy Massacre.

Another problem concerned the lack of authentic military vehicles and tanks in the film. The movie gives the impression that all the German tanks which took part in the Ardennes battle were King Tigers. In fact, of the 1,214 tanks which took part in the initial assault only 150 were King Tigers. Even Peiper's spearhead consisted of only 42 King Tigers, as well as 100 Panthers and Panzer IVs.

When the Germans invaded the Soviet Union in 1941 they were shocked to discover that their Panzer IIIs and Panzer IVs were no match for the latest Soviet tanks, the KV-1 and the T-34. The KV-1 was a heavy tank with very thick armour and the T-34, while being only a medium tank, featured a number of technical innovations including sloped armour, a diesel engine with a compressed air starter which worked in freezing conditions, and a powerful 76.2mm main gun. Sloped armour has two main advantages. It increases the effective thickness of the armour (so a 70mm plate angled at 45 degrees gave an effective armour thickness of 90mm against horizontal projectiles), and it also means some shells are likely to bounce off.

The Germans were quick to respond to the challenge posed by the T-34 and KV-1, and soon came up with two designs which could better them. The first of those was the Panzer VI (Tiger) which first appeared on the battlefield towards the end of 1942. Weighing 60 tons and powered by a Maybach petrol engine, the tank had an 88mm main gun and frontal armour 102mm thick.

The following year another new German tank appeared: the Panzer V (Panther). Although it was lighter than the Tiger at about 50 tons it featured sloped armour (copied from the Soviet T-34) and a powerful, high-velocity Kwk 42L-70, 75mm gun which was a better armour-piercer than the KwK 36 L/56, 88mm gun fitted to the Tiger.

By 1944 an improved version of the Tiger known as the Tiger II or *Konigs Tiger* (Royal Tiger or Bengal Tiger), which the Allies referred to as the 'King Tiger', was in full production. This effectively combined the best features of the Tiger and Panther tanks as it had very thick, sloping armour. The angled front glacis plate of a Tiger II was 150mm thick which meant it was invulnerable to most tank and anti-tank guns in the Allied arsenal. In theory a British 17-pounder gun firing APDS (Armour Piercing Discarding Sabot) ammunition could penetrate the frontal armour of a Tiger II at short and medium ranges, but no instances were ever recorded in WW2 of a King Tiger's frontal armour being penetrated by a tank or anti-tank round. Allied tank crews who successfully knocked out Tiger IIs did so by hitting the thinner side plates.

In 1964 when the film was planned, research by the film-makers showed that of 492 King Tigers built, only two survived: one at the Aberdeen Proving Ground at Maryland in the USA, and a second at the Tank Museum at Dorset in England. Neither were in running order. (In 2017 seven King Tigers are now known to exist, including one buried under a road (!) and a running example at the Musees des Blindes at Saumur in France.)

The only solution was to employ another type of tank which was vaguely similar to the King Tiger, and the producers chose the American M47 Patton which at that time was operated by the Spanish Army. The M47 was a development of the wartime T26/M26 Pershing, which was a heavy tank mounting a 90mm gun and designed to be the equal of the German Tiger and Panther tanks. Twenty M26 Pershings were sent to the European Theatre in February 1945 and performed impressively in combat.

The only modification that was made to these Spanish M47s in the film was the application of an overall medium grey paint scheme and the application of German crosses and codes to the turret sides. However, this was inaccurate as from 1943 onwards German tanks were painted a desert sand colour at the factory, over which was often sprayed camouflage stripes in reddish brown and green.

The M47s could theoretically have been modified to more closely resemble King Tigers by cladding their hulls and turrets with flat sheets of metal or plywood. This method turned M24 tanks into mock Panthers for *Is Paris Burning?* (1965). A similar technique was employed in *A Bridge Too Far* (1977) to make Dutch Leopard tanks resemble Panthers.

Interestingly, in 1965 the Spanish Army still possessed 20 WW2 vintage German Panzer IV tanks which could have been employed in the filming as they were still in running condition. In December 1965 (after filming had concluded), 17 of them were sold to Syria, who subsequently sent them into action against the Israelis in the 1967 'Six Day War'. The three remaining Panzer IVs were retained in Spain and were considered for some sequences in *Battle of Britain* (1969). In the end they were not employed in these shots and M47s appeared in these scenes, which in any case ended up on the cutting room floor.

Another problem concerned American tanks. In December 1944 the standard US tank was the M4 Sherman, which had either a 75mm M3 gun or a higher-velocity 76mm M1 weapon. In addition, US forces also operated the M18 Hellcat tank destroyer with a 76mm gun, the M10 tank destroyer with a three-inch cannon, and the M36 tank destroyer with a 90mm weapon. Unfortunately the Spanish Army did not operate any of these types, and the closest thing they could offer was the M24 Chaffee light tank.

First seeing service in December 1944, the M24 was a light reconnaissance tank which weighed 18 tons and with armour only 15-38 mm thick. Designed to replace the earlier M3 and M5 Stuart light tanks, which had a puny 37mm main gun, the M24 had a reasonable punch in the form of a lightweight M6 75mm gun which was based on a cannon fitted to the B25H Mitchell bomber.

Fast and reliable, the M24 was popular with crews and had a top speed of 35mph. Some M24s are still in military service today, and Norway only retired the type as recently as 1993. At the time of filming of *Battle of the Bulge*, Spain had 31 Chaffees.

Ironically, Spain's neighbour Portugal operated a number of Sherman tanks in the sixties. These vehicles – which were Canadian-built 'Grizzly' versions of the M4A1 tank – were finally retired in the 1980s, and some were sold to collectors. However, in 1965 it would probably have been impractical to borrow these tanks from Portugal for filming in Spain, though another option might have been to make the film in Yugoslavia which operated Sherman tanks and M10 tank destroyers. Eventually the Spanish Army supplied 500 vehicles for the film, including 75 tanks and armoured vehicles.

The film begins with a graphic slide reading 'Overture', with two and a half minutes of specially-composed music by Benjamin Frankel. This was a common feature of so-called 'roadshow' presentations in the sixties, which had overtures and intermissions with special caption slides and seats which were pre-bookable in advance.

The titles then follow in the form of colour graphics depicting tanks, vehicles, guns and soldiers. Some of these images are of correct tanks for the period and the eagle-eyed viewer will spot a couple of American Shermans and a solitary German StuG III among the inaccurate M47s. Benjamin Frankel's title theme draws heavily on the *Wehrmacht* song *Panzerlied*, first composed in 1933 by Kurt Wiehle and Adolf Hoffman, about which I will be saying more later.

The film proper then starts with some breathtaking panoramic aerial shots of a lone US Army Cessna L-19 Bird Dog reconnaissance plane (a type which flew in 1949) flying above the woods and snow-covered hilltops of what is supposed to be the Ardennes forest as a voice-over informs us that it is December 1944. The British 8th Army has reached the German border in the north while General Patton's 3rd Army is to the south. (This is not entirely correct, as the British 8th Army was in Italy at that time and the British forces in that area were actually the 21st Army Group. Also the 3rd

Army was only one part of the US 12th Army Group commanded by General Omar Bradley.) The voiceover is by American actor William Conrad, who is best known for playing the portly detective in the American TV series *Cannon* (1971-76).

The Cessna has tandem seating for only two people, and sitting in the rear cockpit is US Army intelligence officer Lieutenant Colonel Daniel Kiley (Henry Fonda). Like most Allied servicemen, the pilot – Joe (Robert Woods) – is sure that the Germans are on the point of giving up, but Kiley is unconvinced as the Germans still have six million men under arms.

A lone Mercedes 230 cabriolet staff car appears on the winding road below, driven by Conrad (Hans Christian Blech). In the back seat is Colonel Martin Hessler (Robert Shaw), one of Germany's top tank commanders. Kiley orders the pilot to buzz the vehicle so he can take a few photos, greatly alarming Conrad who thinks he is about to be attacked. Finally the American pilot does a head-on pass at the car and revs his engine to make the German Officer look up, enabling Kiley to get a good picture of his face.

His nerves shot, Conrad skids off the road, runs away from the car and takes shelter in a broken building. Hessler though, is unperturbed. As he points out to Conrad, the Cessna was an unarmed reconnaissance aircraft which was no threat. He also chides him for leaving the engine running, as Germany is very short of fuel. As the Cessna banks away and heads back to base, the camera tracks to one side to reveal a large number of King Tiger tanks, covered with foliage, hiding in the nearby woods. At this point Benjamin Frankel's ominous music hints at the significance of this revelation.

The next scene is an excellent miniature shot of a bomb-damaged German town. The camera reveals a swastika flag dangling from a broken building, and then the camera tracks slowly right to reveal a devastated urban landscape. As was the norm in traditional special effects of this era, the model buildings in the foreground were constructed in three dimensions while those in the background were two-dimensional flats. A miniature German Army truck moves from right to left in a distant street as Colonel Hessler arrives at a steel entrance door, which opens to reveal a corridor leading to an underground bunker. Hessler goes downstairs and passes through a second metal door. Eventually he comes to a door marked 'O.B.' and finds himself in a large, well-furnished room with leather armchairs, settees and paintings.

General Kohler (Werner Peters) greets Hessler and notices he is considerably leaner than when they last met. 'The Russian Front does not put meat on a man's bones', replies the Colonel as he remarks on the bunker's central heating, crystal chandeliers and oil paintings. Hessler then asks if a bed can be found for his driver Conrad, who is tired. General Kohler asserts that Germany is not finished. 'A few stones may be knocked down, but the country is strong', he says, and points out that Germany 'is like an iceberg' as one can only see what is above the surface.

Kohler then shows Hessler large pewter models of the wonder weapons which he believes will win the war for Germany. First of all he reveals a model of a revolutionary jet fighter which has a single engine within the fuselage, an air intake in the nose, and unswept wings. The only two jet fighters deployed by the Nazis in WW2 were the twin-engined Messerschmitt Me 262 *Schwalbe* and the single-engine Heinkel He 162 *Volksjager* (People's Fighter), but the model looks like neither of them. Kohler then shows Hessler a miniature of a Fieseler Fi 103 V-1 Flying Bomb, which he describes as a 'rocket'. In fact the V-1 was an early cruise missile, effectively an unmanned winged aircraft with a pulsejet engine mounted above the rear of the fuselage. The model is also an inaccurate representation of this weapon, as the nose is too short and blunt whereas a real flying bomb had a longer, more pointed nose. Also, the engine is too small in proportion to the rest of the aircraft. Kohler then points out a miniature of the V-2 missile, but this is also wrongly proportioned as it is too fat in the middle.

Finally Kohler proudly presents a model of the latest German tank, the King Tiger which he points out has 'two-and-a-half times the firepower and double the armour of the American tanks'. The miniature is actually of an American M47 Patton, the type of tank that portrayed the Tiger II in the movie. Also, only the Allies referred to this tank as the 'King Tiger'. The Germans called it either the 'Tiger II' or the 'Royal Tiger'. As this model is the same size as the miniatures in the special effects sequences in the movie (about three feet long), it is likely to have been made from the same moulds and sprayed silver for this scene.

Hessler is only partially impressed, saying that all this proves is that Germany is a great toymaker. 'Toys are for children. Let me show them to you', Kohler proclaims as he leads Hessler along the corridor. Suddenly a platoon of American GIs arrive in the corridor followed by a German Officer, Von Diepel (Karl-Otto Alberty), who announces that they are actually a special squad of English-speaking German soldiers who will be parachuted behind enemy lines while wearing US uniforms. The unit will be led by Lieutenant Shumacher (Ty Hardin), a German who had lived in Texas for 12 years. Hardin (whose real name was Orison Whipple Hungerford, Jr.) was an American actor best known as the star of the ABC/Warner Brothers TV series *Bronco* (1958-62).

Von Diepel quizzes Shumacher about American baseball players and finds his knowledge to be flawless. He then asks him his opinion of Adolf Hitler. Shumacher is reluctant to speak out, as he knows his opinions may offend some Germans who are present, but under pressure declares that the Nazi leader is 'a crazy Austrian housepainter, a madman who thinks he knows more than the German General Staff and is leading Germany to complete destruction'. General Kohler is displeased at these remarks but Hessler grins, saying that the Lieutenant should be congratulated on his reflexes.

Kohler takes Hessler further along the corridor and opens another steel door with a key. They ascend some stairs and find themselves in a control room. It looks rather like the operations rooms employed by the RAF's Fighter Command during the Battle of Britain. On the far side of the room is a large map showing north-west Europe. Kohler explains that the plan involves an advance from the River Meuse to the port of Antwerp in only four days. This will split the Allied armies, and he estimates that it will take them 18 months to recover. By that time Germany will have achieved air superiority with jets and will have other more significant weapons that can destroy cities with a single blast (a reference to nuclear weapons, though by this point in the war Germany had already lost the race to build an atomic bomb).

Colonel Hessler points out the snags of the plan, namely that the Allies have control of the air. Allied aircraft will bomb his tanks and machine-gun his troops, but the General asserts that there will be no planes in the air to interfere with the operation. Hessler wonders if this is another secret weapon, but the General reveals that it is nothing more than a weather report. He gives Hessler a bulletin from Spitzbergen weather station which indicates that a low-pressure area will move into north-west Europe on 16 December. This will result in low cloud and fog which will ground all aircraft.

Kohler then points to a clock on the far side of the control room which has a rather odd face. Instead of being numbered from one to 12 it is a 50-hour clock, and the general explains that the German army only has sufficient supplies for 50 hours of full-scale attack.

Hessler is then taken to a German army yard outside the bunker. About 30 brand-new King Tiger tanks are lined up for inspection with their crews. Unfortunately the buildings in the background display signs of Spanish architecture (such as terracotta roofs) and the blazing sunshine, clear blue skies and very short shadows indicate that this scene was shot in the summer.

The next scene is set in the Belgian town of Ambleve on a large outdoor set constructed in Spain at a cost of $500,000. The only indication that it is supposedly mid-December comes from a few scattered patches of artificial snow on the ground as a Jeep draws up outside the Hotel D'Ambleve, which is being now a divisional HQ. Benjamin Frankel's theme at this point has a Christmassy feel to it.

Lieutenant Colonel Kiley jumps out the Jeep and goes into the HQ building. A Christmas tree is being set up in the foyer as he hands in the camera film from his recent photo reconnaissance mission for urgent processing. He is met by Colonel Pritchard (Dana Andrews) and then goes into another room which is occupied by his commanding officer, General Grey (Robert Ryan). A second Christmas tree has been set up in the commander's office. Grey is behind his desk reading intercepted German messages sent by Field Marshal Keitel, who is specifically looking for officers and men who speak English. Kiley sees this as confirmation that the Germans are going to attack the allies very soon as they may be preparing a 'fifth column'. (The term 'fifth column' describes a group of persons who undermine a larger group from within, and originated during the Spanish Civil War.)

Colonel Pritchard is dismissive of his claims, and mentions that Kiley's pre-war experience was in the civilian police force. However, General Grey is at least willing to listen to him and asks him why he thinks that the Germans might be mounting an offensive.

Kiley points out that the Germans are still undefeated, but Pritchard starts to argue with him. At this point one of General Grey's aides enters with some photographic prints which have been developed from the film Kiley brought in a few moments earlier (a piece of remarkably fast processing!). One of the photos shows Colonel Hessler's face, but at this point the Americans don't know who he is. Another photo shows a King Tiger tank concealed in a wood, but Pritchard again dismisses this, saying that 'one Tiger doesn't make a jungle' and that General Patton's 3rd Army will be attacking in the Sahr region in the south in two days' time, and that they wouldn't be doing this if an attack was imminent.

But Colonel Kiley suggests that HQ could be wrong and asks for more information on the German officer who was spotted in one of these aerial photographs. General Grey also suggests that Kiley goes to the front line to capture some German prisoners for intelligence-gathering purposes.

Meanwhile, back in the underground bunker HQ in Germany, Hessler is enjoying a lavish meal. Conrad enters the room and Hessler asks his driver to join him for a glass of wine. Hessler is now in a relaxed mood and asks Conrad to speak his mind. It is clear that his driver is war-weary and cynical about the chances of Germany's success in the coming conflict. 'The hope that there is one more chance, that is the illusion. No, it is an illusion you must give up.'

But Colonel Hessler replies testily:

'Four years ago we overran Poland in a month. We went to Paris in 39 days; that was not an illusion. We conquered the Crimea. When I have a brigade of tanks, that is reality.'

But Conrad remains sceptical and mentions the incident earlier with the reconnaissance aircraft.

'How sure can we be of the men who drive the tanks?' he asks.

Hessler is upset by his colleague's comments and gets on the phone, indicating that he wants to see his tank commanders. Soon afterwards they all assemble in a large room in the underground bunker. Nazi slogans are painted on the walls including *Der Sieg wird un Sein* (The Victory Will Be Ours) and *Wir Kapitulen nie* (We Never Capitulate). All the Panzer commanders wear black uniforms, which is correct for the period. During the war this led to many Allied soldiers mistaking German tank crews for SS soldiers.

Hessler has reservations about the apparent youth of the tank commanders, but General Kohler points out that they are ready to die for him. He instructs the tank commanders to sing the *Panzerlied* ('The Tank Song'). This was not written specially for the movie but was a genuine *Wehrmacht* song, composed in June 1933 by Adolf Hoffman with lyrics by Kurt Wiehle. This song became the unofficial anthem of the German Armoured Forces in WW2. It has three stanzas and in the film the tank commanders actually sing the first stanza three times. An English translation of the lyrics of the first stanza is as follows :

> *Whether it storms or snows, whether the sun smiles on us,*
> *The day burning hot, or ice cold the night,*
> *Dusty are our faces, but joyful is our mind, yes our mind,*
> *Our tank roars here in the storm's wind*
> *Our tank roars here in the storm's wind.*

The commanders comply and start to sing the song, stamping their right feet as they do so. Hessler asks Conrad to sing as well and the two of them eventually join in.

Since its use in the film, the song has proved very popular with the modern-day German Army. The author also witnessed a group of historical re-enactors singing the song while portraying German *panzergrenadiers* at the 2009 'War and Peace Show' at Beltring in Kent. However, in 2017 the German Minister of Defence Ursula von Leyen formally banned the song because of its Nazi connections!

Meanwhile Kiley is approaching the American front line in his Jeep. The vehicle – which is a post-war M39 with a single-piece windshield instead of the split screen of wartime Ford and Willys models – carries the US military number 2542 and is painted in green and brown camouflage. This was the standard Spanish Army camouflage scheme in 1965, and American markings were simply applied over it as was the case with most of the vehicles employed in the film. In the European theatre in WW2, US Army vehicles were painted an overall olive drab and tanks were often given a coat of temporary whitewash during snowy conditions.

The Jeep is forced to stop, as the road is partially blocked by an American Sherman tank 'Bargain Basement' commanded by Sgt Guffy (Telly Savalas). Contemporary jazz is playing on the tank's radio as Guffy tells his driver to get the armoured vehicle off the road so that the officer can pass. But the tank is piled high with boxes of what Guffy describes as 'merchandise', including Lucky Strike cigarettes, bottles of Scotch whisky and French champagne, perfume and nylon stockings, and in the hurry to get the Sherman off the road, some boxes fall to the ground and break open. As Guffy attempts to sort out the mess and re-stack the items, one crew member complains about the fact that they haven't seen much action. All the crew wear the correct US Army tanker's uniform for the period.

Soon afterwards, Kiley's Jeep drives up to the bunker on the Siegfried Line, which has been taken over by the US Army. The Siegfried Line (aka the Westwall) was a set of fortifications which marked the western border of Germany and was comparable to the well-known French Maginot Line. In the autumn of 1944 the US Army advanced as far as the Siegfried Line, taking over some of the bunkers, but didn't go any further.

Kiley enters the bunker (known as 'Hindenburg'), which has 'under new management' painted on it, and knocks on the door demanding entry. He notices that there is no sentry. Inside the bunker, a large group of American soldiers are trying to make their accommodation as homely as possible. They are burning wood in a potbellied stove and listening to Christmas carols on the radio. They have even set up a Christmas tree inside the bunker, and washed uniforms are hanging out to dry on a line. Kiley is welcomed by Major Wolenski (Charles Bronson), who offers him some fresh coffee as he warms himself by the stove. Wolenski observes that the Germans don't have any heating in their own bunkers and are forced to exercise outside to keep warm.

Kiley has a proposition for the Major. He intends to take some soldiers out on a night patrol to pick up a few prisoners for interrogation. As he is outlining his plan, the tough Sergeant Duquesne (George Montgomery) unblocks one of the windows and attempts to shoot some nearby Germans with a sniper rifle. He only fires one round before Lieutenant Weaver (James MacArthur) tells him to stop shooting. MacArthur was an American actor who is best-known for playing Danny 'Danno' Williams in the long-running TV police show *Hawaii Five-o* (1968-80). His presence in the show led to the famous catchphrase 'Book 'em, Danno', as uttered by Detective Captain Steve McGarrett (Jack Lord).

However, Sergeant Duquesne's zeal cannot be dampened that easily, and he suggests taking the men outside for field drill. However, Lieutenant Weaver is not keen on this because of the cold weather. All of this has been observed by Kiley, who suggests that this particular Sergeant leads the patrol. Wolenski agrees and says he will pick the rest of the volunteers required for the mission. As it will be four hours until dark, he suggests that Kiley might like to have some whisky in his coffee and offers him some 'half-and-half'. Kiley asks him to simply 'sweeten it', as he does not want to drink too much alcohol before a mission.

Back at the German underground bunker, Colonel Hessler is in his room when there is a knock at the door. A blonde lady, Elena (Barbara Werle), has come to see him. She has been sent by General Kohler and describes herself as a 'courtesan first-class'. Elena chides the Colonel for not offering her a drink and mentions that the General admires his reputation with the ladies. However, Colonel Hessler rejects her advances and sends her away. Barbara Werle was an actress who was also the girlfriend of William Foreman, the owner of the Cinerama process and Cinerama theatres. Her main credits at that point were minor roles in two Elvis Presley movies, *Tickle Me* and *Harum Scarum* (both 1965). At Foreman's insistence, she appeared in this brief scene in *Battle of the Bulge* as a way of advancing her career.

The next scene is set in the underground control room, where a large plotting table has been installed complete with a map and model tanks. The Germans are preparing to launch their operation. Meanwhile, the American patrol has captured some German prisoners during its foray near the Siegfried Line. The men return as Colonel Pritchard arrives. He inspects one of the prisoners using a hurricane lamp and is dismayed at the poor quality of the troops. He examines one of the Germans' rifles and notices that there is grease in the barrel, and that is has never been fired. He concludes that the Germans are now so short of infantrymen that they are sending children to the front line.

However, Lieutenant Colonel Kiley believes it is all a trick. He thinks that these young, inexperienced troops could have been planted in the front line to mislead Allied intelligence. He also notices that all the prisoners are carrying lengths of rubber hose, though the reason for this does not become clear until later in the film.

Pritchard and Kiley then argue, with the former suggesting that he is going to recommend that he is transferred to a desk job in Washington. Later, Kiley drinks coffee with Major Wolenski. The intelligence officer is convinced he is correct in his assumptions. Wolenski then hands a message to Kiley that has arrived from HQ. It gives details of the German officer that Kiley photographed from the Cessna reconnaissance aircraft. He is Colonel Martin Hessler, a highly-experienced Panzer commander who has been transferred from the Russian front. Wolenski then makes his feelings clear about Nazi Germany. He feels that the Allies now have a chance to completely wipe out Germany and turn into 'a prairie' suitable only for buffaloes.

The next scene shows a twin-engined transport aircraft flying across a night-time sky. It is easily identifiable as an American Douglas C-47. There is then a quick cut to a shot of German paratroopers in American uniforms exiting from the door on the port side of the fuselage of a German Junkers 52/3m transport plane. This scene was filmed in the studio with a mock-up fuselage section, although it could theoretically have been shot with a real aircraft as the Spanish Air Force owned a number of CASA 352s (licence-built Junkers 52s) at the time the film was made and two of these aircraft appeared in the film *Battle of Britain* (1969). The parachutists land heavily on the ground, in a scene shot 'day for night' in the studio, and start cursing in German but their leader, Lieutenant Schumacher, orders them to speak entirely in English from that point on.

Back at the German HQ, General Kohler learns that the German paratroopers have landed, and there is a quick cut to a shot of a German parachutist wearing a white snow smock climbing a telegraph pole to cut telephone wires. This part of the plot is entirely accurate, as a unit of German troops disguised as Americans – led by SS Officer Otto Skorzeny – infiltrated Allied lines during the Battle of the Bulge in a mission known as Operation Greif. They also drove a number of captured American vehicles and two Panther tanks which were modified and painted to look like American M10 tank destroyers.

A large formation of King Tiger tanks is assembled in the woods near the American frontline. The one nearest the camera has the code R-01 on the side of its turret. After a ten to one countdown in the control room the Panzers start to roll forward accompanied by several halftracks (American M3s rather than the correct Sd. Kfz.251s), one of which is towing a large caravan.

In the 'Hindenburg' bunker nearby, the American troops are woken by the sound of running tank engines and squeaking tracks. All the troops get out of their bunks, grab their weapons and leave the bunker in a hurry. One soldier tries the field telephone but the line is dead (thanks to the work of Shumacher's men).

In a nearby farmhouse the crews of two American Sherman tanks – namely 'Bargain Basement' commanded by Sgt Guffy, plus 'Blondie' – are woken by the noise and run to man their vehicles. The two vehicles start up and move forward to meet the attackers.

As the American troops fan out in the snow to take on the advancing Germans, Major Wolenski shows one of the GIs how to fit a rifle grenade onto his M1 Garand and mutters that this should have been covered in basic training. The German King Tiger tanks leave the cover of the woods and advance towards the American infantry. One soldier fires his bazooka at the nearest King Tiger but the round simply bounces off the left side of the turret and the infantryman is hit by return fire. The bazookas in the film were all Spanish-made M-65 rocket launchers, a modern weapon with a calibre of 3.5 inches rather than the historically correct M1, M1A1 and M9 wartime bazookas which fired a relatively small rocket of only 2.36 inch calibre. The M-65 in this scene was fitted with an armoured shield rather like that installed in the *Panzerschreck*, the German copy of the bazooka which had a calibre of 88mm.

Major Wolenski picks up the discarded bazooka and decides to take on the King Tiger himself. Colonel Kiley (who is accompanying him) makes it clear that he wants to see inside the tank. As the King Tiger R-01 trundles forward, Wolenski fires the anti-tank rocket launcher and scores a hit on the Tiger's left track. This damages the links and brings the Tiger to a halt. In military parlance, Wolenski has scored what is known as a 'mobility kill'. Colonel Hessler orders the tank to slew off the road so that the others can get past, giving Colonel Kiley an opportunity to capture it. Carrying a hand grenade and an M3 'grease gun' (a 0.45 inch calibre sub machine gun), Kiley approaches the tank and kills the commander (who is standing in the hatch) with a short burst of fire. He then throws in a grenade to kill the rest of the crew and pokes his head inside the hatch. He can hear Colonel Hessler speaking on the radio. Hessler calls the tank '104', even though the code on the turret is 'R-01'. Incidentally, in the German system of tank numbering 'R-01' indicates a regimental commander's tank, so this code should be on Hessler's vehicle.

Meanwhile, the two Sherman tanks we saw a few moments earlier prepare to engage the Tigers. 'Blondie' is soon knocked out, but Sergeant Guffy in 'Bargain Basement' returns fire and notices that his rounds simply bounce off the thick armour of the King Tigers.

'Is it's like hitting them with tennis balls', exclaims the American tank commander.

Suddenly one of the King Tigers rams 'Bargain Basement' and overturns it (an excellent miniature shot), and Guffy is forced to exit from the commander's hatch and crawl away to safety. In the meantime Sergeant Duquesne keeps firing rifle grenades at the advancing German force, but the projectiles are too small to damage the German tanks.

Back at the German control room, word is received that the American resistance has proved weak and that the tanks are now fording a river. The battle is not entirely one-sided however, as one German tank commander is hit by machine gun fire as he stands in his hatch. The Americans retreat, leaving their vehicles behind. One Jeep is apparently left blazing but this is achieved by the non-destructive method employed in films, namely placing a propane gas burner directly behind the vehicle, creating the illusion that it is on fire.

Sergeant Duquesne and Lieutenant Weaver are arguing about whether they should surrender, but the tough experienced sergeant insists they should 'stay loose' and they head to the motor pool where they can pick up a Jeep.

The German advance continues and, in a caravan towed by a halftrack, Hessler is addressing some of his commanders. The first phase of the attack has been successful, but they must cross the Our River as soon as possible. Hessler subsequently speaks to General Kohler on the radio. The General offers his congratulations on his initial success, but Hessler is still concerned about the Our River bridge and asks if Lieutenant Shumacher's men have seized it yet. The General points out that that unit's primary mission is to disrupt communications, but all the same he promises Hessler that the bridge will be secured.

Hessler now has a headache and opens a sliding door to go into the other room in the caravan where he asks Conrad for a painkiller. Suddenly the caravan is shaken by an explosion. The vehicle has struck a mine, and all the commanders in the other part of the caravan have been killed. A King Tiger draws up beside the wrecked vehicle – it is tank R-01, the same one which was supposedly knocked out by Major Wolenski's bazooka earlier in the film.

Hessler is angry that his column wasn't preceded by men carrying mine detectors, but Von Diepel says that that simply wasn't possible as they are advancing too rapidly. The Colonel angrily replies that from now on the infantry will go ahead of the tanks.

Back at the Divisional HQ in Ambleve, the Americans are in a state of near-panic. General Grey says he needs detailed information on the strength of the German forces which are attacking. Kiley arrives and points out that the Germans have 'crack troops and brand-new equipment that can chew up anything we've got'. Grey reiterates that if they knew where Colonel Hessler was heading, they would discover the objective of the entire attack. At the moment the Germans are probing at five separate points along an 85-mile front.

Grey guesses that one likely objective must be the Our River, as it has the only bridge that can take the weight of heavy tanks. Kiley says he will get there as fast as possible, but Grey warns him to be careful as he has ordered the bridge to be blown.

The next shot shows a convoy of American vehicles retreating over the Our River bridge. In the foreground stands an American soldier with his back to the camera. It is Lieutenant Schumacher, and he is observing the scene very carefully.

Sergeant Duquesne and Lieutenant Weaver draw up in a Jeep. The Sergeant is wrong-footed by the road signs as the one pointing to Ambleve is directing him down what he believes to be the road to Malmedy. He realises that someone has moved the signs and starts to argue with two MPs who are directing traffic (including Lieutenant Shumacher), who insists he is wrong. Eventually he heads down the road suggested by the MPs, even though he knows it is incorrect.

Meanwhile, Guffy and his driver jump off a US Army GMC truck as he needs to collect some of his 'merchandise' as Major Wolenski crosses the Our River bridge in another vehicle. He sees some MPs fixing explosive charges to the bridge and knows something is wrong, though he can't put a finger on it. The MPs establish that Wolenski's vehicle is the last one in the column, and then Schumacher contacts Hessler's tank column on his 'walkie-talkie' radio to inform them that the bridge has been secured.

Suddenly a US Army Dodge Weapons Carrier drives up. It contains six sappers tasked with blowing the bridge, but Lieutenant Shumacher says the job is already in hand and shows them his men applying charges to the bridge. But the Lieutenant in charge of the squad becomes concerned when he sees one of Schumacher's men wiring a detonator incorrectly and decides to check out the rest of the work. Without hesitating, Schumacher and his men gun down the American soldiers.

Some miles away, American vehicles are in a traffic jam by the roadside, having been wrongly directed by Schumacher's fake MPs. Major Wolenski consults a map as Kiley arrives. The American Colonel soon twigs that the road signs at the Our River bridge have been moved, and asks Wolenski if he had noticed anything odd about the MPs who were directing traffic. Wolenski thinks for a moment and then realises that he had seen MPs placing explosive charges, something that was not normal practice. He tells Kiley, who puts out an urgent radio message to warn that the MPs at the Our River are really German soldiers and that the bridge had not been blown.

Kiley drives off as a single American Sherman tank arrives at the Our River bridge. The tank commander notices the dead bodies of the sappers and asks Shumacher what happened. The Lieutenant explains that they were attacked by a German patrol, but the tank commander is sceptical of this claim as there are no dead Germans. Suddenly the tank receives an urgent radio message. The MPs are really Germans!

Schumacher's men open fire on the tank, but the commander ducks down inside the turret as the Sherman rolls forward. The tank, appropriately named 'Kraut Killer', moves ahead and sprays the Germans with bullets from its co-axial and hull-mounted thirty-calibre machine guns. The commander reappears in the hatch and joins in, firing the powerful fifty-calibre gun mounted on top of the turret. Most of the Germans are killed but a few survive by diving into the river, including Lieutenant Schumacher himself.

Suddenly the spearhead of the German tank force arrives on the scene and two King Tigers trundle onto the road. The American Sherman tank fires two shells at the leading Tiger, but they bounce off its thick armour and the US vehicle is immediately knocked out by a single 88mm round from the Tiger.

The bridge is now blocked by the blazing hulk of the Sherman, and Hessler is angry at the delay. A soldier explains that they are preparing to tow the wrecked vehicle off the road, but Hessler has no time for such a lengthy procedure and orders the tank to be blasted out of the way. The Sherman is hit by three further 88mm rounds and is then shoved over the side of the bridge by a King Tiger, destroying the parapet in the process. This scene was done 'for real' at the Puento Rio Eresma near Segovia, rather than using a miniature, and includes some impressive subjective camerawork via a 70mm camera attached to the right-hand side of a Tiger. For the scene where the Sherman hulk crashes through the stonework, the original masonry was carefully removed and replaced with Styrofoam blocks. If you look carefully you can see some of them floating on the water!

As the Germans are disposing of the wrecked Sherman, Von Diepel arrives in a halftrack. He points out that the advance is already three hours behind schedule and Hessler proclaims that the Americans are learning how to retreat.

As the German column rolls over the bridge, Kiley arrives in a Jeep with his driver, Murphy. He tells him to send a radio message to inform HQ that the Our Bridge is intact and then borrows his rifle. He intends to assassinate Colonel Hessler, but his bullet misses and goes through the windscreen of a German lorry. This has unintended consequences, as the truck skids to one side and some of its load of fuel drums spills over the side of the Our Bridge. Kiley sees this through binoculars and notices that the drums are floating, indicating that they are empty.

As the Americans continue to retreat, the Jeep 'Kansas Express' – requisitioned by Sergeant Duquesne and Lieutenantt Weaver – has broken down. The Sergeant opens the bonnet and declares that the breakdown is due to a carburettor failure. Suddenly the two soldiers hear the sound of an approaching German halftrack and they take cover in nearby shrubs. Seeing the abandoned Jeep with its bonnet up, the *Panzergrenadiers* stop their vehicle and search the surrounding area. Hiding nearby, Sergeant Duquesne prepares to throw a grenade at the enemy soldiers, but Lieutenant Weaver panics and surrenders and the Sergeant is forced to do likewise. He is angry as he feels he could have taken out the Germans. Back at the control room in the German HQ, General Kohler is receiving reports that the Americans are in headlong retreat with many prisoners taken.

In a snow-covered field near Malmedy, a German lorry discharges a truckload of prisoners who start to stretch their legs. Another German truck reverses towards them and – without warning – an MG42 machine- gun mounted in the rear opens fire. Duquesne and Weaver run for their lives but although the Lieutenant reaches the safety of the trees, the Sergeant is hit and dies instantly. This incident really happened (on 17 December 1944) and subsequently became known as the 'Malmedy Massacre'. Although there was no snow on the ground at the time of the mass shooting, snow soon fell and covered the bodies. As depicted in the film, the slaughter is a bit like the massacre near the end of *The Great Escape* (1963) as it involved a single machine gun mounted in the rear of a truck, but in reality two Panzer IV tanks used their machine guns to kill the prisoners.

In the town of Ambleve, American forces continue to retreat while Sgt Guffy meets his Belgian black market trading partner Louise (Pier Angeli) in a bedroom in the Ambleve Inn which is stacked full of merchandise, including chickens and eggs. Guffy realises he will have to leave as the Germans are coming, but Louise says she is staying as she has lived through German occupation before and believes she can handle it. Louise also tells Guffy she is in love with him, a revelation which leaves the American Sergeant gobsmacked.

'But I never laid a finger on you.'

'That's why.'

Still stunned, Guffy kisses Louise and then leaves.

Meanwhile, the German spearhead is approaching Ambleve, and Hessler views the town (an impressive miniature) through binoculars. He orders his tanks to take up positions to bombard the buildings.

In the town of Ambleve, General Grey comes to a tough decision. There are to be no more retreats, and all units except for tank formations are to stand and fight. Every man who can carry a rifle will be compelled to do so.

Outside the Divisional HQ at the Hotel D'Ambleve, Colonel Pritchard apologizes to Kiley for his misinterpretation of intelligence information and admits he was wrong, while General Grey requests some heavy artillery in the form of 155mm guns. The weapons are to be moved to the front by rail car as the Americans still hold the railway lines.

The next few minutes of footage shows the guns being moved by train and are the first shots in the film which really don't depict the weather conditions in Belgium during the Ardennes offensive, as they show a sun-scorched landscape and clear blue skies. They almost look almost like stock footage from a Western. In these scenes there are many subjective point-of-view shots taken by an Ultra-Panavision 70mm camera fixed to the front of the train as it speeds downhill, through woods and tunnels and across girder bridges. Some of these shots were speeded up to make them more exciting and were designed to showcase the ultra-widescreen Cinerama process, which would have been thrilling to watch on a cinema screen back in the sixties. Again, these sequences were shot at the request of Cinerama owner William Foreman and edited into the film.

Unfortunately the train's departure has been spotted by the Germans, and a single King Tiger tank (a very convincing miniature) is despatched to deal with the problem. It rolls onto the tracks and – standing at the mouth of a tunnel – fires a single 88mm round at the oncoming engine which is totally destroyed.

Back at Ambleve, the Americans are preparing their defences which include artillery pieces of different calibres, mortars, machine guns and bazookas. Colonel Hessler's tanks are positioned on the skyline in line abreast formation, and open fire on the town as Major Wolenski orders the cooks to discard their aprons and grab some rifles as every man is needed to defend the town. The German tanks roll forward accompanied by infantry, but soon the Wehrmacht troops take heavy casualties from the defenders' fire. Mortar bombs and shells burst among the attacking troops and soon they are driven back with heavy losses.

On a ridge overlooking Ambleve, Colonel Hessler takes stock of the situation as General Kohler arrives in a Mercedes staff car accompanied by two BMW motorcycle/sidecar combinations and a rather inaccurate replica of a VW Type 82 Kubelwagen, which was reportedly created from a Citroen 2CV.

The General wants Hessler to attack, but the experienced Colonel says this might result in heavy losses and they go into Hessler's caravan for a chat. General Kohler is displeased as – according to his schedule – his column should be two kilometres west of Ambleve by now.

General Kohler suggests bypassing Ambleve but Hessler says he would prefer a night attack with all his armour. He shows Kohler a chocolate cake which had been taken off an American Private that day. It had been made in Boston and was still fresh. Hessler postulates that if the Americans have fuel and planes to ship chocolate cake across the Atlantic then they can have no concept of defeat. He then asks permission to reduce Ambleve to ashes. Kohler agrees, but stipulates that Hessler attack by 0400 hrs.

In the original cinema version of the film, there is an intermission at this point complete with special caption slide and music. After the intermission the film resumes with a panoramic shot of King Tiger tanks lined up on the skyline, another scene that would have looked particularly impressive in Cinerama.

General Grey and Colonel Pritchard prepare to leave the town as the Germans attack. This time the infantry are behind the tanks. The Americans put up stiff resistance, bombarding the Tigers with petrol bombs. As the German tanks adopt a nose-up attitude to climb over log barricades, American troops place slabs of plastic explosive on the thinner armour of their undersides. Before he leaves, Kiley gives Wolenski back his M1 rifle.

Despite intense resistance, the Germans capture Ambleve and their flag is hoisted over the former US Forces HQ as American prisoners are marched through the town. Three nuns ask Hessler for medical supplies, but he says he has none to spare though he is willing to let them have captured American supplies. Suddenly Hessler is nearly hit by a bullet fired from a nearby window. German troops soon capture the sniper, who is revealed to be a teenage boy. His father begs for mercy as he is an only child. Hessler orders the boy to be released but declares that the father should be shot instead.

Von Diepel then informs Hessler that the senior American officer wants to speak to him urgently. Hessler asks his rank and is told that he is a Major, before he goes into his caravan where Conrad has laid out a spread of wine and fine foods obtained In Ambleve. Hessler declines the excellent food and asks Conrad to serve him the same rations as his men as he needs to know how long they can go on. He then tells Conrad that he has a Christmas present for him – news that his two sons have both been promoted to First Sergeants.

Major Wolenski enters the caravan in a belligerent mood. He tells Hessler about the Malmedy Massacre and wants an assurance that his men will be treated in accordance with the Geneva Convention. He wants this in writing or else his men may riot, killing some of the German occupiers in the process. Hessler replies to the Major's demands in an equally assertive fashion. There will be no written orders and there will be no riot. Wolenski warns him that if anything happens to his men he will hold him responsible and that there are always survivors from every massacre.

Hessler responds by saying that he has never tolerated threats and realises that the American is trying to provoke him. If he doesn't return to his men they will know that they will have to riot so he asks Von Diepel to take him back.

After the Major has left, Hessler calls General Kohler on the radio and asks him to confirm whether American prisoners were massacred at Malmedy. Kohler says that SS units were operating in the area and were responsible for the killings. The Colonel is aghast, as he realises that news of the massacre will stiffen resistance and turn the beaten American soldiers into avengers.

Some miles away General Grey, Colonel Pritchard and Lieutenant Colonel Kiley look on as a convoy of US vehicles drive along a muddy road. Grey concedes that his men have taken a beating, but they are not a rabble. His plan now is to retreat to the west bank of the River Meuse and dig in. At least they will get the Germans' feet wet. Grey asks Kiley for his opinion. The Germans have made mistakes before. Where did they go wrong this time?

Suddenly, Sergeant Guffy's tank trundles along the road. The engine is stuttering as it is almost out of petrol. Employing his last dregs of fuel, the driver slews the tank off the road. Guffy jumps off his vehicle and screams at the crew of a passing truck which is laden with fuel drums. The lorry stops and a soldier throws one of the heavy containers of petrol out the back. It lands in a large puddle with a splash and soaks Guffy with muddy water. Guffy screams at the squaddie who then leaps out and punches him in the face before handing him a rubber tube. Guffy and his crew then get to work siphoning the petrol into jerrycans to make it easier to refuel the tank.

Kiley and Pritchard see this and start thinking as General Grey asks them what is on their minds. The German prisoners captured at the Siegfried Line were all carrying lengths of rubber hose and at the Our River, Kiley had witnessed a German truck carrying empty fuel drums. Perhaps the Germans are short of fuel and are depending on captured supplies to keep them going?

Grey realises this may be the answer to their prayers and he asks one of his aides to obtain three pieces of information, namely the fuel consumption of a Tiger tank (actually two gallons per mile), the distance from the Siegfried Line to the Meuse, and an estimate of the fuel reserves of the German Army.

Back in the German control room, the officers receive news that the Belgian town of Bastogne is now surrounded while, in the town itself, a German motorcycle/sidecar combination with a white flag attached approaches an American outpost. The German Commander wishes to negotiate surrender terms with the Americans. The American officer in charge orders him to be blindfolded and taken to the command position.

Later, at the German control room, General Kohler receives the reply from the American commander. It is only one word: 'Nuts'. This incident really did happen at Bastogne on 22 December and the officer responsible for the brief reply was General McAuliffe, though his name wasn't mentioned in the film as a consequence of the legal case between Columbia Pictures and Warner Brothers.

That evening some American soldiers who have got cut off from their unit take shelter in a broken building where they discover Lieutenant Weaver. They ask him whether they should surrender and he says they should not. 'Stay loose,' he says. The Malmedy Massacre and the death of Sergeant Duquesne have stiffened his resolve.

At the new US Forces temporary HQ, Sergeant Guffy asks if anyone knows what has happened to the Ambleve Inn, and is told that it has been completely destroyed. As he starts to leave he meets General Grey and asks him a rhetorical question: 'When are they going to let us fight?'

Colonel Pritchard gives General Grey the information he requested earlier, leading the General to conclude that the Germans are short of fuel. He decides to commit his tanks with the aim of intercepting the German spearhead nine miles east of the fuel depot. A brief shot follows showing American tank crews mounting their vehicles. General Grey, though, is dismayed at the current foggy conditions which will make it hard for the Americans to find the German spearhead, and he communicates these concerns to Kiley.

Meanwhile, the German armoured column continues its advance. In his caravan Hessler is delighted that his column is in the lead and is pleased to learn that he is to be decorated by Hitler. Conrad though is more cynical.

'Have we won the war?' he asks.

But the German Colonel says 'no' and indicates that it will go on and on and on indefinitely, which to him is a good outcome. He indicates that – as far back as 1941 – key German military figures knew that the Reich could not possibly win the war, but now they have achieved a kind of victory as the world is not going to get rid of them.

'When do we go home?' asks Conrad.

'This is home!'

Conrad then asks about his two sons, and Hessler replies that they will become German soldiers and he will be proud of them. Hessler is left feeling very upbeat by the conversation, and asks Conrad to give him the delicacies he had offered him at Ambleve.

Some miles away Kiley is forced to take drastic measures to locate the German column and he persuades his pilot, Joe, to take him aloft in his Cessna. Joe is very concerned about this risky bit of flying in dense fog, but Kiley points out that if they can't locate the column then it won't be possible to deploy tanks and the Germans will have to be stopped by infantry, resulting in huge casualties.

Joe responds to this 'below the belt' argument and soon the pair are airborne, searching for the German column. Kiley points that if they could pick up a landmark it would greatly aid navigation.

'We'll pick up a landmark all right,' says Joe. 'Right on the kisser!'

Kiley asks Joe to cut his engine and then he listens out the open window to see if he can pick up the sound of the German column. Eventually Kiley finds the fuel depot and guesses that the German spearhead is due south of it. At 400 feet altitude, Joe cuts the engine again and Kiley first hears and then sees the German column.

Kiley orders Joe to start the engine again and fly away to safety as he gives a position report over the radio, but within seconds the plane is hit by anti-aircraft fire and crashes next to the fuel depot where an injured Kiley is rescued by American soldiers.

At the German HQ, General Kohler receives word from the weather station at Spitzbergen that the low pressure area is now moving away from north-west Europe and the skies are due to clear. This means the date must be 22 December 1944.

Back in Hessler's caravan, Conrad is in the next room. He informs the Colonel that he wants to be transferred to other duties 'for personal reasons', as this is his legal right. But Hessler presses him further and discovers that Conrad has become cynical about the war and has realised that his commanding officer has become obsessed with it. 'You like the war... you are a traitor and a murderer', he says.

Hessler is aghast at the revelations and says that the only reason he is not having him court-martialled is their past respectful friendship. Suddenly Von Diepel arrives and informs Hessler that their scouts have sighted a brigade of medium tanks. Hessler thanks Von Diepel for the update and asks him to assign Conrad to fuel truck duties.

At the American HQ Grey hears that the Germans are advancing towards the American tanks. They have taken the bait and Grey's plan is to make the Panzers burn up as much fuel as possible.

On a sun-scorched landscape with blue skies, the American Shermans prepare to attack the advancing Tigers. Their plan is to position their vehicles in a gulley at the bottom of a steep slope, and then fire upwards to hit the German tanks' thinner underbelly armour as they rise to cross the crest of the ridge. These battle scenes were filmed at the US Army Yakima firing range in Washington State in the USA, though many shots were achieved using miniatures.

The commander of the American formation orders his tanks to hold their fire until the Germans are within effective range and instructs the gunners to load with 'hypershot' – a nickname for HVAP (High Velocity Armour Piercing) ammunition which was issued to American tanks from late 1944 onwards. HVAP shells had a greater armour-piercing capability than the standard 76mm AP rounds but were in short supply, so most American tanks only carried a couple of such shells. HVAP ammunition was only manufactured for the 76mm gun (and the larger 90mm weapon fitted to the M26 Pershing tank and the M36 tank destroyer), so this line of dialogue indicates that the American tanks in the film were supposed to be 76mm armed M4s rather than 75mm gun tanks.

Inside his tank Hessler orders his men to attack in staggered formation. The American commander waits until the German Tigers are cresting the ridge and then orders his men to blast them. Several Tigers are hit, and the American commander orders his men to fire one more round and then get off the ridge. A very impressive helicopter shot follows as the camera tracks from one side to the other, showing the large number of tanks in this sequence.

A large number of miniature tanks were employed in these sequences, which were overseen by Art Director Eugene Lourie. The models were three feet long with two horsepower motors and were constructed by Charles Henri-

Assola. These small tanks were remotely controlled with separate commands to make them go forward or backwards, rotate their turrets, and fire their guns. The main cannon even had a working recoil mechanism.

As the Americans retreat, Hessler destroys a damaged Sherman while the American commander orders his more nimble vehicles to get in among the Germans so that they can't fire without hitting one another. Sergeant Guffy sees a tank with a pennant on its antenna and decides to attack it, but his Sherman 'Bargain Basement' is hit by a round from Hessler's tank which blows off most of the turret. Interestingly, 'Bargain Basement' was Guffy's tank when it was rammed and overturned by a Tiger much earlier in the film. Guffy wants to continue the fight but, as he has no functioning main gun, he is ordered to return to the assembly area as the Tigers destroy most of the remaining Shermans.

Back at the American HQ, General Grey receives news of the huge losses suffered by his tanks. But the battle has not been in in vain, as he knows it will have forced the Germans to burn up much of their scarce fuel. Meanwhile, Hessler is forced to return to the nearest German petrol depot – where Conrad is now working – to refuel. After topping up his fuel he orders 15 tanks and all available empty trucks to proceed to the nearby American fuel depot, which he intends to capture intact.

A few miles away, Sergeant Guffy is also heading to the American fuel depot to refuel his battered Sherman when he comes across Lieutenant Weaver and three other soldiers. Guffy still wants to fight as he still has a single thirty-calibre machine gun (which he holds in his arms) and two belts of ammunition, but Weaver persuades him that he is in no condition to take on enemy tanks. The four soldiers climb on board the tank and it heads to the fuel depot.

Hessler's tank column closes in on the fuel dump as General Grey receives word that the Germans are only four miles from the depot. He telephones the installation and orders that all fuel supplies be burned to stop them falling into the hands of the Germans. But unbeknown to the General, the person taking the call is none other than Lieutenant Shumacher, who is still alive and in command of a number of men. Shumacher hangs up the 'phone and orders his men to dispose of the bodies of the Americans who were manning the depot.

In the German control room, General Kohler hears that Hessler's tanks are only 3km from the depot as Guffy's damaged Sherman draws up outside the gates of the installation. Lieutenant Schumacher orders his men to hold their fire and let him do the talking. He offers to fill up Guffy's tank and get the Americans on their way as soon as possible, but Lieutenant Weaver recognises him and tells Guffy to get his machine gun ready to fire.

Lieutenant Weaver asks Shumacher if the road to Ambleve still leads to Malmedy. Instantly Shumacher attempts to open fire on the Americans, but they are too quick for him and he and his men are cut down by a hail of bullets with Guffy spraying rounds from his machine gun.

Nearby, a wounded Kiley hears the shooting and gets up from his sick bed to meet the new arrivals. Lieutenant Weaver sees Hessler's tanks coming up the road and realises that they are intending to capture the fuel supplies. He orders his men to set fire to the depot as Kiley arrives. But how are they going to deal with the approaching Panzers? Employing Guffy's Sherman as a bulldozer, the Americans roll some ruptured drums of petrol downhill towards the German tanks and then ignite them with bullets and grenades. The leading Tigers are consumed in the flames, and Hessler looks through a vision slit only to see a full drum of petrol rolling towards his tank which subsequently explodes in flames.

Two Jeeps arrive at the depot. General Grey gets out of one of them and surveys the scene with satisfaction. He learns that the Germans have abandoned their tanks due to lack of fuel and are walking back to Germany. The films ends with a shot of Conrad abandoning his rifle and most of his kit and marching back to the Fatherland followed by a panoramic view from a helicopter showing the abandoned battlefield. A caption informs viewers that 'places, names and action have been synthesised in order to convey the spirit and essence of the battle'. This is an interesting point. Screenwriter/Producer Milton Sperling claimed the film only covered the first week or so of the Battle of the Bulge, yet early in the screenplay we are introduced to the '50-hour clock' implying that the film ends on 18 December. Yet many of the events depicted in the movie happened much later than this, for example the 'Nuts' incident which occurred on 22 December.

Battle of the Bulge had its world premiere at the Pacific Cinerama Dome Theatre in Hollywood, California on 16 December 1965, which was the 21st anniversary of the battle. It was generally well-received by critics and was the most popular film at the UK box office in 1966. The score by Benjamin Frankel was nominated for a Golden Globe Award.

Not everyone was impressed, though, and the former President Dwight D. Eisenhower (who was the Allied Supreme Commander in 1944 and 1945) came out of retirement to hold a press conference at which he denounced the film for its mistakes. Though it may be inaccurate, *Battle of the Bulge* remains one of the most exciting and spectacular films ever made about the Second World War.

Battle of the Bulge (1965) Production Credits

Production Team

Director: Ken Annakin

Screenplay: Philip Yordan, Milton Sperling, John Melson

Cast

Lt. Col. Dan Kiley: Henry Fonda

Colonel Hessler: Robert Shaw

General Grey: Robert Ryan

Colonel Pritchard: Dana Andrews

Sergeant Duquesne: George Montgomery

Lt. Shumacher: Ty Hardin

Louise: Pier Angeli

Elena: Barbara Werle

Major Wolenski: Charles Bronson

Conrad: Hans Christian Blech

General Kohler: Werner Peters

Lieutenant Weaver: James McArthur

Von Diepel: Karl-Otto Alberty

Sergeant Guffy: Telly Savalas

Eddy: Steve Rowland

Joe (Kiley's Pilot): Robert Woods

Major Burke: Charles Stalnaker

Mother Superior: Janet Brandt

Nun: Quinn Donoghue

American MP: Carl Rapp

Narrator: William Conrad

Announcer: Robert Rietty

Production

Producers: Milton Sperling, Philip Yordan

Executive Producers: Dino De Laurentis, Sidney Harmon

Music

Composer: Benjamin Frankel

Cinematography

Director of Photography: Jack Hildyard

Art and Design

Art Director: Eugene Lourie

Costume Designer: Laure Dezarate

Makeup Department

Makeup Artists: Trevor Crole-Rees, Jose Maria Sanchez

Production Management

Unit Managers: Leon Chooluck, Juan Estelrich, Miguel Perez

Production Supervisor: Bernard Glasser

Production Managers: Tibor Reves, Gregorio Sacristan

Second Unit Director or Assistant Director

Assistant Directors: Luis Garcia, Jose Lopez Rodero, Martin Sacristan

Sound Department
Sound Editor: Kurt Hernnfield
Sound Recordists: David Hildyard, Gordon McCallum
Re-Recording Mixer: Otto Snel
Sound: Alban Streeter

Special Effects
Special Effects: Basilio Cortijo, Richard Parker, Kit West
Special Effects Chief: Alex Weldon
Special Effects Assistant: Antonio Baquero
Miniatures: Francisco Prosper, Henri Assola

Stunt Department
Stunts: Ken Buckle, Nosher Powell
Stunt Double: Jack Cooper

Camera and Electrical Department
Camera Assistant: Ronald Anscombe
Second Unit Photography: John Cabrera
Camera Operator: Dudley Lovell
Aerial Photography: Jack Willoughby

Costume and Wardrobe Department
Wardrobe: Charles Simminger

Editorial Department
Supervising Editor: Derek Parsons
Post-production Executive: Lester A. Sansom

Music Department
Conductor/Composer: Benjamin Frankel
Orchestra: The New Philharmonic Orchestra

Other Crew
Dialogue Coach: Janet Brandt
Production Coordinator: Lou Brandt
Military Advisors: Lt. Col. Sherman Joffe, Lt. Col. Luis Martin DePozuelo, Maj. Gen Meinrad Von Lauchert
Script Supervisors: Joy Mercer, Marie Wachsman
Title Designer: Wayne Fitzgerald
Technical Advisor: Edward King

Metro-Goldwyn-Mayer presents
a Jerry Gershwin-Elliott Kastner picture
starring
RICHARD
BURTON
CLINT
EASTWOOD
MARY URE
Alistair MacLean's
epic adventure story
of a wartime mission that
cannot succeed—but
dare not fail...
"WHERE
EAGLES
DARE"

5

WHERE EAGLES DARE

(1968)

Winkast Film Productions/
Gershwin-Kastner Productions

Director: Brian G. Hutton
Producer: Elliott Kastner
Screenwriter: Alistair MacLean

W*HERE Eagles Dare* isn't just a war film. It straddles more than one genre, as it can also be considered a spy thriller or an action movie. Indeed, its scenes of Allied agents mowing down pursuing German troops in large numbers using just submachine guns and a few bags of explosives presages the great action pictures of the eighties, particularly *Rambo: First Blood Part II* (1985) and *Commando* (1985).

Film critic Barry Norman once described it as 'the best film of its kind ever made', and the movie has a large number of celebrity fans – including film directors Steven Spielberg and Quentin Tarantino – plus a fan website dedicated to the film (*www.whereeaglesdare.com*). *Where Eagles Dare* was also the zenith of writer Alistair MacLean's career. It was his first original screenplay, and formed the basis of a novel which was published in 1967. Thus the oft-mooted claim that the film was 'based on a novel by Alistair MacLean' is totally incorrect.

The roots of the film go back to late 1965, when American film producer Elliott Kastner – who with Jerry Gershwin had recently formed Winkast Film Productions – was keen to get Alistair MacLean to write an original screenplay for a Second World War action adventure. At that point MacLean had written ten novels, starting with *HMS Ulysses* in 1955. However his last book had been *Ice Station Zebra* (1963) and, since its publication, MacLean had given up writing to run three hotels which he owned (including the 'Jamaica Inn', which featured in the Daphne Du Maurier novel of the same name). Eventually Kastner spoke to him on the 'phone and found that he wasn't very interested in his proposal. However, the two did agree to meet at MacLean's house in Hazlemere, Surrey in October 1965, and a deal was struck in which the writer received an advance of $10,000 to be followed by a further $100,000 on completion of the first draft. In addition, MacLean was given the rights to novelise the film. In fact *Where Eagles Dare* proved to be the most profitable thing MacLean ever did, and to this day his estate receives royalties from both the book and the film.

By March 1966 MacLean had written a first draft screenplay entitled *Adler Schloss* (aka *Schloss Adler*), which is German for 'Eagle Castle.' Kastner didn't like the title and abbreviated a line from Shakespeare's *Richard III*: 'Where eagles dare to perch' to create the well-known title.

One problem with MacLean's original screenplay, though, was that it was far too long at 240 pages. The usual rule of thumb is that one page of screenplay is equivalent to a minute of screen time, so almost half the material had to be trashed. As anyone who has read MacLean's books will testify, that particular author had a tendency to excessive wordiness, taking several pages to describe something that a modern writer would deal with in a couple of paragraphs. In MacLean's first draft a whole hour of screen time elapsed before the team of agents even got to Germany. Working with the film's young director, Brian G. Hutton, Kastner threw out about half of MacLean's script, simplifying scenes and eliminating a lot of superfluous dialogue.

A former actor, Hutton was a young and relatively inexperienced director who had made only three films to date: *Wild Seed* (1965), *The Pad and How to Use It* (1967), and *Sol Madrid* (1967) which starred David McCallum. But Kastner knew he had great talent and the two of them worked together to refine the script.

For the lead role of Major John Smith, Kastner planned to cast Welsh actor Richard Burton who was still considered a box-office draw despite his well-known problems with alcoholism. At that time he was married to actress Elizabeth Taylor, who he had first met while making *Cleopatra* (1963).Their subsequent affair and marriage made headline news at the time, and the tabloid press was usually more interested in their off-screen antics than their films. Other actors who were considered for the part included Michael Caine and Marlon Brando. Caine was at the time under contract to producer Harry Saltzman and was due to participate in his blockbuster *Battle of Britain* (1969) which was due to start filming in the spring of 1968, but his schedule would have allowed him to feature in both films.

Eventually Kastner opted for Burton, who was offered a flat fee of $750,000 plus 10% of the film's profits, a deal which resulted in him making more money from this film than from any other project he was ever involved in. However, the actor wanted a say in casting. It had been Brian Hutton's intention to cast Leslie Caron as British agent Mary Ellison and Clint Eastwood as Lieutenant Shaffer, but Burton wanted Mary Ure as Ellison and Richard Egan as Shaffer. Ure was the wife of actor and writer Robert Shaw, and had worked with Burton on the film *Look Back in Anger* (1959). It was also rumoured that Ure and Burton had had an affair some years before, and that this was another reason he wanted her in the film. Elizabeth Taylor was aware of this past relationship and this was supposedly the reason she subsequently visited the film set frequently as she didn't want the flames of a previous romance to be rekindled!

Eventually Kastner proposed that both Mary Ure and Clint Eastwood should be in the film, and Burton readily agreed. At that time Eastwood had starred in the TV series *Rawhide* (1959-65) as Rowdy Yates, and had also featured in three 'Spaghetti Westerns' directed by Sergio Leone but had yet to achieve Hollywood stardom. All the same he was offered $300,000 for six months work on the film. The rest of the cast were mainly established British character actors with the exception of 30 year-old Ingrid Pitt, a Polish-born actress who was later to appear in several Hammer horror films and also achieved some success as a writer.

The next stage in pre-production involved scouting potential locations in Germany, Austria and Switzerland. MacLean's script involved Allied agents infiltrating the 'Schloss Adler', which he envisaged as being a huge fortress sitting atop a large plug of volcanic rock and accessible only by cable car. This was possibly a bit of plot recycling by MacLean, as the fortress next to the gun cave in the novel *The Guns of Navarone* (1957) was also described as being situated on top of a large plug of volcanic rock.

Eventually the production team found the ideal location, namely the castle at Hohen Werfen (German for 'High Werfen') situated on top of a high rock which overlooked the village of Werfen in Austria, about 25 miles from Salzburg. The only snag was that it didn't have a cable car, and access was by a narrow single-track road (which isn't seen in the film). Winkast Film Productions considered building a working cable car system just for the movie, but the costings were astronomical. Eventually the problem was solved by filming the lower cable car scenes at Ebensee, 31 miles away, and creating a full-sized working upper cable car station in a soundstage at MGM Studios in Borehamwood, complete with two replica cars which exactly matched those at Ebensee. In addition, some cable car scenes were shot on the backlot at MGM and inside the studio, using miniatures.

The screenplay called for a large number of stunts including high falls, a fight on top of a cable car, chases and explosions galore, so Winkast called on the services of 72 year-old Yakima Canutt who was one of the world's most experienced stunt arrangers. A total of 65 stunt performers were employed on the production. At that time only the James Bond films had used that many stunt persons, particularly the most recent offering *You Only Live Twice* (1967) which reputedly used every available stuntman in the UK.

One prominent stunt performer in the film was Alf Joint, who doubled for Richard Burton in most of the action scenes in the film as he strongly resembled the Welsh actor. Indeed, Brian G. Hutton eventually commented that the film should really be billed as '*Where Eagles Dare* starring Alf Joint with a few select close ups by Richard Burton', while Clint Eastwood once remarked that the film should be titled '*Where Doubles Dare*'. Although he was supposedly making a film with Richard Burton, he hardly saw him as in most of the action scenes his part was played by Joint.

Joint specialised in high falls and was already a veteran stunt performer. He played the Mexican thug who is thrown into a bath and then electrocuted by Sean Connery's James Bond in the pre-credits sequence of *Goldfinger* (1964). Clint Eastwood had his own stunt double in the film: Eddie Powell, an exceptionally tall stuntman who had doubled for Christopher Lee in many of his films including *The Mummy* (1959).

Another notable stunt performer was 27 year-old Gillian Aldam, who doubled for Mary Ure in many scenes. As she looked very like the Scottish actress, the camera could film her up to about four feet away without the audience noticing. Indeed, all the location scenes towards the end of the movie – including those showing Ure firing a submachine gun out the rear of the bus – are in fact of Aldam. In 1981 Aldam married pilot John Crewdson, who had done a lot of stunt flying in films. He had performed the ultra low-level beat up of RAF Bovingdon in a B-17 for *The War Lover* (1962), and a simulated belly landing of a Mosquito at the same location for *633 Squadron* (1964). Unfortunately Aldam was widowed in 1983 when Crewdson died in a helicopter accident. Aldam is still working in her 70s, and one of her more recent film credits was the James Bond epic *Skyfall* (2012).

Filming started in Austria on New Year's Day 1968 and, as there was insufficient accommodation in Werfen (which was playing itself in the film), the production team stayed in a number of hotels in the Salzburg area while Mary Ure, her husband Robert Shaw and their three children rented a house for a few months. Ebensee was used for scenes of the lower cable car station, while another Austrian village – Lofer – was employed for shots of the *Zum Wilden Hirsch* tavern and the garage containing the Alpine Postbus, which plays a key part in the plot.

The film opens with a panoramic view of the snow-covered Bavarian Alps. Bright red titles in a Gothic style are superimposed on the picture as Ron Goodwin's theme starts with just a few beats of a snare drum. A tiny dot appears in the exact centre of the screen and as it flies directly towards the camera we discover that it is a German Junkers Ju 52/3m tri-motor transport, painted in snow camouflage of wavy grey/green stripes over a white base colour, with the squadron codes 'CN + 4V'. The aircraft flies over the camera (which was mounted in the side door of a stationary, hovering Sud Aviation Alouette II helicopter) as Ron Goodwin's orchestra starts playing the main section of his magnificent theme, probably the greatest score ever written for a war movie. It was Brian Hutton's suggestion to have the music start quietly so as not to mask the sound of the aircraft approaching. Most of the location shots in the movie take place at night and were shot 'day-for-night', as was the norm in the sixties.

As the theme music and titles continue, the action cuts to scenes of the Junkers flying low over the mountains, interspersed with point-of-view shots taken from the Alouette camera helicopter. The aircraft used in this sequence was a genuine German-built Junkers 52/3m registration number A-702 supplied by the Swiss Air Force, one of three purchased from Nazi Germany in 1939 and which were still in service in 1968. All three transports served with the Swiss Air Force until 1981 and were saved from scrapping, eventually being refurbished and operated by a private organisation called *Ju-Air* which used them for pleasure flights. The Junkers 52 which appeared in *Where Eagles Dare* made another screen appearance in the 2007 Tom Cruise film *Valkyrie*, in which it played Hitler's personal aircraft.

As the title sequence ends, there is a cut to a mock-up of the interior of a Junkers 52 which was constructed at MGM British Studios in Borehamwood, Herts. The shot starts with a view through the windscreen of the aircraft – complete with spinning propeller – and then the camera tracks back to reveal a 1940s-style instrument panel with illuminated indicator lights, throttle levers and dials. The pilot (who is called Carpenter) is played by Australian actor Vincent Ball. Born in 1921, he served as an airman in the Royal Australian Air Force during WW2 and played the part of a pilot flying an aircraft in several war movies and TV series. In Alistair MacLean's novelisation of the screenplay, the pilot was 'Wing-Commander Carpenter' and the aeroplane was an Avro Lancaster, a serious inaccuracy since this type was never used to drop paratroops.

The camera continues to track back to reveal that the aircraft contains seven paratroops wearing white snow camouflage smocks, plus an RAF dispatcher (an airman delegated to help the paratroops exit the plane). Their leader Major Smith (Richard Burton) looks at the two coloured light bulbs next to the aircraft's main door. The red light is flashing, meaning a drop is imminent. As the camera focuses on the bulb there is a cut to a similar flashing red light in the ceiling of a briefing room in England some hours before (a beautiful directorial touch). The camera moves down to reveal the same soldiers we saw a moment earlier in the plane, only now they are wearing British Army uniforms. Also in the room are Admiral Rolland (Michael Hordern), head of MI6, and Colonel Turner (Patrick Wymark), an MI6 officer who has spent three years working undercover in the German High

Command. In reality the head of MI6 during WW2 was Sir Stewart Menzies, and most of its functions were taken over by the Special Operations Executive (SOE) for the duration of the war.

Colonel Turner gets to the point. The previous night, an RAF Mosquito aircraft taking the American General Carnaby from Britain to Crete, crash-landed at Oberhausen airfield in Bavaria. The General was on his way to the Mediterranean island to discuss plans for the Second Front with his Russian opposite number when 'a wandering Messerschmitt patrol' attacked the Mosquito. The same night there was a saturation raid on Nuremberg, so there shouldn't have been a German fighter within miles of the General. As a historical footnote, Turner's comments may refer to the huge RAF raid on Nuremberg on 30th/31st March 1944 which means that the events of the film take place between 31st March and 2nd April 1944.

This section of the screenplay is not grounded in reality. In the spring of 1944 Crete was still occupied by German forces and so would not be an ideal place for a meeting! In addition, no American General would attempt to reach the eastern Mediterranean by overflying Germany – the risk of being shot down would be too great. Also, the Mosquito was singularly unsuited to the task of carrying passengers as it had a very cramped cockpit with just two seats for a pilot plus a navigator. During the war, Mosquitos occasionally carried a single passenger in the bomb bay – who had to endure conditions of extreme discomfort – but a more usual mode of transport for an American General would be a roomy transport aircraft such as the Douglas C-54 Skymaster and the most likely route would involve flying to Gibraltar and then to French North Africa and from there to the Middle East.

Turner and Rolland are convinced that the General must have been taken to the *Schloss Adler* ('Castle of the Eagles'), since it is only 10 miles from the airfield and the HQ of the German Secret Service in Bavaria. As he knows the plans for the second front he must be rescued before he can talk.

Sergeant McPherson (Neil McCarthy) asks about the possibility of sending in paratroops, but is told that a whole battalion would be required and that there isn't time to arrange this. Turner also explains that stealth and secrecy will be needed for the success of the mission. There is to be one American on the mission, Lieutenant Schaffer (Clint Eastwood), who is a member of the American Rangers Division (an error, since there are only Ranger battalions not divisions). All the soldiers can speak fluent German, but talk only in English during the film. (The audience is supposed to imagine that everyone is speaking in German and, although this may seem odd, you soon get used to it.)

Christiansen (Donald Houston) has his concerns and suggests a simpler solution, namely to 'whistle up a Pathfinder squadron of Lancasters, load them up with ten-ton bombs' and destroy the castle, but Rolland rejects his suggestion, pointing out that such a plan might tempt General Eisenhower to launch his second front against the British! The 'ten-ton bomb' referred to by Christiansen would be the 22,000 lb 'Grand Slam' weapon invented by Barnes Wallis. But these munitions were not employed until the closing stages of the war and were dropped only by specially-modified 617 Squadron Lancasters and not Pathfinder aircraft, which were only involved in target marking. Sergeant Harrod (Brook Williams) then asks why the man (i.e. Carnaby) is so important, and

Rolland explains that if he is not rescued there will be no second front that year.

The action then moves back to the interior of the Junkers, where the paratroopers are preparing to jump. As the green light flashes, the dispatcher throws out three supply canisters attached to a parachute and the seven soldiers then leap out. The parachute sequences in the film were shot near San Moritz in Switzerland, and all the jumpers were members of a French parachute club.

After the soldiers have left the plane, another previously unseen member of the team, Mary Ellison (Mary Ure), enters the cabin via a door leading to a hidden compartment at the rear of the aircraft. (In MacLean's novelisation, she is hiding in a wooden crate inside the fuselage!) She jumps from the Junkers and lands by parachute some distance from the other soldiers.

Smith instructs his men to bury their parachutes and locate the three all-important supply canisters. There is a problem, though: Sergeant Harrod is missing. Schaffer reports that he last saw him drifting towards the trees. His body is soon located, lying in the snow, and Smith discovers a bruise on the back of his neck which suggests he was killed by another member of the team after landing.

Berkeley asks if they should bury the body, but Smith says that won't be necessary. Instead he covers it with his parachute, knowing that it will soon be coated with deep snow. Before leaving Harrod's body, he removes his radio codebook from his tunic pocket.

He then suggests the team take shelter for the night in a barn about a mile from their present position. As it is in a high Alpine pasture, it is never occupied between September and May. Later, inside the barn, Smith extends the telescopic aerial of his radio set and claims to have left the code book in a pocket in Sergeant Harrod's tunic. Christiansen offers to fetch it but Smith insists on going himself, saying that if he is not back in an hour the team should fire flares to guide him back. He considers this a safe plan, as there are no Germans within five miles.

But instead of walking a mile to Harrod's body, Smith merely enters an adjacent barn. Almost immediately he is challenged by a gun-toting Mary Ellison, who orders him to halt and turn around. She is relieved to see him. 'You took your time getting here', she says, before chiding him for failing to provide her with hot-water bottles or an electrically heated flying suit during her long journey in the freezing Junkers Ju 52.

Smith then mentions that his radio operator, Harrod, had been killed, and Mary is curious to know what happened. Smith says he had been hit forcibly on the back of the neck, which was then broken to make it look like a parachuting accident. He then tells Mary that the team plan to move into the village of Werfen at first light, and that she should meet him in the woodshed next to the *Zum Wilden Hirsche* tavern at 8.00 p.m. Mary wonders how he knows so much, but Smith refuses to divulge further information even though the two of them had worked together for three years.

'I thought you loved me.'

'I can't help what you think', replies Smith.

The two then kiss and embrace.

Later Smith returns to the other barn where he finds Schaffer checking over his MP-40. He suggests that the Lieutenant gets some sleep, and the tired American soldier gratefully complies. Smith tries the radio but can only get static.

The next morning the six soldiers march through the snow until they are on a steep wooded slope facing the *Schloss Adler*. Smith instructs his team to drop their rucksacks and asks Schaffer to come forward with him while the others stay behind the tree line. They gaze at the castle and then set up their radio set. Smith then utters the immortal line 'Broadsword calling Danny Boy', words that have since entered cinema folklore (and appeared on T-shirts), even being used in the 2010 *Doctor Who* story *Victory of the Daleks*. Eventually 'Danny Boy' (in this case an RAF radio operator) answers, and Smith subsequently speaks to Admiral Rolland aka 'Father Macree'. Smith reports that his position is in woods to the west of the castle and reports that Harrod is now dead as a result of enemy action. He then tells Rowland to stand by and hangs up.

Back in England, Colonel Turner turns away from the radio, looking rather disconsolate. At this point the soundtrack features the noise of two De Havilland Mosquito aircraft flying past at low level, suggesting that the British HQ is near an airfield. These sound effects were recorded at RAF Bovingdon in 1963 during the making of *633 Squadron* (1964). But Turner is confident of Smith's success: 'Some people have a sixth sense, he has a sixth, seventh and eighth sense. He's our best agent'. Rolland, though, isn't so sure. As he says: 'Even if he is our best agent, the whole operation is impossible now'.

Meanwhile, back in Bavaria, Schaffer is studying the *Schloss Adler* through powerful binoculars. A shot of the view as seen through the binoculars was simulated in post-production using a superimposed black mask. Rather cleverly, this is actually footage of the 60-foot model of the *Schloss Adler* which was created on the backlot at MGM Studios and included a working miniature cable car and upper station, features which the real castle employed in the production never had.

Schaffer then shifts his view to the area around the foot of the mountain, where he spots an army barracks surrounded by a wire fence. German soldiers are marching as a truck drives past, and guards patrol the perimeter with Doberman Pinschers. Schaffer wonders how they could get through the fence if they had to, and Smith points out that fences 'can be climbed and cut'. 'Not this one', replies the Lieutenant: 'It's probably got 3,000 volts running through it'.

The next shot of the army barracks – ringed by huts, snow-covered trees and tanks – is actual location footage of soldiers marching, combined with a matte painting by Douglas Adamson. Suddenly there is the sound of a powerful piston engine, and the two soldiers look up to see a helicopter coming in to land in the courtyard of the *Schloss Adler*. This is one of the most famous anachronisms in cinema history. Both the Allies and Germans did have a few semi-experimental helicopters in WW2, but neither side had anything that looked like this. The machine is an American Bell 47, a type which first entered service in 1947. The actual example used in the film is thought to have been obtained in Switzerland, and was painted dark grey with Luftwaffe markings and fake framing over the Perspex cockpit bubble to make it look less modern.

One wonders why it was necessary to have the helicopter in the story anyway, since its only function was to transport General Rosemeyer (Ferdy Mayne) to the castle. He could simply have arrived by cable car and it would have made no difference to the plot. In the film it is implied that the only other way to and from the castle is by cable car, though Alistair MacLean's novelization makes it clear that there was a single-track road to the castle which was often blocked in winter.

General Rosemeyer, the head of the German Secret Service, exits the helicopter and is introduced to his colleagues including Colonel Kramer (Anton Diffring) and the fanatical Nazi, Major Von Hapen (Derren Nesbitt). Von Hapen wears a black SS uniform with a huge number of medals (including some relating to WW1) and a Nazi armband, but claims to be an official of the Gestapo (whose members wore civilian clothes). Rosemeyer walks into the castle accompanied by Colonel Kramer and announces that he wants to have a few hours sleep before interrogating General Carnaby. He also wants to keep Von Hapen out of the loop for the time being, as he doesn't want the Gestapo 'cluttering up things with their torture chambers'.

Meanwhile, in Werfen the six commandos cross the railway line and enter the luggage store at the railway station. (In MacLean's book, Smith has a set of skeleton keys for this purpose.) Quickly they leave their rucksacks on shelves and strip off their white snow smocks to reveal field grey German uniforms beneath them.

They then leave the luggage store and cross the bridge to the village. Smith and Shaffer, who are dressed as officers, walk in front while the other four, who wear privates' uniforms, follow close behind. There is a sentry box ahead and a soldier is checking papers. Deciding to bluff his way through, Smith loudly tells Schaffer a story about how he's written many times to a girl he met on leave and hopes he will be the one she remembers. Although he's speaking in English, the audience has to pretend he is talking in fluent German. The ruse works, and the sentry lets the Allied soldiers through the checkpoint without checking their papers. 'What was her name, anyway?' mutters Schaffer. 'Fred', replies Smith.

The commandos make their way through the snow-covered village and, as they do, a dark grey open-topped armoured personnel carrier carrying several soldiers trundles past them. The tracked vehicle is a 1958 Saurer SpzA1, which (like much of the hardware used in the film) was supplied by the Austrian Army. Eventually, the commando team enter the *Zum Wilden Hirsch*, a local tavern and guesthouse. Only the exterior of the building was used, with the interior being a detailed period set built at MGM Borehamwood Studios. The inside is heaving with soldiers, and the only waitress on duty Heidi (Ingrid Pitt) is struggling to serve everyone with large steins of lager.

A seated Smith calls Heidi over and makes her sit on his knee. He then whistles a few bars of a song to her, which is really a password to let her know he is (like her) a British agent. Smith then whispers some instructions in her ear – she is to meet him in the adjacent woodshed in five minutes, but first she must slap him in the face. Heidi does as she has been told and runs off.

A German Major (John G. Heller) sitting opposite is appalled at Smith's boorish behaviour and says that his conduct 'does not become an officer of the Wehrmacht', but Smith bluffs his way out of the situation, claiming that his name is 'Major Bernard Himmler' and he should mind his own business. The German officer is shocked.

Smith rises from the table and meets Schaffer at the bar, where he explains that he had got out of a difficult situation by claiming to be Himmler's brother. He then makes his way next door to the woodshed, where Mary Ellison is waiting. Immediately he tells Mary to take her clothes off, but he doesn't have sex in mind. Instead, he explains that she has to change her clothes to take on the role of Maria Schenck, Heidi's cousin, who is going to be employed at the *Schloss Adler* as a domestic. Her cover story is that she comes from Dusseldorf, but had to give up her original job due to TB. False identity papers and travel permits are already in her case.

Smith then reveals that General Carnaby's plane had crash-landed at Oberhausen airfield the previous day, riddled with machine gun bullets. 'British machine gun bullets. But then, a hole is a hole is a hole, as they say.' This is the first indication in the film that the whole rescue mission is a set-up, but exactly how a Mosquito could safely fly to Germany riddled with bullets is never explained.

Smith then explains more about the plan, revealing that General Carnaby is none other than a former actor Corporal Cartwright-Jones who knows 'no more about the Second Front than I know about the back end of the moon'. This part of the plot may have been inspired by the real-life story of actor M.E. Clifton James, who was used as a double for General Bernard Law Montgomery during WW2 and later wrote a book *I Was Monty's Double*, which was eventually turned into a film of the same name in 1958 and starred James, playing himself.

As Smith is finishing his explanations, Heidi arrives at the door. Smith explains that she has been 'our top agent in Bavaria since 1941' and (looking at her cleavage) remarks 'what a disguise!' Smith leaves the woodshed, and immediately discovers a German forage cap in the snow. Nearby, lying beside a VW Kubelwagen, he finds the bloodied body of McPherson.

A few moments later, Smith is back in *Zum Wilden Hirsch* where he discusses the latest developments with Schaffer, who points out that any one of the team could have slipped out to commit the murder as the place was so busy. He then implores Smith to come clean about what is really happening. As Smith starts to tell Schaffer the British plan, the camera tracks up to reveal Mary arriving through the doors. Heidi greets her and introduces her to Major Von Hapen, who offers to escort her to the castle with Heidi. Carrying a suitcase, Mary goes upstairs to Heidi's room at the tavern. Once inside, Heidi shows Mary a map of the *Schloss Adler.*

Suddenly three German vehicles arrive outside *Zum Wilden Hirsch* – a motorcycle with sidecar, a truck, and a staff car. A squad of troops jump out the truck and burst into the tavern, led by an officer who announces that he is looking for 'four or five Alpenkorps deserters'. Incidentally, the 'Alpenkorps' was disbanded at the end of WW1, and the equivalent unit in WW2 was knowns as the 'Gebirgsjager'. Sitting at a table in the tavern, Smith decides their best chance is to surrender immediately, and Shaffer points out they stand a better chance of escaping outside. Smith immediately goes up to the officer to surrender, and is told that he and Shaffer are to accompany him while the others will be transported in a truck.

Meanwhile, Von Hapen, Mary and Heidi have arrived at the lower cable car station, supposedly in Werfen but actually filmed at Ebensee. There is a brief point-of-view shot of the *Schloss Adler*, filmed on the backlot at MGM Borehamwood Studios using the 60-foot miniature and painted artwork flats. Von Hapen rings the upper station to tell them to send down a cable car.

As the three passengers ascend in the cable car, Smith and Schaffer are being transported along a winding, slushy Alpine road in an Audi staff car. Smith is sitting in the middle of the back seat with the officer to his left and a soldier to his right. Schaffer is in the front with the driver to his left and a squaddie to his right. Their destination is not mentioned, though in the novelization it is made clear that they are heading for the nearby Alpenkorps barracks. The two Allied soldiers realise their best chance of escape is there and then, and communicate non-verbally with each other using the car's rear view mirror.

Schaffer bends down, claiming to be tying his bootlace, and then shoves the soldier to his right out the door. Immediately Smith grabs the other guard's MP-40. There is a brief burst of fire which kills two more Germans and the car crashes, causing the remaining soldier to go flying through the windscreen. Smith and Schaffer emerge from the vehicle unscathed while all the Germans are dead. Quickly, Schaffer picks up the deceased German who is lying in the road (an obvious dummy) and dumps him in the car. Then the two soldiers push the car back, turn it round and shove it over the cliff. True to the tradition of action movies, the car explodes as it falls down the steep slope and lands in a gully.

As this is happening, Mary, Heidi and Von Hapen arrive at the *Schloss Adler* where they are met by Lt Anne-Marie Kernitser (Olga Lowe), who asks to see their papers. As they make their way to their rooms Colonel Kramer arrives, feeling rather pleased with himself. He mentions that five Army deserters have been arrested in the village. Von Hapen is initially uninterested, but is furious when he learns that this was just a cover story and that in fact it was a group of British agents that had been caught. Kramer points out that they had rung his office and his bedroom to tell him of the imminent arrest, but he could not be found. However Von Hapen is not satisfied with Kramer's explanation, saying that it is his job to find him. 'My job is to find you, not to search every guest house in the village', replies Kramer. A furious argument ensues, reflecting the very real tensions which existed during the war between the Abwehr (German Military Intelligence), the SS and the Gestapo.

As Kramer and Von Hapen are arguing, Heidi and Mary arrive in her bedroom. Heidi gives her fellow agent the items she needs: an automatic pistol, field glasses, a ball of string and a lead weight.

Meanwhile, Smith and Schaffer have arrived back at the luggage store at Werfen station, where they retrieve their rucksacks and the radio. Smith calls England using his call sign 'Broadsword' and the radio is answered immediately by an RAF sergeant who summons Admiral Rowland. Smith gives a brief report on the situation; two of the team are dead and three captured. He is entering the castle within the hour, and Rowland is to have transport standing by.

'Pull out, Broadsword', says Rowland.

'You must be joking.'

'That is an order!'

Suddenly the transmission ends. Turner is furious, saying that it is all his fault, while Rowland speculates that the Germans have penetrated MI6.

Back in Werfen three German vehicles – a truck, a motorcycle/sidecar combo, and a VW Kubelwagen – draw up outside the luggage store, and a squad of German troops jump out. The two Allied soldiers see them and quickly set booby traps using special TNT bombs which can be triggered by tripwires. After preparing the explosives, the pair escape via a window at the back of the property. A moment later, the Germans enter the luggage store and trigger the devices which blow up in a series of massive explosions. In the resulting confusion the two soldiers escape. Schaffer kills two German soldiers – one with a knife, the other with a silenced pistol shot – and the two Allied commandos escape on a BMW motorcycle/sidecar combo. Most of these motorcycle scenes were shot with stuntmen doubles intercut with some studio shots of Burton and Eastwood, which used very convincing back projection. To give greater depth to the shot, real flames were added in front of the motorcycle in the studio. The script originally called for Burton to drive the motorcycle and Schaffer to sit in the sidecar, but Clint Eastwood suggested they swop places as Burton was too drunk to control the bike. Burton's alcoholism was to be a problem during the production, as he would often sit up all night drinking while wearing his Nazi uniform resulting in him being unfit for filming the next day. As a result many of his scenes were shot with his double, Alf Joint.

At one point during the filming his drinking buddies Richard Harris and Peter O'Toole arrived on set, and the three of them disappeared on a bender which lasted a few days. Burton's drinking also caused the production to overrun slightly when studio work commenced at MGM Borehamwood Studios in the spring of 1968.

Smith and Schaffer head out of Werfen, and stop on the road between the town and Oberhausen airfield to fix TNT bombs to a few trees and telegraph poles by the side of the road. Tripwires are stretched between them and marker posts at the side of the road and – using a two-position toggle switch on the bombs, which can be set for 'delay' or 'contact' – the soldiers set them to detonate a certain number of seconds after the tripwire is triggered. Thus there is no danger of the bombs being set off by passing traffic.

As Smith and Schaffer are setting the bombs a cable car arrives at the lower station and Heidi gets off. As she walks away a German soldier (Karl-Otto Alberty) looks at her admiringly. Alberty played a more prominent role as a Tiger tank commander in Brian G. Hutton's next film *Kelly's Heroes* (1970).

Smith and Shaffer arrive back in Werfen and visit a local garage, in which they find a large red Alpine Graf & Stift post bus fitted with snow chains and a huge snowplough. Smith instructs Shaffer to put the remaining rucksack in the bus while he checks that the engine will start.

As the two soldiers leave the garage, a VW Kubelwagen and an Opel Blitz truck containing Christiansen, Barclay and Thomas cross the bridge on their way to the lower cable car station. When they arrive, the prisoners get out and board the car accompanied by Captain Muller and some armed guards.

Just as the car departs, Smith and Shaffer climb onto its roof. The prominent electric hum at this point was a stock sound effect also used in many Gerry Anderson puppet series to depict submarines, spacecraft and other vehicles. The two soldiers ride the top of the cable car all the way to the *Schloss Adler* as Ron Goodwin's dramatic musical cue 'Ascent by Cable Car' plays. This stunt was done for real with Alf Joint doubling Richard Burton and Joe Powell standing in for Clint Eastwood while the actors themselves did close-ups in the studio.

As the cabin heads slowly towards the castle, Mary enters her bedroom, looks out her window with binoculars and sees Smith and Shaffer on top of the cable car. As the vehicle approaches the upper station, the two climb onto a metal fairing on top of the car's wheels in preparation for what comes next. These cowlings were added by the production team as a safety feature to prevent the stuntmen getting mangled by the wheels and also gave them somewhere to sit, as though on horseback.

As the car enters the upper station, the two soldiers jump onto the sloping snow-covered roof, securing themselves with ice axes. This scene was filmed in a huge set which took up an entire soundstage at MGM, complete with a miniature forced-perspective landscape with tiny trees and a very realistic painted backdrop. Shaffer starts to slip over the edge of the roof but is saved by Smith, who grabs his outstretched hand and pulls him back. As this stunt was potentially dangerous, cardboard boxes and mattresses were placed on the studio floor and a safety net was provided for Clint Eastwood.

Recovering their composure, the two soldiers climb onto the roof of the station and pick up the end of a weighted length of string which Mary has thrown down to them. They attach a rope to this, which Mary hauls up, and the two soldiers climb up the side of the castle to Mary's room. Finally the rope is used to haul up one of the rucksacks while the other is left where it is for future use.

As Richard Burton was an alcoholic and chain-smoker, and very unfit, he could not climb up even a few feet of rope, so he had to simulate this by standing on a platform which was slowly lifted up with a crane. His fit co-star Clint Eastwood had no problems with this scene, however.

The agents quickly empty the rucksack, which contains two MP-40 submachine guns, some spare magazines and several TNT bombs. Mary puts some of the explosives in her small black suitcase, while Shaffer is given the task of crippling the helicopter to prevent the Germans flying out General Carnaby.

A few moments later, Shaffer approaches the castle's *Funkraum* (radio room) and shoots the operator dead with a silenced pistol. Meanwhile, outside in the courtyard Smith tells the helicopter pilot that there is a 'phone call for him in the radio room. As the pilot leaves, Smith chats to a German officer (Ian McCulloch). Glasgow-born McCulloch made a number of memorable TV appearances in the seventies and eighties, including roles in *Colditz* (BBC, 1974), *Secret Army* (BBC, 1977) and *The Professionals* (LWT, 1980). He also played Greg Preston in the original version of *Survivors* (BBC, 1975) and then made a number of Italian zombie movies in the eighties, *Zombie Flesh Eaters* (1979), *Zombie Holocaust* (1980), and *Contamination* (1980).

Shaffer promptly stabs the pilot as soon as he arrives in the radio room, and then he and Smith decide to see how General Carnaby is getting on. Moving stealthily, they take up positions, unobserved, in the minstrel's galley overlooking the main hall of the castle (the 'Gold Hall') where Carnaby is being interviewed by Colonel Kramer and General Rosemeyer as they sip cognac together.

Carnaby (Robert Beattie) has so far held out and has refused to give out any information other than name, rank and serial number. Rosemeyer tries to be as reasonable as possible, pointing out that he has tried to persuade the German High Command that the mere fact he has been captured will force the Allies to change their plans. Colonel Kramer then threatens to use drugs on Carnaby to get the information out of him. Carnaby is sceptical about whether Scopolamine will work, but Kramer points out that other drugs can be used. Scopolamine is better known as Hyoscine in the UK and has similar effects to Atropine. Its main use nowadays is as a premed in anaesthetics. Its use as a 'truth serum' did not start until well after WW2, and in any case such 'truth drugs' are now considered to be totally ineffective. In the novelisation, Carnaby is threatened with a combination of Scopolamine and Mescaline, which is a hallucinogenic drug. Scopolamine is also mentioned in the film (but not the book) *The Guns of Navarone* (1961), which is probably where MacLean got the idea from. The 'phone then rings, and Kramer answers it. Putting the receiver down, he says he has 'interesting news'.

As developments continue, Mary is in her room preparing the bombs when someone knocks on the door. Slamming the lid of her case down to hide the explosives, she answers the door. It is Von Hapen, who wants to offer her some 'Bavarian Hospitality' as a former armoury in the castle has been turned into a café. He suggests they have some drinks together and chat about Dusseldorf.

The action then shifts back to the Gold Hall where Thomas, Christiansen and Barclay are now sitting round the table drinking cognac. It is clear they have been working for the Germans. Christiansen asks if Smith is now dead, and Kramer says 'it is being looked into'. He also tells Carnaby the situation has now changed and he should talk, but the General still refuses. Lieutenant Kernitser starts to prepare her drugs, but Smith and Shaffer suddenly come down the steps from the minstrel's galley. Both are carrying MP-40s. Suddenly Smith points his gun at Shaffer and tells him to drop his weapon and sit down. Shaffer is taken aback by his colleague's *volte face*, but Smith puts him down with an off-the-cuff remark: 'You're nothing but a punk, and a pretty second-rate one at that!'

Smith then drops another bombshell, pointing out that scopolamine would have no effect on General Carnaby other than proving he was in fact Corporal Cartwright-Jones, an actor. He then says that the drugs would work better on the three captured British soldiers (Barclay, Christiansen and Thomas). He then claims that his true identity is Major Johann Schmidt, SS Military Intelligence in Stuttgart.

As the revelations continue, an obviously stressed Mary is having a rather uncomfortable time in the cafe as she struggles to make a conversation with Von Hapen about Dusseldorf. At this point Von Hapen utters one of the classic lines of dialogue from the movie: 'Strange; I seem to remember the cathedral was on the *other* side of the square'.

Mary thinks quickly before replying: 'I haven't been to Dusseldorf for three years. It's easy to forget', she says, looking very nervous.

'Fraulein, you look distracted.'

Actually they are both wrong, as Dusseldorf doesn't have a cathedral! Mary then offers the excuse that she is tired from her long journey and has a headache. Von Hapen apparently accepts her explanation and suggests they have one more Schnapps before he escorts her to her room.

Back in the Gold Hall, the plot thickens. Smith mentions that Shaffer is an OSS assassin. (OSS stands for the 'Office of Special Services', which was the American equivalent of the British SOE – Special Operation Executive. It was replaced by the CIA after WW2.) He also mentions that Thomas, Christiansen and Barclay were MI6 agents impersonating German operatives who had been captured. He then asks General Carnaby to give his real name and serial number. Smith then shoots the edge of Carnaby's chair and the American finally admits that he is indeed Cartwright-Jones, a Corporal in the US Army. Smith then reveals that the next stage of the operation was for the three agents to be taken to Germany where they would infiltrate the High Command.

Rosemeyer says he finds all of this very interesting, but asks for proof that what Smith is saying is true. Smith agrees to do this, and says that the proof comes in three parts:

First, what is he doing here unless all he says is true? What does he possibly have to gain?

Secondly, if these people are really who they say they are, they must know the name of the top German agent in Whitehall. Why don't we ask them?

Christiansen angrily replies that they all worked through contacts, so they didn't know who the orders were coming from. Smith then shows Kramer a notebook containing the name of the Germans' top agent in Britain. The Colonel looks at it and agrees the information is correct.

Smith then offers the third part of the proof of his identity. He asks for a call to be put through to Major Wilhelm Wilner (Guy Deghy), Field Marshal Kesselring's Chief of Intelligence in Italy. Kramer complies, and a few moments later the Major is woken by his aide who tells him he has an urgent 'phone call from Colonel Kramer at the *Schloss Adler* in Bavaria.

Wilner is told that a man there claims to be Major Johann Schmidt. Can he describe him? Wilner says that will not be necessary. He should ask Schmidt to bare his right forearm. What can be seen? Kramer reports that there are two parallel scars 2 cm apart. Wilner says he should ask Schmidt how he got them.

'I was born with them.'

'That is correct. Then tell him he is a traitor.'

'Tell him he is renegade.'

'That is Schmidt. No doubt about it.'

His identity established beyond doubt, Smith then points out that the genuine Thomas, Christiansen and Barclay would know the names of all the German agents in Britain and should be able to write down a list of them. He asks Lieutenant Kernitser for some notebooks and pencils.

As these amazing developments continue, Von Hapen escorts Mary to her room and bids her goodnight. But as soon as the door has closed, his facial expression changes. He is suspicious that something is going on, but doesn't know what it is.

Back in the Gold Hall, the three agents finish writing the names and addresses in the notebooks and hands them to Smith who passes them to Kramer. Smith makes eye contact with Shaffer and glances briefly at his discarded gun, implying that he is to get ready to use his MP-40 which is lying on the floor.

'Now compare them to my original', says Smith as he passes his single notebook to Kramer. The Colonel flicks through the Major's notebook and discovers it is blank. He realises he has been duped and calls for a guard, but Smith immediately shoots him with his silenced pistol. Shaffer grabs his MP-40 and holds the Germans at gunpoint.

'Second rate punk, eh?'

'Sorry, that's all I could think of in the spur of the moment.'

'Thanks, that actually makes it worse.'

Kramer soon realises what has happened. Barclay, Christiansen and Thomas are actually who they claim to be – German agents. And Smith now has three notebooks, each of which contains the names and addresses of all the German agents in Britain. Smith confirms that MI6 had been suspicious of the trio for some time and also that Major Wilmer Wilner honestly believed him to be his top agent in Italy. He had been fed useless and out-of-date information for years.

Suddenly Von Hapen appears, gun in hand. He has heard some of the conversation but doesn't know exactly what is happening, so he tells everyone to keep still. Exploiting his confusion, Smith claims he and Schaffer have just uncovered a plot to assassinate the Fuhrer, a masterstroke as SS and Gestapo officials were extremely paranoid about this particular issue.

Kramer angrily retorts that what Smith has suggested is 'preposterous', but Smith continues to feed Von Hapen's paranoia by claiming that in his pocket he has the names of all the conspirators. 'You may not believe me, but you'll certainly believe these names if you will permit me to show them to you', says Smith as he moves to stand directly in front of Shaffer who now cannot be seen by Von Hapen.

As the tense standoff continues, Mary arrives outside the door to the Gold Hall carrying her suitcase of explosives. She opens the door, distracting Von Hapen momentarily. As the German turns his gaze to see who has entered the room, Smith ducks allowing Shaffer to shoot him with his silenced Walther PPK pistol. Kramer and Rosemeyer try to intervene, but they are also shot by the Lieutenant while the guard is killed by Smith with a pistol shot. Lieutenant Kernitser makes a break for the door where she is confronted by a pistol-wielding Mary. Shaffer promptly shoots her in the back.

'We need to create confusion.' says Smith.

'Major, right now you got me as confused as I ever hope to be', replies Shaffer.

Smith unfolds the set of plans of the castle, which Mary has brought in her case. He intends to plant bombs in various parts of the castle including the armoury, the destruction of which will cause secondary explosions. The team start to leave the hall, taking the three traitors with them, while

Cartwright-Jones makes himself useful by arming himself with Von Hapen's gun.

As the three traitors are shepherded through the corridors of the castle, Smith goes into a file storage room and hides a time bomb behind two box files (which appear to have been glued together to make the task easier), while Schaffer installs some tripwire-triggered explosive devices in the Gold Hall. Later he walks into the armoury carrying a large case. 'At ease', he says before opening the case, pulling out a pistol, killing two guards and throwing a time bomb through the bars of one of the weapon storage areas. He then takes the 'phone off the hook. He also throws a time bomb into a quadruple 20mm flak emplacement.

Meanwhile, the rest of the Allied agents are ascending a wooden staircase leading to the radio room (the castle appears to have two of them, since this isn't the one next to the courtyard we saw earlier). 1940s-style music – composed by Ron Goodwin and treated to sound like a poor quality AM transmission with fading and static – emanates from the room as the operator twiddles with the dial. Shaffer comes up the stairs and slowly enters the room, watched by Smith. He is planning to creep up on the operator and stab him. But things don't go to plan. Failing to find a station he likes, the operator turns off the radio, which was masking the sound of Shaffer's approach. Then the American Lieutenant steps on a creaky floorboard, alerting the operator who turns round and sees him. Smith immediately shoots him with his silenced pistol, but not before the operator has pressed the alarm button. Sirens sound all over the castle and troops start running towards the radio room.

Shaffer destroys the nearest wall speaker by smashing it with the butt of his MP-40, but klaxons elsewhere continue to sound the alarm. German soldiers ascend the stairs to the corridor which leads to the radio room as Shaffer prepares to hold them off with his MP-40. Smith is frantically trying to make contact with his British HQ using the castle's transceiver as the first wave of German troops move slowly along the corridor, weapons in hand. Suddenly Shaffer jumps out and kills them all with a burst from his MP-40.

The MP-40, which plays a key part in the plot of the film, was a highly effective submachine gun which first saw action with German forces in 1940. It replaced the earlier MP-38 and MP-36 weapons, and is often incorrectly described by some writers as a 'Schmeisser' (after gun designer Hugo Schmeisser, who wasn't actually involved in the creation of the MP-40). MacLean's novelisation of the film repeatedly describes the weapons as 'Schmeissers'.

Further waves of German troops follow and Shaffer takes shelter round the corner, holding his gun at arm's length and firing sideways to shoot back without exposing his body to enemy fire. Then the Germans try a different tactic, setting up an MG42 light machine gun on a tripod and spraying the corridor with fire. Suddenly the bomb in the armoury explodes, setting off secondary explosions. The MG42 crew are momentarily distracted by the blast, giving Shaffer an opportunity to jump into the corridor and spray them with bullets from two MP-40s – one held in each hand (something that would be impossible due to the recoil).

Smith continues his efforts to contact his HQ in England while more bombs explode. Finally Admiral Rowland speaks to him.

'Do you have it?'

'Yes, we have it all!'

'All sins forgiven.'

Suddenly the radio goes dead as a German officer (Derek Newark) cuts the power. Newark was a popular British character actor at the time, having appeared as the caveman Za in the very first *Doctor Who* story in 1963, later returning in the Jon Pertwee era to play Greg Sutton in *Inferno* (1970). Meanwhile, the Germans try new tactics to flush out the agents, throwing Model 25 stick grenades, but Shaffer simply throws them back and they explode, killing more troops. This scene may seem far-fetched but actually happened many times in WW2. German stick grenades had a four to eight second fuse (depending on model), while the British Mills bomb had a four second one. Experienced troops would often hold onto long-fused grenades for a few seconds before throwing them to make it impossible to chuck them back.

The Germans throw a few more grenades and this time Shaffer retreats into the radio room, bolting the door behind him to shield everyone from the blast. They hang a rope out the window, force Thomas to climb down it and then hide in the adjacent room, shutting the door behind them. The Germans blast their way into the radio room, see the rope tensing, look out the window, spot Thomas abseiling down the wall and shoot him dead with an MP-40. Then they rush out the radio room thinking the other agents have already rappelled down the castle wall.

Once the Germans have gone, the team emerge from their hiding place. Smith tells Shaffer to retrieve the rope as they will need it. As the agents flee along the corridor, Shaffer kills some more Germans with his MP-40. As Smith closes a large door behind him, he is shot in his left hand which is left bleeding.

The team go to a room upstairs, where they untie the hands of the two traitors and everyone puts on warm parkas.

These garments – which were reversible and had camouflage on one side and white on the other – were specially made for the film and weren't actually issued to German troops during WW2. Smith throws a rope out the window and the team – including the two traitors – abseil down the side of the castle as bombs continue to explode and fires break out. The agents make their way to the roof of the cable car station and Shaffer climbs inside via the roof of a stationary cable car. He quickly jumps down and runs up the corridor which connects the station with the courtyard, shutting and bolting the pair of doors at the top of the passage and also a second one at the lower end of the corridor. There are now two sets of locked doors between the German troops and the agents.

Shaffer then works the cable car controls and brings the car (with the two traitors on top) into the station. But the two enemy agents see an opportunity to trick Shaffer. Berkeley jumps from the roof of the cable car onto the concrete and pretends to have injured his ankle. When Shaffer goes to his aid, Christiansen leaps on top of him and the two bad guys kick him unconscious. Christiansen grabs his silenced Walther PPK and screams at Smith.

'We've got him, Smith.'

Christiansen then offers Smith a deal. If he will let him and Berkeley go down in the cable car then they won't kill Schaffer. Smith says he will only agree to this if they show him Shaffer to prove he is still alive. But the resourceful Major has no intention of admitting defeat that easily. As the cable car leaves the station, he tucks one of the TNT time bombs inside his parka and jumps onto the roof of the vehicle. He intends to blow up the cable car while the two agents are on board.

As he secures the bomb to the suspension bracket, the two enemy agents hear the sound of him scrabbling about and Christiansen blindly fires a few rounds through the roof of the car. All the bullets miss, and soon the gun is empty. Christiansen and Berkeley then climb out the windows to fight Smith, who ends up lying prostrate on the roof of the car. Christiansen tries to grab onto his legs but the Major kicks him in the face several times, causing severe facial injuries. Meanwhile, he is also attacking Berkeley with his ice axe and gives him a deep flesh wound in his left upper arm. The enemy agent is so badly wounded that he crawls back into the cabin, nursing his left arm. The Major then kicks Christiansen, who falls to his death via a very effective blue screen travelling matte shot. These cable car fight scenes – some of the most exciting ever committed to celluloid – may have been inspired by similar sequences in the Rex Harrison movie *Night Train to Munich* (1940) which (at the time of writing) can be seen in its entirety on YouTube. They may also have influenced the fight between Jaws and James Bond atop a cable car in *Moonraker* (1979).

Now Smith can concentrate on setting the bomb. After setting the timer he selects 'delay' on the two-position toggle switch and prepares to jump onto the other cable car which is ascending from the lower station. Smith waits until the other car is almost level and then jumps the gap, grabbing the edge of the car roof with his fingers. He almost falls off, but manages to pull himself onto the roof. Slowly, Smith's car makes its way up to the castle while the other descends as the seconds tick by. Suddenly the lower car explodes, fortunately without damaging the cable.

All these fight scenes were performed for real using three stuntmen, with a second cable car fitted out as a camera platform. Although the second unit (directed by Yakima Canutt) spent several weeks on this one scene, much of the resulting footage had to be discarded as the winter light was too poor and so the scenes were recreated at MGM Borehamwood Studios using the brand-new front projection process which was first developed for the 'Dawn of Man' scenes in *2001: A Space Odyssey* (1968). All the same, some of the cable car fight scenes in the final print were those shot on location and almost as dangerous as they looked, although the stuntmen were actually attached to the cars by hidden steel cables.

For the scene where Smith prepares to jump from one car to another, the ascending car in the background was a two foot-high miniature which was added using blue screen technology to produce a travelling matte. The exploding cable car was real though, and the cables had to be covered with asbestos to prevent them being damaged.

As Smith continues his journey back to the *Schloss Adler*, Shaffer starts to recover consciousness, watched by Mary and Cartwright-Jones who are still on the roof of the station. By now the Germans have realised what is happening and are trying to break down the door at the top of the corridor.

Shaffer brings the car into the station and Smith, Cartwright-Jones and Mary board it. By this time the Germans have broken through the first door and have now turned their attention to the second one at the bottom of the corridor. (This is a bit of plot recycling from Alistair MacLean, as a similar scenario appears in *The Guns of Navarone* where the Germans have to break down heavy doors to reach the cave containing the gun battery.)

As the Germans continue to pound on the steadily weakening door, Schaffer sets the controls to send the cable car to the lower station and then jumps on board. Meanwhile, a strong force of German troops has arrived at the lower station and takes up positions to riddle the oncoming car with bullets. This must be one of the great cliffhangers in movie history. Will the Germans break through the door before the cable car reaches the lower station? And even if they don't, the agents will surely be shot by the 'reception committee' which is waiting?

But the resourceful Smith has a solution. Fixing time bombs to the inside of the cable car, he sets them to go off in just three and a half minutes, and unscrews the light-bulbs inside the car so that the Germans can't see what they are doing. Eagle-eyed viewers may notice at this point that Smith turns the bulbs clockwise to unscrew them, and this action has appeared on the internet as a 'goof'. In fact this is incorrect, as (for decades) bulbs in various forms of public transport in Austria and Germany have had reverse threads to stop people stealing them and taking them home.

As the agents make their preparations, Heidi arrives at the garage containing the bus. By this point the cable car is crossing the icy river that runs through the village and – as the lower station nears – the four agents jump into the freezing water. This stunt was done for real with Gillian Aldam doubling Mary Ure while close-ups were shot using a mock-up of the river bank at MGM Studios in Borehamwood. The point-of-view shot looking down on the river just prior to the jump was created using a very realistic miniature.

Finally the Germans in the *Schloss Adler* break into the upper cable car station, but they are too late. At almost the same moment, the cable car makes its final approach to the lower station. The German officer commanding the squad of troops orders his men to open fire with rifles, MP-40s and

MG42s. The bombs in the car promptly explode, wiping out all the troops.

Some miles away, the Junkers Ju-52 we saw earlier is flying down a valley on its way to Oberhausen airfield. 'We'll make it, will they?' says the pilot, Wing Commander Carpenter.

Meanwhile, the Allied team have swam ashore and have made their way to the garage where Smith gets behind the wheel of the red Alpine Post Bus and starts the engine. He reverses the coach and then smashes through the wooden doors with the huge metal snowplough which he also uses to destroy a line of Wehrmacht motorcycles. Germans troops in the village fire at the bus, and Shaffer and Mary smash the rear window and shoot back.

A German officer 'phones Oberhausen Airfield and asks to be put through to the commandant's office as a German convoy consisting of trucks, Kubelwagens and motorcycle/sidecar combos chases after the bus. As Smith heads towards the airstrip along a winding, slushy road, the Germans appear to be catching up, but then the Major veers to both sides of the road in turn and slices through five separate tripwires causing the bombs to explode after a time delay has elapsed. Several trees fall, plus one telegraph pole which results in telephone communication with the airfield being cut. Then Smith hits another wire, causing a huge tree to fall across the road and halting the Germans. But using great initiative, the Alpenkorps troops manage to steer a single BMW motorcycle/sidecar combo round the obstruction to continue the chase.

Now the bus is nearing the airfield and as it crosses a wooden bridge, Smith realises that if they blow it up, further pursuit by the Germans will be impossible. Schaffer and Smith jump out and attach time bombs to the underside of the bridge while Mary watches the road from the shattered rear window of the bus. As the two agents are furiously working against time, the Germans explode the tree trunk further back the road allowing the pursuit force to continue the chase. Suddenly the motorcycle/sidecar combo arrives at the bridge and is expertly shot up by Mary using her MP-40.

His work done, Smith runs back to the bus and starts it up, closely followed by Shaffer. The first vehicle in the German convoy – a Kubelwagen – appears and is shot up by Shaffer. As Shaffer races to board the now-moving bus by the rear door a second VW starts to cross the bridge which promptly explodes, wrecking the German vehicle. The other German vehicles in the convoy are forced to stop on the far side of the bridge. The VW Type 82 Kubelwagen (which was the most common German vehicle used in *Where Eagles Dare*) was a lightweight utility car based on the original VW Beetle. 50,000 of them were built during WW2, and a large number of versions were produced including the amphibious Schwimmwagen. 16 Kubelwagens were used in the film, some being original wartime examples and others modern fibreglass replicas based on VW Beetle running gear. Only two of the Kubelwagens survived the rigours of filming.

The next shot shows Oberhausen airfield (actually Aigen in Switzerland), where four German fighters are sitting on the snow-covered tarmac. The aircraft are all North American AT-6 Harvard trainers, which had been operated by the Swiss Air Force until 1967 and were due to be scrapped. Their engines had already been removed and to make them more closely resemble Focke-Wulf Fw 190 fighters they were fitted with three-bladed propellors with spinners and dummy wing guns, and the rear portion of the elongated cockpit canopy was removed. By this point in the filming schedule, spring had arrived and much of the snow was starting to melt. This particularly affected the bus chase scenes and a number of remedies were used to address the problem. Many truckloads of real snow were brought in from higher regions and were spread on the roads. Also, the local fire brigade put down foam and snow was also simulated with tons of Epsom salts.

Nearby, Smith stops the bus close to the entrance of the airbase and awaits developments. Within minutes the Junkers Ju-52 arrives in the area, and Wing Commander Carpenter radios Oberhausen Control tower claiming he is from a Junkers squadron and is carrying out a night navigation exercise. He has lost one engine and requires clearance for an immediate emergency landing. The controller accedes to his request and the aircraft touches down on the runway, but then does a U-turn at the end and revs all three engines in preparation for a fast take-off. Immediately Smith starts the bus's engine and crashes through the perimeter fence. He uses the coach's snowplough to wreck the four German fighters and then makes a bee-line for the Junkers while under fire and hotly pursued by Kubelwagens and trucks. The control tower officer desperately tries to contact 'Fighter Wing 126' for assistance, but is cut down by a hail of fire from the back of the bus. Shaffer also hits the leading VW, which overturns.

Smith brings the bus to a halt as close as possible to the rear door of the Junkers, behind the port wing, and then fires his last rounds at another Kubelwagen as the rest of his team board the plane. Eventually the VW explodes in a ball of flame and overturns, and Smith races to the plane. Slamming the door behind him, Smith tells everyone to lie flat on the floor as Carpenter puts the throttles 'through the gate' and the Junkers slowly accelerates down the runway hotly pursued by the remaining German vehicles. As the lumbering transport finally lifts off, a few rounds hit the side of the fuselage and the port cockpit window, but as Carpenter pulls back on the control column the aircraft soon climbs out of range.

The crisis over, Colonel Turner examines Barclay's notebook and is astonished to learn that there were three traitors. But then Smith drops a bombshell.

'One name is missing.'

'What name is that?'

'I have it in this notebook. Earlier I showed it to Colonel Kramer and he agreed it was the name of their top agent in Britain.'

Colonel Turner looks at the first page of the notebook. It has his name on it.

Smith then mentioned that Admiral Rolland had suspected him for some time. That was why he brought himself and Mary back from Italy, as they were the only people he could trust. Turner had picked Smith to lead the mission as he thought he was a double agent, but Rolland knew he was not – yet for Turner, he was the perfect choice.

Turner realises the game is up. But he has one last card to play, because he is holding a loaded Sten sub machine gun. However, Smith points out that it was Admiral Rolland who handed him the weapon and he ensured the firing pin was removed. Turner pulls the trigger. Nothing happens, and then Schaffer grabs his MP-40 and holds the Colonel at gunpoint. Smith points out to Turner that he faces a trial followed by death by hanging, but he has an alternative. Turner thanks him, walks to the door, opens it and jumps out. Schaffer then closes the door.

'Is that it?' he says to Smith.

'That's it.'

'Do me a favour. The next time you have one of these things, make it a British operation.'

'I'll try it.'

Mary attends to Smith's hand wound and the film ends with a view of the Junkers Ju-52 flying over the Alps.

Where Eagles Dare premiered in the UK on 4 December 1968, but didn't go on general release till March 1969. It was very successful, making $21 million against a final budget of $7.7 million. It wasn't as profitable in the USA as *The Dirty Dozen* (1967) – also made in the UK by MGM – and this was probably explained by the fact that American cinema audiences generally don't like British war movies. Nonetheless, it remains hugely popular in Europe and attracted a large audience when it was first shown on BBC 1 on 26 December 1979.

Elliott Kastner and Jerry Gershwin's production company, Winkast, made nine more films with the last being *Angel Heart* (1987). One notable picture was *When Eight Bells Toll* (1971), a Bond-style action thriller written by Alistair MacLean and starring a young Anthony Hopkins as Royal Navy officer and spy Philip Calvert. It was based on MacLean's 1966 book and was the only one of his novels to be set in his native Scotland.

Richard Burton continued to be dogged by alcoholism for years after making *Where Eagles Dare,* but had reportedly given up drink by the time he made *The Wild Geese* (1978), regarded as one of his best pictures. He died in 1984, shortly after completing work on his final picture, the George Orwell adaptation *1984.* Three years later, Alistair MacLean died at the age of 64 and was buried just a few yards from Richard Burton in a plot in Celigny, Switzerland.

Mary Ure also suffered from bouts of heavy drinking and had been addicted to sleeping pills since 1960. In 1975 she died from an overdose of barbiturates after performing in Don Shaw's play *The Exorcism.* To this day, no-one is certain whether this was a deliberate suicide attempt or just an accident. Her husband Robert Shaw – who was also an alcoholic – died of a heart attack three years later.

A remake of *Where Eagles Dare* has been mooted over the years, but I would consider this a great mistake as the original achieved excellence in so many areas – stunts, photography, special effects, acting, scripts, direction and music – that it is hard to see how it could be bettered. It is without a doubt one of the greatest war movies ever made.

Where Eagles Dare (1968)
Production Credits

Production Team
Director: Brian G. Hutton
Screenplay: Alistair MacLean

Cast
Major Smith: Richard Burton
Lt. Schaffer: Clint Eastwood
Mary Ellison: Mary Ure
Colonel Turner: Patrick Wymark
Admiral Rolland: Michael Hordern
Christiansen: Donald Houston
Berkeley: Peter Barkworth
Thomas: William Squire
Carnaby: Robert Beatty
Sgt Harrod: Brook Williams
Sgt Jock MacPherson: Neil McCarthy
Carpenter: Vincent Ball
Col. Kramer: Anton Diffring
General Rosemeyer: Ferdy Mayne
Von Hapen: Derren Nesbitt
Colonel Weissner: Victor Beaumont
Heidi: Ingrid Pitt
Telephone Orderly: Richard Beale
Cable Car Engineer: Roy Beck
German Officer: Ivor Dean
Major Wilhelm Wilner: Guy Deghy
German Officer on Stairs: Jim Dowdall
Sgt. Hartmann: Max Faulkner
German Soldier: Harry Fielder
German Major: John G. Heller
German Woman: Lyn Kennington
Young German Soldier: Nigel Lambert
Lt. Anne-Marie Kernitser: Olga Lowe
German Officer: Ian McCulloch
German Radio Operator: Terence Mountain
German Major: Derek Newark
Waiter: Jim O'Brady
German Officer at Airfield: Anton Rodgers
German Soldier: Peter Roy
Helicopter Pilot: Bill Sawyer
German Officer (Ammo Store): Jack Silk
Cable Car Operator: Philip Stone
Inn Keeper: Jim Tyson
Airport Control Operator: Ernst Walder

Producers
Producer: Elliott Kastner
Associate Producer: Dennis Holt
Executive Producer: Jerry Gershwin

Music
Composer: Ron Goodwin

Cinematography
Photographer: Arthur Ibbetson
Film Editor: John Jympson

Art Direction
Art Director: Arthur Mullins

Costume Design
Costume Designer: Arthur Newman

Makeup Department
Makeup artist: Tony Sforzini

Production Management
Production Supervisor: Ted Lloyd
Unit Manager (Second Unit): Tom Sachs

Second Unit Director or Assistant Director
Assistant Director: Colin M. Brewer
Second Unit Director: Yakima Canutt
Assistant Director (Second Unit): Anthony Waye
Second Assistant Director: Patrick Clayton
Second Assistant Director (Second Unit): Chris Kenny

Art Department
Set Dresser: Arthur Taksen
Assistant Property Master: Mickey Lennon

Sound Department
Sound Editor: Jonathan Bates
Sound Recordist: John Bramall
Dubbing Mixer: J.B. Smith
Foley Artist: Richard Best Jr
Assistant Foley Artist: Peter Dobson
Sound: Michael Hickey

Special Effects
Special Effects: Fred Hellenburgh, Richard Parker
Photographic and Visual Effects: Tom Howard

Stunts
Stunt Doubles for Key Players:
Mary Ure: Gillian Aldam
Robert Beatty: Tom L. Dittman
Richard Burton: Alf Joint
Clint Eastwood: Eddie Powell, Bill Sawyer
Other Stunt Performers: Peter Brace, Tim Condren, George Lane Cooper, Jack Cooper, Jim Dowdall, Roy Everson, Max Faulkner, Harry Fielder, Tex Fuller, Romo Gorrara, Richard Graydon, Rick Lester, Jimmy Lodge, Dave Newman, Terence Plummer, Joe Powell, Nosher Powell, Terry Richards, Doug Robinson, Jack Silk, Paul Stader, Jimmy Thong, Les White, Dave Wilding, Terry Yorke

Camera and Electrical Department
Second Unit Cameraman: H.A.R. Thomson
Camera Operator: Paul Wilson
Photographer (Aerial Unit): Douglas Adamsson
Gaffer: Bob Bremner
Grip: Denis Fraser
Camera Operator (Second Unit): Ginger Gemmel
Still Photographer: John Jay
Focus Puller: Allan Jones
Electrician: Edward Michael Perry
Camera Operator (Second Unit): Kelvin Pike
Clapper Loaders: Graham Scaife, David Wynn-Jones

Music Department
Conductor: Ron Goodwin
Orchestrator: Brian Couzens

Other Production Crew
Continuity: Penny Daniels
Dialogue Coach: Alfredo Lettieri
Assistant to Producer: Marion Rosenberg
Production Assistant: Raymond Becket
Military Advisor: Brian L. Davis
Process Projectionist Trainee: Steve Pickard

**It's hard to believe that after
The Rape of Poland, The Fall of France,
The Blitz of London and The Siege
of Leningrad, one of the final blows of
World War II came at a little iron bridge.**

DAVID L. WOLPER
presents

"THE BRIDGE AT REMAGEN"

A dot on the map. A motion picture as big as history.

starring
GEORGE SEGAL / ROBERT VAUGHN / BEN GAZZARA / BRADFORD DILLMAN / ANNA GAEL / Guest Star E. G. MARSHALL

Screenplay by RICHARD YATES, WILLIAM ROBERTS Screen Story by ROGER HIRSON Produced by DAVID L. WOLPER Directed by JOHN GUILLERMIN Music ELMER BERNSTEIN

PANAVISION™ **COLOR** by DeLuxe

69/251

6

THE BRIDGE AT REMAGEN

(1969)

Wolper Pictures

Director: John Guillermin
Producer: David L. Wolper
Screenwriter: Richard Yates and William Roberts, from a story by Roger Hirson

THE *Bridge at Remagen* is one of the most underrated films about the Second World War. Filmed in Czechoslovakia in 1968, it set new standards for realism in war movies which have only been bettered in recent years by high-budget productions such as *Saving Private Ryan* (1998) and *Fury* (2014). At the time though, the film performed poorly at the US box office, largely because of public disenchantment with the Vietnam War, even though the script reflected the rather cynical attitude towards the military that was prevalent at the time.

As in *Fury*, the movie is set in the final stages of the Second World War in Europe when both the Germans and Allies were questioning the wisdom of sacrificing lives when the outcome of the conflict was already obvious. Unfortunately Hitler had vowed to fight for every inch of territory and never surrender, something that features prominently in the screenplay which also depicts soldiers on both sides as being exhausted by years of fighting. The company of US soldiers in *The Bridge at Remagen* are tired and war-weary, and seem to be more interested in food, booze, women, money and sleep than in winning medals.

The film was based on the non-fiction book *The Bridge at Remagen: The Amazing Story of March 7, 1945* by Ken Hechler, which was turned into a screenplay by Richard Yates and William Roberts and dealt with the capture of the Ludendorff Bridge across the Rhine by the US 9th Armoured Division which allowed the Americans to put several divisions across the Rhine and shorten the war.

The producer was David L. Wolper, who began his career by selling independent feature films to broadcasters. Later, Wolper specialized in historical documentaries with the first being *The Race for Space* (1960). After producing several documentaries, including *007: The Incredible World of James Bond* (1965), Wolper turned his hand to feature film making. His first movie was *The Devil's Brigade* (1968) starring Cliff Robertson and William Holden, which was closely followed by *The Bridge at Remagen.* Wolper had actually owned the rights to Ken Hechler's book for many years, and development work on the movie had begun as early as 1962.

Although only Richard Yates and William Roberts received an on-screen credit, many other writers contributed ideas and the script went through many drafts over the years. The screenplay had its origins in a five-page story outline prepared by Warren Fitzgerald Ambrose. Then in 1965, Roger Hirson produced a first draft which included a scene in which the US soldiers encounter a group of Polish prostitutes in Stadt Meckenheim. One of them, originally called Raya (later changed to Karla) had a liaison with Lt. Hartman, although in the final version of the script she became an unnamed French girl played by Anna Gael.

Further work was carried out by William Roberts and in October 1967, just a few months before shooting was due to begin, Ray Rigby – a British writer and WW2 veteran – was brought in to polish the script. Rigby had co-written (with R.S. Allen) the play *The Hill*, on which Sydney Lumet's 1965 film was based. He also co-wrote the screenplay for Michael Anderson's *Operation Crossbow* (1965), about British attempts to counter the German V-weapon programme. Rigby's main task on *The Bridge at Remagen* was to improve the dialogue and characterization. He also came up with the idea of the film opening with an American armoured column charging towards the Oberkassel Bridge.

Another writer who worked on the movie was Rod Serling, best known for TV series *The Twilight Zone* (1959-64). Although he was paid $250,000 for a complete draft, his work remains uncredited to this day and it is unclear whether any of his ideas were used in the final cut of the film.

The director was John Guillermin. Born in the UK in 1925, one of his earliest movies was *I Was Monty's Double* (1958) – which had the US title *Hell, Heaven or Hoboken* (!) – and starred John Mills in a tale about the wartime exploits of actor Clifton James, who successfully impersonated General Bernard Montgomery as part of a British Intelligence operation. Another early success was *Tarzan's Greatest Adventure* (1959), which starred Gordon Scott as the titular hero and a young Sean Connery as O'Bannion. Later Guillermin directed *The Blue Max* (1966). This film – which is covered in detail in my book *Planes on Film* (2016) – was praised for its realistic portrayal of WW1 air battles and convinced Wolper that Guillermin was the right man for the job.

For the key role of Major Paul Kreuger, Wolper chose American actor Robert Vaughn who had just achieved international fame as spy Napoleon Solo in the hugely successful TV series *The Man from UNCLE* (1964-68). Incidentally, while Vaughn was making *The Bridge at Remagen* in Czechoslovakia his former co-star in *The Man from UNCLE*, David McCallum, was in England filming *Mosquito Squadron* at RAF Bovingdon and MGM Studios, Borehamwood. At the same time this was happening, *Battle of Britain* (1969) was being filmed at various English locations, so the summer of 1968 was a boom time for war film production.

Vaughn might have seemed an odd choice in a film in which most of the Germans were played by well-known German actors, but one thing that influenced the producers was Vaughn's fluency in German, having learned the language as part of his Ph.D. candidacy at the University of Southern California. In fact Vaughn was not eventually required to speak German in the film, though he adopted a convincing accent. Another actor who was considered for the part of Kreuger was a young Anthony Hopkins, who was just about to make his screen debut in *The Lion in Winter* (1968).

Other actors who played prominent roles in *The Bridge at Remagen* included Ben Gazzara, George Segal, E.G. Marshall and Bradford Dillman. At that time Gazzara was well-known in the UK and the USA for playing Paul Bryan in the TV series *Run for Your Life* (1965-68) – produced by Paul Huggans – which lasted three seasons. This series had an interesting premise: the lead character had discovered he had leukemia and had only 18 months to live, so decided to spend the rest of his life travelling the globe in search of adventure.

This 'man on the move' format had previously been explored in the hit TV series *The Fugitive* (1963-67), starring David Janssen, which was also produced by Roy Huggans. Dillman was also well-known at the time for appearing as a guest star in numerous TV series including the final two-part *The Man from UNCLE* episode entitled *The Prince of Darkness Affair.*

All the characters which appear in the final film are fictional, though most of them were based on real people. In some cases two characters were merged into one (a familiar cinematic trick – see my previous book *Planes on Film* for an explanation of the origins of the 'Johnny Sanderson' character in the 1956 film *Reach for the Sky*) to simplify the plot, and many characters underwent several name changes during the evolution of the script. Towards the end of this chapter I have listed the main characters in the film and the real people they were based on.

Originally it had been planned to make the film in West Germany, but the Bonn Government refused permission on the grounds that the production would cause too much disruption to traffic on the Rhine so producer David L. Wolper had to look elsewhere. Eventually he found a bridge at Davle, 15 miles south of the Czech capital Prague on the Vltava River which had a similar girder structure to the one at Remagen, although it had two arches compared to just one at the Ludendorff Bridge. Once two fake stone towers had been added at each end and cladding added to the fenestrated girder structure, it made a passable stand - in for the Ludendorff Bridge, though a fake 60-foot-long railway tunnel through a hill at one end of the bridge had to be built at a cost of $250,000. The real Ludendorff Bridge had been built by the Germans using Russian PoWs between 1916 and 1919 in order to allow them to send troops to the Western Front more easily. It was constructed as a rail bridge, but with wooden planking added to enable it to accommodate wheeled vehicles as well.

Wartime US tanks were not available in Czechoslovakia, so the Austrian Government supplied eight M24 Chaffee tanks, three Ford M8 six-wheeled armoured cars, eight GMC 'Deuce-and-a-half' trucks, six Jeeps, and hundreds of M1 Garand rifles. The Czech Army also provided a number of vehicles for the film including OT-810 halftracks and Praga RN trucks.

The film is also remembered for the real-life drama which unfolded during its production, namely the Soviet invasion of Czechoslovakia in August 1968 which disrupted filming. In his autobiography *A Fortunate Life* (2008), actor Robert Vaughn devotes an entire chapter to this episode.

Vaughn arrived in Prague on 10 June 1968, having recently completed work on *Bullitt* (1968), and was pleased to discover an air of optimism in the Czech capital. A new leader – Alexander Dubcek, 46 – had taken over from his hard-line Communist predecessor Antonin Novotny in January that year. Dubcek immediately ordered a programme of reforms including the release of political prisoners, the introduction of a free press, a truly democratic opposition party, and the possibility of free elections. Dubcek had the right idea (socialism with a human face), but at the wrong time because the Cold War was at its height and the Soviet regime viewed these developments in one of its satellite states with great unease. Negotiations between the Soviet leader Leonid Brezhnev and Dubcek took place, but the Russians' patience eventually snapped and – on the night of 20/21 August 1968 – Soviet tanks rolled into Prague to 'normalize' the situation.

Dubcek's bodyguard put up some resistance, but he was shot dead by Soviet troops and the Czech leader was trussed up and taken to the Ukraine lying on the floor of an armoured car. After a week of interrogation and torture he was returned to Czechoslovakia, where he spent the next eighteen years as a clerk in a timber yard.

The filming of *The Bridge at Remagen* was disrupted by these events, and Robert Vaughn – along with most of the cast and crew – was held under house arrest at the International Hotel in Prague. After a week of intense diplomatic pressure from the American Government, the entire crew was allowed to leave Czechoslovakia in a fleet of taxis, although Vaughn's uncompleted Ph.D. manuscript was left behind at his room at the Park Hotel. It was eventually returned to him some months later.

Eventually the film was completed in Austria, Germany and Italy, where a replica of a section of the Ludendorff Bridge was built at the Pope's summer residence at Castle Gandolfo near Rome.

Amazingly, the Russians eventually allowed the Second Unit back to Czechoslovakia to film a few scenes under the watchful eye of the Soviet military. All the M24 tanks and other military vehicles were shipped back to Austria by rail flatcar, even though the Soviets had earlier made accusations that they were part of an invasion force under the control of the CIA. Most of the film was made on location, but a few interiors were shot at the Barrandov Studios in Prague and in Hamburg.

The film opens with a shot of a heavily-laden troop train carrying German casualties as a caption informs us that it is March 1945 and the location is the Obercassal Bridge. A further caption then states that 'in the final months of WW2, the armies of the Third Reich are in full retreat across the great moat that guards the heart of Germany – The River Rhine'.

As the train gets closer to its destination, we can see that it is carrying wounded German soldiers and is bedecked with Red Cross flags. German sappers preparing the bridge for demolition look on apprehensively as it gets nearer. Most of the extras in these scenes were Czech students, while 300 men of the Czech Army were also used in some sequences.

Suddenly there is a cut to a fast-moving American armoured reconnaissance column consisting of M24 Chaffee light tanks, GMC trucks, M8 armoured cars, Dodge Weapons Carriers, Jeeps and White M3 halftracks speeding along a road towards the bridge. This scene illustrates the qualities of the M24 Chaffee which, with a top speed of 35 mph, was one of the fastest tanks of WW2. Other speedy armoured vehicles of this era were the British Cromwell (40 mph) and the American M18 Hellcat tank destroyer (50 mph). Indeed Field Marshal Montgomery once said that if the German forces in the Battle of the Bulge had been equipped with British Cromwells they might have reached Antwerp.

Introduced in late 1944, the M24 was one of the first Allied tanks to have automatic transmission and replaced the earlier M3 and M5 Stuart light tanks. Fitted with a lightweight 75mm cannon, the M24 fired the same ammunition as the larger M4 Sherman and thus packed a good punch for its size. On one occasion in early 1945 two M24s came across a German Tiger I and knocked it out by repeatedly hitting the turret with 75mm high explosive rounds. Although the shells didn't penetrate the Tiger's thick armour, they caused several 88mm shells inside the turret to 'cook off', resulting in the loss of the tank.

M24s have appeared in several films. In *Battle of the Bulge* (1965) they played Shermans, in *Is Paris Burning?* (1965) they were modified to look like German Panthers, and in *The Day the Earth Stood Still* (1951) they were the US tanks which surrounded Klaatu's flying saucer.

Many of the shots in this sequence were taken from cameras fixed to the tanks and vehicles, others from a helicopter. The aerial shots in particular are quite breath-taking, and illustrate the technical advances that were made in helicopter-mounted cameras during the sixties. The most common camera helicopter used during this period was the French-made Sud Aviation Alouette II which was one of the earliest choppers to have a gas turbine engine, offering less vibration than earlier piston types. Improved camera mountings for use in helicopters were also invented in the sixties, and were even featured on the BBC's *Tomorrow's World* programme.

As the American column races towards the bridge at about 25 mph (quite fast for armoured vehicles), it comes under fire from the opposite bank as the Germans open up with artillery, including powerful 88mm guns. Explosions start falling on the road, and some US vehicles are hit. Suddenly the bridge itself is shrouded by a series of explosions as it blows.

The film then cuts to a shot of a map of Western Germany as the camera zooms in on Oberkassel. In a German HQ, Generaloberst Von Brock (Peter van Eyck) reviews recent developments with dismay. The Americans were only 100 metres away from capturing the bridge at Oberkassel over the Rhine. Only one bridge is left standing over the river – the railway bridge at Remagen – and the General has orders to destroy it.

'What a brilliant plan to shorten the war. Just do what the enemy wants!' says the General just before the titles roll.

What we have just witnessed is a pre-credits sequence as spectacular as anything in a James Bond movie, and illustrates the influence that that series of Eon films had on movies in other genres. Pre-credits sequences had been used occasionally in films for decades before *Dr No* (1962), but the success of that film and the use of increasingly lengthy and spectacular pre-credits scenes in subsequent Bond productions meant that they became an almost obligatory feature of most films made in the sixties and early seventies.

Yellow titles then roll over aerial footage of the bridge at Davle in Czechoslovakia, which makes an excellent stand-in for the one at Remagen. Refugees and German troops are streaming eastwards over the bridge to escape the advancing American army. The helicopter-mounted camera then reveals the nearby town. It is all inspiring footage, which nowadays would be done much more cheaply with a radio-controlled drone.

After the titles there is another helicopter zoom shot of a US Army Willys MB Jeep travelling at speed along a country road. It arrives at a US Army encampment, where military vehicles of all kinds are parked including M24 tanks, M8 armoured cars, M3 halftracks, Jeeps, and Dodge weapons carriers. Several destroyed German vehicles also lie about abandoned, including an overturned VW Type 82 *Kubelwagen* scout car which was a made-for-movie replica based on a VW Beetle car as evidenced by its running boards (which no real *Kubelwagen* ever had). Some of the US Jeeps have vertical metal bars welded to their front bumpers. This is entirely accurate for the period, as these were fitted to snap wires which might be stretched across the road in the hope of decapitating soldiers travelling in Jeeps.

General Shinner (E.G. Marshall) gets out of his Jeep and briefs Major Barnes (Bradford Dillman) on his next mission. At least 50,000 German soldiers are trapped to the west of the Rhine, and he wants his men to carry out an armed reconnaissance towards the river. However, he is not expected to capture any bridges.

Nearby, Lieutenant Phil Hartman (George Segal) is shaving in the open air using a wing mirror ripped from a vehicle, while his colleague Sergeant Angelo (Ben Gazzara) is looting a dead German soldier in front of a mud-splattered *Wermacht* Horch 901 troop carrier.

'You're a pig', says Angelo.

'I love you too', replies the Sergeant, who justifies his action by saying that 'everyone makes a profit out of the war'. Angelo is like a darker, less comedic version of Don Rickles' character Crapgame in *Kelly's Heroes* (1970). Having finished his shaving, Hartman gives the order for his men to move out and they set off in an assortment of vehicles, including the captured Horch.

On the other side of the Rhine, a staff car arrives at a local German Army HQ. A couple of German halftracks can be glimpsed in the background. Although they look like authentic Sd. Kfz 251s they are in fact OT-810s, a post-war Czech-made version of the same vehicle.

The main differences between a genuine Sd.Kfz 251 and an OT-810 were that the original German vehicle had a petrol engine whereas the Czechs fitted a diesel, and also that the Sd.Kfz 251 was open-topped while the OT-810 had two large armoured flaps which could be closed over the troop compartment to turn it into a fully enclosed vehicle like a modern APC. The two OT-810s are also painted grey with faded rust and black camouflage stripes which is wrong for the period as, from 1943 onwards, German armoured vehicles were painted sand yellow with green and brown camouflage stripes.

The staff car comes to a halt and Major Paul Kreuger (Robert Vaughn) gets out. He goes into the German HQ where he meets General von Brock who briefs him on the situation, which is perilous. The Russians have reached the Elbe (a script error, at they had only got as far as the Oder by early March) and 75,000 men are trapped to the west of the Rhine. Their only means of escape is the Remagen Bridge, but letting it fall into American hands would be disastrous as it would allow US forces into Germany itself.

Von Kreuger is therefore ordered to blow the bridge, although the Major himself suggests it would be sensible to delay this to allow as many Germans as possible to escape back to the Fatherland. He is told that 1,500 men are available to defend the bridge, and he is to report there the following morning.

To the west of the Rhine, Hartman's men are conducting their armed reconnaissance along a country road. The Lieutenant orders his vehicles to stop short of a farmhouse as he suspects a trap. A second Jeep with Captain John Colt (Paul Prokop) in the passenger seat draws up beside Hartman. Colt dismisses Hartman's concerns and orders his driver to go to the farmhouse. They have only travelled a hundred yards before there is an explosion to the left of their Jeep. A couple of seconds later the vehicle suffers a direct hit and both occupants are killed. Hartman is visibly shaken by the death of his friend, but now knows for sure that the farmhouse contains enemy troops who must be eliminated. He orders his men to 'bring the Kraut car up', a reference to the captured Horch. Sergeant Angelo wonders if Colt's Jeep was blown up by a landmine, but Hartman is sure that an anti-tank shell was responsible.

As Hartman stuffs grenades in the pockets of his battledress, he orders Angelo to take an M3 halftrack filled with soldiers across the field to the farmhouse while he goes down the road in the Horch. Exactly why Hartman uses the Horch is never made clear, although it can be assumed that he is thinking that it may momentarily confuse the German gunners who might be reluctant to fire on one of their own vehicles in case it is manned by friendly troops.

The Horch sets off down the road as Angelo's men cut across the field. Suddenly Hartman's driver Corporal Grebs (Bo Hopkins) spots a German soldier in an upstairs window, aiming a *Panzerfaust*, a hand-held anti-tank weapon. Hartman tells Grebs to 'give it everything you've got'. The sudden increase in the vehicle's speed spoils the aim of the German gunner, who misses with two consecutive shots. In reality it would be very hard to hit a speeding vehicle with a *Panzerfaust*, as its hollow-charge bomb would travel relatively slowly in a curved trajectory and such weapons were usually only effective against slow-moving or stationary targets at very close range.

First introduced in 1943, the *Panzerfaust* replaced the earlier *Faustpatrone* and was a very effective hand-held anti-tank weapon. Unlike the American bazooka and the British PIAT (Projector Infantry Anti Tank), it was not a reloadable weapon. One it had been fired, the operator simply threw it away and picked up another one.

The operating principle was also different from the bazooka and PIAT. Whereas the bazooka fired a rocket and the PIAT fired a hollow-charge bomb from a spigot mortar, the *Panzerfaust* used a gunpowder charge to fire a large, shaped-charge warhead attached to a wooden pole with pop-out fins. Thus the *Panzerfaust* was really a type of recoilless gun rather than a rocket launcher.

The first model was the *Panzerfaust 30* which – as the name suggests – had a range of 30 metres. Further improved models with greater range and explosive power followed, namely the *Panzerfaust* 60, 100, 150 and 250 models. Even the *Panzerfaust 30* could penetrate 140mm of armour, while the 150 model could pierce a thickness of 320mm which meant the weapon could knock out any Allied tank provided it was used at short range. The Americans were very impressed with the weapon and used large number of captured *Panzerfausts* during the Normandy campaign and the Battle of the Bulge as they considered it to be superior to their own bazookas. This was largely because the *Panzerfaust* used a much larger explosive warhead than the PIAT or bazooka. The bazooka typically made a hole in a tank just half-an-inch in diameter, whereas that left by a *Panzerfaust* hit was typically three-and-a-half inches across.

As the Horch is closing in on the farmhouse, Angelo's halftrack arrives in its rear yard, spraying the defending German soldiers with deadly fifty-calibre bullets from the vehicle's M2 Browning machine gun. Soldiers spill out from the vehicle and kill the remaining defenders with their M1 Garand rifles, while one GI throws a grenade. Within a couple of minutes all the Germans are dead.

Angelo hears some chickens clucking and suggests they investigate the barn. Chickens mean eggs, a much-prized commodity in WW2. Hartman then checks out the kitchen and finds a German MP-40 submachine gun. He fires a short burst at the table, smashing a few bottles, and then sits down to eat some chicken wings and bread and drink some wine.

Major Barnes arrives and orders the men to move on to the town of Stadit Meckenheim. Barnes also tells Hartman that with the death of Colt he is now the acting CO.

A few hours later it is dark as Major Kreuger sits in the front passenger seat of his staff car, which is stopped at a checkpoint. Kreuger notices that several German soldiers are being shot by a firing squad. An SS Officer checks his papers and explains that the deceased Germans were guilty of desertion, but Kreuger is staggered. As he smokes, his driver offers the opinion that this shocking development indicates that the war is lost. All the SS officers in the movie wear black uniforms, which is incorrect as by this point in the war the SS had switched to field grey outfits, with the exception of SS tank crews.

Meanwhile, Hartman's patrol has reached Meckenheim, a sequence which was clearly shot 'day for night'. The vehicles split into two separate units and enter the town from different directions, meeting in the square. The German Army have gone, and so Hartman gives orders for his men to bed down. The GIs burst through the doors of what they think is a *Gasthaus*, but discover it is the local jail. Hartman takes the governor's office while the rest of his men rest in the cells.

Soon there is a commotion at one end of the jail and Sergeant Angelo discovers that his men are ogling an attractive young female (Anna Gael) who is being held prisoner. Angelo orders his men to leave the cell and sits down. He reassures the girl that he means no harm and offers her some chocolate. Suddenly Hartman arrives and asks the girl what she is doing in the jail. She explains that she is actually French, but was arrested by the Germans.

Hartman is too exhausted to be interested in the girl – attractive though she may be – and tells her to go. He then returns to his room to sleep. The girl is there and offers to sleep with him, asking if he has any cigarettes. She explains that she had lived with a German soldier, but he had been killed in the Ardennes offensive. She takes off her top so that Hartman can see her bare breasts. (As this film was released in 1969 and the producers didn't want it get an 'X' certificate, we only get a brief side view of Gael's left breast. At this point in time British and American censors were still quite prudish, something that was to change within a few years. For example, Hammer's version of *The Mummy* (1959) had extra scenes featuring bare-breasted handmaidens which were only included in foreign releases of the film.)

The French girl puts her top back on just as Angelo arrives. 'Privilege of rank, Lieutenant?' he quips. However, Hartman has other things on his mind and tells the Sergeant, much to his dismay, that they have orders to move out and keep moving forward until they encounter the Germans.

'Where that might be?' asks Angelo. Hartman doesn't answer, and merely looks at one town on the map: Remagen.

The action then switches to Remagen itself, where a staff car is crossing the bridge. The car arrives at the German HQ and Major Kreuger gets out. He is met by Captain Carl Schmidt (Hans Christian Blech) who is in charge of the town's defences. He reports that the bridge is secure, and then gets on the field telephone to summon Captain Otto Baumann (Joachim Hansen) who is in charge of the demolition work. Baumann reports that it is proving difficult to install the explosive charges and cables because so many refugees and soldiers are streaming over it. The bridge really needs to be closed to allow this work to take place. Kreuger, though, is adamant that at the moment the priority is to keep the bridge open.

Kreuger then reviews the defences at the bridge and discovers that most of the forces that are supposed to be defending it no longer exist. For example, 600 Polish and Russian volunteers have simply vanished. Only 200 men are left to defend it, including the sappers.

'You realise that what you are saying is treason', says Kreuger.

'No, only the truth', replies Schmidt.

At this point the 'phone rings and Kreuger asks for two Panzer battalions to be sent at once. He then enquires about explosives, asking if they are in place. Baumann reports that 600kg are on their way.

Kreuger looks out the windows and notices the twin stone towers at each end of the bridge. He is informed that two heavy machine guns have been placed in each. An old barge is moored in the river, and Kreuger suggests putting some weapons on it.

Later, Kreuger reviews the defences on the high ridge overlooking the bridge. Three 88mm guns have been installed plus multiple machine guns. On the bridge itself, Kreuger views the master switch controlling detonation and observes that the electrical cables which are being wired to the explosives are protected by a thick steel pipe. The circuit is tested every hour and, in addition, there is a back-up incendiary fuse which can be lit to trigger the explosives. Satisfied at what he has seen, Kreuger announces that he is going into town to review the civil defences.

Suddenly the air raid siren sounds and three USAAF aircraft – two B-25 Mitchells and a solitary P-51 Mustang – appear in the skies above the bridge. In fact, only one B-25 was used in this sequence and for one shot the image of the single aircraft was duplicated in post-production. Furthermore, the B-25 used in this scene has incorrect USAAF markings for the period, as it has a red dot in the centre of the white star. This particular style of roundel was dropped in 1942 to avoid confusion with Japanese 'meatball' markings. In any case, the B-25 Mitchell was never used by the USAAF in the north-west European theatre during WW2.

The bomber used in these scenes was B-25N 44-29121, US civil registration N86427, which at that time was owned by Ralph Johnson of Compass Aviation Inc., Richmond, VA. It was painted in an early war scheme to commemorate the Doolittle Raid on Tokyo on 18 April 1942. It was eventually acquired by Jeff Hawke, and flown across the Atlantic in May 1978 as one of five B-25s used in the filming of *Hanover Street* (1979) at Bovingdon and Little Rissington. N86427 was 'Brenda's Boys' in that film, and the following year it took part in the Sean Connery movie *Cuba* (1980) which was filmed in Spain. The aircraft now resides in the Spanish Air Force Museum at Cuatro Vientos. All the aircraft footage in *The Bridge at Remagen* was shot from the ground by a Second Unit in the USA and edited into the film. The identity of the P-51 used in these sequences remains unknown to this day.

Bombs fall around the bridge and several sappers fall into the river, but no damage is done. Later, after the US planes have departed, Kreuger calls at a local *Gasthaus*. The owner, Herr Holzgang (Heinz Reincke), is in charge of civil defence and is clearing up the mess caused by the air raid. He asks his wife Greta (Sonja Ziemann) to fetch some glue to repair a damaged porcelain ornament.

Kreuger picks up one of Holzgang's precious ornaments, pretending to admire it. Then he lets it drop to the floor where it smashes into several pieces. Kreuger has made his point in a non-verbal way. Germany is facing invasion and this is no time to worry about porcelain. Every available man must be rounded up to defend the town. Holzgang points to a photo of his son who died at Stalingrad, implying that he himself has made enough sacrifices, but Kreuger is unimpressed, pointing out that Germany has already lost four million sons in the war.

Suddenly there is the sound of explosions. Kreuger gets on the 'phone and asks to be put through to the command post at the bridge. The call is answered by Hartman, who tells the Major that the man he wants to speak to is dead. Kreuger subsequently learns that an advance spearhead of American troops is attacking the town from positions on high ground overlooking the bridge. There is no news of the two promised Panzer battalions.

Meanwhile, some of Hartman's men have occupied a church bell tower overlooking the bridge. The Lieutenant is amazed to see that the bridge is intact with hundreds of German troops fleeing across it to safety. He asks for Major Barnes to come up, and the Americans briefly wish they had a camera as they are expecting the bridge to blow any moment. However, Private Glover (Frank Webb) points out that he has already sold his camera to Sergeant Angelo.

Barnes realises that the Americans have an opportunity at their fingertips. If they shell the bridge and bring up tanks, they can trap six enemy divisions on the west bank of the Rhine. Barnes promises Hartman a unit citation if they can pull it off, and Hartman replies – in a rather sarcastic tone of voice – that there is 'nothing my boys would appreciate more'.

Standing on the bridge, Kreuger looks up at the church bell tower using binoculars and sees Hartman looking back at him through his own field glasses. As the situation is deteriorating, Kreuger asks Captain Schmidt to transfer the command post to the railway tunnel. The 'phone rings to tell Kreuger that the explosives have now arrived, but the crates contain only an insufficient quantity of Donarit, a civilian-grade explosive.

As this is happening, several more M24 tanks arrive on the high ground overlooking the bridge and engage the German 88s and machine guns on the opposite bank as German sappers start to install the newly-arrived explosives. A German halftrack carrying a squad of soldiers crosses the bridge. The two hinged armour panels which can be used to form the roof of an OT-810 can be clearly seen in this scene.

As the Germans continue with their preparations, M24 tanks trundle into the town of Remagen. All these scenes were shot in the Czechoslovakian town of Most, which was due to be demolished and rebuilt elsewhere to allow coal mining to take place. For a fee of $20,000 the filmmakers were allowed to destroy a number of buildings, resulting in some very authentic footage. The Czechs were also keen to use up a large supply of explosives which they had retained since WW2, and the explosions were quite spectacular.

The first two M24s are hit by *Panzerfaust* bombs fired from a first floor window, but the two following tanks engage the gunner with machine gun fire and 75mm shells and the threat is soon eliminated, allowing the tank unit to move forward.

Holzgang orders his family to take shelter in the cellar of the *Gasthaus*, but his 14 year-old son goes upstairs carrying an MP-40 submachine gun. He is determined to make a last stand as the M24s rampage through the town, shooting everything in sight. They easily crash through barricades of cars and masonry that have been erected by the civil defence forces as Hartman's men shelter in a shell crater. Eventually the defenders surrender, and the American soldiers are shocked to realise that they consist entirely of old men (members of the *Volkssturm*, the German Home Guard) and boy soldiers of the *Hitlerjugend*, the Hitler Youth.

One GI captures a prisoner who has a bloodied bandage over his left eye, but as he is moved out both men are killed by a burst of machine gun fire from an upstairs window. The American troops storm the house and Angelo bursts into a room where he sees a figure standing at a window clutching an MP-40. He kills him with a single burst and then turns the body over with his foot and is shocked to discover that the assailant is a teenage boy. As Angelo is still reeling with shock over what he has done, Hartman arrives.

'Come on, you can loot him later', the Lieutenant says brusquely. Angelo takes great offence at this remark and points his gun at the Lieutenant before he recovers his composure and leaves the room.

Hartman later confronts the innkeeper, Holzgang, about the identity of the boy who shot one of his men, and discovers that it was his 14 year-old son, Rudi. 'I ordered him not to resist', says Holzgang, but the American officer is not impressed.

'So you hate Hitler, eh?'

'It has been a tragedy for Germany. I hate the terrible war. I'm a man of peace. I'm an innkeeper.'

Hartman doesn't comment and merely rips the Nazi party badge off Holzgang's lapel.

As Hartman is playing hardball with the innkeeper, German Army sappers have finished placing explosives under the bridge. Kreuger orders the bridge to be blown, but there is a problem as a train carrying munitions is heading north on the west bank of the river. In earlier drafts of the script the train's flatcars were carrying secret rocket weapons, but this idea didn't survive to the final cut of the film.

The train has only a few hundred yards to go till it crosses the bridge. Kreuger hopes to let it cross before triggering the explosives, but the US Army has other ideas as several M24s are heading south on the riverbank road on the west bank and are intending to intercept the train before it can cross the river. Eventually the American tanks blast the train with their 75mm guns at close range before it can go over the bridge and it stops, emitting clouds of smoke and steam. The M24s now start to cross the bridge but have to halt at a large crater. As Kreuger retreats for the safety of the railway tunnel, he drops his gold cigarette case.

More M24s have now arrived on the ridge overlooking the bridge and they start to shell it, but Brigadier General Shimmer orders them to cease fire as he realises there is an opportunity for his troops to capture the bridge intact. He gives Barnes an order to send his men across the bridge. They have to cut every wire and cable they can find and throw the explosives into the water. These scenes of American troops pulling detonation charges from the underside of the bridge were filmed near Hamburg after the production was forced to leave Czechoslovakia.

Barnes gives the order but Hartman is cynical, suggesting that the Major should lead the men himself as he considers the job too risky. Angelo takes things even further and hits Barnes, resulting in the American officer threatening him with a court martial.

Despite their concerns, the Americans advance slowly across the bridge, taking cover behind the vertical metal girders as they go. At the other end of the bridge, the Germans have set up three MG42 machine guns which lay down a withering volley of fire. Both the MG42 and its predecessor the MG34 were used in the film. These weapons had a reputation for very high rates of fire which could be anything between 900 and 1,500 rounds a minute depending on the type of bolt that was fitted. However, though this could have a demoralizing effect on Allied troops who used weapons with a slower cyclic rate (e.g. the British Bren fired at just 500 rounds per minute), this high rate of fire could cause problems with barrel overheating, requiring frequent barrel changes. In addition, with their voracious consumption of ammunition, the MG34 and MG42 tended to run out of rounds very quickly.

Most of the machine guns used in *The Bridge at Remagen* were 'gas guns', which looked like the real thing but were worked by propane gas ignited by a spark plug. This meant that the sound of the gun firing had to be dubbed onto the soundtrack in post-production. In the case of the MG34 and MG42 weapons, stock 'rat-a-tat-tat' machine gun sound effects were used instead of the real sound which that type of gun made, which was often described as being like a buzz-saw or a piece of canvas ripping.

Seeing what is happening, Brigadier General Shinner orders his mortars to fire smoke shells to cover the advance. Taking advantage of the cover offered by the smoke, Kreuger retreats into the railway tunnel and warns everyone to lie down and cover their ears to protect their eardrums from the pressure wave. German sappers connect up wires to a detonator plunger and push it, but nothing happens. Captain Schmidt soon realises what is wrong; the detonation cable has been severed by a shell hit, and the steel pipe lies smoking in a crater. The only solution now is to light the emergency fuse.

Under heavy American fire, two German soldiers advance towards the centre of the bridge towards the incendiary fuse.

As the American soldiers are trying to pick off the two Germans, one GI sees Kreuger's discarded cigarette case and tries to pick it up, but he is hit. One of the two Germans is also shot and killed, but the second reaches the location of the emergency fuse, lifts up a flap and lights it using a flare pistol.

The Americans realise what has happened and evacuate the bridge. Within seconds the bridge explodes. There are massive amounts of smoke and a few bits of superstructure fall off (courtesy of a miniature shot in which a thin wire attached to a section of girder can be seen), but when the smoke clears it is evident that the bridge is still intact. Hartman is relieved that his men are still alive. Realising that the attempt to blow the bridge has failed, Captain Baumann rails about the poor quality of the explosive that was sent.

As this is happening, Hartman and his men are advancing across the bridge and the American Lieutenant finds a dead German soldier with a gold cigarette case in his right hand. Hartman realises he died trying to retrieve the case and pockets it himself, not knowing who it originally belonged to.

In the railway tunnel nearby, Kreuger is shocked at the failure of the Germans' attempt to blow the bridge and asks for an urgent message be sent to General von Brock, advising that the bridge be bombed by the Luftwaffe as soon as possible and that reinforcements be sent.

Time is running out for the Germans, though, as a US Army Caterpillar D7 bulldozer starts to fill in the first of a number of craters which are preventing tanks from crossing the bridge. Kreuger estimates that the Americans will have tanks across the bridge by the morning.

As night falls, Hartman gives cigarettes to his men from the gold case he acquired earlier and then puts it back in his left breast pocket. At almost the same moment, deep inside the railway tunnel, Kreuger realises his cigarette case is missing.

Suddenly the German troops in the river barge open fire with MG42 machine guns. The Americans respond by sending four troops round the back of the barge by boat and then flinging in two grenades. In the ensuing gun battle all the Germans are killed, but one US soldier is shot and Angelo falls into the river and is presumed drowned. Hartman is furious at this unnecessary loss of life, and takes his revenge by clubbing a German corpse with a rifle butt.

In the railway tunnel Kreuger is trying to rally his remaining troops. He orders the men to divide into two squads, one to be led by himself and the other by Captain Schmidt. Each man is to carry as much ammo as possible.

Unfortunately one man panics and starts to run away, only to be shot in the back by Kreuger. Schmidt is mortified and points out that 'dying animals bite at their own wounds'. But Kreuger is unrepentant and orders Schmidt to hold out as long as possible so that he can get to HQ and find some reinforcements.

At the local HQ, the Germans are packing up and preparing to withdraw as Kreuger arrives. He asks to see General von Brock but is told that he is unavailable. SS General Gerlach (Gunter Meisner) tells him that he has been sent by the Fuhrer and wants an explanation as to why the bridge was not blown as instructed. Kreuger replies that the reason was simply that he wasn't given enough explosives to do the job properly but the General is unimpressed, saying that he delayed the destruction of the bridge for too long. Kreuger urges the General to counter-attack, but the SS officer says that Remagen is no longer his concern and that he is being placed under arrest.

Back on the Ludendorff Bridge it is still dark. Hartman's men are still lying in a small crater near the eastern end of the bridge. He asks everyone to call out their names and confirms Angelo is missing. At the western end of the bridge some M24 tanks advance as Hartman moves forward, bullets dancing around his feet. Dead bodies and the detritus of war are everywhere. Captain Schmidt emerges from out of the darkness, a white flag in his hand to offer his surrender. Hartman accepts his offer and asks for all his men to come out of the tunnel with their hands on their head.

At that moment a large formation of M24 tanks, M8 armoured cars and M3 halftracks clank forward and illuminate the scene with their headlights. A crowd of people emerge from the railway tunnel (including many civilians) as Captain Schmidt mentions that in peacetime he was the schoolmaster in Remagen. These scenes were filmed at the mock-up bridge in Italy in late 1968.

Major Barnes appears and chides Hartman for his reckless courage under fire. But he has good news as well, as he informs him that his men are being moved back for a rest. They will also receive a unit citation. Suddenly Angelo – who was presumed dead earlier – appears wearing a German tunic. Hartman offers Angelo a cigarette from his gold case.

Some miles away, Kreuger is about to face a firing squad. He is led to an upright post made from a railway sleeper and offered a last cigarette. Just before he dies, he hears the sound of aircraft and asks whether they are 'ours or theirs'. He is told they are enemy planes. 'But who is the enemy?' he asks, before he is hit by a volley of rifle bullets.

Back at the Ludendorff Bridge, US troops have erected a sign which reads 'Cross the Rhine with Dry Feet Courtesy of the 9th Armoured Division'.

As Captain Schmidt is being led away by a GI, he notices Hartman offering Angelo a cigarette from Kreuger's gold cigarette case and politely asks where he got it. 'From a friend', replies the American Captain. The film ends with a high angle crane shot of American vehicles crossing the bridge and, as the camera tracks upwards, a yellow caption informs viewers that the bridge finally collapsed on 17 March 1945, which was ten days after its capture.

The Bridge at Remagen was released on 25 June 1969 to mainly positive reviews. It did not do well at the box office though, taking only $1.6m at the US and Canadian box office against a production cost of $4.5m. Among film and military enthusiasts, however, it remains a highly regarded production.

Character names in *The Bridge at Remagen* and the real people they were based on

Character Name	Based on
Lt. Phil Hartman	Lt. Karl Timmerman
Major Paul Kreuger	Major Hans Scheller
Sergeant Angelo	Sergeants Alexander Drabik and Joseph De Lisio
Major Barnes	Major Murray L. Deevers
Brigadier General Shinner	Brigadier General William Hoge
Generaloberst von Brock	Generalleutnant Walter Botsch
Hauptmann Karl Schmidt	Hauptmann Willi Bratge
Hauptmann Otto Baumann	Hauptmann Carl Friesenhahn
Lt. Pattison	Lt. Emmett James Burrows

The Bridge at Remagen (1969) Production Credits

Production Team
Director: John Guillermin
Story: Roger O. Hirson
Screenplay: Richard Yates, William Roberts

Cast
Lt. Phil Hartman: George Segal
Major Paul Kreuger: Robert Vaughn
Sgt. Angelo: Ben Gazzara
Major Barnes: Bradford Dillman
Brigadier General Shinner: E.G. Marshall
General Von Brock: Peter van Eyck
Captain Carl Schmidt: Hans Christian Blech
Holzgang: Heinz Reincke
Captain Otto Baumann: Joachim Hansen
Greta Holzgang: Sonja Ziemann
French Girl: Anna Gael
Lt. Zimring: Vit Olmer
Corporal Grebs: Bo Hopkins
Private Bissell: Robert Logan
Corporal Jellicoe: Matt Clark
Private Slavek: Steve Sandor
Private Glover: Frank Webb
Lieutenant Pattison: Tom Heaton
Captain John Colt: Paul Prokop
General Von Sturmer: Richard Munch
SS General Gerlach: Gunter Meisner
SS Corporal: Rudolf Kalina
Private Manfred: Rudolf Jelinek
Colonel Dent: Fritz Ford
Rudi: Pavel Solty
Kreuger's Driver: Rolf Jahncke
German Lieutenant: Zdenek Braunschlager
Lieutenant Eckert: Jan Schanilec
Vaclav Neuzil: Sergeant Becker
Volkssturm Soldier: Vladimir T. Gottwald
Kleindarstellerin: Heikedine Korting
German Mounted Infantry Lieutenant: Karel Mares

Production
Producer: David L. Wolper
Associate Producers: Julian Ludwig, Theodore Strauss

Music
Composer: Elmer Bernstein

Cinematography
Director of Photography: Stanley Cortez
Film Editors: William T. Cartwright, Harry Knapp, Marshall Neilan

Production Crew
Casting: Lynn Stalmaster
Production Designer: Alfred Sweeney
Art Director: Bohuslav Kulic
Makeup Artist: Miloslav Jandera

Production Management
Production Managers: Horst Meyer, Ottavia Oppo, Jiri Pokorny
Executive Production Manager: Milton Feldman

Second Unit Director or Assistant Director
Assistant Director: Reggie Callow
Second Unit Director: William Kronick

Art Department
Property Master: Donald B. Nunley
Construction Coordinator: Hendrik Wynands

Sound Department
Sound Mixer: Hans Ebel, Al Overton
Boom Operator: Don Wortham

Special Effects
Special Effects Supervisor: Logan Frazee

Stunts
Stunt Supervisor: Hal Needham
Stunts: Fritz Ford, Gary McLarty

Camera and Electrical Department
Camera Operators: Cecil Cooney, Gordon Meagher

Costume and Wardrobe Department
Wardrobe: Frank Balchus

Editorial Department
Post-production Coordinator: George Fredrick

Location Management
Location Auditor: Yannoulla Wakefield

Music Department
Conductor: Elmer Bernstein
Musician (Harmonica): George Fields
Music Copyist: Albert Glasser
Orchestrator: Jack Hayes
Score Remixer: Michael J. McDonald
Orchestrator: Lee Shuken

Other Crew
Executive Secretary: Jean Baker
Production Secretary: May Capsaski
Technical Advisors: Ken Hechler, Col. Cecil Roberts
Continuity: Marion Mertes
Controller: Robert Pedersen

Supervising Story Consultant: Theodore Strauss

Production Secretary: Irmgard Von Ruexleben

CLINT EASTWOOD
is the leader of
KELLY'S HEROES
They set out to rob a bank...
and damn near won a war instead!

7
KELLY'S HEROES

(1970)

Metro-Goldwyn-Mayer/Avala Films/
The Warriors Company/Katzka-Loeb Productions

Director: Brian G. Hutton
Producers: Sidney Beckerman and Gabriel Katzka
Screenwriter: Troy Kennedy Martin

KELLY'S *Heroes* is a film which straddles several genres. It can be considered an action movie, a war film, an anti-war picture, a comedy, a thriller, a black comedy, or a heist movie. Although not an entirely serious film, it features more accurate WW2 tanks, vehicles and equipment than the Oscar-winning *Patton* (1970) which premiered the same year and purported to be a serious account of that American General's exploits in North Africa and north-west Europe. Most of the military hardware in *Patton* is wrong for the period, the locations don't look right, there is little action, and the script has an anti-British and anti-Montgomery bias which is probably explained by the fact that it was partly based on *A Soldier's Story*, the memoirs of the notoriously Anglophobic American General Omar Bradley.

I remember feeling very disappointed in *Patton* when I first saw it in early 1971. My reaction on seeing *Kelly's Heroes* for the first time in August 1976 (six years after its initial release) was totally different. I was thrilled by the action sequences. I laughed at the jokes. I loved the musical score and was very impressed by the accuracy of the military hardware. There were real Sherman tanks, correct WW2 Jeeps with split windscreens, M5 halftracks mounting 75mm guns, and even what looked like German Tiger tanks.

At the time of its release, screenwriter Troy Kennedy Martin, director Brian G. Hutton and star Clint Eastwood were all disappointed in the final cut of the film as 20 minutes of footage was excised by studio executives to reduce its running time. In addition, Kennedy Martin was also unhappy at the way Hutton had handled certain scenes which he felt diminished the anti-war message of his original screenplay.

Despite these criticisms, the film has a cult following and even though it features a mix of styles – as indicated above – it somehow all pulls together. It makes an interesting comparison with the disastrous film version of *Catch-22* (1970) which – though based on a cult anti-war novel and featuring stunning aerial scenes – somehow doesn't work.

Kelly's Heroes started life as a 'spec' script (an unsolicited screenplay) by film and TV writer Troy Kennedy Martin. Born in Rothesay on the Isle of Bute in Scotland in 1936, Kennedy Martin did National Service in the 1950s and then carved out a career in television. One of his earliest successes was the BBC's police series *Z-Cars* (1962-78) which he co-created, and which set new standards in social realism as it depicted policemen as fallible human beings with personal problems.

In the late 1960s Kennedy Martin tried his hand at screenwriting, leading to what was probably his greatest achievement, the screenplay for the original version of *The Italian Job* (1969) starring Michael Caine which – like *Kelly's*

Heroes – was about a gold bullion robbery. His next film project, *The Warriors*, was re-titled *Kelly's Warriors* and finally *Kelly's Heroes*, and dealt with a bank heist behind enemy lines in WW2 France. The script, for which he was paid $250,000, drew on elements of his only novel *Beat on a Damask Drum* (1959), which also dealt with a bank robbery by soldiers.

The film was made entirely on location in Yugoslavia (without any studio work) over a period of nearly six months beginning on 30 June 1969. At that time that European country was a Communist State run by Marshal Tito, and offered two distinct advantages to filmmakers. One was that profits generated from showings of previous films made in that country could not be taken abroad but could be used to fund new productions, resulting in budget savings. Another was that the Yugoslavian Army owned a large number of WW2-vintage American tanks and vehicles, plus some Soviet T34/85 tanks, which could be used in filming.

Of particular interest to the filmmakers was the fact that the Yugoslavian Army still had some M4 Shermans – the standard medium tank used by the US Army in WW2 – which at that time were very hard to find. That was the reason that most WW2 epics such as *Battle of the Bulge* (1965) and *Patton* had to use Korean War-era armoured vehicles. It was this ready availability of WW2 hardware that had led to Yugoslavia being considered as a possible location for both *The Guns of Navarone* (1961) and *A Bridge Too Far* (1977), and one wonders why *Battle of the Bulge* and *Patton* were never made there rather than Spain? The Yugoslavian Army even owned three working replicas of German Tiger I tanks which had been constructed (using Soviet T34/85 tanks) for the film *The Battle of Neretva* (1969), and the fight between these three tanks and a solitary M4 Sherman is the highlight of *Kelly's Heroes.*

The star of the film was Clint Eastwood, who had just made *Where Eagles Dare* (1968) and whose career was on the up. He was backed by a strong cast including Telly Savalas, Donald Sutherland, Carroll O'Connor and Don Rickles, who at that time was a well-known stand-up comedian.

The original director was to be Don Siegel, but he had to pass on the opportunity as he was still involved in post-production on *Two Mules for Sister Sara* (1970). The directorial reins were therefore handed to Brian G. Hutton who was recommended by Clint Eastwood, who had just finished making *Where Eagles Dare* with him and was impressed by his organisational skills.

In fact, many of the mainly British crew on *Where Eagles Dare* also worked on *Kelly's Heroes* including stunt arranger Alf Joint, stuntman Eddie Powell and film editor John Jympson. Although most of the cast were American, only a few of the crew were. The director of photography was a Mexican, Gabriel Figueroa, while the special effects co-ordinator – mainly pyrotechnics, as there were no miniatures or matte shots in the film – was a German, Karl Baumgartner. Baumgartner had previously provided the impressive bangs in *The Longest Day* (1962), and was known in the film industry as Karl 'Boom Boom'.

One of the cameramen was Bruce Surtees, who later worked on many of Clint Eastwood's subsequent pictures and whose trademark was shots taken with a very long lens. Another notable crew member was 18 year-old American John Landis, who made his own way to Yugoslavia via London and got a job as a production assistant at $75 a week. Landis also appeared as an extra in two scenes and much later became a highly-acclaimed film director with his most famous movie probably being *An American Werewolf in London* (1981).

The film was made in the Istrian peninsula of Yugoslavia, in what is now Croatia. The town of Vizinada became 'Claremont', while other scenes were shot in Obrenovac, Beocin, and the coast south of Trieste.

The movie opens with a tracking shot of a stationary German column in a village five miles west of the French city of Nancy. It is night-time, and raining heavily. The vehicles include VW Type 82 Kubelwagens, trucks towing 88mm guns, and what look like Panzer Mark VI (Tiger I) tanks. The armoured behemoths rev their engines and emit large plumes of oily smoke from their rear-mounted exhausts, giving away the fact that they have diesel engines (real Tigers had Maybach petrol motors but the replicas, based on Soviet T34/85s, used in the film were diesel-powered).

In the middle of the convoy sits a single US Army Willys MB Jeep. Its engine is running and its windscreen wipers are in action. No-one is paying much attention to it (which is probably quite accurate, as the Germans used a lot of captured vehicles). Private Kelly (Clint Eastwood) is sitting in the driving seat with Colonel Dankhopf (David Hurst), a captured German military intelligence officer, in the front passenger seat and a GI in the rear, armed with a rifle.

As Kelly sits waiting for the convoy to start moving, a passing German soldier looks through the window. He is not suspicious about the vehicle but, as he looks through the rain-streaked windscreen, he sees the two Americans inside and deduces that something is wrong.

Kelly realises the game is up and quickly swerves his vehicle to one side, tearing through the village at high speed and splashing soldiers standing at a field kitchen as Lalo

Shifrin's catchy theme song 'Burning Bridges', sung by the Mike Curb Congregation, begins. Shifrin was one of the USA's most prolific film and TV composers, having written the theme and incidental music for the original *Mission Impossible* TV series (1966-73) and the film *Bullitt* (1968) among many other compositions. His theme tune for *Kelly's Heroes* perfectly captures the film's essence, as it suggests military action with added elements of comedy and parody.

As an American artillery barrage continues to fall nearby, Kelly drives into a barn where his platoon is billeted. Inside the barn are several soldiers including the platoon sergeant Big Joe (Telly Savalas) and some of the unit's vehicles, including an International Harvester M5 halftrack mounting a heavy 75mm gun.

Big Joe is on the radio to Mulligan (George Savalas), complaining about the inaccuracy of his artillery barrage which is threatening his men. He asks him to lift it. George Savalas was Telly Savalas's brother, and the two of them later worked together on the TV series *Kojak* (1973-78).

As Kelly has coffee, he is told that the Germans are about to push over the canal. Meanwhile, Big Joe starts to interrogate the German colonel but he is not interested in details of troop movements; he only wants to know about the availability of hotels and women in Nancy, which the American 3rd Army intends to capture soon. The Colonel replies that he thinks the Hotel Majestic is the best in the area. Colonel Dankhopf warns Big Joe that a major German offensive is imminent, but the Sergeant is uninterested.

Joe Consults his 1939 Michelin Guide and discovers that the Majestic has a three-star rating as Kelly rummages through the Colonel's briefcase. He discovers clerical files which indicate that the Germans are planning a large convoy of trucks to take unspecified items from France to Germany in a mission called 'Operation Tannenbaum' (Fir Tree).

Kelly realises further interrogation is required and decides to get the Colonel to talk by getting him drunk on brandy. As the questioning continues, Big Joe goes to see his superior Captain Maitland (Hal Buckley) who is in an adjacent barn, looking over a captured yacht. Joe is dismayed to learn that his unit is being pulled out of the front line and won't be involved in the final push on Nancy. Instead, fresh soldiers from the 3rd Army will be used for this task.

Joe is appalled at this news, as he is concerned that his sex-starved men need to meet some women otherwise they will start 'freaking out with each other'. But Maitland is unconcerned, as he is more interested in his yacht and wonders if it will fit in the hold of a B-17. (The Boeing B-17 Flying Fortress was an American bomber and didn't have a 'hold', only a small bomb bay which wasn't big enough to take a vessel of that size.)

Suddenly Cowboy (Jeff Morris) announces that three German tanks are coming up the road. Maitland gives orders that the unit is to withdraw from the barn and take up new positions on the other side of the canal. He also orders Cowboy to engage the tanks with the unit's halftrack-mounted 75mm gun, but the American soldier is reluctant to do this as they have spent hours polishing the weapon and don't want it to go rusty in the rain. (This is similar to the gag in an episode of the BBC sitcom *'Allo 'Allo* (1982-92), when German Officer Lieutenant Gruber announces that he put away his armoured car in the garage as he 'had just polished it and it looked like rain').

The two M5 halftracks exit the barn by crashing through the closed wooden doors, wrecking them in the process, while Kelly snaps the canvas roof on his Jeep closed. Meanwhile, Colonel Dankhopf has got really drunk and starts to spill the beans about Operation Tannenbaum. Kelly finds a disguised gold bar in his briefcase and asks where it came from. The inebriated German reveals that there are 14,000 of them in a bank in the French town of Claremont, 25 miles East of Nancy. (The fictitious town of 'Claremont' is believed to be based on the real-life 'Clermont-en-Argonne', which is in the Lorraine region of France.)

The last of the Americans exit the barn just before it explodes. Kelly tries to save Colonel Dankhopf but they get separated and, as the German staggers about drunk, he is hit by machine gun fire from the bow-mounted MG34 of a Tiger tank which has just crashed through the barn. As explosions fall all around them, the American vehicles beat a hasty retreat.

The next morning it is warm and sunny as Kelly drives up to a US Army stores base in a Jeep with a thirty-calibre Browning machine-gun mounted in the rear. He meets Mulligan, who immediately apologizes for the inaccuracy of his artillery barrage the previous night. But Kelly isn't bothered about that. Instead he has a proposition for him. He wants him to arrange an artillery barrage against a crossroads at grid section seven. Mulligan says he doesn't have authorisation, but Kelly shows him the gold bar. 'You won't forget. You're a good man, Mulligan.'

The next scene – filmed at Novi Sad – is one of the most visually spectacular in the film and depicts General Patton's 3rd Army advancing on Nancy. As Kelly's platoon look on, a huge American armoured column drives past consisting of M4 Sherman tanks, Ford M8 six-wheeled armoured cars, Jeeps, GMC 'Deuce-and-a-half' trucks, Dodge Weapon Carriers, M5 halftracks and M6 tracked high-speed tractors. I counted ten working M4 Sherman tanks in this scene, which is more than were used in *A Bridge Too Far* (1977).

Five single-engined fighter aircraft fly over. Although from a distance they look like North American AT-6 Harvards they are in fact Ikaras Type 522 'Soko' trainers, a type which saw extensive service with the Yugoslavian Air Force from 1955 onwards. With their radial engines they make a passable stand-in for USAAF Republic P-47 fighter-bombers.

Big Joe tells Kelly that they have been ordered back to map reference MS473, but Kelly disagrees and tells him he needs to fix up transport papers for him and his men as they are going after the gold.

Later, the platoon is resting at a nearby farmhouse when Captain Maitland and his entourage draw up in a Jeep and an M5 halftrack. He is about to leave for Paris on a shopping trip. As Paris was liberated on 25 August 1944 and Nancy was captured on 15 September 1944, this indicates that the events in the film must take place between these two dates.

Much to Big Joe's dismay, the Captain informs him that he and his men are to have three days' rest at this location. Special services will call round with some newspapers and magazines. But Big Joe isn't happy because they are 10 miles from the nearest town; there is 'no booze, no women and no action!' Maitland simply tells Big Joe to use the time to 'get himself a suntan'. He also warns Joe to avoid the local women, as all the men carry guns. He also tells him that the penalty for looting is death, before driving off in an M6 high-speed tractor with the yacht in tow.

Meanwhile, Kelly has arrived at the local Divisional Trains Area Dump where he meets 'Crapgame' (Don Rickles), whose real name is never revealed in the film. (In some other scenes he is referred to as 'Hustler'.) Crapgame is sitting at a wooden table among crates of stores, but it is obvious that he is involved in a bit of black marketeering on the side.

Kelly gets straight to the point. He wants Crapgame to supply him with weapons and equipment comprising 15 Thompson submachine guns, two thirty-calibre Browning machine guns, two bazookas, ammunition for all these weapons, field rations and intelligence reports.

Crapgame asks Kelly what is in it for him, and the American Private shows him the bar of gold he retrieved from Colonel Dankhopf. Crapgame is intrigued and immediately gets on the 'phone to obtain a quotation for the current price of gold on the Paris market. He asks Kelly how many more are available and he reveals that there are 14,000 in a bank which is behind enemy lines. Crapgame agrees it is the perfect crime.

A couple of minutes later the 'phone rings and Crapgame answers. He has the quote he requested, which reveals the price of the full stash of 14,000 gold bars is $1.6m. Crapgame then asks Kelly what else he needs, and a voice pipes up from behind some crates in the background.

'You could probably use some armour', says Oddball (Donald Sutherland), who has been having a liaison with a local girl. Sutherland's character Oddball, a bearded, long-haired hippy who keeps going on about 'negative waves', clearly belongs in 1967 San Francisco, not 1944 France. His anachronistic appearance in the film is very similar to most of the characters in *Monty Python and the Holy Grail* (1975) and *Monty Python's Life of Brian* (1979), who displayed modern-day attitudes in historical settings to great comic effect.

Oddball reveals that he has three Sherman tanks outside, and he is willing to show them to the two soldiers. (The M4 Sherman was the standard American medium tank of WW2, and first saw action with the British at the Battle of El Alamein in October 1942. However, although a modern-day historian or armour enthusiast would refer to the vehicle as a 'Sherman tank', in WW2 a US soldier would probably call it just an 'M4 tank' as it was the British, rather than the Americans, who tended to give names to tanks. The same applies to most WW2 aircraft, as the 'Dakota' was really the British name for the C-47.)

Oddball then reveals that the commanding officer of his outfit had been decapitated by an '88' (a German 88mm tank or anti-tank gun) three weeks earlier. However, he wasn't too unhappy about that as his CO had been 'trying to get everyone killed' since his unit landed at Omaha Beach some weeks earlier. Oddball saw his tank unit as being defensive in nature – if the Germans threatened Paris or maybe New York then they would spring into action. 'But for $1.6 million, we can be heroes for two days'. Kelly isn't sure about the offer, but Oddball points out that a Sherman 'can give you a nice edge'.

Oddball then takes Kelly and Crapgame outside to view his tanks. Kelly is taken aback by what he sees. As the crew members of one tank clean the inside of the main gun barrel with a rod, others are lying about relaxing in the sun, drinking red wine and listening to music. Meat is cooking on a rotating spit as rustic music plays on an old-fashioned wind-up gramophone. Local women are hanging washing up to dry on clothes lines which have been strung between the tanks.

Oddball introduces the two soldiers to his chief mechanic, Moriarty (Gavin MacLeod), who has tuned up the engines of the three M4s to make them 'the fastest tanks in the European theatre, forwards or backwards'. Oddball then demonstrates a unique feature of his tanks – an extension tube which can be fitted over the gun barrel to make the standard 76mm gun look like a 90mm weapon and hopefully frighten off the Germans. This is an interesting point. When the M4 Sherman was first introduced in 1942 it carried a 75mm M3 gun which was based on a French weapon dating back to 1897. Although this was reasonably effective against the Panzer III and IV tanks, it soon became apparent that this would not be an adequate weapon for dealing with the newer German tanks such as the Tiger and Panther and a more powerful gun – the 76mm M1 with a longer barrel and higher muzzle velocity – would be needed.

Development work on the 76mm gun started in 1942, but it was found that the original rounded Sherman turret was really too small for this new weapon, resulting in a cramped operating space, so a new, larger and more angular turret – the T23 (taken from the aborted T23 tank) – was fitted to give the crew more room.

None of these improved 76mm gun Shermans took part in the initial landings in Normandy – though 200 of them were held in reserve in England – but in July 1944 a request was made for 76mm Shermans to be sent to France to counter German Panther tanks. Thus by September 1944 small numbers of 76mm-armed Shermans were reaching front-line units in France.

The Sherman tanks which were used in *Kelly's Heroes* were a post-war variant known as the M4A3E4 which employed the earlier, rounded turret, retro-fitted with the later 76mm M1 gun. The resulting hybrid vehicles thus looked visually similar to the British Sherman Vc Firefly tanks which mounted the British 17-pounder, long barrelled 76.2mm gun in the original turret. This has led to incorrect reports on the internet that the Shermans used in *Kelly's Heroes* were Fireflies. In fact, Fireflies differed from M4A3E4 Shermans in a number of respects as they carried a muzzle brake on the end of the main gun barrel, had a large armoured box containing the radio protruding from the rear of the turret, and also had the bow gunner's position plated over to provide extra ammunition stowage.

Oddball's comments about the 90mm gun are also interesting. During WW2 the US Army did field a 90mm M3 tank gun which was fitted to the M36 tank destroyer and the M26 Pershing tank, only 20 of which saw action from February 1945 onwards. Because of delays in the introduction of the M26 tank, consideration was given to up-gunning Shermans with the 90mm weapon but this never happened. As to Oddball's remarks about a fake 90mm gun possibly scaring off the Germans, it should be noted that the British had the opposite experience with the Sherman Firefly, as German tanks tended to target them selectively as they were considered a greater threat. The British responded by painting the underside of the last few feet of Firefly gun barrels light blue with a wavy edge to make it look as though they had the smaller 75mm gun, the exact opposite of the strategy Oddball used! Oddball shows Kelly two other unique features of his tanks, namely a number of 76mm shells filled with pink paint and also a speaker mounted on the left side of the turret which can blast out loud music.

In the meantime, Big Joe is giving orders to his platoon. They are to do their laundry, have a shave and shower, and get to work on the farmhouse to make it look like a nightclub. A bar is to be set up and he will find some booze and dirty movies.

Back at the supply depot, Crapgame is busy with his calculating machine and discovers that he has made a mistake. The value of the cache of gold isn't $1.6 million – it is $16 million! Kelly is pleased at this revelation, but mentions to Crapgame that he will need petrol for his mission.

He wants to go ahead that night at 2200 hrs, but Oddball says he and his boys have something on that evening and they agree to execute the mission the following night. Before Kelly leaves, he lets Crapgame retain the bar of gold.

Once Kelly has left, Crapgame tells Oddball a bit about Kelly's back story. He was a Lieutenant until he was asked to take his men up the wrong hill. His patrol suffered a heavy loss of life and Kelly was made the scapegoat and demoted to Private. Oddball chuckles when he hears this revelation. Crapgame then gets on the 'phone to Hogan in Intelligence to acquire some aerial photos as Oddball asks to borrow the gold bar so he can show it to his men.

Meanwhile, a Jeep draws up outside the farmhouse where Kelly's platoon is billeted. Big Joe gets out, leaving another soldier sitting in the passenger seat. He is carrying a large pile of film cans, presumably the 'dirty movies' Joe was talking about earlier.

Big Joe learns of Kelly's plans and confronts him, but the rest of the platoon stick up for him. Little Joe (Stuart Margolin) points out that they have been risking their necks for 50 dollars a month but Kelly has got everything figured out. He even has armour support in the form of three Shermans from the 321st.

Big Joe asks who is in command of the Shermans and when he learns it is Oddball he goes ballistic, calling the tank commander a 'freak' and a 'nut'. He points out there are rules and regulations which affect soldiers, the most important of which is that you don't stick your neck out unless you have to.

But Kelly is adamant that he and the rest of the platoon are going on the mission to steal the gold and if Big Joe won't lead them then he will. Joe asks about Captain Maitland, and Kelly assures him that everyone will assume he has been sent to the front lines.

Big Joe thinks things over for a moment or two and then relents. It is a wonderful piece of acting from Savalas, because he has clearly made a sea change in his thinking but it is all conveyed through a change in his facial expression, not through dialogue. The rest of the platoon whoop with delight.

The next scene is set the following night at a crossroads at 10.00 p.m. It is dark as Kelly awaits Mulligan's artillery barrage, which will cover their advance to an enemy-held town a quarter of a mile ahead. Their force consists of two Jeeps and two M5 halftracks. All the vehicles' headlights have been partially blacked out with tape, leaving just a thin horizontal strip of light showing. A few miles away, Mulligan's alarm clock rings. He awakens, gets on the 'phone and orders the mortars to fire.

As mortar bombs start to fall on the village, the American convoy moves forward. Kelly's men use their Thompson submachine guns to kill any German soldiers they can see. One of their halftracks knocks down a telegraph pole (this was actually an accident during filming, but looked so good it was kept in) and a VW Kubelwagen is rammed by the passing vehicles.

Meanwhile at General Colt's HQ, the American commander (played by Carroll O'Connor) is looking at a photo of his opposite number, General Vogel of the German 2nd Armoured Division. He brands him a 'loser', and then berates his officers for their current inaction. One of his officers (Read Morgan) points out that there is half a Panzer division between their forces and Nancy, but Colt mentions that that particular formation had 'no gas'. This is a very valid point, as by this stage in the war Germany was running short of fuel.

The officer also points out that the 'Air Corps' is blowing up the bridges by day while the Germans are rebuilding them at night (this is an error, as the US Army Air Corps became the US Army Air Force on 20 June 1941). The Lieutenant also mentions that orders had been received the previous night for artillery fire to be directed towards a crossroads. He can't explain this and Colt is dismissive of his claim, believing that he is making excuses. The Lieutenant also can't find aerial photos of the Nancy region, and is at a loss to explain their absence.

Some miles away, Oddball and his other two tank commanders are looking at these very same missing photos and discover an intact railway bridge they can use. Although it is designed for trains, Oddball believes his Shermans can cross it. As he puts it, they will 'swing onto the tracks and cross the mother bridge'. Moriarty, though, is worried the bridge won't be there and Oddball replies with one of the most fondly remembered lines from the movie: 'Don't hit me with those negative waves so early in the morning. It's a mother beautiful bridge and it's going to be there'.

The next scene is set in a wooded area on a hilltop. The camera tracks down as the sound of a piston-engined aircraft is heard in the distance. In the background, Kelly's platoon's halftracks and Jeeps are camouflaged with foliage. The men are resting and re-stocking their packs with fresh magazines for their Thompson submachine guns. Crapgame is offered a cardboard box containing K-rations, but doesn't want any. He does, though, take some water from a jerrycan as Kelly is told that Big Joe wants to see him at the command Jeep.

Joe is concerned that the all-important bridges they need may have been blown, but Kelly suggests the solution is to arrive at dawn before the USAAF has a chance to bomb them. The Sergeant then asks Kelly how many German troops they are likely to face, and Kelly suggests 30-40 soldiers. Joe asks him how he came up with the figure, and Kelly admits it is the normal support for three Tiger tanks. Joe is aghast and asks Kelly if Oddball knows that he going to be putting Shermans up against Tigers. However, Kelly is confident that the Tigers can be beaten by superior tactics.

Suddenly a single-engined fighter dives on the American troops and starts strafing them. It is one of the five Soko trainers used in the film as a stand-in for USAAF Republic P-47 Thunderbolts. Initially the aircraft attacks using two wing-mounted guns (simulated by strobe lights in the leading edges), although real P-47s actually had eight fifty-calibre Brownings, not two. As the aircraft climbs away we can see it has a natural metal finish with an incorrect USAAF marking on its upper port wing and the number '149' on the upper surface of the starboard wing.

The fighter comes round for another pass, and this time fires two underwing-mounted rockets at the vehicles, impressively filmed from a camera with a wide-angle lens fitted under the fuselage of the plane. Both rockets strike home and destroy all the vehicles – which in fact was quite rare in WW2, because the early unguided missiles used in that conflict were very inaccurate and it has been estimated that only a small percentage of the anti-tank rockets fired by Republic

P-47 Thunderbolts and RAF Hawker Typhoons in Europe actually hit armoured vehicles.

Typhoons could carry eight 25lb or 60lb rockets. American P-47s and P-38s could also fire rockets of a different design. Some P-47s carried 2.36 inch rockets which were mounted in tubes, three under each wing, not the single installation shown in the film. Later, 5 inch HVAR rockets became available, with five being mounted under each wing of a P-47.

All the vehicles are left blazing, though this effect was achieved by the usual film industry method of placing propane gas burners behind each one to give the impression they were on fire. The platoon's radio is also destroyed, but fortunately the men had got most of the weapons and supplies out of the vehicles before they were hit. The platoon resumes its mission on foot, and Crapgame is particularly annoyed that he has to carry one of the thirty-calibre machine-guns.

Some miles away, Oddball's three tanks halt inside a railway tunnel which leads to a marshalling yard. He briefs his commanders by radio and orders them to attack in triangle formation. The railway yard used in this sequence was real, though a fake tunnel (which could only hold two Shermans) had to be constructed.

What follows is probably one of the greatest tank sequences in the history of the movies as the three Shermans engage in an orgy of destruction. Troy Kennedy Martin reportedly hated this scene, which was not in his original script, but I love it.

Without warning, the three tanks emerge from the tunnel and start shooting up everything in sight. One of their first targets is a four-barrelled *Flakvierling* 20mm anti-aircraft gun (as seen in *633 Squadron* and *Where Eagles Dare*). As alarms and klaxons blare (using sound effects previously used in *Where Eagles Dare*), German troops are massacred in large numbers and buildings are blown up. Each Sherman carries a powerful 76mm main gun plus thirty-calibre machine-guns in the bow and mantlet positions which they use to deadly effect.

Trundling slowly through the installation, the tanks destroy most of the wooden buildings and kill the majority of the German troops. Some of the most effective shots in this sequence – which was directed by Second Unit director Andrew Marton – were taken by cameras fixed to the top of the tank turrets.

What also makes this sequence so striking is the use of music supposedly blaring from Oddball's turret-mounted speaker. During the attack, the track used is 'All for the Love of Sunshine'. But as the Shermans drive away, their orgy of destruction complete, the music changes to an instrumental version of 'I've Been Working on the Railroad': a piece of irony if there ever was one.

Some miles away, Kelly's platoon rest before moving off while Crapgame is still moaning about having to carry the thirty-calibre machine gun. In the meantime, Oddball's three tanks have arrived close to their chosen railway bridge by driving along the tracks. Oddball views the scene with satisfaction through binoculars but – just as he is about to give the order to move – two USAAF fighters bomb the bridge, which collapses into the water.

He berates Moriarty over this setback, which he believes is due to his 'negative waves', but the tank crewman is unrepentant, saying that he has had nothing but 'positive thoughts' about the bridge. Oddball then sees that the only solution is to find another bridge. A little later the 'phone rings at the HQ of the 42nd Engineers bridging unit and is answered by a private who calls over Lieutenant Bellamy (Len Lesser). It is Oddball, who is on the 'phone and he starts off by giving one of his dog impressions. 'Woof, woof, woof', barks the tank commander.

'Don't try to be funny', the Lieutenant says. 'What do you want?'

Oddball reports that he is at the *Chez Leon* café 10 miles south of Mesurier and he needs 60 feet of bridge. The sergeant is uninterested until he hears about the gold, but points out that he will need a support unit of 100 guys. Where will he find them? As he turns round the camera zooms in – through the window – on a band of marching soldiers. The Lieutenant has his 'volunteers'.

Some miles away, Kelly's platoon is plodding through a ploughed field when one of the GIs, Grace (Michael Clark), is blown into the air by an explosion. Big Joe realises they have walked into a minefield and tells all his men to get down on the ground and use their bayonets to locate the mines. Eventually they will clear a path to the nearby road.

At a nearby German Army base a Lieutenant (John Heller) answers the 'phone. Someone has reported an explosion in the minefield and they need to investigate. John Heller appeared in director Brian G. Hutton's previous film, *Where Eagles Dare*, in which he played the German Officer who berated Major Johann Schmidt (Richard Burton) over his lewd conduct towards Helga (Ingrid Pitt). Incidentally, a part was written for Ingrid Pitt in *Kelly's Heroes*, but at the last moment her scenes were deleted from the final shooting script.

Meanwhile in the ploughed field, Kelly's men are gradually identifying and marking the mines – but it is a slow, painstaking business. A German patrol leaves the Army base in two trucks led by a VW Kubelwagen. In the background are two M5 halftracks modified to look like German Skd. Kfz 251s. The two lorries are Czech-made Praga RNs, which is entirely accurate as the Germans used a lot of Czech equipment. All the German vehicles in the film are painted dark grey though – as related in other chapters of this book – by 1943 the Wehrmacht was painting all its vehicles desert sand with green and brown camouflage stripes.

Kelly's platoon leaves the minefield and takes up positions behind a drystone dyke on the other side of the road. But two soldiers, Job (Tom Troupe) and Mitchell (Fred Pearlman) are still stuck in the middle of the field, so Kelly tells them to pretend to be dead. Both do as they have been instructed but prepare their weapons – a Thompson submachine gun and a Browning Automatic Rifle (BAR) – for action. As the German patrol arrives, Kelly asks Fisher (Dick Balduzzi) for a grenade.

The Germans halt and their Lieutenant scans the scene through binoculars. There appear to be three dead American soldiers lying in the minefield, but he orders his men to investigate. As the German soldiers move towards the bodies, the US platoon opens fire with their Thompsons and two thirty-calibre machine guns, hurling grenades. Job and Mitchell also defend themselves, but their Browning Automatic Rifle soon jams. The main force of Americans then charges the Germans, and in minutes all the Nazi troops are dead. But it has not been a one-sided battle as Job and Mitchell have also been killed. This scene differed considerably from what was scripted by Troy Kennedy Martin. In his original draft, the Germans were a unit of unfit *Volkssturm* (Home Guard) in their sixties who were massacred, resulting in the Americans feeling remorse for their actions.

That night, in a sombre mood, the platoon takes shelter from the heavy rain in a barn by the road. Suddenly the noise of music can be heard in the distance and a column of US Army vehicles led by Oddball and his three Shermans come clanking down the road. Oddball is playing an instrumental version of 'John Brown's Body' through his tank's speaker.

A truck draws up beside the barn, and Lieutenant Bellamy from the Bridging Unit asks Kelly for details of the deal. He tells him that anyone who makes it to the bank will get an equal share, and Bellamy warns him not to double cross him. Kelly tells his men to jump up on top of Oddball's tank and it sets off down the road.

At US 3rd Army HQ, General Colt is woken by Booker (Ross Elliott) who tells him that there has been some kind of breakthrough on the front. He wants to know which unit is involved. Captain Maitland is carrying a pile of wrapped presents which he has just bought in Paris, but tries to help.

The American officers quickly establish that there is some kind of battle going on at a bridge near Claremont, 30 miles behind enemy lines, but it is pointed out to the General that the unit involved is using unofficial codenames like 'Crapgame' and 'Oddball'.

Colt picks up further information from the radio messages. He learns that two of Oddball's tanks are now out of action. One is in the river and the other is burning. Kelly says they will have to push on towards Claremont with the one surviving tank, which is on the other side of the river as the pontoon bridge is badly damaged.

Bellamy is told he will have to stay with his men and repair the bridge – which will take five hours – while Kelly and his platoon push on with the remaining tank. Colt is ecstatic when he hears the enthusiasm of the men, not realising they are motivated solely by financial gain. He is even more impressed when he hears a gravediggers' unit asking for a share of the action. 'Attack, attack, attack', says Colt, 'and don't worry about your flanks', echoing the views of General George Patton on whom his character was clearly based. Carroll O'Connor later became well-known for playing Archie Bunker in *All in the Family* (1971-79), an American (CBS) version of the BBC's *Till Death Us Do Part* (1965-75).

As Oddball's Sherman moves off with Kelly's men riding on top, Colt prepares to leave his HQ with a box of medals. A few moments later, Oddball's tank is driving through a French village on its way to Claremont as Lalo Schifrin's composition 'Burning Bridges' plays for the second time in the movie. The old man who appears briefly at the roadside in this scene was a local man, Vincent Maracecchi, who died of a heart attack just after this scene was shot. The film company subsequently paid for his funeral. Also appearing in this section of the film were three nuns, one of whom was played by John Landis. In the original cinematic release of the film there was an intermission at this point.

After the intermission there is a brief shot of General Colt and his entourage heading off to Claremont, and then the action moves to the square in the French village where three Tiger I tanks are guarding the bank. This is the first time in the movie that we see all three Tiger replicas clearly. The Yugoslavian Army clearly did a good job converting Soviet T34/85 tanks to look like Tigers, but the replicas weren't perfect reproductions. On a real Tiger I there is a distance of 32 inches between the front glacis plate and the gun mantlet, but on the film replicas the mantlet is almost level with the front vertical armour. Also, the main gun barrel of a Tiger was usually painted the same colour as the rest of the tank but the film versions appear to have shiny black barrels and muzzle brakes. The main clue that the vehicle is not a real Tiger is the wheel arrangement, as the replicas have spaced wheels with a clear gap in between them whereas genuine Tigers had overlapping, interleaved road wheels. Apart from that, though, the Tigers are fairly convincing with every detail of the original reproduced even down to a fake *Zimmerit* coating on the hull. *Zimmerit* was a textured coating applied to German armoured vehicles in the latter stages of the war to prevent magnetic mines from sticking to the hull. The 'key' symbol painted on the rear of each Tiger's turret indicates that they are attached to the 1st SS Panzer Division.

As the German troops guarding the bank go about their business, Cowboy is in a church tower overlooking the square. He contacts Kelly by walkie-talkie and reports that he can see the three Tigers, plus the bank.

On a hill near the village, Kelly, Big Joe, Oddball and his tank crew discuss their options. Kelly wants Oddball to 'keep the Tigers busy' while he robs the bank. Oddball, though, says the only way he can do this is by letting the Tigers shoot holes in them. Moriarty mentions that while in Normandy they were 'assaulted' by Tiger tanks.

Kelly tries to look on the positive side. The Tiger is an 'open country tank' and won't be able to manoeuvre well in the narrow streets. This is a good point, because the dumbest thing you can do with a heavy tank is to put it in a cramped town with narrow streets where infantry can get around it and above it and attack it with satchel charges, sticky bombs, Molotov cocktails, bazookas, anti-tank grenades and other weapons. This is exactly what happens in *Saving Private Ryan* (1998), which is discussed later in this book.

In fact, I would question whether it would have been a wise military decision to use three heavy tanks to defend a bank in the first place. A large squad of infantry backed up with halftracks or armoured cars would have been a wiser choice. This plot point probably came about because most writers don't know much about armoured vehicles and, for many, the only German tank they know is the famous Tiger which accounted for less than 7% of German tank production and has a mythical reputation which isn't matched by its combat record. Tigers were actually encountered very rarely. Between the D-Day landings on 6 June 1944 and the fall of Germany in early May 1945, US Army tankers only encountered Tiger Is on *four* occasions.

Oddball then asserts that 'the weakest point of a Tiger is its ass', and the only way to defeat it using a Sherman is to hit it at point-blank range in the rear. Actually this is a myth which is also incorrectly implied in another recent tank movie, *Fury* (2014).

The Tiger I had an armour thickness of 80mm on its rear plate and 100mm on its front glacis plate. The thinnest armour was actually on the lower side hull which was only 60mm thick. The US Army already knew this as a result of the examination of captured Tigers, including Tiger 131 which was captured intact in Tunisia by British forces in 1943. I will be discussing this issue a little later in this chapter.

Crapgame tells Oddball that this is his chance to become a hero, but the tank commander replies that to a New Yorker 'a hero is a type of sandwich' – a line which inspired one of the posters for the film. Kelly, however, reassures Oddball that he'll be right up on the tank beside him telling him where to go.

At that point Cowboy reports in by radio and Kelly tells him that he is to ring the church bells to give the signal for the US troops to go into action.

Meanwhile, the commander of the troop of three Tigers orders them to start their engines. It is revealed that they normally turn over their engines for 20 minutes every three or four hours, though the reason for this is never made clear. On the Russian Front, German vehicles and aircraft had their engines run frequently to stop them freezing, but this would not be necessary in France in early September and it would be wasteful of fuel, particularly as the Tiger's Maybach petrol engine had a fuel consumption of two gallons per mile.

Covered by the noise of the three tank engines, Oddball's Sherman makes its way downhill and into the village as the American troops infiltrate the village and take up positions. Some of them carry jerrycans of petrol, although the reason for this (e.g. making petrol bombs) is never made clear in the film.

Oddball's Sherman winds its way through the narrow streets of the town and then stops to allow Kelly to get off. The American soldier enters a destroyed building and, moving to the far wall, opens a door slightly. Two of the Tigers can be seen through the gap, and one has its rear end facing the building.

The platoon's sniper Gutowski (Richard Davalos) enters the attic of a building through a hatch and takes up position while Cowboy starts ringing the church bell using ropes. Under the cover of the noise created by the bells, Oddball's Sherman starts up and moves forward as the US troops prepare for action.

Oddball's Sherman enters the half-destroyed building and slowly moves forward, guided by hand signals from Kelly.

Oddball exits the turret and crawls along the top of the gun barrel, going as far as the muzzle brake. The Sherman moves forward very slowly, its muzzle level with a small open window on the side of the building. Its main gun is now pointing directly at the Tiger's rear plate at almost point-blank range, which Oddball had said earlier was the only way a Sherman could knock out a Tiger.

Actually this isn't correct. Apart from the fact that the rear plate of a Tiger I is 80mm thick and therefore the best place to hit such a tank with a 75mm round would be the side, specifically the lower hull where the armour is just 60mm thick, Oddball seems to have forgotten that his tank has a 76mm M1 gun, not the short-barrelled 75mm M3 gun of earlier Shermans.

The 76mm M1 gun didn't have the armour-piercing capabilities of a British 17-pounder or an American 90mm M3 gun, but even with standard ammunition it could penetrate the frontal armour plate of a Tiger I at less than 100 yards' range. So all these tactics involving getting behind the Tiger wouldn't be needed with a 76mm gun. The same error also appears in the film *Fury* (2014), in which tank commander Don 'War Daddy' Collier (Brad Pitt) believes he has to get a shot into the rear of a Tiger to kill it, even though his tank has a 76mm M1 gun.

Another error in the film is that the troops in Kelly's platoons could have attacked the other two Tigers using bazooka rounds and petrol bombs. Even the wartime M1 bazooka with its relatively small 2.36 inch rocket was capable of piercing the side and rear armour of a Tiger I at close range. Earlier in the film Kelly had specifically requested two bazookas, so what happened to them?

A German soldier blows a whistle to tell the three tank drivers to turn off their engines. Instantly Gutowski opens fire with his sniper rifle, quickly followed by the rest of the platoon who use machine gun fire and grenades to annihilate the German garrison. Oddball gives the order to fire, and the rear of the Tiger explodes in a ball of flame.

One of the two surviving Tigers (Number 113) starts up and trundles forward, seeking revenge. It smashes through a building and then comes across Oddball's Sherman which is moving quickly along a village street from left to right. The Tiger's gunner fires but the 88mm round passes behind the Sherman's turret and explodes in the field beyond.

The Tiger tries to get through a destroyed building to catch Oddball's Sherman but gets stuck and has to reverse out and try a different route. Meanwhile, the Tiger previously hit by Oddball explodes as Crapgame tells Cowboy to stop ringing the church bells.

As this is happening, Big Joe is leading Tiger 113 into a trap. He throws a grenade and fires his Thompson to entice the Tiger down a narrow street. Oddball and Kelly see the Tiger and follow it in their Sherman, intending to ambush it from the rear. As they turn to follow the enemy tank they crush a German car, a 1936 BMW convertible. Shooting this scene proved more difficult than might be thought, because in the first few takes the Sherman simply pushed the car away. Eventually the production crew solved the problem by tying the car to the ground!

Eventually Tiger 113 ends up in a narrow street with Oddball's Sherman right behind it. At a range of just 50 feet Oddball's gunner fires, resulting in nothing more than a splash of pink paint over the Tiger's rear plate. The gunner has accidentally loaded one of the paint shells! As he frantically searches for an armour-piercing round to load into the gun, the German tank commander emerges from the turret hatch. Kelly sees what is happening and sprays the enemy tank with bullets from his turret-mounted fifty-calibre gun. The commander slumps dead. Oddball's gunner fires a second time and the rear of the Tiger explodes, destroying the tank.

Meanwhile, having killed most of the German garrison, the members of Kelly's platoon approach the bank but they can't get in. It has thick solid doors and bars on the windows. One wonders why Kelly hadn't thought of this problem earlier and brought some plastic explosive?

Another way to break down the doors might be to use bazooka rounds, which possibly explains why these weapons never feature in the film even though Kelly requested them. If the platoon had bazookas then the next part of the plot would be different.

Meanwhile the surviving Tiger (115) goes on the rampage, destroying numerous buildings in the town while, nearby, Oddball's tank has broken down. The eccentric American tank commander is sitting in a deckchair drinking wine, eating cheese and 'catching rays'. Big Joe asks him why he is not helping, but Oddball says that he 'only rides in them and doesn't know how they work'.

'Woof, woof, woof. That's my other dog impression', he says. Big Joe visits Crapgame, who has been wounded in the recent fighting, and briefs him on the situation. The Hustler suggests they make a deal with the German tank commander.

Some miles away, General Colt arrives at the now-repaired pontoon bridge in his Jeep, where he meets a rather disconsolate looking Lieutenant Bellamy. He asks Bellamy where he comes from, and is told that he hails from Jersey

City. 'You're a helluva soldier and I want to shake your hand', says the General. Before driving off towards Claremont he promises the soldier that he has a medal for him.

Back in Claremont, Moriarty says the fuel pump is 'shot'. Kelly suggests using parts from the knocked-out Tigers, but Moriarty says that won't work. Big Joe then says they should talk to the German tank commander. He has been ordered to guard the bank, but does he know what is in it?

The scene which follows is one of the funniest in the whole movie as it is a parody of Clint Eastwood's Spaghetti Westerns such as *A Fistful of Dollars* (1965). In the hands of a poorer director and composer it might have failed, but it is to the credit of all concerned that it works marvellously.

Kelly, Oddball and Big Joe step out into the town square in a cowboy pose while Lalo Schifrin's music briefly parodies Ennio Morricone's scores for the three 'Man with No Name' Westerns. Oddball even holds his right hand above his holstered gun as though preparing to draw it.

The crew of the Tiger view the three soldiers through the front vision port and the bow MG34 machine gun wiggles about, but they don't open fire. Eventually the tank commander (Karl-Otto Alberty) opens the main hatch and jumps to the ground. Big Joe offers him a cigarette but he refuses as the tank has a fuel leak. Joe then points out that in 30 minutes the American Army will be coming down the road. The commander says he has orders that the bank must not fall into the hands of the 'American Army', but is told that they are not the 'American Army'. Kelly then tells him the bank contains 16 million dollars worth of gold, which is 65 million marks. To get an equal share he only has to crank the turret round and blow the door down. The tank commander accepts the offer and uses his 88m gun to blast into the bank.

The soldiers enter the bank and discover a crate covered by a tarpaulin. At that point the film intercuts repeatedly between shots of the bank interior and those of a band welcoming General Colt's troops. His Jeeps and other vehicles are mobbed by adoring villagers who have been told that Eisenhower (and maybe even General De Gaulle) are among the liberating troops.

As the American troops make very slow progress towards the bank, Kelly's men are loading the gold onto a truck. Oddball has used some of his share to buy the last Tiger, and is up in the turret hatch as the former commander – now sporting a brown leather jacket – prepares to leave. Moriarty is aghast as there is petrol everywhere inside the tank, but Oddball merely dismisses his comments with his usual remarks about 'negative waves'.

Crapgame, meanwhile, has calculated that all the surviving members of the platoon are due $875,000 dollars each. As the platoon escape in a German truck loaded with the gold bars, one of General Colt's men enters the bank. All the gold is gone and there is a cartoon scrawled on the wall which reads: 'Kilroy Was Here. Up Yours Baby'. As has been pointed out in many forums on the internet, one of the flaws in the plot is that the huge number of gold bars stolen in the heist could not be carried in a single truck. Even after deducting the amounts given to Oddball's crew and the German tank commander, the gold would weigh 150 tons which would require a huge fleet of lorries to move. The same error occurs in Ian Fleming's original novel of *Goldfinger*, but this is corrected in the 1964 film version in which the villain intends to irradiate the gold in Fort Knox rather than stealing it.

Kelly's platoon heads off into the sunset as 'Burning Bridges' plays for the third and final time in the film and the credits roll, starting with a 'roll call' of the main players, as was the norm in sixties war films – an idea that was re-used in *Predator* (1987).

Kelly's Heroes premiered at the Pacific Hollywood Theatre on 8 July 1970 and was well-received, making $5.2 million at the US box-office alone set against a budget of $4 million, making it the 24th highest grossing film of 1970.

A single of 'Burning Bridges' sung by the Mike Curb Congregation was released and proved very popular, even reaching Number 1 in May 1971. A novelization of the screenplay by Burt Hirschfeld was also a success.

Despite the popularity of the film, Clint Eastwood was unhappy about the cuts ordered by MGM which he felt undermined the anti-war message of the movie. As a result he never worked for MGM again, and chose to make films using his own production company – Malpaso – which offered him greater creative control. Director Brian G. Hutton only made four further films, with the last being *High Road to China* in 1983. He then gave up directing and went into real estate. He died in 2014. Writer Troy Kennedy Martin scripted four further screenplays for *The Jerusalem File* (1972), *Sweeney II* (1978), *Red Heat* (1988) and *Red Dust* (2004). He also wrote the script for the BBC TV thriller miniseries *Edge of Darkness* (1985). His final TV writing credit was *Bravo Two Zero* (1999). He died in 2009.

Deleted Scenes

20 minutes of footage were deleted by MGM prior to release to give a running time of 144 minutes.

The deleted scenes are as follows:

- Oddball and his men depart their camp to meet Kelly while local girls run around half-clothed.

- As they wait for Oddball and his tanks in a barn at night, Kelly tells Big Joe about the reason he was demoted to private.
- After the minefield incident some of the platoon want to quit, but Big Joe and Crapgame talk them round.
- On their way to Claremont the platoon encounter some German soldiers and naked girls swimming in a pool, but simply ignore them.
- General Colt is in bed with some women when he hears of Kelly's unit's breakthrough.
- Kelly's men find an RAF pilot hiding in a cupboard in Claremont. This part was played by Production Designer Jonathan Barry.
- Kelly finds a wounded German soldier in the ruins of Claremont.
- Big Joe, Oddball and Kelly discuss tactics while standing on a knocked-out Tiger tank.
- As the platoon's captured German truck drives off into the sunset at the end, three US soldiers yell at them to tell them that they are going in the wrong direction. One of these soldiers was played by John Landis.

The whereabouts of this missing footage is unknown, though stills from some of these scenes exist, some of which can be seen in the *Cinema Retro* special on *Kelly's Heroes.*

Troy Kennedy Martin's original screenplay also contains a scene which was never filmed, in which the platoon discover a train full of Jews which is heading to a concentration camp. They face a moral dilemma over whether they should intervene and save the prisoners, or else simply proceed with their mission and leave the Jews to their fate.

Kelly's Heroes (1970)
Production Credits

Production Team

Director: Brian G. Hutton
Screenplay: Troy Kennedy Martin

Cast

Kelly: Clint Eastwood
Big Joe: Telly Savalas
Crapgame: Don Rickles
General Colt: Carroll O'Connor
Oddball: Donald Sutherland
Moriarty: Gavin MacLeod
Maitland: Hal Buckley
Little Joe: Stuart Margolin
Cowboy: Jeff Morris
Gutowski: Ricard Davalos
Petuko: Perry Lopez
Job: Tom Troupe
Willard: Harry Dean Stanton
Fisher: Dick Balduzzi
Babra: Gene Collins
Bellamy: Len Lesser
Colonel Dankhopf: David Hurst
Mitchell: Fred Pearlman
Grace: Michael Clark
Penn: George Fargo
Jonesey: Dee Pollock
Mulligan: George Savalas
German Lieutenant: John Heller
Turk: Shepherd Sanders
German Tank Commander: Karl-Otto Alberty
Booker: Ross Elliott
Third Tank Commander: Phil Adams
French Mayor: Hugo De Vernier
Tanker: Frank L. Garlotta
Supply Sergeant: Harry Goines
German Captain: David Gross
Second Tank Commander: Sandy Kevin
Guest: James McHale
Roach: Robert McNamara
US Lieutenant: Read Morgan
Bonsor: Tom Signorelli
Roamer: Donald Waugh
Old Man: Vincent Maracecchi
MP Sergeant: Paul Picerni
German MP: Zvonko Jovcic
Nun: John Landis
General's Aide: Joe Mantell
Soldier: Lee Miller
German Sturmbannfuhrer: Yves Montand
General Colt's Driver: Tony Wheeler
US Soldier: Jerry Whittington

Producers

Producers: Sidney Beckerman, Gabriel Katzka, Harold Loeb
Associate Producer: Irving L. Leonard

Music

Composer: Lalo Schifrin

Cinematography

Director of Photography: Gabriel Figueroa

Film Editor: John Jympson
Production Design: Jonathan Barry, Aleksandar Milovic
Art Directors: Veljko Despotovic, Vladislav Lasic, Miodrag Miric, Milan Todorovic
Set Decorator: Mike Ford

Makeup Department
Makeup Artists: Trevor Crole Reese, Stanislava Zaric

Production Management
Production Manager: Terry Lens
In Charge of Production: Basil Somner
Production Manager (Yugoslavia): Milenko Stankovic
Location Unit Manager: Michael Profit

Second Unit Director or Assistant Director
Assistant Directors: John C. Chulay, John Landis
Second Unit Director: Andrew Marton
Assistant Director (Yugoslavia): Stevo Petrovic
Third Assistant Directors: Raymond Becket, Jak King

Art Department
Poster Designer: Tom Jung
Property Master: Micky Lennon
Set Dresser: Simon Wakefield

Sound Department
Sound Editor: Jonathan Bates
Sound: Cyril Swern, Harry W. Tetreck, Vladimir Stankovic

Special Effects
Special Effects: Karl Baumgartner

Stunts
Stunt Coordinator: Alf Joint
Stunt Performers: Philip Adams, George Lane Cooper, Joe Dunne, Eddie Eddon, Alf Joint, George Leech, Rick Lester, Jimmy Lodge, Boyd 'Red' Morgan, Slavoljub Plavsic-Zvonce, Eddie Powell, Dragomir Stanojevic

Camera and Electrical Department
Camera Coordinator: Dennis Fraser
Second Unit Cameraman: H.A.R. Thomson

Costume and Wardrobe Department
Wardrobe: Anna Maria Fea

Editorial Department
Assistant Editor: Alan Strachan

Music Department
Musicians: Harry Bluestone, Ray Brown, Dennis Budimir, Larry Bunker, George 'Red' Callender, Conte Candoli, Frank Capp, Buddy Collette, George

Fields, Carl Fortina, Richard Hazard, Milt Holland, Pias Johnston, Artie Kane, Virginia Majewski, Shelly Manne, Tommy Morgan, Larry Muhoberac, Richard Nash, Joe Porcaro, Emil Richards, Howard A. Roberts, Tom Scott, Bud Shank
Conductor: Lalo Schifrin

Other Crew
Transportation Department: Frank Khoury
Technical Adviser: Alexander Gerry
Continuity: Gladys Goldsmith
Production Assistant: Mladen Cernjak
Production Accountant: George Davis
Assistant Chef (Second Unit): Dusan Dimitrijevic
Production Coordinator: Lorraine Fennell
Production Assistants: John Landis, John Larroquette

"THE EAGLE HAS LANDED"

8

THE EAGLE HAS LANDED

(1976)

Associated General Films for ITC Entertainment

Director: John Sturges
Producers: Jack Wiener and David Niven Jr.
Screenwriter: Tom Manckiewicz,
from a novel by Jack Higgins

HENRY Patterson (aka Jack Higgins) was born in 1929 and is a British novelist who (at the time of writing) is still active, having published his most recent novel *The Midnight Bell* as recently as 2016. Having served in the British Army between 1947 and 1949, he became a college lecturer and, in 1959, released his first novel *Sad Wind from the Sea.* Since the late 1960s he has written under the pen-name Jack Higgins.

The Eagle Has Landed was Higgins 35th novel, and was a great success when it was first published in 1975. It employed a technique first used in Frederick Forsyth's debut novel *The Day of the Jackal* (1971) and the subsequent 1973 film adaptation, in which a fictional story was created around a few factual events. In both the film and book *The Day of the Jackal,* the machine gun attack on President De Gaulle's motorcade which opens the story is true, and everything after that point is fiction.

Higgins is said to have been influenced by a conversation he had in the late 1940s with a Russian Officer who revealed that the Germans came close to kidnapping Churchill in 1943. Certainly the Germans did have plans to assassinate or kidnap the British leader, but they were never put into effect. In the same way the Allies had tentative schemes to kill Hitler but these too were never implemented, largely because it was eventually realised that the Germans were more likely to lose the war with him in charge as he was militarily incompetent.

Another influence on Higgins' storyline was undoubtedly the British propaganda film *Went the Day Well?* (1942) – based on a story by Graham Greene – in which 50 German paratroopers posing as British soldiers invade an English village. They are intent on destroying radio-location (radar) stations as a prelude to an invasion, and are eventually beaten off by local civilians with the assistance of the British Army.

As someone who has read and enjoyed a large number of this author's books, I am aware that there are a number of 'Higgins archetypes' which crop up in his work. One of Higgins' favourite tropes is to have a character working for the bad guys, who is actually a very decent person. Examples of these might include the leader of the commando mission, Kurt Steiner, and his men who are all portrayed as brave, chivalrous soldiers. In fact all the Germans in *The Eagle has Landed*, except for Hitler, Himmler and various SS Officers, are depicted as decent individuals just doing their jobs as best they can. IRA man Liam Devlin is another example of this trend, as he is written as a kind, sympathetic intellectual who loves poetry and animals and dislikes killing.

Higgins also uses the same technique in reverse in many of his stories, so in *The Eagle Has Landed* we have two rather unpleasant characters on the Allied side. Colonel Pitts of the US Rangers is not necessarily evil but he is bumptious, vain, arrogant, glory-seeking and incompetent. Local man Arthur Seymour is also a thoroughly nasty piece of work, and in the book *The Eagle Has Landed* (though not the film) he attempts to rape local girl Molly, only being thwarted when Liam Devlin intervenes.

For the key role of German paratroop Colonel Kurt Steiner, producers David Niven Jr and Jack Wiener cast Cockney actor Michael Caine who was no stranger to military roles, having appeared in several war films including *Zulu* (1964), *Battle of Britain* (1969), *Play Dirty* (1969), and *Too Late the Hero* (1970). In a 1977 interview with *Photoplay* magazine, Caine revealed that he had been offered the part of Major John Smith in *Where Eagles Dare* (1968). Caine turned down the role but later regretted the decision, and this was one of the reasons he was keen to play Colonel Steiner.

The other key role in the film was that of Liam Devlin, an IRA operative who was working for the Germans. The producers' original choice was Irish actor Richard Harris but – rather ironically – Harris's numerous outspoken public comments in support of Irish Republicanism led to the producers getting cold feet and the role was given to Canadian actor Donald Sutherland, who had appeared in three classic war movies *The Dirty Dozen* (1967), *M*A*S*H* (1970) and *Kelly's Heroes* (1970). Interestingly, Michael Caine was originally earmarked to play Devlin but was unhappy about portraying an IRA man, so he ended up in the role of Steiner.

Other notable cast members included Anthony Quayle in a cameo role as Admiral Canaris, Donald Pleasence as

Himmler, Robert Duvall as the mission's planner Radl, and Michael Byrne as his assistant Karl. Byrne also starred with Michael Caine as cousins Giles and 'Joe' Vandeleur of the Irish Guards tank regiment in *A Bridge Too Far* (1977), which was filmed in Holland around the same time as *The Eagle Has Landed.*

The director was John Sturges, who had served in the US Army in WW2 and had directed a large number of classic films including *The Magnificent Seven* (1960), *The Great Escape* (1963), *Ice Station Zebra* (1968), and *Marooned* (1969).

Filming started in Finland with the railway sequences in the spring of 1976. This was followed by a small amount of location work near Munich, and then the unit moved to England where most of the film was shot during the long, hot, dry summer of 1976. The village of Mapledurham in Berkshire became Studley Constable in Norfolk, with the only additions required (courtesy of the art department) being a working water wheel and a pub – *The Spyglass and Kettle* – which was destroyed during filming. The other main location was Cornwall which stood in for Alderney. Parts of the RAF base at St Mawgan were used to represent both the airfield on Alderney and a Luftwaffe base in Holland.

A considerable amount of military hardware was acquired for the film including several Jeeps, motorcycles, two British Army trucks and several period cars. Three vintage aircraft were used in the production, namely a Fieseler Storch, an Arado 396, and a Douglas C-47. A wingless Hispano HA-1112 Buchon (Spanish built Messerchmitt Bf109) and an artwork mock-up of a Junkers 52/3m were also employed in the production. All the aircraft were sourced by Doug and Edna Bianchi of Personal Plane Services (PPL) at Booker. PPL had a long involvement with many aviation films including *Those Magnificent Men in Their Flying Machines* (1965), *The Blue Max* (1966), *Mosquito Squadron* (1970) and *Aces High* (1976), to name just a few.

The producers were also fortunate to find a genuine WW2 vintage Motor Torpedo Boat (MTB) which was owned by a group of Sea Scouts in Norfolk. Some restoration was carried out on the vessel to enable it to participate in the production and, after filming, it was returned to its original owners.

The original cinematic release of the film begins with archive footage of the rescue of Italian dictator Benito Mussolini by German troops on 12 September 1943 with a voice-over by actor Patrick Allen. This is immediately followed by the titles.

In the extended version (released on DVD in 2004), the film starts with three captions. The first tells the viewer that about half the film is based on historical fact. The second states that it is left to the viewer to decide which parts are fact and which are fiction.

A third caption then informs the viewer that 'It began in the Bavarian Alps in September 1943' as a helicopter shot shows a fairytale castle in the Bavarian Alps. A German staff car arrives containing SS Reichsfuhrer Heinrich Himmler (Donald Pleasence) who ascends a staircase to meet his colleagues including Adolf Hitler (Peter Miles in an uncredited role) and Admiral Wilhelm Canaris (Anthony Quayle), the head of the Abwehr (German Military Intelligence). Hitler talks briefly with Himmler about Mussolini being rescued, salutes and goes into a room, closing the door behind him.

In another room Admiral Canaris and Himmler have a discussion. Canaris mentions that the Fuhrer was in a good mood as he had just received word that a German commando raid (Operation Oak) led by SS Obersturmbannfuhrer Otto Skorzeny had succeeded in freeing the Italian dictator Benito Mussolini. As this had taken place the previous day, this means the date must be 13 September 1943.

Skorzeny was famous for carrying out the mission to rescue Mussolini and also for leading a number of German troops behind enemy lines – while wearing US uniforms and driving American vehicles – during the Battle of the Bulge in December 1944. As a result of this action, the post-war Allies tried to prosecute him for breaching the Hague Convention but Skorzeny was acquitted and in the early 1960s even worked for the Mossad (the Israeli Intelligence service), becoming involved in the assassination of a number of German rocket scientists who were employed by the Egyptians.

As a result of the success of Operation Oak, Himmler asks Canaris to carry out a feasibility study into the possibility of a commando raid to kidnap Winston Churchill. The title sequence then follows, consisting of red lettering overlaid on aerial shots taken from a helicopter overflying the Bavarian Alps. This part of the titles is therefore very similar to the opening of *Where Eagles Dare* (1968), which was filmed in the nearby Austrian Alps and Switzerland. The final part of the credits sequence shows a Mercedes staff car escorted by two motorcycles arriving at Abwehr HQ. All of these sequences in the first few moments of the film were shot in the Munich area in the spring of 1976.

Admiral Canaris is sitting at his desk as Colonel Radl (Robert Duvall) enters. He is asked to sit down as the Admiral explains that he wants him to carry out a feasibility study into the possibility of kidnapping Winston Churchill and bringing him to Berlin. Canaris says that Hitler will soon forget that he had asked for the study, but Himmler will not. Although he personally thinks the plan is a waste of time, he asks Radl to go ahead. Radl then goes upstairs and talks to his doctor (Ferdy Mayne). Radl has a patch over his left eye and a gloved artificial left hand, suggesting the character may be inspired by Claus Von Stauffenberg, the German officer who tried to assassinate Adolf Hitler with a briefcase bomb in July 1944, and who was the lead character in the Tom Cruise movie *Valkyrie* (2008).

Radl then meets his assistant Karl (Michael Byrne) and orders him to start work on the feasibility study. Karl reports that a German agent (codenamed Starling) living in the Norfolk village of Studley Constable has reported that the British Prime Minister Winston Churchill will be visiting the village that autumn, following a visit to a local RAF Bomber Command airfield.

She is normally contactable via the Spanish Embassy's diplomatic bag and also has a radio. Radl and Karl go next door to the map room where they discover that Studley Constable is only seven miles from a relatively deserted part of the Norfolk coast.

Radl realises that the mission is now feasible, but understands that a very special person will be required to lead it. Consulting their files, they choose Colonel Kurt Steiner, a highly decorated officer in the German *Fallschirmjager* (parachute troops). Steiner had fought in Holland, Norway, Crete and Russia and speaks perfect English, having been educated in the UK.

As an air-raid siren sounds, Radl realises that he has found his man. He then suggests this is an example of Jung's 'synchronicity'; that is, events having a coincidence in time. (Carl Gustav Jung was a Swiss psychologist who proposed a theory of 'synchronicity' to explain meaningful coincidences. Jung's explanation was that all minds in the Universe were connected at a deep level via what he described as the 'collective unconscious'.) So a report of Churchill visiting a Norfolk village, which would normally be of no significance, suddenly becomes very important indeed. Radl then tells Karl to locate Steiner: 'Find this man for me Karl; he's been out of Germany too long'.

The next scene shows a steam train pulling several coaches and flatcars across a snow-covered landscape in Poland. This impressive shot was filmed from a moving railcar on an adjacent track and was lensed in Finland. The train comes to a halt with a jerk, waking one of its passengers – Colonel Kurt Steiner (Michael Caine) – who tells his men that they should get out the train to stretch their legs.

As the German soldiers leave the carriage, two truckloads of Jewish civilians are being herded into goods wagons on another train. Two German sentries try to stop Steiner from walking further and insist he and his men return to the coach, but they immediately become more respectful when they see the Knight's Cross with Oaks Leaves round his neck.

'If memory serves me right, the Polish Army surrendered in 1939. Who are these people?' says Steiner.

'Jews', replies the sentry. 'They put up one of a hell of a fight.'

'What, with umbrellas and crutches?'

As the Jews continue to board the train, one girl breaks free and runs towards Steiner who takes her in his arms. An SS Obergruppenfuhrer (Joachim Hansen) says that he will take the prisoner, but Steiner's men cock their weapons and point them at the SS men. Steiner asks the girl her name. She says she is called Branna. Steiner wishes her luck and places her on a moving flatcar on an adjacent goods train. But Branna's freedom is short-lived and, within seconds, she is shot dead by an SS soldier.

The SS officer confronts Steiner and asks him to identify himself. Steiner explains that he is the Commander of 2 Para detachment. He explains that he has nothing for or against the Jews, but has seen too many people die for a cause. As the confrontation continues, an armoured vehicle – a genuine German StuG III 75mm assault gun – can be seen on the flatcar in the background. Based on the chassis of the Panzer III tank and lacking a revolving turret, the StuG III was nonetheless a highly successful armoured vehicle, destroying more Allied tanks than any other type. Nearly 11,000 StuG IIIs were produced during WW2. The example featured in the film was one of a number operated by the Finnish Army, who were one of the last users of the type. Also visible in the background sitting on railcars are some wooden mock-ups of Panzer Mark V (Panther) tanks draped in tarpaulins.

The SS Officer warns Steiner that he will be court martialled. Steiner in turn asks for clemency for his men, but the Obergruppenfuhrer indicates that will not be possible. Steiner turns to his men and says that 'he can always tell a bastard when he sees one'. This is a very important scene in the film because it establishes that Steiner is a brave, resourceful and principled officer. Though he is humane and patriotic, he clearly has his doubts about the rightness of the Nazi cause.

Back in Germany, Radl and Karl continue to plan the mission, now called 'Case Eagle'. Radl asks if there is further news from Starling, and Karl reports that he has had some difficulty in tracking down Steiner. Radl, however, has located a former IRA man – Liam Devlin – who is teaching at a

University in Berlin and may prove useful in the execution of the mission.

Admiral Canaris then arrives, but is angry that Radl has apparently exceeded his authority as he was only supposed to prepare a feasibility study. Canaris is concerned that Churchill may resist and the abduction may become an assassination; it would be foolish to kill him when Germany had already lost the war. The head of the Abwehr, Admiral Wilhelm Canaris, was a highly controversial figure in WW2. Although he started off as a supporter of Hitler, he became disenchanted with the regime and is believed to have maintained contact with Britain's MI6 throughout the war. He may even have secretly helped the Allies to defeat Hitler. In 1940 his department produced an intelligence report which suggested that the coast of Southern England was defended by 49 divisions and that invasion was therefore impossible. This highly inaccurate report – which greatly exaggerated the extent of Britain's defences – undoubtedly influenced Hitler. Later that same year, Canaris intervened to ensure that Franco did not agree to the passage of German troops through Spain as a prerequisite to an assault on Gibraltar, thus preventing its conquest by the Nazis. In 1944 Canaris was arrested by the SS, and the following year he was executed in a concentration camp.

Canaris's doubts about the Nazi regime are hinted at in the film when he makes the following proclamation:

'This operation could make the Charge of the Light Brigade look like a sensible military operation. Drop it!'

At that point Karl enters the room and tells Radl that Devlin (Donald Sutherland) has arrived. The Irishman greets Radl with the cliché Irish phrase, 'Top of the morning to you'. Donald Sutherland makes a passable attempt at an Irish accent, though critics have pointed out that his accent sounds more like Southern Irish than Northern Irish.

Devlin mentions that the last time he was invited to Section Three he was persuaded to jump out of a Dornier at 3,000 feet. He has twigged that he is going to be asked to go to England and mentions that Brighton is lovely at that time of year, as he coughs on a Russian cigar. Radl then explains that he has a proposition to make to the Irishman. Devlin wonders if he wants him to go back to Ireland, and is asked if he is still a supporter of the IRA. The Irishman counters that he doesn't believe in 'soft hits' and has moral scruples about blowing up women and children. His fight is really with the British Empire, and his goal is a United Ireland. Radl responds that for this to happen, it would be necessary for Germany to win the war. He then explains that he wants Devlin to travel to England to assist in a mission to kidnap Winston Churchill and bring him to Berlin. Suddenly a visitor arrives, SS Stormbandfuhrer Toberg (Roy Marsden), who wishes to see the file on the proposed operation. Marsden was later to find fame in many TV series including *The Sandbaggers* (1980) and *Airline* (1982).

Later, Himmler and Radl meet to discuss the mission, and the Reichsfuhrer says that some people are saying that the proposed mission makes 'the Charge of the Light Brigade seem like a sensible military mission'. Himmler chuckles but Radl remains unsmiling.

He then mentions the fate of Colonel Kurt Steiner, who is facing court martial along with his men over the incident in Finland. Steiner – a veteran of six commando raids – had apparently thrown away his career in a failed attempt to save a Jewish girl. Currently he and his men are serving in a penal battalion on the island of Alderney in the Channel Islands. Hitler has now given his written authority for the mission to go ahead, and Himmler gives it to Radl before wishing him good luck.

The next scene is set in Alderney on a dull day where a Motor Torpedo Boat (MTB) is approaching a harbour. This scene was filmed at Charlestown in Cornwall. Two dead men lie on the deck covered in blankets. Steiner's men are being forced to carry out suicidal raids against Allied shipping in the English Channel using small human-guided torpedoes.

While this is happening, a single-engined, high-winged German Fieseler F.156 Storch observation aircraft lands on the airfield on Alderney and stops beside a wooden watch tower. The aircraft used in this sequence was a French licence-built Morane-Saulnier MS.500 Criquet with an Argus engine which was thus identical to wartime German Storches. Registered G-AZMH it was then owned by the Hon. Patrick Lindsay and based at Booker Air Park in High Wycombe. The Storch was widely used by German forces in WW2, and had a remarkable Short Take Off and Landing (STOL) capability. One of them was used in the rescue of Mussolini mentioned at the beginning of this chapter.

The Storch's propeller stops and Radl and Devlin exit via the starboard door. They are met by the German Commandant of Alderney. The commandant is given orders for Steiner and his men to cease further suicide missions.

Radl meets Steiner at the quayside and explains the proposed mission. While Steiner studies the file, Devlin goes to the pub near the quayside. Radl meanwhile notices the unusual configuration of the 'E-Boat' and the Captain explains that it is actually a British MTB which was captured off the coast of Holland. The vessel used in the production was MTB102, which at that time was owned by a Norfolk Scout

Group. This vessel had a fascinating history as it was built in 1937 and took part in 'Operation Dynamo', the Dunkirk evacuation. Some restoration work was carried out on the boat by the production company (Kelso Films) to return it to full running condition. This included the fitting of twin 20mm Oerlikon guns on the forward deck. Full details of the history of this craft can be found on its website (*www.mtb102.com*).

Incidentally, 'E-Boat' was a term used by the Allies to describe German Torpedo Boats. The Germans themselves referred to them as 'S-Boats' ('Schnell Boats', meaning 'fast boats). The Captain also explains that he is very familiar with the British coastline, as he was the First Mate on a German cargo ship before the war.

Radl explains further details of the plan as the two dead bodies are loaded onto a Mercedes truck. The mission has been approved by none other than Adolf Hitler himself, and Steiner mentions that he had met him when he was awarded the Knight's Cross. He then states that he is under suspended sentence of death and is likely to die eventually. Radl counters that if he carries out the mission then he and his men will pardoned and reinstated to their previous positions.

Steiner thinks for a moment and then offers an opinion. He thinks the mission is feasible as, of all the world's leaders, Churchill is the least protected – unlike the Fuhrer. Radl then points out that the mission may not win the war, but it could force the Allies to negotiate a peace settlement.

As Steiner and Radl are continuing their discussions, Devlin is attempting to have a quiet drink in the pub. But his attire of raincoat and hat makes Captain von Neustadt (Sven-Bertil Taube) mistake him for a Gestapo official and he pours a drink over him. Devlin asks von Neustadt to lick the drink off his thumbs, prompting the German to throw him through the front window just as Steiner, Radl and the MTB captain are walking up the path to the entrance. The three Germans are amused to see the Irishman lying on the ground and Steiner asks him why he is coming along. Devlin replies that he is 'one of the last of the world's great adventurers'.

Steiner chats with Radl and says he will have to get the consent of his men. Devlin is to leave for England that night. The plan is for him to be parachuted into the Republic of Ireland, close to the Northern Ireland border. He is to make his way into Ulster and, from there, travel by ship to England. The German agent (Starling) has found him a job as a Marsh Warden. He will be paid £10,000 up front, and the same amount on completion of the mission.

The next scene is set on Alderney airfield, where Devlin is given a parachute and a pistol. He opts to wear the parachute over his civilian clothes rather than donning a flying suit, as he will be less conspicuous on arrival. At this point Devlin demonstrates his ability to subdue dogs by using whistling sounds combined with hand movements to pacify a German guard dog, a skill that plays a key part in the plot later in the story.

All the airfield sequences in the film were shot at RAF St Mawgan in Cornwall, which at the time was the home to a squadron of RAF British Aerospace Nimrod MR.1 maritime reconnaissance aircraft. This former military airbase is now Newquay Airport, and has been used as a location in many episodes of ITV1's popular *Doc Martin* TV series.

The rather unusual-looking two-seat aircraft which flies Devlin to Ireland is a SIPA S.121, a French-built version of the wartime German Arado Ar.396 trainer. This particular example F-BLKH was supplied by the Amicale Jean-Baptiste

Salis Collection based at the Aerodrome de Cerny-La Ferte Alais 40km south of Paris and was painted in authentic Luftwaffe camouflage for the film.

The pilot explains the technique Devlin must use to exit the aircraft. He is to unfasten the harness and slide back the hood. The pilot will then invert the aircraft and Devlin will fall out. This in fact was the safest method of bailing out of a single-engined aircraft before ejector seats were invented.

The next scene is set in the village of Studley Constable. After a brief establishing shot of the village (filmed from a helicopter), we see Devlin strolling through a field of cows on his way to meet his contact Joanna Grey, aka Agent Starling (Jean Marsh). It is later established that Grey hails from South Africa and her family had suffered at the hands of the British during the Boer War at the turn of the century, leading to her decision to become an agent of Nazi Germany.

Devlin arrives at Grey's cottage and is given a cup of tea. Grey's dog, Patch, runs down the stairs and Devlin again demonstrates his ability to subdue dogs with whistling and hand movements. Grey then briefs Devlin on his duties. He is to be issued with a motorcycle, a shotgun and cartridges plus ration books. His petrol ration is just three gallons per month.

Later Devlin travels into the village on his motorcycle, where he is spotted by local girl Molly (Jenny Agutter) who is preparing her horse-drawn cart for use. He rides to his cottage with its adjacent barn and checks over the property. Then he goes back to the village and has a brief conversation with Molly, who loads milk churns onto her cart before riding off. Jenny Agutter, who plays the 17 year-old girl, was actually 22 when the film was shot. Her most famous roles were as Bobbie in the 1968 BBC-1 TV adaptation of *The Railway Children* and the subsequent 1970 film version.

Devlin goes into the local pub, *The Spyglass and Kettle*, and offers to buy everyone a drink. But his presence angers local man Arthur Seymour (Terence Plummer), who is infatuated with Molly and feels jealous. He threatens Devlin, telling him to leave Molly alone. Eventually the landlord intervenes and asks Arthur to leave. The Englishman leaves with great reluctance, telling the Irishman that the next time they meet he will be the one who will have to depart. Later Devlin makes his way to the local Catholic Church where he meets Father Vericker (John Standing) and his sister Pamela (Judy Geeson), who is a WAAF based at nearby RAF Mildenhall.

The action then moves to Holland, where Steiner and his men disembark from a Junkers 52/3m transport aircraft and make their way to a hangar on the airbase. This scene never appeared in the cinematic release of the film in 1977, and only came to light when it was reinstated (along with a few other scenes) in the extended DVD release in 2004. This particular shot is of great interest to both aviation enthusiasts and students of special effects techniques because although it appears to show a group of German paratroopers walking from a parked Junkers 52/3m in the far distance towards a hangar on the right hand side of the frame – with the front half of a Messerschmitt Bf 109 framing the left-hand edge of the shot – all is not as it seems.

The 'Messerschmitt' is actually one of the ex-Spanish Air Force Hispano HA-1112 M1L Buchons used in the filming of *Battle of Britain* during 1968. This particular example (believed to be C.4K-111) had its wings removed to facilitate cockpit shots at Pinewood Studios, and was retained in open storage on the backlot at the studio for many years. It was still wingless when it was used in the filming of *The Eagle Has Landed* in 1976, so artwork was added to make it look as though it still had wings. It was also fitted with a three-bladed propeller (instead of the four-bladed unit used in most of the *Battle of Britain* Buchons), the upper blade of which can be seen to be bent forwards.

The identity of the Junkers 52/3m which appears in this deleted scene has also been the subject of much discussion on internet forums ever since this extra footage emerged in 2004, with the general consensus being that it was an ex-Spanish Air Force CASA 352, T2B-176, which was then owned by Doug Arnold at Blackbushe. However, in 2014 in his book *Flying Film Stars*, author Mark Ashley concluded that the Junkers was nothing more than a small piece of two-dimensional artwork mounted on a rod which projected near-vertically from a notice board attached to a fence in the foreground of the shot. This was a favourite method employed by special effects expert Les Bowie, who often used blown-up monochrome photos which were pasted on hardboard, cut out, and then coloured by hand with paints. This method was used for effects shots in *Operation Crossbow* (1965), *Battle of Britain* (1969) and *Mosquito Squadron* (1970), amongst others.

Steiner and his men walk into a nearby hangar, where a captured British twin-engined transport aircraft is being prepared for action. In both the book and film the aircraft is described as a 'DC-3', though this was actually the civil designation for this model which was known as the Douglas C-47 Skytrain, though the British tended to use the name 'Dakota'. As the German paratroopers examine their weapons and equipment, Steiner wonders if everything will be ready in time.

The Dakota which appears in the film was sourced by Doug Bianchi and was a Douglas C-47D G-AKNB owned by

Intra Airways, an air cargo firm based in Jersey. The aircraft was painted in authentic RAF colours at Exeter Airport for its use in the movie. After its use in *The Eagle Has Landed* it took part in several films and TV series, and now resides in the USA with the civil registration N59NA.

Meanwhile back in Norfolk, Devlin is riding his motorcycle among the sand dunes on the beach when he sees a horse and then spies Molly. The two chat about Arthur, but Molly makes it clear that she is not interested in him. They flirt and then kiss. Soon afterwards Molly leaves on her horse after asking Devlin if he will be at Mass on Sunday. Back at the airbase in Holland, Steiner and Hans discuss the forthcoming mission. This was another of the deleted scenes which was reinstated in the 2004 DVD release.

In Studley Constable, Devlin returns to his cottage on his motorcycle and sits on a rocking chair while he reads a book. A moment later Molly arrives and, while hanging her coat on a hook, notices Devlin's scarf which indicates that he has been to Trinity College, Dublin. She discovers that he has a middle name (William) and that he likes to write poetry. Devlin then reads her some of his poetry, establishing that he is really an intellectual rather than a man of violence.

In Holland a German technician is painting an RAF roundel on the underside of the aircraft's port wing as Steiner checks the parachutes they will use on the mission. They have been fitted with slots to enable better control of the chutes, as they will have to drop at high tide.

Steiner also explains that he and his men will be wearing German uniforms under their Polish paratrooper smocks and that this will not be a subject for negotiation. If they are engaged in combat, they will fight and die as German soldiers and will not be shot as spies. Radl reluctantly agrees.

Back in Studley Constable, Devlin meets Molly. The two have clearly fallen in love and Devlin tries to put Molly off while explaining that he is not saying these things to make her want him more (an educated man, Devlin clearly understands the principle of 'reverse psychology'). Suddenly a very jealous Arthur arrives and challenges Devlin to a fight. Though much more muscly and stocky than the Irishman, the Englishman is soon trounced by his wiry, agile opponent who is highly skilled in the art of boxing. As Father Veriter arrives, Devlin gives a demonstration of what he calls the 'Holy Trinity' of legwork, timing and hitting. Arthur is left lying stunned on the ground had has to be revived by an onlooker, using a bucket of water.

Meanwhile two vehicles arrive at Devlin's cottage – a 1941 Bedford QLT 3-ton lorry and a 1940 Austin Ten Light Utility truck, both painted dark green with British Army markings. (In Jack Higgins' original novel these were civilian vehicles purchased on the black market which were resprayed in Army colours by Devlin, but in the film the source of these two trucks is never explained.)

Devlin turns up at the cottage and finds Molly there. She has discovered stencils for British Army vehicle markings in the wood bin and realises that he is involved in illegal activities, but at this stage thinks he is simply trading on the black market. The couple embrace.

Over in Holland, Steiner and his men prepare to board the Dakota which will fly them to England. They are all now posing as Polish paratroopers except for Steiner himself, who is playing their English commanding officer. The soldiers board the plane which starts up and taxies towards the runway.

On a Norfolk beach a few miles from Studley Constable, Devlin lays out two large strips of fabric in the shape of a large letter 'L' and weighs it down with stones. He also places a vertical pole with an orange marker at the top of the 'L' and sets up a radio to communicate with the aircraft as the Dakota nears the English coast.

A few miles away Molly returns to Devlin's cottage to be confronted by an angry Arthur who has found a lot of incriminating evidence against Liam including a pistol, the two trucks, Army stencils and petrol ration books. 'I'll have the bastard arrested within the hour', he says as he heads for the door, intent on contacting the police. But Molly has no intention of letting him grass on her lover. She pleads with him not to do this and, when he won't listen, she picks up Devlin's loaded shotgun and blasts the Englishman at close range with a single cartridge. The wound proves fatal and Arthur slumps to the ground dead.

As these dramatic developments are taking place, Steiner's men leap out of the Dakota at low altitude over the Norfolk coast, open their chutes and land in the surf. Curiously, this all takes place in broad daylight whereas Allied clandestine parachute missions were always executed at night to lessen the chance of detection. The parachute jump seen in the film was carried out by an eight-man detachment from the British Army's REME (Royal Electrical and Mechanical Engineers) parachute team of 1976, who made their drop over the Cornish coast.

The paras quickly form up and walk the seven miles to Devlin's cottage, where the Irishman discovers Arthur's dead body. He also examines his shotgun and finds that one cartridge has been fired and has obviously been used to kill Arthur. Steiner orders his men to bury Arthur's body straight away.

In Germany, Radl tells Himmler that 'The Eagle has Landed', indicating that Steiner's force has arrived safely in Norfolk. ('The Eagle Has Landed' was, of course, already famous as the sentence spoken by Neil Armstrong when Apollo 11's lunar module landed on the Moon in July 1969.) Himmler is pleased and says that he will inform the Fuhrer. He then asks Radl for the letter from Hitler he had previously given him, authorising the mission. The German officer hands it over and Himmler promptly rips it up and then puts it in his briefcase, leaving Radl to wonder what is going on.

Back in England, Father Verecker is in the church when one of his parishioners suddenly appears behind him. But where has he come from? The purpose of this scene is simply to introduce the audience to the hidden tunnel linking the church interior to the nearby vicarage, something that plays a key part in the plot later in the story. Incidentally, although the church exterior in the story was real, the interior was a set built on location and installed inside a huge tent.

Posing as Polish paratroopers, Steiner's men are now wandering around the village and soon make friends with the locals, including the gravedigger. The Bedford QLT and Austin trucks arrive in the village and park near the church. Inside, Father Vericker is delighted to discover one of the paratroopers, Corporal Jankowski (uncredited), playing Bach on the organ. Far from being displeased, the Father congratulates the young soldier on his musical skill.

Outside the church Colonel Steiner (posing as British officer Colonel Miller) explains to the Father that his men will be carrying out some manoeuvres in the village. At that point a US Army Jeep draws up and Captain Harry Clark

(Treat Williams) jumps out. He explains that he is from a nearby Rangers unit.

Steiner is taken aback by this revelation as he realises that there is an Allied force in the vicinity he knew nothing about, and which could interfere with his mission. But he keeps his composure and calmly inquires how many men are in the Rangers detachment and exactly where they are. Clark informs Steiner that he has a company of men at Millenhouse, eight miles away. He also mentions that he has a couple of Poles in his unit and perhaps they could meet up with Miller's men sometime. 'Miller' replies that that would be fine, but would have to take place at a later date as his men are busy at the moment. Hans then drives Steiner away in the Austin truck after receiving a reminder to drive on the left.

A few minutes later, Clark's Jeep arrives at the car park outside the Rangers HQ in Millenhouse. One of the vehicles that can be briefly glimpsed in this scene is an M3 halftrack which has been fitted with a machine gun turret. I will be talking more about this highly unusual modification later in the chapter.

Clark races into the office of his commanding officer, Colonel Pitts (Larry Hagman), who is in a foul mood because he has just received some disturbing news. After kicking the wastebasket, Pitts explains what has happened in more detail. He has just received a letter ordering him back to Fort Benning in the USA, which means he will miss the chance to see actual combat as he has yet to fire a gun in anger.

Eight miles away the Poles are carrying out their manoeuvres in Studley Constable, moving from one position to another while covering their comrades. Steiner tells Hans to continue with this charade for another 20 minutes before setting up roadblocks.

Steiner asks Father Vericker about the marshes and is introduced to Devlin. The two pretend they have never met before, while Joanna Grey offers to help and she, Devlin and Steiner drive off in the Austin truck with the Irishman riding in the back. They stop near the house where Churchill will be staying and Grey reveals the latest news on the whereabouts of the British Prime Minister, which is that he has just left King's Lynn. She also mentions that her mother and sister died in a British concentration camp in the Boer War, which explains her antipathy towards the English.

Back in Studley Constable the Poles are continuing with their manoeuvres when a little girl falls into the water beside the mill. One of Steiner's men jumps into the river to save her. Although he succeeds he gets caught up in the water wheel and drowned. As his body is dragged out of the water by the wheel his paratrooper's smock is torn open, revealing a German uniform underneath. This is witnessed by Father Vericker who realises at once what is going on. Steiner quickly takes command of the situation and orders his men to round up all the villagers and lock them in the church.

Meanwhile Pam goes into one of the smaller halls in the church where she finds a distraught Molly, who wants to see the Father. Steiner herds all the villagers into the church and discovers a locked door. He asks Father Vericker what is behind it and is told it is a room containing various pieces of paperwork. He has left the keys for this room at home. Does the Colonel want him to fetch them? Steiner replies that that will not be required.

Next door, Pam and Molly have heard everything. She tells Molly to go to Liam and explain what has happened while she seeks help herself. Molly rides off on her horse to meet the Irishman as Father Vericker leads the villagers in prayer. As this is happening, Steiner is reviewing the mission. Churchill is still on schedule and the 'E-Boat' (the MTB) is off the coast, so the mission is still feasible as anything is possible.

Pam Vericker arrives at Joanna Grey's house in a near-hysterical state, not realising she is part of the plot. She tells Grey what has happened. The South African says she is going to get the keys to her car, but instead pulls a gun on Pam. Grey fires at Pam but she escapes in her car, though wounded in the arm. In terrible pain, Pam drives the few miles to the Rangers' HQ along winding country lanes.

Meanwhile Molly has turned up at Devlin's cottage. The Irishman is perturbed at the latest developments and, saying that he 'can't leave them in the lurch', he rides off on a motorcycle after giving Molly a letter.

From the tower of the church in Studley Constable, Steiner and Captain von Neustadt see Joanna Grey arriving in her car. She informs the two Germans that Pam has gone to the Rangers for help. A furious Father Vericker confronts Joanna over her apparent disloyalty. She had lived amongst the community for decades and has now betrayed them. But the South African woman is unrepentant. Later, Steiner tells Grey to communicate with the E-Boat.

Over at the Rangers HQ, Clark arrives in his Jeep to discover Colonel Pitts gagging for some action. He has been briefed by Pam, who is now in hospital, and so has learned that the Polish paras are really Germans who intend to kidnap Churchill.

However, the Colonel sees this turn of events as an opportunity to grab some glory for himself as he feels he has sufficient forces at his disposal to deal with the Germans. Clark, though, feels that the British War Office should be informed.

Reluctantly the American Colonel agrees to put a telephone call through to the War Office, but as soon as Clark has left he cancels the call. He is determined to get all the credit for leading a successful military operation against the Germans.

Outside the Rangers HQ three Jeeps pull up. Each carries five soldiers (including the driver) and a single bazooka, although this is the later M20 'Super Bazooka' firing a 3.5 inch rocket rather than the correct WW2 vintage M1 2.36 inch bazooka which was much smaller (a common error in war films).

As the three Jeeps set off for Studley Constable, a fourth intercepts the car containing Churchill at a crossroads a few miles short of the village. Clark jumps out and tells Churchill's police guard what has happened.

Colonel Pitts drives slowly into the village with a makeshift white flag attached to his Jeep's radio aerial. He parks outside the church and walks up to the main door. The door opens, and a German soldier emerges. But it is soon apparent that the German doesn't know any English as he answers 'Yes' to every question. Pitts is humiliated and, as he walks back to his Jeep, he displays what can only be described as a 'comedy walk'. The character of Pitts bears some similarities to screenwriter Tom Mankiewicz's previous creation, the redneck Sheriff J.W. Pepper, in the two James Bond films *Live and Let Die* (1973) and *The Man with the Golden Gun* (1974). Pitts calls his colleague Mallory on the radio to order an assault. Mallory feels this should be preceded by a reconnaissance, but Pitts overrules him and orders his three Jeeps to drive into the village.

The American Jeeps speed into the village only to find that Steiner's men are ready and waiting for them with their British 9mm Sten sub machine guns. Soon the Americans come under fire from well-prepared positions, and two of the Jeeps are hit. One ends up in the river next to the mill and the other crashes into a yard. Seven soldiers are killed and some wounded. The only success for the Americans comes when Mallory's team destroys the Germans' Bedford QLT with a bazooka round.

Meanwhile, Churchill has arrived at the Rangers' HQ where he will be safer. British officer Major Corcoran (Maurice Roeves) gets on the 'phone to the War Office, while Captain Clark explains that Colonel Pitts has 'limited combat experience'.

While this is happening, Pitts discovers Joanna Grey's house. He bursts in, pulls out a grenade, removes the pin and slowly ascends the stairs leading to Grey's bedroom. Suddenly the South African woman shoots him with her pistol. He falls down the stairs backwards and drops the grenade. A soldier accompanying him sees what has happened and dives behind a sofa for cover as the grenade explodes. Quickly he recovers his composure and runs up the stairs, spraying bullets in front of him from his M2 carbine. Grey dies instantly. The Rangers in the film are mainly armed with M2 carbines (which didn't appear until 1944) with curved magazines, rather than M1 Garands with straight magazines which would be correct for 1943.

Elsewhere in the village, two of Steiner's men try to reach their comrades in the church. As they drive through the streets in their Austin, they are spotted and hit by an American bazooka round. The vehicle overturns, but the injured paratroopers (including Hans) escape. Curiously, the Austin used in this sequence was damaged but not destroyed, and was later retrieved by a military vehicle enthusiast. At the time of writing, it is in storage awaiting restoration to running order. The Bedford QLT truck used in the film was a complete write-off, though. Steiner looks out the window, sees the burning Bedford, and realises he has no means of escape.

Suddenly a second convoy of American vehicles arrives, consisting of three Jeeps lead by an M3 halftrack with its rear passenger area roofed over and fitted with a fifty-calibre machine gun in a rotating, electrically-driven turret. During WW2, M3 halftracks were fitted with a wide variety of armaments including 75mm anti-tank guns and an open, electrically-driven Maxson turret mounting four fifty-calibre machine guns for anti-aircraft work. The most common armament, though, was a fifty-calibre machine gun mounted on a cupola above the driver's compartment on the right-hand side. The armament shown in *The Eagle has Landed* was entirely fictitious, as was the roofing over of the rear troop compartment. Apparently the turret was made from wood and built specially for the film.

The reason this was done was presumably for plot reasons. At this point in the story the German paras had to face an armoured vehicle which they could not knock out. A standard M3 halftrack could be disabled just by chucking a grenade into it. Any troops in the rear compartment were only protected by armour up to waist level so could be killed by Sten gun fire. A more obvious solution to the problem would have been to use an American armoured car such as the Ford M8, but perhaps one was not available at the time the film was made – hence the use of the inaccurately converted M3.

Displaying the formidable firepower available to him, Captain Clark offers Steiner the chance to surrender but the German officer refuses. Father Vericker points out that the

German plot has failed, but Steiner points out this happened because his men saved a little girl from drowning.

Clark points out that he has nothing left to fight for as Churchill is in a safe place, but Steiner replies that he has hostages. Clark doubts if he will really use them and Steiner agrees with him, ordering his men to let the villagers go. As they depart, a woman thanks Steiner for saving her daughter.

Meanwhile, Devlin fights with Father Vericker before throwing him outside. Why he does this becomes clear in a moment. Steiner says goodbye to Captain Clark, who points out that there is no such thing as death with honour – only death. Once Steiner has shut and bolted the door, Devlin reveals the real reason behind his fight with Father Vericker: he wanted to get his car keys, which he throws at Steiner. He also reveals the presence of the secret tunnel between the church and the vicarage.

In an instant, Steiner realises there is a chance for his men to carry out their mission after all. But Captain von Neustadt offers an alternative plan. Steiner and Hans should escape and complete the mission, while he and the rest of the paras stay behind and hold off the American Rangers as long as possible.

As Steiner and Hans make their escape, one of his men plays a tune on the church organ which is none other than the main theme from the film. The Rangers commence their attack, smashing the church windows and throwing grenades through the broken panes. The M3 halftrack opens fire with its turret-mounted gun.

As the assault continues, Steiner arrives at the vicarage and steals Vericker's car – a 1936 Vauxhall 14/6 – while Devlin leads the way on his motorcycle. Eventually the Rangers burst into the church and kill all the surviving German paras as Steiner arrives at Devlin's cottage.

Back at the Rangers' HQ, Major Corcoran is pleased at the outcome of the assault, but Captain Clark points out that three of the German assault force are still missing – including Steiner and Devlin. A few miles away, the captured MTB draws into a river creek and puts down its gangway. Devlin arrives on his motorbike, followed by Steiner and Hans in the Vauxhall. But Devlin doesn't want to leave as he now has a reason for staying, namely Molly. Hans is also reluctant to go despite his wounded arms, and has to be persuaded by his commanding officer. As the MTB prepares to depart, the crew haul down the White Ensign (the flag of the Royal Navy) and raise that of the Kriegsmarine.

Back on Alderney, Radl is standing at the harbour looking out to sea as Karl arrives with a message from 'Albatross' (Devlin) which is largely unintelligible. He tells Karl to leave, as he realises things have gone badly wrong.

That evening as darkness is falling (achieved with a 'day for night' shot), American troops are hunting for Steiner in the woods near Studley Constable. But the hunter has become the hunted. Steiner parks his car amongst the trees and sees a single soldier (Frazier) who is standing by his Jeep, talking on the radio. Steiner knocks him unconscious with his pistol and then reports in using the correct call sign which he has heard.

A few miles away, two American soldiers approach Devlin's cottage. Seeing the door open and fearing a trap, they decide to send in their two Alsatian dogs. As soon as the two hounds enter the cottage, the Rangers hear a curious whistling sound. Devlin is using his dog-handling skills again. The two men race into the cottage, but both Devlin and the dogs are gone.

In Germany, Himmler receives word that the mission has failed and asks to be put it touch with the SS Commander in Cherbourg. Later, Radl is in the radio room on Alderney when he is arrested by two SS men. The charge is exceeding orders to the point of treason to the state. Radl is taken outside, stood against a breakwater on the beach, and shot.

Meanwhile, events continue to unfold in Studley Constable. Churchill (Leigh Dilley) arrives at the Manor House in a convoy, closely followed by a single Jeep containing Steiner. The guard sees the vehicle and American uniform and lets him in.

Later, Churchill strolls onto the patio at the Manor House (an obvious studio set) with cigar and brandy in hand as Steiner lurks nearby, clutching his Walther P38 pistol. But in a nearby office Major Corcoran and Captain Clark hear that there is some doubt about the identity of an American officer who followed Churchill through the gates in his Jeep. A 'phone call then comes through for Captain Clark about a soldier who has been found unconscious... and his Jeep is missing! 'Jesus God. He's here!' cries Clark as several soldiers and policemen rush towards the patio. But they are too late, as Steiner shoots Churchill with a single bullet before being cut down by a volley of fire.

'Poor sod. No one will ever know what he did!' says a detective who is looking down at Churchill's body. But then he reveals that Steiner had actually killed a double, a variety artist by the name of George Fowler. (This part of the plot may have been inspired by the real-life tale of actor Clifton James, who was General Montgomery's double during WW2. As mentioned in previous chapters, he later wrote a book about his exploits – *I Was Monty's Double* – which was turned into a film of the same name in 1958.) The detective then explains that the real Churchill is in Tehran in Persia for a conference. This is a serious historical error in the film. The scenes in Studley Constable are clearly set in the summer as evidenced by the blazing sun, short shadows and trees in full bloom. Yet the Tehran Conference referred to took place between 28 November and 1 December 1943.

The film ends with shots of Devlin walking in the woods and by the sea with the two Alsatians, which have now become his pets. The MTB has failed to reach Holland and lies beached on the shore (a shot achieved with a matte painting by Ray Caple). His inner dialogue reveals the content of a letter to Molly, which implies they are going to spend the rest of their lives together. The film then ends with a 'roll call' of the key players in the film, as used in many war films including John Sturges' previous WW2 picture *The Great Escape*.

The Eagle Has Landed was John Sturges' last film. At that point in his career Sturges was only taking on directorial work to fund his hobby of deep-sea fishing, and he declined to take part in the post-production editing work. He died on 18 August 1992.

The film premiered in Finland and Sweden on 25 December 1976, though it was not released in the UK until 31 March 1977. It was well-received by critics who appreciated the efforts that had gone into achieving authenticity, although the film critic of *The Observer* – Clive James – said that casting Michael Caine as Kurt Steiner was like having Curt Jurgens play Field Marshal Montgomery!

It remains, though, a well-remembered thriller with a fair amount of action and one of the great WW2 movies of the seventies.

The Eagle Has Landed (1976)
Production Credits

Production Team
Director: John Sturges
Screenplay: Tom Mankiewicz
Original Novel: Jack Higgins

Cast
Colonel Steiner: Michael Caine
Liam Devlin: Donald Sutherland
Colonel Radl: Robert Duvall
Molly: Jenny Agutter
Himmler: Donald Pleasence
Admiral Canaris: Anthony Quayle
Joanna Grey: Jean Marsh
Captain von Neustadt: Sven Bertil-Taube
Father Verecker: John Standing
Pamela: Judy Geeson
Captain Clark: Treat Williams
Colonel Pitts: Larry Hagman
Corporal Kuniski: Alexei Jawdokimov
Hams Altmamm: Richard Wren
Karl: Michael Byrne
SS Obergruppenfuhrer: Joachim Hansen
Churchill's Aide: Dennis Lill
Branna: Leonie Thelen
Hauptmann Gericke: Keith Buckley
Arthur Seymour: Terence Plummer
George Wilde (Publican): Tim Barlow
Laker Armsby: John Barrett
Mrs Wilde: Kate Binchy
Major Corcoran: Maurice Roeves
Sergeant Murphy: David Gilliam
Frazier: Jeff Conaway
Sergeant Brandt: Siegfried Rauch
Narrator: Patrick Allen
Winston Churchill/George Fowler: Leigh Dilley
Motorbike Outrider: Harry Fielder
Dead Diver: Harry Fielder
Sergeant Hayley: Anthony Forrest
Hauptsturmfuhrer Fleischer: Wolf Kahler
Traumer: George Leech
Radl's Doctor: Ferdy Mayne
Adolf Hitler: Peter Miles (uncredited)
German Officer: Malcolm Tierney
Mallory: Kent Williams

Producers
Producers: David Niven Jr, Jack Wiener

Music
Music: Lalo Schifrin

Cinematography
Director of Photography: Anthony B. Richmond

Film Editing: Anne V. Coates

Casting and Design
Production Design: Peter Murton
Art Direction: Charles Bishop
Costume Design: Yvonne Blake
Casting: Irene Lamb

Makeup Department
Makeup Artists: Eric Allwright, Paul Rabiger, Freddie Williamson
Hairdresser: Betty Glasow, Michael Jones

Production Management
Production Supervisor: Basil Rayburn

Second Unit Director or Assistant Director
Assistant Director: David Anderson
Second Assistant Director: Terry Churcher
Second Assistant Director: Michael Stevenson

Art Department
Set Dresser: Peter James
Construction Manager: John Paterson
Property Master: John Chisholm
Sculptor: Brian Muir
Assistant Art Director: Cliff Robinson
Stand-by Property Master: Terry Wells
Stand-by Props: Barry Wilkinson

Sound Department
Sound Editor: Jonathan Bates
Sound Recordist: Robin Gregory
Dubbing Mixer: Gerry Humphreys
Assistant Sound Editor: Jeremy Hume
Assistant Sound Editor: Jeremy Hume
Boom Operator: Terry Sharratt

Special Effects
Special Effects: Roy Whybrow
Special Effects Assistant: Chris Corbould
Matte Artist: Ray Caple

Stunts
Stunt Coordinator: Gerry Crampton
Stunts: Gilliam Aldam, Del Baker, Andy Bradford, George Lane Cooper, Jack Cooper, Gerry Crampton, Jim Dowdall, Steve Emerson, Richard Hammatt, Nick Hobbs, Jazzer Jeyes, George Leech, Rick Lester, Mark McBride, Valentino Musetti, Terence Plummer, Ken Sheppard, Eddie Stacey, Bill Weston
Stunt Double (Michael Caine): Bill Weston

Camera and Electrical Department
Electrician: Derek Suter

Aerial Photographer: Peter Allwork
Camera Operator: James Bawden
Electrical Supervisor: Martin Evans
Camera Operator (Second Unit): Gordon Hayman
Stills: George Whitear
Director of Photography (Second Unit): John Wlicox
Best Boy: Harry Jackson
Focus Puller: Mike Roberts

Costume and Wardrobe Department
Wardrobe Supervisor: Elsa Fennell
Wardrobe Master: Michael Jarvis

Location Management
Location Managers: Ray Freeborn, Ray Frift, Bernard Hanson

Music Department
Music Editor: Peter Watson
Music Preparation: John Graves

Other Crew
Production Accountant: John Beharrell
Aviation Consultants: Doug Bianchi, Edna Bianchi
Assistant to Producer: Penelope Forrester
Unit Publicist: Geoffrey Freeman
German Advisor: Hubert Frohlich
Presenter: Lew Grade
Continuity: Sally Jones
Finnish Production Consultant: Ake Lindman
Historical Consultant: Andrew Mollo
Runner: John Dodds
Set Runner: Paul Tivers

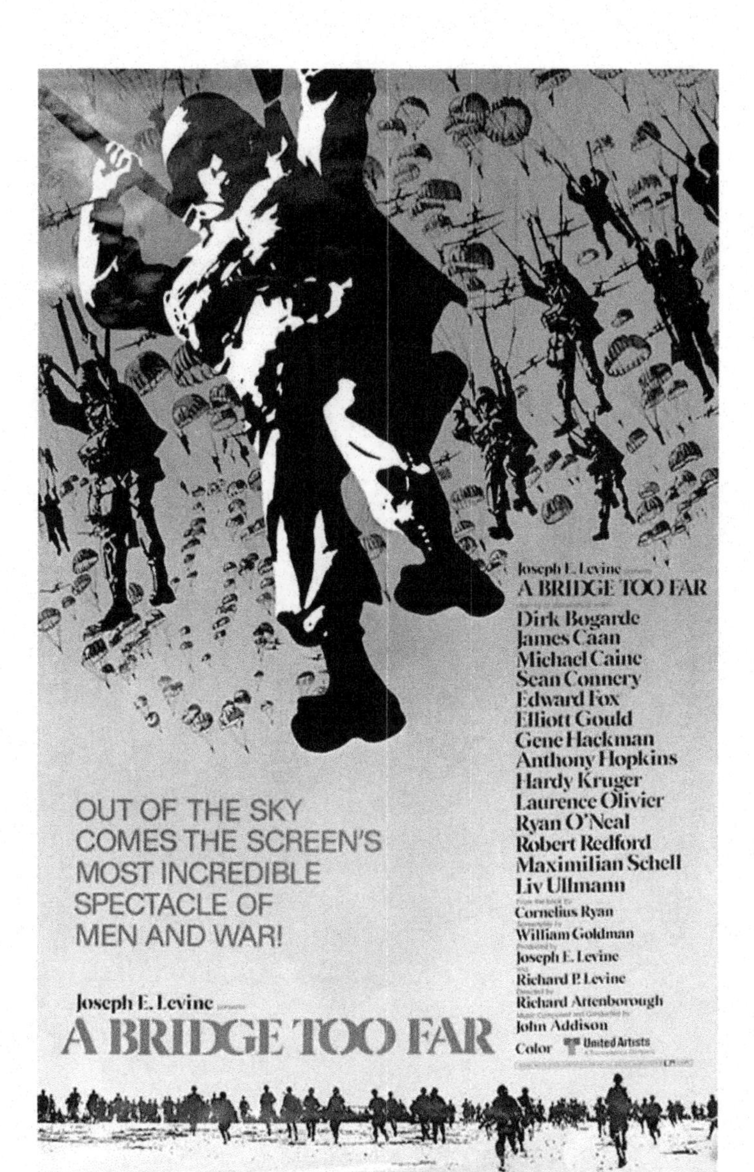
Joseph E. Levine
A BRIDGE TOO FAR
Dirk Bogarde
James Caan
Michael Caine
Sean Connery
Edward Fox
Elliott Gould
Gene Hackman
Anthony Hopkins
Hardy Kruger
Laurence Olivier
Ryan O'Neal
Robert Redford
Maximilian Schell
Liv Ullmann
Cornelius Ryan
William Goldman
Joseph E. Levine
Richard P. Levine
Richard Attenborough
John Addison
Color
United Artists
OUT OF THE SKY
COMES THE SCREEN'S
MOST INCREDIBLE
SPECTACLE OF
MEN AND WAR!
Joseph E. Levine
A BRIDGE TOO FAR

9

A BRIDGE TOO FAR

(1977)

Joseph E. Levine Productions

Director: Richard Attenborough
Producers: Joseph E. Levine and Richard P. Levine
Screenwriter: William Goldman,
from a book by Cornelius Ryan

OPERATION Market Garden – the September 1944 campaign to capture key bridges in Holland, allowing armoured forces to move into Germany – was one of the most controversial battles in WW2. Had it succeeded then history could have been changed, as the war would have ended earlier and the Soviet occupation of East Germany could have been prevented.

Unsurprisingly, it has been the subject of numerous books over the last 70 years, the best-known of which is the lengthy tome *A Bridge Too Far* by Cornelius Ryan, which was first published in 1974. Ryan was an American war correspondent who had previously written the book *The Longest Day* about D-Day, which was itself made into a film in 1961.

In 1975 American film producer Joe E. Levine – who had made almost 500 movies – bought the rights to *A Bridge Too Far*, and on June 26 that year it was announced that the film would be made the following year in the Netherlands.

The director was to be Richard Attenborough and the film was to premiere in June 1977, a tight schedule by any standards. Attenborough was a highly-respected British character actor who had previously directed just two films – *Oh, What a Lovely War* (1969) and *Young Winston* (1971). Both were praised by critics but fared poorly at the box office. The budget for the new film was set at $26m, making it one of the most expensive movies ever made. Levine put up the money for the movie and came out of retirement to oversee its production.

The most immediate problem facing the film makers was the acquisition of sufficient period tanks, military vehicles and aircraft to use in the production. Associate producer John Palmer – who had performed a similar task on *Battle of Britain* (1969) – was given this task with his Aviation Consultant being retired Group Captain Hamish Mahaddie, who had procured aircraft for several films including *The Dambusters* (1955), *633 Squadron* (1964), *Operation Crossbow* (1965) and *Battle of Britain* (1969).

At a very early stage in the production, John Palmer had a meeting with Winston G. Ramsey, editor of *After the Battle* magazine, specifically to enquire about the availability of restored military vehicles. As a result Charles Mann of the Military Vehicle Museum at Lamanva near Falmouth, Cornwall, was given the job of Military Vehicle Coordinator. Mann subsequently put together a fleet of 103 British, American and German vehicles which were acquired from his own collection, the 1939-45 Group, and Bapty & Co.

One problem was finding sufficient German armoured vehicles, particularly tanks. A few genuine German halftracks and armoured cars still existed in running order, but these were too precious to be used in the explosive stunts planned for the film. In addition, in 1975 there were no WW2 German tanks in running condition anywhere in the world. Four reproduction Panther tanks were therefore created in Holland using Dutch Army Leopard 1 tanks as a base vehicle while some AMX self-propelled guns portrayed their wartime German equivalents. In addition, Mann's team built four replica armoured cars and two halftracks in the UK which could be damaged (if required) in stunt sequences. Some replica Kubelwagen scout cars were also created using VW Beetle running gear.

The lend-lease American Sherman tanks used by the British XXX Corps were also a problem. At an early stage in the production, consideration was given to making the whole film in Yugoslavia as its armed forces still used considerable amounts of WW2 equipment, particularly Shermans. The 1970 film *Kelly's Heroes* was made there for that reason. The problem with Yugoslavia, though, was that it would be hard to make it look like Holland and there were no suitable bridges like those at Nijmegen and Arnhem. These could be built for the film, but would be prohibitively expensive. So making the film in Yugoslavia was not an option and shipping Sherman tanks from that country to the Netherlands (even if permission could be obtained) could be costly.

Eventually tank specialist Major John Larminie scoured Europe for running Shermans and spare parts, and acquired nine examples. Four were obtained from the Dutch Army who supplied a 105mm howitzer version which was transformed into a Firefly (a Sherman armed with a British 17-pounder gun) by means of a barrel extension, a turretless bulldozer Sherman which was fitted with a plastic turret to approximate its wartime appearance, and two towable hulks. Five further examples were obtained from Belgium comprising two 'gate guardians' (a 105mm version and a Firefly) from the

Ecole De Troupes Blindees at Arlon, plus another Firefly from a cabbage patch behind the Royal Army Museum in Brussels. Two further late-war examples with 76mm M1 guns were also sourced in Belgium.

To back up these nine genuine examples, a plaster cast was taken of one of the Fireflies and this was used to produce five fibreglass replica Shermans which were mounted on long-wheelbase Land Rovers. These replicas had moving tracks which didn't quite touch the ground, and had another flaw as their gun barrels wobbled when they moved. However, these deficiencies were hardly noticeable in the finished film as the replicas tended to be kept in the background.

One technical error in the film, however, was an absence of Shermans with short-barrelled 75mm guns. When this tank first saw action at El Alamein in October 1942, it was fitted with the American 75mm M3 weapon which was based on a WW1 French design. Later in the war the Americans introduced more powerfully-armed versions of the tank with a long-barrelled, high-velocity 76mm M1 gun in a larger T23 turret. These newer models were not in service with British tank regiments in September 1944. However, in 1943 the British had developed their own improved version of the Sherman mounting the long-barrelled 17-pounder anti-tank gun in a standard Sherman turret. In order to make room for the breech and recoil mechanism, the radio was removed and fitted in a large armoured box which was welded to the back of the turret. In addition, the hull machine gunner's position was removed and plated over to provide extra ammunition stowage.

These vehicles (which were known as Sherman Fireflies) could knock out the latest German tanks and were initially issued on the basis of one per troop of four tanks. Thus in September 1944 one in four Sherman tanks in British armoured columns would be Fireflies while the remainder would have short-barrelled 75mm guns. In the film, though, most of the Shermans appear to be Fireflies with two (featuring more angular and less rounded T23 turrets) having 76mm M1 guns which no British tank had at the time.

Another problem facing the filmmakers was how to depict soldiers accurately. The problem with most extras was that they had not usually received any military training and so did not know how to march, stand to attention, or use a weapon correctly. Attenborough's solution was to hand-pick a core of 50 extras and send them for gruelling military training, just like National Serviceman used to receive. Priority was to be given to actors who had previously served in the armed forces, and a prominent member of this disparate group of thespians – who became known as 'Attenborough's Private Army' (the APA) – was Scottish actor Jack McKenzie, who had served for three years in the Royal Marines and later played military roles in several TV dramas.

Members of the APA appeared in the film as British, American or Polish paratroops, or as German soldiers, depending on the demands of the scene. Thus *A Bridge Too Far* became one of the first films in which members of the cast received Boot Camp-style military training, something that has since become standard practice in the film industry. *A Bridge Too Far* wasn't actually the first film to use 'Boot Camp' training (as is often claimed), as some of the German soldiers in *The Longest Day* (1962) endured a similar regime.

Meanwhile, Hamish Mahaddie was looking for suitable aircraft to participate in the film. In September 1944, British airborne troops used three main types of transport aircraft –

the Short Stirling, the Handley-Page Halifax and the Douglas C-47 (which the British usually called the 'Dakota').

No airworthy Halifaxes or Stirlings existed anywhere, so the producers had to use only the C-47 which was still in service with some Air Forces and airlines in 1976. Eventually eleven C-47s were sourced for use in the production. Four were supplied by the Finnish Air Force, three by the Danish Air Force, two from Air Djibouti, and a further pair – both ex-Portugese examples – was supplied by Vision Air (with one of these being the later C-53 version).

Four North American AT-6 Harvards based in Holland also participated in the production. With their rear cockpits faired over and appropriate paint schemes and markings applied, they appeared in different scenes as USAAF P-47 Thunderbolts, Hawker Typhoons and Focke-Wulf Fw-190s, although the 'Fw-190s' don't appear in the final cut of the film. An Auster III and Spitfire Mk IX were also used in the film (full details are given in Appendix II at the end of this book).

The script also called for a fleet of Allied transport gliders. The main British glider in use at the time of the operation was the large Airspeed Horsa which could carry not just troops but also a Jeep, and light artillery such as the 75mm lightweight air-portable howitzer and the specially-narrowed airborne version of the 6-pounder anti-tank gun. No complete Horsas existed in 1975. Although a single replica had been built for *The Longest Day* (1962), that example had been destroyed during filming and the plans could not be found. However, using a single piece of microfilm supplied by the Imperial War Museum, production draughtsman Tony Rimmington drew up plans to create six non-flying replica Horsa gliders. In addition, a few two-dimensional flat Horsas were created for erection on scaffolding as background set dressing.

Although Arnhem Bridge still existed it was surrounded by modern buildings so could not be used in filming, but the location scouts found a very similar bridge at Deventer on the Issjel river just 35km away. Furthermore, it had a large car park at one end in which replicas of various period Arnhem houses could be constructed.

To create a script, the producers turned to respected American screenwriter William Goldman whose previous credits included *Butch Cassidy and the Sundance Kid* (1969), *Marathon Man* (1975) and *All the President's Men* (1976). Goldman's original draft contained a lot of 'Americanese', but this was subsequently corrected by various military advisors.

The previous film based on a Cornelius Ryan book, *The Longest Day* (1962), had employed an 'all-star' cast. A similar plan was used in *A Bridge Too Far*, with 14 major stars in key roles including Sean Connery, Gene Hackman, Elliott Gould, James Caan, Laurence Olivier and Robert Redford. All of these actors received a reported $250,000 per week for their work on the film, with Redford being paid $2m for what was in effect a cameo appearance. Sean Connery, who had appeared as Private Flanagan in *The Longest Day* immediately before appearing in *Dr No*, was initially reluctant to be involved in the film but changed his mind after reading the book *A Man Called Intrepid* about wartime espionage operations.

Interestingly, his successor as James Bond – Roger Moore – nearly got a part in the film, as he was earmarked to portray General Horrocks but in the end he lost out to Edward Fox. Richard Attenborough also hoped to find a role for his old pal Steve McQueen, who he had worked with on *The*

Great Escape (1963) and *The Sand Pebbles* (1965). McQueen was earmarked to play Major Julian Cook, but when his demands became unreasonable the part went to Robert Redford instead.

On 2 April 1976 a specially-chartered British Rail roll-on, roll-off vessel – the *Cambridge Ferry* – took the 103 military vehicles acquired by Charles Mann from Falmouth to Zeebrugge, and from there by road to Deventer, and on 26 April shooting started. Filming took place over a period of almost six months during the long hot summer of 1976, though the weather had broken by September when the all-important parachuting sequences were lensed. Almost the entire film was shot on location in the Netherlands, with Dutch houses standing in for buildings in England. Post-production work was carried out at Twickenham Studios in London.

The film begins with a monochrome 1940s-looking version of the United Artists logo, followed by some archive footage of flak bursting. Three USAAF Martin B-26 Marauders drop their bombs, and the camera follows the ordnance downwards with the picture freeze-framing just before the weapons hit the ground. A voice over (by actress Liv Ullman) says that it is hard to believe that Europe was like this in 1944. The film then starts again with the bombs exploding on hitting the ground as Ullman (in character as Kate ter Horst) explains that in 1944 the war 'was going Hitler's way' until D-Day 'changed everything'. This is incorrect, as the Germans had suffered a series of defeats from late 1942 onwards and – prior to the D-Day landings – had been driven out of North Africa and Sicily. The Allies were slowly advancing north in Italy, while the Russians had inflicted massive losses on the Wehrmacht on the Eastern Front and were approaching the German border.

Further library footage then follows, depicting the D-Day invasion and the advance into north-western Europe. It is explained that by early September 1944 the Allies had liberated most of France and Belgium, and were preparing to invade Holland. It was at that point that Field Marshal Bernard Montgomery came up with a plan (Operation Market Garden) to 'end the war by Christmas' by capturing several key bridges in Holland and then turning east in order to occupy the Ruhr. One problem though was that two of the Allied Commanders – Montgomery and General George Patton – hated one another and there weren't enough supplies for both the British and US Armies to conduct their own offensives, so priority had to be given to the British plan. Eisenhower reluctantly agreed that the operation could go ahead, but the plan – like so many that had gone before it – was to fail.

This part of the monologue isn't entirely accurate either, as it perpetuates the myth that Monty and Patton were constantly arguing. Although they both had ego problems they didn't really have much to do with one another, and Eisenhower not only approved the plan but was very enthusiastic about it. Even General Omar Bradley – who was one of Montgomery's severest critics – praised the operation, saying it was 'one of the boldest plans of the war'.

The title sequence then follows, consisting of simple white lettering in a military stencil style on a black background accompanied by John Addison's stirring martial theme. It is interesting that a lot of movies made in the late seventies and early eighties had very simple titles which were very often just plain white letters on a black background. The fad for lengthy pre-credits sequences had also passed by this time.

After the titles we see the interior of a dimly-lit house and a caption states that the action is set in 'Arnhem, Holland, September 1944'. A Dutch underground leader (Siem Vroom), his wife (Marlies Van Alcmaer) and son (Erik Van't Wout) are excited as they realise the Germans are in full retreat. There is the noise of tank engines, though to my ear they sound like the engines of American Sherman tanks rather than German Maybach motors. The next scene shows a large group of German soldiers retreating along a canal bank.

Meanwhile a Mercedes staff car draws up outside the German Western Front HQ. An officer gets out, accompanied by his aides. It is none other than the veteran Field Marshal Von Rundstedt (Wolfgang Preiss, who had previously played Major-General Max Pemsel in *The Longest Day*).

Von Rundstedt tries to put a brave face on things, but soon discovers that the Germans lack air support and are short of men, tanks and ammunition. When asked his opinion on what the Germans should do, he mutters that they should 'end the war'. Quickly, the resourceful Field Marshal recovers his composure and asks his intelligence officers when the Allies plan to invade Holland, only to be told that his opponents are being delayed by supply problems. (At that point in the war Antwerp was not operational, as the Germans still held the approaches to the port plus the island of Walcheren, and all supplies had to be transported by road from Normandy.) Von Rundstedt cynically observes that the Germans are 'retreating faster than the Allies can advance'. As the Germans plan their next move, the underground leader's son spies on German vehicles from an attic window and counts the number going past.

The action then moves to General 'Boy' Browning's Airborne Forces HQ in England (a scene which was actually filmed on location in Holland), where the officer is holding a briefing for the other Generals commanding the Allied Airborne Army – namely Major General Maxwell Taylor (Paul Maxwell) of the 101st Airborne, Brigadier General James M. Gavin (Ryan O'Neal) of the 82nd Airborne, Major General Roy Urquhart (Sean Connery) of the British 1st Airborne, and Major General Stanislaw Sosabowski (Gene Hackman) of the Polish 1st Airborne.

Browning (Dirk Bogarde) explains Field Marshal Montgomery's plan to end the war in less than 100 days. They are going to fly 35,000 men over 300 miles and then drop them behind enemy lines in Holland to capture key bridges. 'It's all about bridges', says Browning. These will be seized with 'thunderclap surprise' and a 'carpet' of airborne troops laid over Holland, enabling the British XXX Corps with 20,000 vehicles (including tanks) to advance north from the Belgian border.

General Maxwell Taylor's 101st Airborne Division will land in the Eindhoven area, the 82nd (commanded by General Gavin) will capture Nijmegen while General Urquhart's Paras will seize the most northerly objective, the bridge at Arnhem. The plan involves XXX Corps driving 63 miles in just two days to link up with the British troops at Arnhem.

Browning then realises he hasn't mentioned the role of the Polish paratroops and – rather apologetically – has to explain to General Sosabowski that he will also be taking his men to Arnhem. He then mentions that the operation will be mounted the following Sunday (which in fact was September 17).

One criticism I have of the movie is that although locations are given on screen via captions, no actual dates or times are shown, unlike other movies based on historical events, e.g. *Tora, Tora, Tora* (1970) which has frequent captions giving dates and times. Sosabowski is sceptical about the chances of the operation succeeding, but says he will be ecstatic if it works.

Meanwhile at the German Army HQ in Holland, Field Marshal Von Rundstedt is studying a map table and wondering which Allied Commander will lead the forthcoming assault – Montgomery or Patton? Field Marshal Model (Walter Kohut) suggests Patton as he is their best commander, and the Germans laugh with Von Rundstedt suggesting that he 'would have preferred Montgomery, but doesn't think Eisenhower is that stupid'. This is one of a number of 'anti-Montgomery' comments in the movie. In the meantime he suggests pulling back Bittrich's Panzer Corps (two divisions) to somewhere quiet, far from the front line, and chooses Arnhem.

The next scene is set at an unspecified airfield used by Allied Airborne Forces in England, but was actually shot at Deelen – north of Arnhem – which was a Luftwaffe base during the war and is mentioned as such in the movie. General Browning departs in an Auster III light aircraft in authentic RAF markings while General Gavin discusses the forthcoming mission with Captain 'Harry' Bestebreurtje (Peter Faber), a Dutchman serving with the 82nd Airborne.

Several of the C-47s used in the production can be seen in the background along with four North American AT-6 Harvards modified to look like USAAF Republic P-47 Thunderbolts by fairing over the rear cockpits, fitting dummy machine gun barrels to the wing leading edges and applying

WW2 USAAF camouflage and markings. Gavin points out that the Germans had tried to take Nijmegen Bridge in 1940 but had got slaughtered.

As the two soldiers are fretting about the operation, the underground leader's son we saw at the start of the movie is preparing to carry out some espionage. He persuades a German soldier to let him cycle down a country road on the pretence that he wishes to visit a female friend to collect a birthday present. In fact he wants to get a closer look at some German staff cars which are parked outside a house. Later, when he gets home he sketches the checked pennant on one of the cars which enables his father to deduce that Field Marshal Model must have been holding a meeting.

Back in England an intelligence officer, Major Fuller (Frank Grimes), expresses his concern about reports from the Dutch Resistance which mention a large number of German armoured vehicles in the Arnhem area. Browning dismisses his concerns, stating that the opposition is likely to consist of 'Hitler Youth and old men on bicycles', but reluctantly agrees to sanction an aerial photoreconnaissance mission of the area. In reality the Intelligence Officer involved was called Brian Urquhart, but the name was changed to Fuller as it was thought to be too confusing to have two characters called Urquhart in the cast.

The next scene is set in England where an unnamed RAF Officer (Jeremy Kemp) shows Major General Urquhart and General Sosabowski blow-ups of aerial reconnaissance photos of the Arnhem area. Kemp was a well-known character actor at that time, and specialised in playing military types. He had played a WW1 German airman in *The Blue Max* (1966), a German Officer in *Zeppelin* (1970), and an imprisoned RAF photo-reconnaissance pilot in the second series of the BBC series *Colditz* (1974).

The RAF Officer makes the point that the British are very short of transport aircraft and can't afford to lose a single one. Urquhart then looks at one of the blow-ups and suggests a field near Arnhem Bridge as being an ideal landing zone, but the RAF officer rejects the suggestion on the grounds that the land is too soft for gliders as their nosewheels will dig in, causing them to crash. Urquhart then suggests an alternative area to the north of the town, but that is also rejected by the RAF officer as it will bring his aircraft within range of anti-aircraft guns situated at the Luftwaffe airfield at Deelen.

Urquhart despairs, but then the RAF officer announces that he has found the ideal landing zone. The only snag is that it is eight miles west of Arnhem; a three-hour march for men wearing full kit and carrying a lot of equipment. General Sosabowski is unimpressed and approaches the RAF officer to check he is not really wearing a German uniform.

Back in Holland the young bespectacled Dutch boy we saw earlier is riding his bike along a country road when he is buzzed by an RAF Spitfire carrying out a low-level aerial reconnaissance. The aircraft, Mark IX MH434, then owned by Adrian Swire, had previously appeared in *The Longest Day* (1962), *Operation Crossbow* (1965) – in which it also played a PR Spitfire – and *Battle of Britain* (1969).

In *Operation Crossbow* it wore a PR blue colour scheme, but for this appearance it retained its normal fighter camouflage and D-Day invasion stripes and was flown by former British aerobatic champion Neil Williams, who had flown Mosquito TA634 in *Mosquito Squadron* (1970) and a Stampe-based SE5A replica in *Aces High* (1976). In December

1977 Williams was killed with his wife while flying a CASA 2.111 (Spanish-built Heinkel He 111) back to the UK.

After carrying out a pass to take pictures, the Spitfire waggles its wings and returns to England as the boy notices what the pilot has just seen – several German armoured vehicles, including two Panther tanks.

Back in England, General Urquhart is briefing his commanders. In view of the distance between the dropping zone and Arnhem Bridge, a squadron of Jeeps equipped with twin Vickers machine guns is to be carried in some of the gliders and will race ahead to secure both ends of Arnhem Bridge and hold them until the rest of the troops arrive. The Vickers guns referred to by General Urquhart were not the well-known bulky WW1-era weapons based on the Maxim gun, but much lighter Vickers 'K' gas-operated machine guns which were ideal for mounting in Jeeps. At the start of WW2 these were the standard weapons fitted to RAF bomber aircraft, but within a couple of years they were replaced by the even more effective belt-fed Browning 0.303 in guns. The SAS liked the Vickers 'K' guns as they worked well in sandy conditions and had a high rate of fire, so they mounted these weapons on Jeeps in twin mounts and used them to destroy parked Axis aircraft in raids on enemy airfields in North Africa. The main snag of the 'K' gun was that it used drum magazines containing just 100 rounds, which was enough for only six seconds firing.

Browning explains how XXX Corps will pass through areas controlled by the American 101st Airborne, then the 82nd Airborne zone, and finally link up with British paras at Arnhem. But General Sosabowski remains sceptical about the mission's chances of success. 'What about the Germans?' he says. Having seen the efficiency of the Wehrmacht at first hand, he is convinced that the Germans would put up stiff resistance, a prediction which proved to be entirely correct. However Browning dismisses his fears, claiming that the few troops in the Arnhem area will be 'second class'.

Sosabowski then says that he had been thinking of asking Browning for a letter stating that he had been ordered to carry out the mission, in case his men were massacred. Browning looks astonished and asks Sosabowski if he wants such a letter, but the General replies that he does not actually want one... because in the event of a massacre it would make no difference.

Meanwhile in a radio storage room, Major Steele (Stephen Moore) and Lieutenant Cole (Peter Settelen) are discussing possible problems with the tactical radio sets to be used in the forthcoming operation. They worked well in the desert, but will they function correctly in the damp, low-lying terrain of Holland?

As these issues are being discussed, Major Fuller is attempting to show General Browning three low-level photos that have been taken by the PR Spitfire. Fuller is not used to working the epidiascope (a device which projects images onto a screen using a photographic print rather than a transparency), and initially shows the first picture upside down. All it shows are trees.

The General is relieved that it only shows a picturesque view of the Dutch countryside. 'It's clearer in the next one', says Fuller as he puts up the next photo which clearly shows six armoured vehicles (including two Panther tanks) sitting on the edge of a wood, covered with foliage to camouflage them.

'Next', says Browning, clearly perturbed. The third print shows the vehicles in greater detail. The General walks up to the screen and inspects the enemy armour. 'I wouldn't worry about these. I doubt if they're fully serviceable.'

'They've got guns', replies Fuller.

'So have we!'

Browning also dismisses Fuller's claim that the Germans wouldn't bother to camouflage unserviceable vehicles, saying that this would be 'standard procedure'. He then gets angry, saying that many airborne operations have been cancelled in the past few weeks and that 'this time the party is on'.

Dirk Bogarde's portrayal of General Browning attracted a lot of criticism at the time of the film's release, with some critics saying that the General was unfairly made the 'fall guy' for all the failings of Operation Market Garden. His widow, the writer Daphne Du Maurier, was particularly angry at the way he had been portrayed, but no legal action against the film-makers was feasible as it is impossible to libel the dead. However Dirk Bogarde, who had served under General Browning during WW2, later expressed regret at the way he had depicted the General in the film, which he confirmed was nothing like the way he actually was. In fact Browning had some misgivings about the operation, and warned Montgomery that they might be going 'A Bridge Too Far'.

The action then moves to Leopoldsburg on the Belgian/Dutch border, where General Brian Horrocks (Edward Fox) is arriving to address his officers at a local cinema. Although Colonel John Waddy has mentioned that 20 Jeeps were used in the making of the film, I counted about 40 of them in this scene which was filmed in a square in Deventer.

Horrocks takes the stage to address his men and gives a stirring speech to motivate them. It is such a good piece of public speaking that I referenced it in one of my books, *The*

Craft of Public Speaking (2016). Quickly Horrocks outlines the plan. Three Airborne Divisions consisting of 35,000 men are to fly from 24 airfields in southern England to seize bridges in Holland. The American 101st will land near Eindhoven,the 82nd at Njimegen and the British 1st Airborne and the Poles will take Arnhem bridge.

Meanwhile XXX Corps will cross the Dutch border and head north, aiming to reach Arnhem in two to three days, with the latter's bridge being the last one between Allied forces and Germany itself. Horrocks then describes the whole operation as being 'like one of these American Westerns' with the Germans being the bad guys, the Paras the besieged homesteaders, and XXX Corps the US Cavalry coming to the rescue'. The officers laugh and clap in approval. It is a brilliant speech, and an object lesson on how to deliver an arresting presentation. Edward Fox later revealed that General Horrocks was his favourite film role. In the DVD commentary, screen writer William Goldman explained that he used the 'Western' metaphor to explain the operation in simple terms to 1977 audiences who would then be familiar with cowboy movies. He also said that this method wouldn't work nowadays, as such movies have fallen from favour.

Back in England, Colonel Frost (Anthony Hopkins) is discussing the forthcoming operation with his batman Private Wicks (Paul Copley), saying that perhaps he should pack his dinner jacket, shotgun and golf clubs. Paul Copley was the son of veteran actor Peter Copley, whose most memorable role was as Dr Warlock in the classic *Doctor Who* story *Pyramids of Mars* (1975).

Meanwhile in a tent at a US Army camp 'somewhere in England', the young Captain Glass (Nicholas Campbell) expresses his fears about dying to the calm and experienced

Staff Sergeant Eddie Dohun (James Caan). Dohun reassures him that he won't die, but Glass asks him to guarantee that statement.

'OK, I guarantee you won't die', says Dohun.

As Dohun is placating Glass, Major Fuller is asked to take a walk outside his HQ by an Army Medical Officer, Colonel Sims (Gerald Sim). Fuller admits to being exhausted but claims he is not ill. He still thinks that Operation Market Garden should be cancelled, but is told that that would not be possible.

In reality, General Browning got rid of Major Brian Urquhart by ensuring he was sent on sick leave, but in the film Fuller subsequently takes part in the parachute drop on Arnhem – something that is never explained.

The next scene is set early in the morning of Sunday 17 September. As the sun rises, General Gavin and Staff Sergeant Dohun look at the sky while General Urquhart plays golf. As is widely known, Sean Connery learned to play golf while making *Goldfinger* (1964) and has been a keen player ever since.

The next few minutes of footage are some of the most impressive in the film, for aviation enthusiasts at least, and might be described as 'Dakota porn'. Hundreds of paratroopers descend from trucks and board the C-47 transports while others get inside Airspeed Horsa gliders as mock-Hawker Typhoons fly overhead to the accompaniment of some stirring music by composer John Addison. Addison was a respected British film composer who had actually taken part in 'Operation Market Garden' as a tank commander in XXX Corps, and had written the score for several British war movies including *Reach for the Sky* (1956). This particular track is called 'Air Lift' on the soundtrack LP and CD. Richard Attenborough originally considered making the film without music and asked Addison to avoid scoring the action sequences, and as a result there are only 30 minutes of music in the whole movie.

General Maxwell Taylor waves goodbye from the doorway of a C-47, recreating a pose from an actual wartime photo, and the aircraft start their engines and taxi out. Although only 11 Dakotas were used in the production, split-screen matte photography methods were employed by visual effects maestro Wally Veevers to multiply the number of aircraft on screen. The first two rows of Dakotas in this shot are real, but the large number in the background were created using a matte painting.

Other Dakotas pull Horsa gliders along the runway. Although no Horsas actually flew for the movie, one of them was towed at speed along a runway by a Dakota while a point-of-view shot from a Horsa's cockpit was achieved using a LET L-13 Blanik sports glider which really was towed aloft by a C-47.

The Dakotas taxi to the end of the runway and then take off in formation as an insert shot shows the throttles being pushed forward (although one aviation expert has pointed out that the levers shown being manipulated were actually propeller pitch levers). All these scenes were shot at Deelen airfield close to Arnhem, and all the aircraft made several take offs. Once these multiple shots were edited together it gave the impression that scores of planes were used in the production.

One error in the film was that all the Dakotas were painted a sand brown colour instead of the correct olive drab. This was supposedly done so that the aircraft would show up better against the Dutch heathland during the parachute drop sequences. One wonders why this was thought necessary. In the opening title sequence of *Where Eagles Dare* (1969), the Junkers Ju 52/3m aircraft is easily seen against the snow-covered Austrian mountains despite being painted in a (fictitious) white and dark grey winter camouflage scheme. Furthermore, there would only have been a potential problem if the subsequent parachuting scenes were filmed from above looking down on the aircraft, when in fact they were mainly shot from below with the sky providing the background.

The vast aerial armada heads towards the English coast, and Wally Veevers's split-screen matte techniques are again used to multiply the number of aircraft on screen. One particularly impressive shot shows the view from the nose of a Horsa. A towing rope and Dakota glider tug appear in the centre of the screen with a huge number of Horsas and Dakotas in the far distance behind them. This effect was achieved by carefully cutting out colour photos of Horsas and Dakotas and sticking them on glass, the same method that was used to create the huge formation of Heinkels overflying London in *Battle of Britain* (1969). Curiously, no miniature work at all was used in *A Bridge Too Far* and – apart from a few split-screen and matte shots by Wally Veevers and his colleagues – the entire film was done 'in camera'.

As the vast formation flies over Belgium, it is observed by General Horrocks and Colonel Joe Vandeleur (Michael Caine), who gets into a Humber Scout car and makes his way to the Dutch border where a huge column of British armoured vehicles of XXX Corps are preparing to move into Holland. As the aircraft approach their drop zones, the Dakotas are buffeted by flak and Staff Sergeant Dolan has to reassure Captain Glass. This fuselage interior scene was shot in Holland using a wooden mock-up of a Dakota fuselage. A similar set of the inside of a Horsa glider was used for the sequence in which General Urquhart feels airsick as he approaches the landing zone. South of Arnhem, General Bittrich (Maximillian Schell) watches in awe as the vast aerial armada flies over his position. Enviously, he wishes that he could command such powerful forces himself.

As the Dakotas overfly their designated dropping zones, hundreds of airborne troops start to drop from the aircraft. This is probably the most impressive parachuting sequence in the history of the movies, and was filmed simultaneously by 25 cameras. Cameras were fitted inside some of the Dakotas, filming inside the fuselage and cockpit, out the astrodome, under the belly, and over the port wing. Other shots were taken from gliders and from a Piper Aztec light aircraft (which was painted sand brown in case it appeared in shot) and an Alouette camera helicopter. A second Aztec and two Cessna light aircraft were also used as additional camera ships. Cameras were also mounted on two of the parachutists themselves, and others were fitted in 'cherrypickers' on the ground and in camouflaged hides. Although 11 Dakotas were obtained for the production, no more than nine managed to get airborne at the same time (a common problem in aviation films), but when all the footage from multiple cameras was edited together the effect was stunning. All these shots were filmed using men of the British Parachute Regiment who made three separate drops in September 1976 using modern PX parachutes. Some additional, smaller scale drops were made by Belgian paras, from a modern Lockheed C-130, to depict US Airborne troops.

As the paratroops continue to land in their dropping zones, Horsa gliders can be seen lying on the ground in the background. This is inaccurate, as separate landing zones were assigned to the gliders to avoid accidents. Also, only one type of glider is seen in the film – the large British Airspeed Horsa, which was also used by US Forces – when in fact the smaller American Waco CG-4A was also used in the operation, as were a number of huge British Airspeed Hamilcars which could carry a 7-ton load such as powerful 17-pounder anti-tank guns and Universal Carriers. The Hamilcar could also deploy the Tetrarch light tank armed with a 2-pounder gun, though none were used in this particular operation.

Meanwhile, Field Marshal Model starts to panic when his Aide (Michael Wolf) reports that parachutists are dropping all over Holland. He fears that the parachutists must be after him, and decides to flee his HQ.

On the Belgian border, Lieutenant Colonel 'Joe' Vandeleur is sitting atop a Humber Scout car as a large column of British Sherman tanks of XXX Corps, backed up by M3 halftracks, Universal Carriers and other vehicles, prepares to advance into Holland. The most distant vehicles in the column were modern Dutch Army Leopard tanks and AMX self-propelled guns, giving the impression of a huge force.

In the American 101st Airborne Division dropping zone near Eindhoven, General Maxwell Taylor watches as Horsa gliders in US markings discharge their cargos of Jeeps and trailers. Meanwhile, Lieutenant General Bittrich orders Major General Karl Ludwig (Hardy Kruger) to get to Nijmegen as fast as possible with whatever forces he can muster. Ludwig was a fictional character based on two different people, Generals Harmel and Harzel.

In the 82nd Airborne drop zone near Nijmegen, General James Gavin lands heavily and injures his spine. Later as he makes his way through a wood, he is nearly killed by an enemy soldier and is only saved by the timely intervention of his Dutch friend Harry, who shoots the German with his rifle.

On the landing zone, General Urquhart learns that Frost's men are on the way to Arnhem Bridge on foot but hears that there is bad news about Major Freddie Gough's squadron of special Jeeps. Most of the gliders carrying them were lost, and the few special Jeeps that did arrive were shot up in an ambush. Urquhart realises that the plan is starting to unravel already. To rub things in, a nearby lunatic asylum has been bombed in error and the inmates are wandering through the woods. One of them (with dark hair, beard and glasses) is played by Richard Attenborough in a Hitchcock-style cameo.

Meanwhile on the Dutch border, Lt Colonel 'Joe' Vandeleur checks his watch as he prepares to give his XXX Corps armoured column the order to move off. The advance is preceded by a devastating artillery barrage. This is represented by a battery of 25-pounder field guns supplied by the Dutch Army. The 25-pounder was one of the most remarkable weapons used by British Forces in WW2. Designed as a field gun and howitzer (i.e. for high-angle indirect fire at considerable range), it was also employed as a stopgap anti-tank gun in North Africa in 1941-42, firing a solid shot, as the contemporary 2-pounder gun could not penetrate the armour of the latest German tanks. Once the 6-pounder anti-tank gun became available from May 1942 onwards, the 25-pounder reverted to its former roles. The weapon remained in service with the British Army for some decades after the war, and the last active examples were only retired by the Irish Army fairly recently. Ammunition for this weapon is still manufactured in Pakistan.

After allowing the 'creeping barrage' to move forward, 'Joe' Vandeleur gives the order for his tanks to advance using the words 'get moving' (the same words the real Vandeleur used), and the column moves forwards. Before too long the column is spotted by the crews of two German anti-tank guns hidden in woods near the road, and they engage the leading Shermans which burst into flames, bringing the entire column to a halt. Some of the tanks try to get off the road to escape annihilation, while others rotate their turrets to shoot at the enemy forces. At this point in the film, three tank hulks supplied by the Dutch Army – an M47 Patton, an M24 Chaffee and an M10 Wolverine – are used to depict knocked-out Shermans. These scenes of the XXX Corps breakout were filmed at the Dutch Army's tank training ground at Amersfoort. Soon the Germans are attacked with machine guns and the tanks' main guns, while soldiers fire back with their personal weapons. Vandeleur orders his tanks to fire purple smoke shells to mark targets in the woods for air strikes.

Suddenly some 'Hawker Typhoons' (actually modified Harvards) appear over the armoured column and bank to port to drop 500lb bombs (in reality, modified fire extinguishers) on the enemy positions. These mock Typhoons don't really look much like the genuine article as they have 550hp radial engines, heavily framed canopies and green-and-dark earth camouflage, whereas the real Hawker fighters had 2000 hp Napier Sabre in-line engines, four 20mm cannon, bubble canopies and green and grey camouflage.

In 1976 only one complete Hawker Typhoon (MN235) existed in the world, in the RAF Museum, but at the time of writing (2017) there is a project in England to rebuild a Typhoon (RB396) to flying condition by 2024, using a crashed example to provide parts. There is a second similar project in Canada using Typhoon JP843.

Director of photography Geoffrey Unsworth used a lot of smoke in the film. White smoke created by heating a special oil was used in most scenes to create an atmospheric haze, while old car tyres were burned to generate black smoke. In fact 10,000 old car tyres were burned during the making of the movie, something that would not be allowed nowadays under Health & Safety legislation.

Eventually the enemy troops are defeated by massive firepower and the Germans are forced to surrender, but much damage had been caused to the British force which has been delayed. A 'dozer' Sherman pushes an M24 hulk (representing a Sherman) off the road as the column prepares to get moving again. Lt Col Giles Vandeleur (Michael Byrne) asks his cousin Joe how they can be expected to advance over such a narrow road only to be told that the section they are on is 'the wide part'! In the meantime, a German soldier investigates a crashed Horsa glider full of dead troops and finds a large folder marked 'Not to be taken into the Air'. It is the entire plan for 'Operation Market Garden'.

Back at the main dropping zone, eight miles from Arnhem, General Urquhart receives further bad news from Major Steele. The VHF radio sets have been delivered with the wrong crystals and are quite useless. It is therefore impossible to contact Colonel Frost to let him know what has happened.

Problems with the radios were indeed a major factor in the failure of the operation but the 'crystals' explanation given in the film is a gross over-simplification. In that era, crystals were used to set the frequency of a radio set as an alternative to manual tuning. But the 'wrong crystals' problem only involved three American Jeeps that were designated as 'contact cars' to communicate with aircraft and order air strikes. There were a number of other factors which affected the performance of radios in the Arnhem area. The tactical sets of that era had a very low power output and limited range. In addition, some had batteries which needed recharged and the local low-lying, damp terrain with thick woods and an iron-rich soil contributed to problems with establishing radio communications. Even today the Dutch Army has difficulties using tactical radios in this part of Holland. Urquhart orders Moore to get the problems with the radios sorted out 'before we have a disaster on our hands', and is brought tea by Corporal Hancock (Colin Farrell).

The next scene is set in General Bittrich's former HQ in Arnhem which has been taken over by Field Marshal Model. Bittrich is keen to blow up the bridges at Nijmegen and Arnhem as it will thwart the Allies' plans but Model believes they don't actually want the bridges. If they had intended to take Arnhem Bridge, why would they have landed 12km away?

Meanwhile Colonel Frost's men are marching into Arnhem, and are greeted by large numbers of civilians who are delighted to see them. These include local woman Kate ter Horst (Liv Ullman) and her family, who wave enthusiastically at the soldiers.

As Colonel Frost and his men continue their long trek towards Arnhem, a squad of paratroopers from the 101st Airborne led by the cigar-chomping Colonel Bobby Stout (Elliott Gould) – a fictional character based on the real-life Bobby Sink – are running towards the Son Bridge. They are determined to capture it before the Germans can demolish it. They have almost made it when the bridge blows up. A huge splash of water drenches the American soldiers, extinguishing Colonel Stout's cigar. 'Shit!' he exclaims. As Stout is wondering what to do, General Urquhart heads towards Arnhem in a Jeep in an attempt to make contact with other elements of the British 1st Airborne division.

Meanwhile, Colonel Stout drives up to the 101st Airborne's temporary HQ where a radio operator gleefully informs him that the Grave Bridge has been captured, but Stout tells him that is of little consequence as the Son Bridge has been destroyed. He asks the operator to send a message to XXX Corps asking for some 'Bailey Stuff' to be sent forward, a reference to the prefabricated Bailey Bridge (of which more later) and to meet him in Eindhoven.

The next scene shows XXX Corps tanks slowly moving north as Colonel Vandeleur proposes stopping for the night. Post-war analysts have since criticized XXX Corps for stopping overnight only a few hours after the advance began, but with the Son Bridge destroyed and not yet re-bridged the advance would have had to stop anyway.

Back at Model's HQ in Arnhem, Ludwig shows Bittrich the captured plans for 'Operation Market Garden' which reveal all the objectives, dropping zones and timetables. All the Germans have to do to foil the operation is to blow up Nijmegen Bridge. But Model is sceptical, suggesting that the plans are fake and were intended to be found as part of a deception operation. Model's deduction is not unreasonable, particularly as the British had pulled off such a ruse in 1943 when they arranged for the corpse of 'Major William Martin' to be washed ashore in Spain. Martin had a briefcase attached to his wrist by a chain which contained letters confirming that the Allies intended to invade Greece and not Sicily. 'Operation Mincemeat', as it was known, was entirely successful and was described in detail in Ewan Montague's post-war book *The Man who Never Was* and the subsequent 1956 film adaptation.

In the interim, General Urquhart has stopped on the outskirts of Arnhem to discuss the situation. He has only walked a few yards from his Jeep when it is catapulted into the air by an explosion. Machine guns open up from all sides. He is surrounded.

The light is failing as Frost's men finally arrive at Arnhem Bridge and commandeer a house as their temporary HQ. As they are waiting for the owner to answer the doorbell, the Colonel realises that his DPM Airborne smock is not ideal camouflage for an urban environment. Frost subsequently goes upstairs and surveys the bridge from a balcony. The paras now hold the north end, but for the operation to succeed they will have to capture the southern end as well. Major Carlyle suggests they assault the bridge as soon as possible before it is too dark. The character of Major Carlyle was based on Major Allison Digby Tatham-Warter.

A few minutes later the British paras walk onto the bridge, guns at the ready. At first it looks as though they are going to cross the bridge unmolested, but then a machine gun in a pillbox at the base of the west arch of the bridge opens up on them. The British troops return fire with their Bren guns while others throw smoke bombs to cover their retreat. They have been driven back with casualties.

Later, under cover of darkness, two of Frost's men creep up to the pillbox and attempt to knock it out with a flamethrower. Unfortunately they miss their target – the bunker's tiny slit – and the tongue of flame ignites an ammunition store to the left of the target. There is a huge explosion and the paint on the bridge catches fire. To achieve this effect, asbestos pads were fitted on the bridge's archwork and flames were created with piped calor gas. Seeing the flames, Frost blows his hunting horn, much to the amusement of General Bittrich who can hear the commotion from his vantage point on the south side of the bridge.

The next morning, Bittrich's Panzer troops prepare to dislodge the paras from the north side of the bridge using a fleet of armoured vehicles commanded by Captain Grabner (Fred Williams). This incident, which is often described as 'Grabner's Charge', is one of the most famous actions of the Arnhem battle and is one of the highlights of the film. The real attack involved 21 vehicles, but director Richard Attenborough cut this down to 16. One of the problems facing the filmmakers was a shortage of genuine German armoured cars and halftracks, so many of them were replicas created using converted Land Rovers and other vehicles. Some of the VW Kubelwagens were genuine, others were reproductions using a VW Beetle chassis which was logical since the original 1940 Kubelwagen was a military derivative of the early Beetle car. The small tracked Marder self-propelled gun in this sequence was a modified Hotchkiss Brandt, while two of the SD.Kfz 251 Hanomag halftracks were replicas – one was an expendable version designed to be blown up, while a second was a fully-running version created by combining a British Universal Carrier with the front end of a Commer van. This particular vehicle survived the filming and was subsequently used in *Force 10 from Navarone* (1978), *Hanover Street* (1979), and *Highlander* (1985).

The real attack went on for three hours, but for the film it was tightly edited down to just three minutes of screen time. It begins with the German panzergrenadiers mounting their vehicles and setting off. As the British troops prepare to repel the attack, director of photography Geoffrey Unsworth uses a long lens to depict the first German vehicles appearing above the hump in the centre of the bridge. Gradually rising through a heat haze, the halftracks and armoured cars look like sea monsters raising their heads above the ocean.

One British para looses off a single round from his Lee-Enfield rifle, prompting Frost to order everyone to wait for the command to open fire. Just when it seems the Germans are on top of them, Frost orders his men to start shooting. Immediately the British soldiers open up with Lee-Enfield rifles, Bren guns, Sten guns and PIAT anti-tank weapons. The PIAT (Projector Infantry Anti Tank) was one of the most unusual weapons of WW2. It did not fire a rocket like the American bazooka. Nor was it a recoilless gun like the German Panzerfaust. Instead, it employed the principle of the spigot mortar to project a 5.5 lb hollow-charge warhead at the target.

The spigot mortar was a type of gun in which the barrel was attached to the rear of the projectile. A metal rod at the front of a spring fitted into this, and the munition was fired by an explosive cartridge in the rear of the bomb (inside the barrel) which was detonated by the powerful spring. Before the first round could be fired, the spring had to be cocked manually. After this, the recoil from each cartridge exploding re-cocked the spring and a fresh round could be inserted by a loader (as depicted in the film), allowing quite a high rate of fire to be achieved. The spigot mortar principle was also used in the highly effective British 'Hedgehog' multi-barrelled anti-submarine mortar, which was so effective that it was bought by the US Navy.

The other piece of technology used in the PIAT was the 'hollow charge' (also known as the 'shaped charge'). In the late 19th century it was found that explosive charges were more effective against armour plate if the surface facing the metal was hollowed out (a scientific discovery known as the 'Munroe Effect'). This resulted in the explosive blast being 'focused' into a narrow beam, which enabled a relatively small charge to penetrate quite thick armour. By the early 1940s the first practical weapons to use this discovery appeared, employing a cone-shaped depression in the nose of the warhead which was lined with copper. When it hit the target and exploded, the copper cone turned into a thin jet of molten metal which could pierce thick armour. Even though the PIAT only had a 5.5 lb warhead it could penetrate 75mm of armour, and thus could pierce the side armour of even the heavier German tanks such as the Tiger and Panther.

The PIAT had a couple of advantages over the American bazooka (which also used a hollow-charge warhead), as it could be fired in a confined space without any backblast and also had a more powerful explosive charge. The main disadvantages of the PIAT were that the launcher was heavy, the initial cocking of the spring was difficult as the operator had to stand upright, and it had a powerful recoil which could injure the operator's shoulder. In addition, the recoil sometimes failed to re-cock the spring, meaning that the difficult manual cocking operation had to be repeated.

One inaccuracy in the film is that it is implied that the PIAT was the only anti-tank weapon used at Arnhem. In fact the Horsa gliders brought in a number of 6-pounder anti-tank guns, which could be towed by Jeeps or Universal Carriers, and some even more effective 17-pounders were delivered by the larger Hamilcars. Five 6-pounders are known to have been used by Frost's men to repel Grabner's assault on Arnhem Bridge on 18 September, but this was not depicted in the film. Although three 6-pounders were acquired for use in the movie, only two of these appear in the background of one shot and none are seen firing.

Grabner is shot by a sniper and his troops retreat with heavy losses, having had all their vehicles knocked out. One

Kubelwagen replica rolls over, revealing that it is fitted with a roll bar to protect the stuntman, while four armoured car replicas crash into each other. A Marder and a halftrack appear to be blazing – an effect achieved by piping calor gas flames behind the vehicles in order to avoid damaging them, allowing re-takes. In fact this scene was re-staged many times over a three-week period, during which the bridge had to be closed to traffic and a temporary passenger ferry provided for commuters.

Frost's men have won this round, but he knows further attacks will follow. As he visits a temporary hospital that has been set up in a nearby building, he is shocked to discover that one of the troops captured in the attack is from an SS Panzer division and not the 'Hitler Youth and old men on bicycles' that he had expected.

In another part of Arnhem, General Urquhart and a few fellow officers are hiding in a house and decide to make a break for it. Unfortunately one of his colleagues is shot, and they are forced to duck into a house for cover. As Urquhart is examining his wounds on a kitchen table, a German soldier walks past the window. Initially he doesn't notice the British troops, but then does a double take and returns. He is promptly shot several times through the window by General Urquhart using his pistol. To achieve this scene, the window was broken with a ball bearing and the stuntman playing the German soldier was protected by a sheet of perspex.

Urquhart and his colleagues then flee the building. After running through the town for a few minutes, a Dutch civilian beckons them to come into her house where they hide in the attic. But then, to their dismay, a German Panther tank parks outside the house which makes escape impossible. (In reality, the vehicle involved back in 1944 was a self-propelled gun.) The 'Panther' which appears in this scene was actually a modern Dutch Army Leopard 1 which was converted to resemble a wartime German tank by having flat plates applied to its turret sides along with armoured skirts, a muzzle brake and a turret-mounted MG42 machine gun.

Like all the German armoured vehicles in the film, the four 'Panthers' were painted light grey, which was inaccurate. Up to 1943, German military vehicles were painted dark Panzer grey (or 'desert sand' for vehicles used in North Africa), but from mid-1943 onwards the base colour applied at the factory was a sand yellow which was often oversprayed in the field with varying patterns of dark green or reddish brown camouflage. Curiously, the four German tanks used in *A Bridge Too Far* are referred to as 'Panzer IVs', or 'Tigers' in some accounts of the making of the film, though they are obviously intended to look like Panthers.

Back in England an RAF Met Officer (Denholm Elliott) has disappointing news for General Sosabowski. His paratroops cannot depart from their English air bases because of fog, and the General asks why his men cannot be moved to another aerodrome which isn't fogged in. The Met Officer says that his request is not unreasonable but, since fog tends to move, it is possible they could move to a new departure point only to find the fog has 'preceded' them.

In the meantime, XXX Corps tanks have reached Eindhoven just 48 miles from Arnhem, where they are surrounded by cheering crowds. Colonel Bobby Stout meets Colonel 'Joe' Vandeleur and asks if XXX Corps has any 'Bailey Crap'. Stout is pleased to hear that they do have bridging equipment, and explains that his American troops have cleared a side road through Eindhoven to allow the engineers and the equipment to bypass the crowds.

Some miles away at the 82nd Airborne's HQ in Nijmegen, Captain 'Harry' Bestebreurtje tells General Gavin that the Germans are moving large numbers of troops and tanks to Nijmegen to prevent the bridge from being taken.

As this is happening, Staff Sergeant Eddie Dohan discovers that his Captain has been shot in the head and is presumed dead. But he refuses to accept what he has been told and drives off into the countryside to recover his Captain's body. Placing the unconscious officer in the passenger seat, he drives through a wood which is full of enemy troops. At one point he is surrounded and switches off his engine as he waits for the Germans to move on. Eventually he sees his chance to escape, turns on the engine and drives through the woods while swerving to avoid enemy vehicles and troops. Avoiding a hail of hostile fire, he manages to get back onto a road which takes him to a US Army field hospital.

A US Medical Officer (Arthur Hill) refuses to even examine Captain Glass as he thinks he must be dead, so Dohan pulls out his Colt 0.45 service revolver and forces him to inspect the wounded Captain. To his astonishment the Colonel finds he is alive, and then operates to remove a bullet from his head and save his life. After the successful operation, Dohan hands over his pistol to the Colonel and offers to submit to arrest. But the Colonel simply asks for an MP, Sergeant Rafferty (Garrick Hagon), to arrest him, count from one to ten and then release him,

As the light is falling, Colonel Bobby Stout is supervising the construction of a temporary bridge over the Son. The 'Bailey Bridge' was named after its inventor, Donald Bailey, and was a wood-and-steel prefabricated construction which could be erected quickly. Many are still in place today and it is possible to walk over one at the Imperial War Museum at Duxford, near Cambridge.

A real Bailey Bridge was used in the film, supplied by the Dutch Army with some extra sections provided by the British Army of the Rhine. Some Dutch Army officers and NCOs participated in the construction, but ordinary servicemen could not be used as they had long hair which they refused to get cut. However, the 50 men of the APA made up for the lack of numbers.

The sappers work through the night, illuminated by floodlights, to get the bridge constructed as the men of XXX Corps sleep by their tanks. The effectiveness of this scene is greatly increased by the musical track which accompanies it ('Bailey Bridge'), which suggests people working fast against the clock. Eventually the bridge is ready. 'Roll the fuckers', says Stout as the first Sherman crosses the bridge. For reasons of cost, the bridge used in the film was not constructed to a specification which would allow it to take the full 30-ton weight of a Sherman tank, so for scenes showing tanks fully crossing the bridge the lighter fibreglass Sherman replicas were used. As these shots were filmed at sunrise the deception is not noticeable, though eagle-eyed viewers will notice that the gun barrels of the fibreglass tanks wobble around like crazy when the vehicles are moving, making them easy to spot.

At this point a caption reveals that XXX Corps have 39 miles to go until they reach Arnhem. The tanks continue to move forward, and General Taylor drives his Jeep beside Vandeleur's tank and informs him that they are now passing into an area controlled by the 82nd Airborne. A little while later the armoured column passes over the Grave Bridge, where they are cheered on by American paratroops. Now they only have 22 miles till they reach Arnhem.

Back in Arnhem, Colonel Frost is in his temporary HQ in a house overlooking the bridge when he hears a tank approaching. He is sure it must be XXX Corps and broadcasts the news to his elated men. But as the tank gets nearer he realises it is the wrong colour and shape to be a British vehicle. It is a German Panther!

Quickly he tells his men to take cover and directs the two-man crew manning a PIAT on the roof to fire at the enemy tank. Their first round falls short and explodes harmlessly in front of the Panther. The two soldiers change their position as the tank rolls past. They fire a second bomb at the rear of the vehicle as it drives past but this also misses.

As this battle is raging some airborne troops attack the crew of the Panther which is parked outside the house where General Urquhart is trapped. The soldiers' assault is successful, and General Urquhart is released. (In reality there was no attack, as the German self-propelled gun eventually drove off.) Urquhart asks for a Jeep, as he wants to reach his HQ.

The next scene is set at the British 1st Airborne Division HQ at the Hartenstein Hotel, where Urquhart is briefed on the situation. Frost and his men are holding the north end of the bridge and the Poles are due to arrive. However, the bulk of the British Airborne troops are surrounded and are running short of food, ammunition and water. Few supplies are arriving, as the Germans have overrun the drop zones. To cap it all, the radios are not working, so they can't tell the RAF pilots what is happening.

Outside the hotel the British troops have set up burning markers on the ground to attract the pilots' attention, but the aircrews ignore them as they are under orders to disregard signals from the ground. Four Dakotas in RAF markings fly over the Hartenstein Hotel dropping supply containers which land behind the German lines. Then a fifth Dakota flies low over the British troops, its port engine smoking. It dives behind the trees and disappears behind a huge orange fireball, having apparently crashed. In the original cinema release of this film the starboard wingtip of the aircraft can be seen as the Dakota climbs after the explosion has subsided, revealing how this common camera trick was done, but in subsequent DVD and Blu-Ray releases a few seconds of footage have been cut, preserving the illusion that the plane actually crashed.

The Dakota pilot in this sequence was John Hawke, a former Flight Lieutenant in the RAF who had done a lot of film flying. He flew one of the Mosquitos, plus a Nord 1002, in *633 Squadron* (1964), and was also responsible for bringing five North American B-25 bombers to Britain in 1978 for the filming of *Hanover Street* (1979). He also flew the B-25 camera plane in *Battle of Britain* (1969).

As the explosion clears, the troops spot a single parachute container land about 200 yards away. One British Private, 'Ginger' Marsh (John Salthouse), sees an opportunity to acquire some supplies and runs towards the metal cylinder. Against all the odds, he makes it to the metal tube without getting shot, hoists it onto his shoulder and runs back to the Hartenstein Hotel. He is about halfway back with the canister when a shot rings out and he falls dead. The container bursts open, revealing that it is filled with nothing more than red berets. John Addison's music track for this sequence (which was apparently based on a true incident) is called 'Futile Mission'.

Meanwhile, a large German force has arrived to defend Nijmegen – watched by Major General Ludwig – while back in Arnhem the house commandeered by Colonel Frost is now full of wounded men. The house owner's mother – who clearly is affected by dementia – puts on a hat and goes to call a taxi, only to be promptly cut down by German machine gun fire.

As the situation deteriorates, the British Medical Officer Colonel Weaver (Richard Kane) approaches local resident Kate Ter Horst to ask if her house can be used as a temporary hospital. He is accompanied by Dr Spaander (Laurence Olivier), a fictional character who represents a number of real people. Kate ter Horst readily agrees to the suggestion. As the British soldiers walk into the house, one of them inadvertently steps on a clockwork train, stopping it and hinting at the carnage to come. A similar symbolic trick was used by James Cameron in *The Terminator* (1984), when the titular character destroys a toy truck early in the movie.

Back at Arnhem Bridge, Frost is called upstairs by one of his men. He goes onto the roof, where he sees a German soldier waving a white flag. He has been sent by General Bittrich, who is suggesting a surrender as there is no point in continuing fighting. Major Carlyle answers on Frost's behalf, saying that they (the British) don't have facilities to take them all prisoner, so he will have to decline the offer. The German retreats, looking rather peeved. These lines were originally scripted as dialogue for Anthony Hopkins' character to deliver but, when the real Colonel Frost objected to them, it was agreed that it would be OK if they were spoken by Major Carlyle. News of the British rejection of the surrender offer is given to General Bittrich. Sitting in his staff car, he grimly orders his men to 'flatten Arnhem'.

German Panther tanks roll through the town, destroying buildings as they do so. In a desperate attempt to stop the German advance, Dutch civilians create makeshift barricades from rubble, broken furniture and even dead bodies. Suddenly there is a rifle shot, and a young boy falls dead. It is the underground leader's son we saw earlier in the movie. With tears in his eyes, his father lifts up his dead son and puts him on the barricade as an armoured car appears in the background, twin machine guns firing. Though this scene may appear contrived, it was actually based on fact.

Back at the XXX Corps HQ, Generals Gavin, Horrocks and Browning walk outside as they discuss the tense situation at Nijmegen Bridge. Gavin is in a tetchy mood as he asks for tank support to enable the bridge to be taken, and Horrocks agrees to this. He also requests assault boats to cross the river, and asks if XXX Corps can provide them. Horrocks says he will look into it. Later four trucks carrying boats – a Fordson WOT 6 and three Bedford QLs – are taken out of the XXX Corps column and given priority to move forward.

As dusk falls, Gavin goes to meet with Major Julian Cook (Robert Redford) and briefs him on the mission. He is to lead a river assault by two companies in small boats to capture the north bank of the Rhine adjacent to the bridge at Nijmegen, allowing it to be taken. 'I need someone who is tough enough, experienced enough and dumb enough. Start getting ready', says Gavin. Redford was paid $2m for his relatively brief appearance in the film, but was such a box-office draw at that time that this expenditure was considered worthwhile.

As Major Cook and his men try to sleep, the four trucks containing the boats continue on their journey north. They cross a Bailey Bridge and soon afterwards one of the

Bedford QLs is hit by a shell. The other trucks simply drive round it. The number of available boats has now been reduced by a quarter. In reality, 32 boats took part in the assault.

Furthermore, the delays in getting the boats north has had an impact on the planned assault. It will now have to take place in daylight instead of at night. Gavin and Vandeleur agree that his tanks will provide fire support for the operation, including the laying of a smoke screen.

At dawn, Cook briefs his men. The assault is planned for 10 a.m. but the trucks are delayed by heavy traffic and enemy action, and the operation is put back to noon. Eventually the three trucks finally arrive, and the American paras rush to unload them. They are dismayed to find that the boats are flimsy collapsible craft with plywood bottoms and canvas sides, which will offer no protection from enemy fire.

'What did you expect? Destroyers?' says Cook.

In fact the boats used in the mission were part of the kit for assembling Bailey Bridges and were not specialised assault craft, although this is not explained in the film.

Quickly the American troops carry the boats to the river and jump in. The craft lack outboard motors and don't even have enough oars, so some of the soldiers have to use their rifle butts as paddles (though the craft used in the film actually had concealed engines). From the south bank, Vandeleur's Sherman tanks fire smoke shells to cover the assault, but the wind blows much of the smoke away and the Americans come under attack from German machine guns, mortars and artillery. Some of the boats are sunk and many paras are killed, but enough make it to the north bank to enable them to overrun the enemy positions. Close-up shots were filmed at a specially built outdoor water tank.

Soon the American soldiers have captured the north end of Nijmegen Bridge and start to pull out all the wires they can find. At this point, four British Sherman tanks storm the bridge and start firing at enemy snipers high in the arches using their co-axial Browning 0.303 inch calibre machine guns.

This section of the film isn't entirely accurate. What actually happened was that Major Cook's men captured the Nijmegen *railway* bridge, to the west of the *road* bridge. Soon afterwards the tanks of the Grenadier Guards armoured division captured the road bridge. In 1976 this led to some misreporting in the British press by journalists who had witnessed these scenes being shot and somehow thought that what was being filmed was American paratroopers and British tanks fighting at Arnhem Bridge. Richard Attenborough had to write to the press to correct this misconception. He also deleted a scene where Robert Redford waves on the British tanks.

As the British tanks cross the bridge, Major General Ludwig orders it to be blown but the explosives fail to detonate. There is a 'goof' at this point, as one of the tanks seen crossing the bridge is one of the Leopard/Panther replicas, footage originating from earlier in the movie with the scene of German reinforcements arriving to reinforce Nijmegen. Major General Ludwig is devastated. The Allies are now only 18km from Arnhem, and he can't see how anything can stop them now.

Back in Arnhem, the radios have started working and Frost is finally able to speak to Urquhart. Both men realise they are in a desperate situation as they are short of food, ammunition and medical supplies. The only solution is for the XXX Corps tanks to arrive soon.

The next scene is set just to the north of Nijmegen Bridge as dusk is falling. Four Sherman tanks are parked on the main road as Major Julian Cook remonstrates with an unnamed Major of the Grenadier Guards (John Stride). Cook is furious that the British tanks have stopped for the night and have no intention of moving anywhere. The British Major defends his position, saying that he has no orders to move and that he needs infantry support to proceed further as his tanks will otherwise be picked off easily by German anti-tank guns. The infantry is currently fighting in Nijmegen, and once they arrive he will move on. Cook is not mollified by these comments and points out that his unit had taken 50% casualties capturing the bridge. Why does he have to do everything by the book?

This conversation really happened, but between Captain T. Moffatt Burris of the US 82nd Airborne Division and Captain Peter Carrington of the Guards Armoured Division (who eventually became a Tory MP and Minister in the Thatcher Government, and later a Peer). The incident is recorded as happening at 6.30 p.m. on Wednesday 20 September 1944. Burris became increasingly irate and at one point used a string of expletives, calling Carrington a 'yellow-livered coward', and threatened him with his Thompson submachine gun. Eventually Carrington responded by shutting himself inside his tank to avoid further verbal abuse.

Ever since the war, controversy has raged over whether XXX Corps could have made a greater effort to bash through to Arnhem, particularly as it is now known that the Germans had very few forces between Nijmegen and Arnhem to stop them. Captain Burris has remained unrepentant in his views ever since, particularly as – prior to the river assault – General Horrocks had given him a personal assurance that if he captured the Nijmegen Bridge, XXX Corps would pull out all the stops to get to Arnhem as fast as possible, something which they plainly did not do.

Back in Arnhem, Frost's defensive positions are collapsing. Now wounded, Frost lies in a cellar and asks Major Carlyle why he always carries an umbrella. The Major replies that he always forgot passwords and by carrying one people would know he was English.

As German tanks continue to flatten Arnhem, Frost tells Private Wicks to try and escape as they are now out of ammunition. Later General Bittrich arrives in a staff car to accept Frost's surrender. The British Colonel is clearly exhausted and depressed as Bittrich offers him a bar of chocolate. 'It is good', he says. 'Your aircraft dropped it this morning.'

As Frost's men surrender, the Polish paratroops are dropped south of the river but many of them are killed by massed German machine gun fire as they float to Earth and the survivors are cut off from the main British force. Kate ter Horst's house is now full of wounded men, and she reads from the Bible as Dr Spaander does his best to treat them.

At Elst, just five miles from Arnhem, a British armoured column comes under attack. One Sherman is knocked out and has to be pushed off the road by a bulldozer.

Back in Arnhem, Dr Spaander meets General Urquhart and suggests a brief ceasefire to allow wounded British troops to be treated in German hospitals. At the Polish Airborne Division's HQ on the south bank of the Rhine, a British soldier arrives. He has swam the river to give General Sosabowski a message from Urquhart. He wants the Poles to cross the Rhine to strengthen his forces, who are within a small thumb-shaped defensive perimeter at Oosterbeek with their backs to the river. General Sosabowski agrees and says they will make the crossing that night.

As darkness falls, the Poles attempt to cross the river using rubber boats which are winched across but they are soon detected, a German flare is fired into the sky, and many of the Poles are killed by machine gun fire. The next morning Dr Spaander is driven through Arnhem in a captured British Jeep. He is appalled at the devastation and carnage. It was Richard Attenborough's idea to show the horror of Arnhem through the reactions and facial expressions of the world's greatest actor.

The Dutch doctor is taken for a meeting with Major General Karl Ludwig, who initially declines his request for a ceasefire saying that 'there is a battle and we are in the process of winning'. Spaander replies that 'winning or losing is not a concern; living or dying is'. All he is asking for is a ceasefire of one or two hours, after which the killing can resume. Eventually General Bittrich intervenes and a ceasefire is agreed.

From a church tower just a mile from Arnhem, Generals Browning, Gavin, Horrocks and Sosabowski plus Lieutenant Colonel Vandeleur view the town and consider their options. Vandeleur feels that they should try to bash through to Arnhem, but Horrocks thinks it is now too late and all the remaining airborne troops should be withdrawn. The various officers then give their opinions on what went wrong with the operation. Gavin thinks it was the delay at Nijmegen. Vandeleur believes it was the narrow road leading to Nijmegen, while Horrocks considers that it was the road after Nijmegen and Browning blames the fog. General Sosabowski though, comes up with a different explanation. He says that 'when man decides to play the war game, everyone dies'. His comments are typical of the kind of 'anti-war' speech that bedevilled many war movies of the period.

In Arnhem, General Urquhart is dismayed to learn the decision that has been made but agrees to carry out his orders. The wounded are left behind with some manning radios to maintain the pretence that positions are being occupied. That night, in pouring rain, the surviving British paras cross the Rhine. Some travel in boats while others swim the river.

The next morning Urqhuart arrives at Browning's HQ in Holland looking exhausted and bedraggled. Browning's batman asks him if he would like to change his uniform, but the General declines. This is entirely accurate, as Urquhart wanted him to see how unkempt he looked after his ordeal.

Browning is sympathetic to Urquhart's plight, saying he had done everything he could. 'Did everyone else?' replies Urquhart. Browning then offers Urquhart a bed upstairs, but the General declines the offer. 'I led 10,000 men into Arnhem and came out with 2,000. I don't feel like sleeping.'

Browning then says that Monty is proud and pleased at the outcome and feels the operation was '90% successful', a remark that astonishes Urqhuart. 'What do you think?' he says. Browning concedes that he had told Montgomery that 'we might be going a bridge too far'. This is entirely correct, though it was a remark made *before* the operation, not *after* it.

The final scene of the film shows wounded British soldiers lying in the grounds of the Hartenstein Hotel as Kate ter Horst leaves her house with a handcart piled high with her possessions. Helped by Dr Spaander, she pushes the cart against the skyline as the sun sets and the end titles roll.

The film premiered on 15 June, 1977 and received generally favourable reviews. Although it did well in the UK and

Europe it did not fare well in the USA and made only $50,750,000 in box office receipts set against a budget of $26 million. Similarly, the film won several BAFTA awards but was not even nominated for a single Oscar. The film was criticised for its negative portrayal of British military types and in his autobiography *Hamish: The Story of a Pathfinder* (1989) the film's aviation advisor, Hamish Mahaddie revealed that he asked for his name to be removed from the credits because he was unhappy at the way certain people had been portrayed in the movie.

William Goldman himself felt that the film's relative failure in the USA was because the American public wasn't interested in accuracy (ironically, many critics wrongly believed the film was inaccurate), and of course despite the number of Americans in the cast it was still a British war movie, which the American public generally don't like. Goldman also felt that audiences in the USA were put off by the film's bleak tone. Speaking personally, I prefer this film to *Saving Private Ryan* (1998), which I feel is very sentimental and – apart from the opening sequence – not really set in the real world. *A Bridge Too Far*, in my personal opinion, is the better movie of the two.

The film also re-ignited the controversy about all the things that went wrong with the operation. My own father Dr Peter Barron, who was a Captain in the Royal Army Medical Corps in Belgium at the time of Operation Market Garden, once told me that the main problem was that 'the whole plan was based on the assumption that there would be no resistance'. Both General Urquhart and Colonel Frost later considered that the plan could have worked if the entire assault force had been dropped in one day by asking the RAF to do two lifts on Sunday 17 September, and also by ensuring that all the British and Polish paratroopers were dropped close to Arnhem Bridge. Other military experts have suggested that the operation might have succeeded if the British had taken some Tetrarch light tanks with them, which could have been carried in the Hamilcar gliders. These could have rushed to Arnhem Bridge and held it until Colonel Frost's men arrived. These would have been less vulnerable to ambush than Freddie Gough's Jeeps.

More recently, other historians have postulated that the operation might have succeeded if Colonel Frost's men had used folding bicycles which would have enabled them to reach Arnhem Bridge in just one hour, preventing German reinforcements from crossing the bridge and reaching Nijmegen which would have enabled the XXX Corps tanks to reach them much sooner. The British had developed special folding bicycles for use by airborne troops but – like the Tetrarch tanks – they were not taken on the Arnhem operation.

However, the most recent assessment of Operation Market Garden in Key Publishing's *Arnhem Special* in 2014 concluded that the most important objective of the mission was actually Nijmegen Bridge, which provided a springboard for future offensives into Germany. This makes General Browning's comments about 'going a bridge too far' and Montgomery's view that the campaign was '90% successful' more understandable. Regardless of various military experts' views on the operation's flaws and whether it should even have gone ahead, there is no doubt that *A Bridge Too Far* is one of the greatest war movies ever made.

A Bridge Too Far (1977) Production Credits

Production Team
Director: Richard Attenborough
Screenplay: William Goldman
Original Book: Cornelius Ryan

Cast
Underground Leader: Siem Vroom
Underground Leader's Wife: Marlies Van Alcmaer
Underground Leader's Son: Erik Van't Wout
Field Marshal Gerd Von Rundstedt: Wolfgang Preiss
General Gunther Blumentritt: Hans Von Borsody
Café Waitress: Josephine Peeper
Lt General Frederick Browning: Dirk Bogarde
Major General Maxwell Taylor: Paul Maxwell
Major General Roy Urquhart: Sean Connery
Brigadier General James M. Gavin: Ryan O'Neal
Major General Stanislaw Sosabowski: Gene Hackman
Field Marshal Walther Model: Walter Kohut
Captain 'Harry' Bestebreurtje: Peter Faber
German Sentry: Hartmut Becker
Major Fuller: Frank Grimes
RAF Briefing Officer: Jeremy Kemp
Lt. Col MacKenzie: Donald Pickering
Brigadier Lathbury: Donald Douglas
Lieutenant Cole: Peter Settelen
Major Steele: Stephen Moore
Lt General Brian Horrocks: Edward Fox
Lt. Col. J.O.E. Vandeleur: Michael Caine
Lt. Col. Giles Vandeleur: Michael Byrne
Lt Col. John Frost: Anthony Hopkins
Private Wicks: Paul Copley
Captain Glass: Nicholas Campbell
Staff Sergeant Eddie Dohun: James Caan
Colonel Sims: Gerald Sim
US Private: Harry Ditson
Organist: Erik Chitty
Vicar: Brian Hawksley
Corporal Hancock: Colin Farrell
Major Carlyle: Christopher Good
Private Morgan: Norman Gregory
Corporal Davies: Alun Armstrong
Private Dodds: Antony Milner
Private Clark: Barry McCarthy
Sergeant Matthias: Lex Van Delden

Lt General William Bittrich: Maximilliam Scnell
Field Marshal Model's Aide: Michael Wolf
Major General Karl Ludwig: Hardy Kruger
Irish Guards Lieutenant: Sean Mathias
German Private: Tim Beekman
British Padre: Edward Seckerson
Kate ter Horst: Liv Ullman
Jan ter Horst: Tom Van Beek
Dutch Villagers: Bertus Botterman, Henny Alma
Colonel Stout: Elliott Gould
US Radio Operator: Ray Jewers
British Radio Operator: Geoffrey Hinsliff
Lt. Cornish: Keith Drinkel
Old Dutch Lady: Mary Smithuysen
Her Son: Hans Croiset
Captain Grabner: Fred Williams
German Lieutenant: John Peel
Sergeant Clegg: John Judd
Trooper Binns: Ben Cross
British Medical Officer: Hilary Minster
Private Andrews: David English
Sergeant Towns: Ben Howard
Captain Cleminson: Michael Graham Cox
Elderly Dutch Couple: Johnan te Slaa, Georgette Reyevski
Young Dutch Couple: Pieter Groenier, Adrienne Kleiweg
RAF Met Officer: Denholm Elliott
US Sergeant: Peter Gordon
US Medical Colonel: Arthur Hill
Lt. Rafferty: Garrick Hagon
US Engineer: Brian Gwaspari
Grenadier Guards Lieutenant: Stephen Rayment
British Corporal: Tim Morand
Private Gibbs: James Wadroper
Colonel Barker: Neil Kennedy
Private 'Ginger' Marsh: John Salthouse
Glider Pilot: Jonathan Hackett
Regimental Sergeant Major: Stanley Lebor
Private Galloway: Jack Vincent
Private Long: Milton Cadman
'Taffy' Brace: David Auker
Doctor Spaander: Laurence Olivier
Colonel Weaver: Richard Kane
Private Stephenson: Toby Salaman
British Staff Colonel: Michael Bangerter
Grenadier Guards Colonel: Philip Raymond
Boat Truck Driver: Myles Reithermann
Major Julian Cook: Robert Redford
US Captain: Anthony Pullen
US Padre: John Morton
US Lieutenant: John Ratzenberger
German Lieutenant: Patrick Ryecart
Captain Krafft: Dick Rienstra
Sergeant Whitney: Ian Liston
Private Gordon: Paul Rattee

Sergeant Tomblin: Mark Sheridan
Sergeant MacDonald: George Innes
Grenadier Guards Major: John Stride
British Medical Orderlies: Niall Padden, Michael Graves
Private Simmonds: Simon Chandler
Private Archer: Edward Kalinski
Corporal Robbins: Shaun Curry
Sergeant Treadwell: Sebastian Abineri
Corporal Merrick: Chris Williams
Flute Player: Andrew Branch
British Staff Major: Anthony Garner
Dutch Priest: Feliks Aron
Soldiers: Stuart Blake, Ray Boyd, Stephen Churchett, Jon Croft, Patrick Dickson, Adrian Gibbs, Jason Gregory, Stewart Guidotti, Patrick Hannaway, Brian Haughton, Anthony Howden, David Killick, Dan Long, Gerald Martin, Edward McDermott, Tony McHale, Jack McKenzie, Francis Mughan, Ricard Ommanney, Peter Quince, Robin Scobey, Farrell Sheridan, James Snell, Michael Stock, David Stockton, Paul Vaughan-Teague, Jason White, Mark York
German Officer (uncredited): Anthony Robb
Colonel Frost's Aide: Frank Jarvis

Producers
Producers: Joseph E. Levine, Richard P. Levine
Associate Producer: John Palmer
Co-producer: Michael Stanley-Evans

Music
Music: John Addison

Cinematography
Cinematography: Geoffrey Unsworth
Film Editing: Antony Gibbs

Production and Design
Casting: Miriam Brickman
Production Design: Terence Marsh
Art Direction: Stuart Craig, Roy Stannard, Alan Tomkins
Costume Design: Antony Mendleson

Makeup Department
Chief Hairdresser: Ronnie Cogan
Makeup Supervisor: Tom Smith
Makeup Artists: Ernest Gasser, Nick Maley

Production Management
Production Manager: Terence A. Clegg
Production Manager (Second Unit): Richard Bamber

Unit Manager: Grania O'Shannon
Production Supervisor: Eric Rattray

Second Unit Director or Assistant Director
Assistant Directors: Roy Button, Steve Lanning, Geoffrey Ryan, Peter Waller
Assistant Director (Second Unit): Bert Batt
First Assistant Director: David Tomblin
Second Assistant Director: Andy Armstrong
Second Unit Director: Sydney Hayers

Art Department
Construction Manager: Peter Dukelow
Set Dresser: Peter Howitt
Production Buyer: John Lanzer
Property Master: Jack Towns
Sketch Artist: Michael White
Standby Painter: Michael Guyett
Drapesman: Chris Seddon

Sound Department
Sound Editor: Peter Horrocks
Dubbing Mixer: Gerry Humphreys
Sound Recordist: Simon Kaye
Dubbing Mixer: Robin O'Donoghue
Sound Boom Operator: David Stephenson
Sound Editor: Les Wiggins

Special Effects
Special Effects Supervisor: John Richardson
Special Effects Technicians: Ron Cartwright, John Evans, David Harris
Special Effects Coordinator: George Gibbs
Supervisor (Second Unit): Ian Wingrove

Visual Effects
Optical Effects: Wally Veevers

Stunts
Stunt Arranger: Alf Joint
Assistant Stunt Arranger: Vic Armstrong
Stuntmen: Roy Alon, Joe Amsler, Vic Armstrong, Dickey Beer, Marc Boyle, George Lane Cooper, Jim Dowdall, Joe Dunne, Stuart Fell, Nick Hobbs, Billy Horrigan, Alf Joint, George Leech, Valentino Musetti, Doug Robinson, Tony Smart, Alan Stuart, Rocky Taylor, Michael Turk, Chris Webb, Henry Weissenman, Bill Weston, Jason White
Stunt Driver: Rick Lester
Stunt Double (Ryan O'Neal): Gregory Hodal
Stunt Double (Robert Redford): Paul Weston

Camera & Electrical Dept
Clapper Loader: Steve Barron
Camera Grip: Frank Batt
Aerial Photography: Robin Browne
Camera Operator (Second Unit): Wally Byatt
Camera Assistant: John Campbell
Second Aerial Camera Operator: John Cardiff
Chief Rigger: Nobby Clarke
Second Camera Operator: Ken Coles
Electrical Supervisor: Jack Conroy
Camera Operator (Second Unit): Lou Lavelly
Camera Operator: Peter MacDonald
Parachute Cameramen: John Partington-Smith, Dave Waterman
Still Photographer: Bob Penn
Lighting Cameraman (Second Unit): Harry Waxman
Set Photographer (Second Unit): Frank Connor
Lighting Technician: John Fenner
Additional Photography: Geoff Glover

Costume and Wardrobe Department
Wardrobe Master: John Hilling
Wardrobe Mistress: Margaret Lewin

Editorial Department
Colorist: Chris Lamie
Assistant Editors: Brian Mann, Chris Blunden

Location Management
Location Manager: Norton Knatchbull

Music Department
Conductor: John Addison

Transportation Department
Military Vehicle Co-ordinator: Charles Mann

Miscellaneous Crew
Armourer: Bill Aylmore
Title Design: Joe Caroff
Production Assistant: Sheila Collins
Military Advisors: Major General John Frost, General James M. Gavin, Frank A. Gregg, Lt. General Sir Brian Horrocks, Brigadier J.O.E. Vandeleur, Colonel J.L. Waddy, Major General R.E. Urquhart, Brian L. Davis
Production Assistant: Judy Humphreys, Dena Vincent
Production Consultant: Gabriel Katzka
Presenter: Joseph E. Levine
Chief Technical Advisor: Kathryn Morgan Ryan
Production Accountant: Arthur Tarry

Dutch Liaison: Cornelius Van Eijk
Continuity: Connie Willis
Production Runner: Matthew Binns

Meteorological Advisor: Peter Davies
Marine Coordinator: Michael Turk

A STEVEN SPIELBERG FILM
tom hanks
saving private ryan
edward burns matt damon tom sizemore
the mission is a man.
DREAMWORKS PICTURES AND PARAMOUNT PICTURES PRESENT
AN AMBLIN ENTERTAINMENT PRODUCTION IN ASSOCIATION WITH MUTUAL FILM COMPANY TOM HANKS "SAVING PRIVATE RYAN"
EDWARD BURNS MATT DAMON TOM SIZEMORE BONNIE CURTIS AND ALLISON LYON SEGAN JOHN WILLIAMS
JOANNA JOHNSTON MICHAEL KAHN, A.C.E. TOM SANDERS JANUSZ KAMINSKI, A.S.C.
STEVEN SPIELBERG & IAN BRYCE AND MARK GORDON & GARY LEVINSOHN ROBERT RODAT
STEVEN SPIELBERG

10

SAVING PRIVATE RYAN

(1998)

*Paramount Pictures/DreamWorks Pictures/
Amblin Entertainment/Mutual Film Company*

Director: Steven Spielberg
Producers: Ian Bryce, Mark Gordon,
Gary Levinsohn and Steven Spielberg
Screenwriter: Robert Rodat

S*AVING Private Ryan* is an epic war film set during the invasion of Normandy in June 1944. Unlike the earlier movie *The Longest Day* (1962), it does not attempt to be a comprehensive account of Operation Overlord. Instead, the first 27 minutes of the film deals with the landings on Omaha Beach, an operation which nearly ended in disaster for the US Forces involved. The middle section of the film deals with an American patrol's search for the elusive Private Ryan, whose three brothers have all died in action, and the last part of the film is a bit like *The Alamo* (1960) and *Sahara* (1943), in which a group of soldiers hold a position against overwhelming odds. The film is best remembered for its highly realistic battle scenes and its unflinching depiction of violence, which influenced many subsequent productions such as *Black Hawk Down* and *Pearl Harbor* (both 2001). It was also one of the first movies to use 'washed out' colour, a stylistic trend which has even been employed in other genres, including recent James Bond movies such as *Spectre* (2015).

The film started life in 1994 as a script by Robert Rodat. The plot concerned Private James Francis Ryan being removed from combat duties in Normandy when his three brothers die in action. The storyline was based on a number of true incidents – including that of the Niland brothers – and followed a ruling by US President Franklin D. Roosevelt that, if a family lost more than two sons in combat, any remaining siblings should be brought home. Roosevelt's decision was a result of the case involving the five Sullivan brothers, all serving on the cruiser *USS Juneau*, who were lost in action off Guadacanal in November 1942. Incidentally, this true story was itself made into a film – *The Sullivans* (aka *The Fighting Sullivans*) – in 1944.

Rodat's script was sent to producer Mark Gordon who passed it on to Steven Spielberg, regarded as one of the world's greatest film directors. Spielberg had a lifelong fascination with WW2, which was at least in part due to his father Arnold's experiences during the war when he had served as a radio operator in USAAF North American B-25 aircraft in Burma and India. At age 16 the young Spielberg had made his first war movie *Escape to Nowhere* in the Californian desert. Another of his early amateur productions was *Fighter Squadron* which used abandoned WW2 fighters at Sky Harbor Airport in Phoenix, plus stock gun camera footage which the teenage Spielberg purchased at his local drugstore.

Spielberg decided that the film was to be as authentic as possible and so shooting it in the USA was not an option. It was also impossible to use the real Omaha Beach because of the huge memorial at the site, plus a lot of modern redevelopment which included a power station, so another location had to be found.

Spielberg originally intended to film the Omaha Beach sequences in Sheringham, Norfolk, but that was ruled out as well after John Major's Government and the Ministry of Defence proved uncooperative, particularly regarding the provision of extras from the Regular and Territorial Armies.

Eventually the producers opted to film the Omaha beach sequences in the Republic of Ireland, which offered a number of incentives to filmmakers. A number of major film productions had been shot there including Mel Gibson's *Braveheart* (1995) and two war movies, *The Blue Max* (1966) and *The McKenzie Break* (1970). The Irish Army was more than happy to assist the film-makers, and 850 reservists plus civilian battle re-enactors played American and German soldiers.

The location chosen to represent Omaha was Ballinesker Beach, Curracloe Strand, Ballinesker just east of Curracloe, County Wexford, Ireland. The topography was similar to that at Omaha, as the wide sandy beach was overlooked by grassy high ground on which German pillboxes could be built. Replica beach defences were installed along the waterline plus acres of fake barbed wire, which was made from rubber to avoid causing injuries to the actors.

A large bunker made out of wood and plaster was built on the site, based on an accurate model built by Tom Sanders in Hollywood, and various machine guns and artillery pieces were installed as part of the beach defences. These were supplied by Steve Lamonby of Plus Film Services and included a Skoda 105mm artillery piece, MG 42 machine guns and a German 20mm Flak 38 weapon.

One problem was finding enough period landing craft. At one point the producers considered building new vessels for the film, but suitable boats were eventually found. Two British LCMs (Landing Craft Mechanised) were discovered in the Boston Boatyard in Oreston, Plymouth, and were restored to correct WW2 configuration by former Royal Marine James Wakefield. For the film these wore the codes PA30-10 and PA30-31 indicating they were from the US troopship APA 30, the *Thomas Jefferson*. Ten of the smaller LCVP (Landing Craft Vehicle/Personnel) were located, sitting in the desert in Palm Springs, and were shipped to the UK where they were reconditioned for use in the film by Robin Davies' team from Square Sail in St Austell, Cornwall. In addition, a derelict landing craft was patched up so it could be blown up in certain scenes, while a section of one was constructed for use in underwater sequences shot in a water tank. A Russian civilian vessel based in Scotland was also acquired specifically to land tanks on the beach, although this ship doesn't appear in the final cut of the film.

A large number of period military vehicles were employed in the production including Willis MB Jeeps, M3 halftracks, GMC 'Deuce and a half' trucks and Dodge weapons carriers. Two genuine M4 Sherman tanks were sourced and fitted with mock-up deep wading snorkels for a scene where American armour lands on Omaha Beach, but this footage was deleted from the final cut of the film which only includes a brief glimpse of a single Sherman at the end of the movie.

Various German military vehicles were also sourced for the film including an Opel Blitz truck, a Horch staff car, five motorcycle-sidecar combinations, three Kettenrad motorcycle-halftracks and an Sd.Kfz. 251 halftrack. (A full listing of the vehicles used in the film can be found in Appendix III at the end of this book.)

As had been the case with *A Bridge Too Far* (1977), it proved impossible to find any genuine wartime German tanks in running condition. However, the script called for a tank assault on Captain Miller's squad in the final section of the movie. The solution was to build replicas of German armoured vehicles using readily available types.

Art Director Alan Tomkins, who had previously worked on many classic British war films including *The Heroes of Telemark* (1965), *Battle of Britain* (1969), *A Bridge Too Far* (1977) and *Memphis Belle* (1990), had designed a replica Russian T-54 tank – using a British Alvis Saracen armoured car – for the Bond film *GoldenEye* (1995). Tomkins originally thought that a T-55 could be used to create a reproduction of a German Tiger I tank, but was informed that the earlier T34/85 would be a better base vehicle as it had the same barrel height as a Tiger and its all-round dimensions were slightly smaller than the German vehicle, making it ideal for conversion.

Eventually Steve Lamonby and his team from Plus Film Services – working from drawings made by Tomkins – built two replica Tiger Is over a wooden framework applied to the Russian tanks. Much assistance was provided by the Tank Museum at Bovington in Dorset, who allowed detailed photos and measurements to be taken of their preserved example – Tiger 131, which had been captured by British forces after being disabled by a British Churchill tank in Tunisia in 1943.

As a result the two mock Tigers were near-perfect in every detail. The only feature of the Tiger which couldn't be replicated was its roadwheels. A real Tiger has interleaved, overlapping roadwheels, while the film reproductions had the spaced roadwheels of a T34.

If you have read the chapter on *Kelly's Heroes* (1970) in this book, you will know that the three Tigers used in that film were also created using T34/85 tanks, resulting in incorrect reports on the internet that the Tiger replicas in *Saving Private Ryan* were the same ones used in the earlier film. This is not true, and the fate of the three *Kelly's Heroes* Tigers is unknown.

The screenplay also called for two Marder III self-propelled guns. One was built specially for the film by Steve Lamonby using the chassis of a Panzer 38 (t) found in Czechoslovakia, while the second was a cosmetically-modified Swedish SAVM/43 self-propelled 105mm gun which also used the Panzer 38 (t) chassis. The Panzer 38 (t) was a German adaptation of a pre-war Czech tank manufactured by Skoda. Large numbers were captured when the Germans invaded Czechoslovakia in 1939, and were used by the Wehrmacht during the Blitzkrieg in 1940. Although the tank soon became obsolete, the chassis was used in a number of German self-propelled guns including the Marder III.

About 2,000 historically accurate firearms were used in the production, including M1 Garand rifles, M1 carbines, Thompson submachine guns and BAR (Browning Automatic Rifles). 500 of them could fire blanks, while the remaining 1,500 were lightweight rubber replicas which could be carried by extras. As few original uniforms from the 1940s existed, thousands of new ones were created by various manufacturers and then artificially aged to give a correct worn-in look.

The musical score for the film was composed by Spielberg's long-time collaborator, John Williams, and at the director's request there was no music during the battle scenes which make up a considerable portion of the movie. This makes an interesting comparison with *The Guns of Navarone* (1961), in which only ten minutes of screen time lack music.

Tom Hanks was cast in the key role of Captain Miller. Oher actors who were considered for the role were Harrison Ford and Mel Gibson. Private Ryan was played by Matt Damon, who at that time was relatively unknown. Later, Damon was to achieve worldwide fame through the series of Jason Bourne movies starting with *The Bourne Identity* (2002). The other seven members of Miller's rescue squad consisted of Sergeant Horvath (Tom Sizemore), Corporal Upham (Jeremy Davies), Tech/4 Wade (Giovanni Ribisi), Private Caparzo (Vin Diesel), Private Jackson (Barry Pepper), Private Mellish (Adam Goldberg) and Private Reiben (Edward Burns).

All the actors playing Miller's eight-man rescue team attended a ten-day 'boot camp' prior to the start of filming, run by former US Marine Dale Dye who also appears in the film as an officer in the War Department casualty section. Dye ran a company called Warriors Inc. and forced the actors to live under canvas, eat army rations and do intensive training, including weapons handling. Matt Damon was deliberately excluded from this course so that the other actors would feel resentment towards him (which they did).

Apart from the Omaha Beach sequences, most of the film was made in a huge outdoor set which had been created at the former British Aerospace factory and airfield at Hatfield. During WW2 the facility had been owned by the De Havilland Company which built the famous wooden Mosquito bomber. Hatfield's large grounds were also the location for Dale Dye's 'boot camp'. This outdoor set, which included a fake river and bridge, was used to depict two different ruined French villages – Ramelle and Neuville.

The former British Aerospace offices at Hatfield appear in the film as the War Department casualty section in Washington. while the director's suite on the first floor became General Marshall's office. The huge building at Hatfield became a temporary studio, with the former aircraft hangars in particular being used to store vehicles and equipment.

The budget was set at $70m, with $11m set aside for the Omaha Beach sequences. The film was shot in just 59 days in the summer of 1997, which was a remarkably short time compared with other epics such as *Battle of Britain* (1969) and *A Bridge Too Far* (1977) which both took about six months to film.

The film opens with simple white titles on a black background, followed by a close-up of the American flag fluttering in the wind. An elderly man (Harrison Young) wearing a light blue casual zipper jacket, polo shirt and grey slacks walks along a path in a cemetery, closely followed by his wife and family members. Beside the US flag, a French tricolour is blowing in the wind. It is a dull, overcast day.

The location is the cemetery for the American war dead near Omaha Beach in Normandy, France, and the date is the present day (1998). The old man stops at one particular tombstone and falls to his knees as we see a shot of hundreds of white crosses. At this point we can't see the name on this particular gravestone as the camera zooms in on the man's eyes. The picture then morphs to a close-up of Captain Miller's eyes as he commands a company of US Rangers heading towards Omaha Beach on 6 June 1944. Spielberg's camera moves suggests that the old man is an aged Captain Miller, but all is not as it seems as we will discover later.

Captain Miller takes a swig of water from his canteen as soldiers around him vomit profusely with seasickness. Miller's right hand is shaking because of the stress of the situation. Within minutes he could be dead or seriously wounded.

As the boat prepares to land, one Private kisses his crucifix. Suddenly the ramp at the front of the boat drops and the soldiers rush forward. Almost immediately many of them are killed by murderous fire from well-sited German MG 42 machine guns, while others find themselves in deep water. They are not even safe underwater, as some of the machine gun rounds go under the surface and hit them. These underwater sequences were filmed in a specially-built water tank at the Hatfield location and included a mock-up of the bottom of a landing craft. However, there is a goof here as the water tank looks at least ten feet deep whereas the water depth at that point on the shore was no greater than chest height – if it was really as deep as shown then how could most of the troops have managed to wade ashore? It has also been scientifically proven that bullets that hit the surface and then travel underwater are no longer dangerous as they slow down so much. Despite the historical and scientific inaccuracies of this scene, it was shamelessly copied by director Michael Bay for the strafing sequences in *Pearl Harbor* (2001).

Despite the intense fire, most of the troops make it ashore. Some carry their rifles in clear plastic bags to keep them dry. Steven Spielberg wondered if this might be an anachronism as he believed plastic bags didn't exist in 1944, but period photos of the real operation show some troops carrying their weapons in transparent bags though the material would have been a form of cellophane rather than polythene.

Troops continue to swarm ashore but many are killed or wounded by bullets, mines and artillery shells. Some of the soldiers lose arms and legs. These highly realistic shots were achieved by using 30 real amputees who were fitted with fake silicone limbs which could then be blown off. One soldier is lying close to death with his intestines hanging out. Another soldier is carrying a flamethrower and is burned alive when his fuel tank is hit (something that has also been proven to be a scientific impossibility). The noise of the explosions and gunfire temporarily deafens Miller, who hears a ringing sound in his ears.

Many of these scenes were shot by Spielberg himself using a hand-held camera without any advance storyboarding. Spielberg simply pretended he was a newsreel cameraman at Omaha and filmed whatever caught his attention. Cinematographer Janusz Kaminski employed a 90 degree shutter for these scenes to produce a staccato effect. In addition, a vibrating image shaker was applied to the camera and the protective coating was removed from the camera lenses to soften the image. Finally, the film was desaturated by a bleaching process in post-production, resulting in the colour saturation being reduced by 60%. This gave the footage a unique period feel. Spielberg's intention was that the film should look like faded colour newsreel footage from 1944, a technique that has since been copied by many other directors.

Miller realises the only way for his Company to escape total annihilation is to move forward closer to the seawall where they can shelter in hollows and gain some protection from enemy fire. He asks his radio operator to send a message to the effect that the first wave of troops has been ineffective, they don't hold the beach, and that no DD tanks have made it ashore.

The DD tank was an amphibious version of the M4 Sherman which floated by means of a flimsy vertical canvas screen which was erected around the hull, and propelled itself in the water using two screws driven by the engine. The main snag of the DD tank was that it could only be used safely in calm waters, as a single large wave could swamp the vehicle and cause it to sink. At Omaha Beach the DD tanks were launched too far out to sea and in rough conditions. As a result most of them sunk and only a few reached the shore. However, some DD tanks did get ashore and some others – plus a number of standard Shermans – were eventually landed on the beach by flat-bottomed craft.

At the eastern end, two out of 29 DD Shermans which were launched at sea managed to get ashore, while three more were landed directly on the beach. In addition, 16 standard (non-DD) Shermans were landed at Omaha. At the western end, 29 DD Shermans and 14 standard Shermans were landed directly on the beach.

Though many of these tanks were subsequently knocked out by German anti-tank guns, the film gives the incorrect impression that the troops landing on Omaha were completely devoid of armoured support. Some British historians (such as Max Hastings) have suggested that the Americans would have suffered fewer casualties at Omaha if they had used the full range of specialized armoured vehicles developed by the British and known as 'Hobart's Funnies', but other experts disagree on this point as they insist that such vehicles would have been less useful at Omaha than they were on the other invasion beaches. Another error in the film is that no DUKWs are seen at Omaha, but this is purely due to the fact that – with the change in filming locations – it wasn't possible to hire these vehicles at short notice.

One soldier is hit in the helmet by a German bullet and survives. As he takes off his headgear another bullet strikes his head, killing him. Army Medics do their best to attend to the many casualties as other soldiers bring up Bangalore Torpedoes to blow up the barbed wire. Quickly they fit the tubular sections of the explosive device together, attach the detonation cable and explode the barbed wire which is blocking their path. The soldiers now charge forward to a sheltered position below the pillboxes. From this safe location, Miller attaches a small mirror to a bayonet, using chewing gum, and views the German defences without exposing himself to enemy fire. He can now direct a coordinated attack on the enemy strongpoints.

Private Reiben uses his BAR (Browning Automatic Rifle) to fire a few bursts at a sandbagged machine gun nest, while Private Jackson kills the remaining Germans in that position with his Springfield M1903A4 sniper rifle. With the defences immediately in front of them neutralised, the Rangers advance up the hill and attack the bunkers from behind. German soldiers running out the rear entrances of the pillboxes are shot without mercy, grenades are thrown inside, and – to finish them off – a flamethrower is used to torch the inside of the bunker. Having taken substantial casualties, the Americans are in no mood to show leniency to their opponents, and are delighted to see their adversaries being roasted alive. Some blazing German bodies fall out the slit of the bunker and land on the ground, while two Germans who are trying to surrender are shot.

Sergeant Horvath takes out a cylindrical metal tin with a screw top, labelled 'France', and puts some sand in it. In his pack he already has a number of tins of soil, each labelled with countries he has served in during the war such as 'Italy' and 'Sicily'. Miller takes a drink from his canteen as he looks at the shoreline. 'Quite a view', he says as the camera does a close-up on his eyes. Bodies are strewn along the shoreline and on the beach, accompanied by a lot of dead fish. These were highly convincing silicone dummies made from body casts of real people. For a moment the camera lingers on one soldier who is lying face down in the bloodstained surf. The lettering on his backpack reads 'Ryan S.'

In the US Army Casualty Office in Washington, a large number of typists are composing letters informing next-of-kin that their sons have been lost in combat. One eagle-eyed secretary spots something that needs to be passed on to her superior. Private Sean Ryan has just died at Omaha Beach. His brother Peter has been killed at Utah Beach, and another sibling – Daniel – has been killed in action in New Guinea. There is a fourth brother who is with the 101st Airborne in Normandy and – following the case involving the five Sullivan brothers who were all killed in action – it is the policy of the War Department that the surviving sibling (in this case James Francis Ryan) must be brought home.

Later, in Iowa an olive green US Army Buick staff car winds its way up a road towards the Ryan farmhouse. This shot was filmed at Tan Hill Farm at West Kennett, just south of Avebury. Both the farmhouse and the adjacent barn were two-dimensional plywood cut-outs designed by Art Director Alan Tomkins. The only section of this set which was built in three dimensions was the front porch. Mrs Ryan (Amanda Boxer) is washing the dishes when she sees the car approaching and has a good idea what this means. The car stops outside her front porch and a US Army officer and a priest get out to deliver the devastating news in the form of three telegrams. The woman slumps on her doorway in shock.

Back in Washington, General George Marshall (Harve Presnell), the US Army's Chief of Staff, is apprised of the situation. He recognises that it is vital that an attempt is made to find Private James Ryan, but an officer points out that he could be anywhere in Normandy and a rescue mission may not be feasible. Marshall is unmoved though, and reads out a letter that someone else had sent to a mother who had lost five sons in battle. He concludes by revealing that the writer was none other than former US President Abraham Lincoln. This well-known 'Bixby letter' was an unscripted addition by Steven Spielberg, and was an actual letter allegedly sent by President Abraham Lincoln to Lydia Parker Bixby who was thought to have lost her five sons during the American Civil War. Historians have since questioned the veracity of this famous document since at least two of Bixby's sons survived the war, and the letter may actually have been written by Lincoln's assistant private secretary, John Hay.

'The boy's alive. We're going to find him', announces General Marshall.

In Normandy it is now 'D-Day plus three' (June 9) and the Americans have consolidated their position on Omaha Beach. Thousands of troops and vehicles are streaming ashore. Landing Craft Tanks (LCT's) are discharging hundreds of tanks and trucks directly onto the shore while an armada of naval vessels lies just out to sea, protected by a forest of barrage balloons (an excellent digital matte shot by Industrial Light and Magic).

A Rangers officer is wet-shaving as Captain Miller patiently waits to speak to him. Coffee is poured and a thick, bully-beef sandwich sits on a plate awaiting consumption. Miller then briefs the officer on the current situation using a map. His men have destroyed several German 88mm gun emplacements, which had previously accounted for some Sherman tanks and 'Deuce-and-a-half' GMC trucks. His unit had sustained some casualties though – 35 dead and two wounded.

The Rangers officer then tells Ryan that he has another assignment for him – to find Private James Francis Ryan, whose location is presently unknown. Miller briefs Sergeant Horvath about the task and then chooses another six soldiers to accompany them on the mission. Their initial destination will be Neuville.

The squad sets off across open country on foot. Originally the eight-man team was to travel in a Jeep towing a trailer but, after shooting considerable footage using these vehicles, director Steven Spielberg elected to have them execute their mission on foot. One short scene showing the squad travelling by Jeep and trailer does survive in the final cut of the movie.

Miller's team make their way across the damp Normandy countryside and end up marching in heavy rain. This shot was filmed at Screen in the Irish Republic, a few miles inland from the Omaha Beach set. Eventually the squad makes their way to the wrecked village of Neuville, which has only been partially liberated by US troops. A contingent of Germans is hiding amongst the destroyed buildings, blaring out crude propaganda from loudspeakers, such as 'the Statue of Liberty is kaput'. Miller deploys his men to counter the German forces in the town, but Private Caparzo is hit by a sniper and slowly bleeds to death. Private Jackson locates the enemy sniper. Both eyeball each other through their telescopic sights but Jackson fires first and puts a round through his opponent's sight. The German dies instantly. This scene was inspired by the real-life exploits of US Marine sniper Carlos Hatchcock, who achieved 93 kills in Vietnam and reportedly killed a North Vietnamese sniper by putting a bullet through his opponent's telescopic sight. Hatchcock was also one of the inspirations for the character of Martin Riggs in *Lethal Weapon* (1986).

Miller's squad advances through the town. Abandoned German equipment, including a Horch Staff car and a 20mm cannon, is strewn everywhere as Miller collects Caparzo's dog tag. As the US troops rest they knock over a heavy wooden beam which hits an exterior wall of a building, causing it to collapse, revealing several German troops. For a few seconds the two groups of soldiers gaze at each other in amazement before the Americans open fire, killing all the enemy troops.

Later, Miller finds a soldier called James Francis Ryan (Nathan Fillion), and gives him the bad news that his brothers are all dead. Ryan is traumatized but then reveals that his brothers were still at school. Miller asks a few more questions and soon discovers that he has got the wrong Private Ryan, as the one he is speaking to is from Minnesota, not Iowa. The soldier he is looking for is from Baker Company of the 506th Parachute Infantry Regiment, part of the 101st Airborne Division.

Miller discusses the current situation with Captain Hamill (Ted Danson) who is concerned that Caen has not yet been taken despite it being earmarked for capture by the British on the first day of the invasion. He then makes a disparaging comment about General Bernard Montgomery, saying that 'that guy is overrated'. This comment did not go down well with British veterans of the Normandy campaign, who complained that the film implied that the D-Day invasion was purely an American affair. Apart from this one snide remark, British, Canadian and French forces are not mentioned at any point in *Saving Private Ryan.*

There are no functioning hotels in the destroyed French town, so Miller suggests his squad rest in the church for three hours before setting off again. He talks to T/Sgt Horvath and reveals that to date he has lost 94 men who were under his command, but that perhaps that sacrifice had saved twenty times that number. 'That's when you start to rationalize', he says. A moment later Miller is sound asleep, and his men are astonished at his ability to take a nap under combat conditions.

The next morning the squad sets off on foot across the French countryside. There is a continuity error at this point, as eight soldiers are seen; there should only be seven, as Caparzo has been killed. Soon Miller's men come across a field which is strewn with wrecked American WACO CG-4A gliders. All have been damaged by anti-invasion poles which have been erected to deter landings by glider. Six WACO replicas were built for the film using a surviving example in the Museum of Army Flying at Middle Wallop as a template. One glider contains the body of a dead Brigadier General in his Jeep, and Miller learns that the disaster was caused by the fitment of armour plate in the floor of the glider. Though it protected the officer from flak, it made the glider too heavy, causing it to become uncontrollable and crash. 22 men had died in the resulting accident, and the WACO pilot hands over all the dog tags for Miller's men to examine. But James Francis Ryan isn't among the dead.

Miller speaks to one of the 101st Airborne Division troops to find out if he knows Ryan, but the soldier is temporarily deaf due to a German grenade exploding next to his head so Ryan has to write his questions down on a pad. He discovers that James Francis Ryan was in a detachment from the 101st which missed their drop zone by 20 miles. He is believed to be in the area of the crucial (and fictional) Ramelle Bridge, which must be held to prevent German armoured divisions from launching a successful counter-attack against the advancing Americans.

Later, Miller's squad heads across open country and comes across a damaged German radar station which is defended by several troops in a sandbagged MG 42 machine gun post. This scene was shot in Thame Park in Oxfordshire. Miller decides to knock out the machine gun nest, but Privates Mellish and Reiben are aghast at this decision as they feel they are taking an unnecessary risk since they could simply bypass the installation and proceed with their mission.

Nonetheless, Miller's men obey their orders and bravely attack the radar station, but things don't go to plan. Some of the grenades chucked by Miller's men are picked up and thrown back at them, and Tech/4 Wade receives massive abdominal wounds and dies.

All the Germans are killed except for one (Joerg Stadler), who is captured. Shaking with fear, he pleads for his life to be spared, saying that he loves America. He mentions Betty Grable and does an impersonation of 'Steamboat Willie' (from this point in the script this soldier is referred to by that name). Incidentally, *Steamboat Willie* (1928) was a short Walt Disney animated film which featured the debut of Mickey Mouse.

'Steamboat Willie' even denounces Hitler in an attempt to placate his captives, and says he is sorry about the death of Wade. Miller doesn't have the facilities to take him prisoner and is too humane to shoot him so he blindfolds him and orders him to walk towards the Allied lines where he can surrender.

There are now only six men left in the squad and some start to question the futility of the mission, particularly Reiben who threatens to quit. But T/Sgt Horvath pulls a gun on him, and Miller in turn reveals that he used to be a teacher of English Composition in civilian life. Eventually the members of the squad back down and agree to continue with their mission.

Some time later, the squad of six soldiers is marching through a field when Miller hears the unmistakable sound of an armoured vehicle. The US troops take cover as a German Sd. Kfz.251 halftrack trundles into view. It has only gone a few yards when there is a small explosion against the left side of its hull. About twenty seconds later the engine compartment explodes; there is a ball of orange flame, and the vehicle comes to a halt. Several German soldiers spill out of the halftrack and are gunned down by Miller's men. Miller wonders who was responsible for knocking out the vehicle. A moment later he has the answer as three paratroopers from the 101st Airborne Division emerge from hiding in the long grass. One of them, who is clutching an M1A1 2.36 inch bazooka, is none other than Private James Ryan from Iowa. The Sd. Kfz.251 used in this sequence was actually a Czech OT-810 with its roof panels removed. To simulate the bazooka hit, the front armoured plate was removed and replaced with an MDF panel backed with a loop of Primacord explosive, with the fireball effect achieved using propane gas. This bazooka used in this scene was a historically accurate M1A1 which fired a relatively small 2.36 inch rocket. Most WW2 films use later models of the bazooka, such as the M20 3.5 inch 'super bazooka' which didn't see action until the Korean War. Armourer Simon Atherton couldn't find any surviving M1 or M1A1 bazookas, so replicas had to be made for the film.

A little while later, in the square of the destroyed town of Ramelle, Miller tells Ryan about his mission. He explains that, as all his brothers are dead, he is to return to the

USA. But Ryan is not willing to comply as he feels his job is to stay with his comrades in arms and defend Ramelle against the expected German onslaught.

Miller and Horvath are somewhat taken aback by Ryan's unexpected reaction and debate what to do. Eventually they decide their only option is to join forces with the paratroopers and defend the bridge until American reinforcements arrive. Miller reviews their weaponry. They have two Browning thirty-calibre machine guns, 11 Hawkins mines, 17 grenades, two bazookas with eight rounds, some explosive, and various small arms including M1 rifles and Thompson submachine guns. They have some mortar bombs, but no launching tube.

Miller thinks the best plan would be to entice the expected German tanks down the narrow street where they can be attacked from the side and rear using weapons such as Molotov cocktails and sticky bombs. He suggests that some sticky bombs can be made by filling a woollen sock with Composition B (an explosive consisting of 60% RDX and 40% TNT), attaching a simple pyrotechnic fuse, and coating the sock with axle grease.

Knocking out the lead tank in an advancing column will 'create a 60-ton road block', according to Miller (with 60 tons being the approximate weight of a Tiger tank). But how does Miller know at this point that the first tank to come down the road will be a Tiger I? It is statistically more likely that it would be a Panther, a Panzer IV, a Stug III, or any number of tank destroyer types. During WW2 Allied troops encountered Tigers quite infrequently as so few were made, and many of the sightings of 'Tigers' were actually of Panzer IVs.

As some of his men get to work preparing sticky bombs, others haul a thirty-calibre machine gun to the top of the bell tower using a rope. In a war-damaged café, Miller tries to get some coffee from the machines on the counter but the urns are empty. As the troops prepare for the impending attack, one of them plays an Edith Piaf record *Tu es Partout* (French for 'you are everywhere') on a wind-up gramophone. He explains that the song is about a woman whose lover has left her, yet she keeps seeing him everywhere she goes.

Ryan and Miller sit among the ruins of the abandoned town, and the Private reveals that he can't see the faces of his dead brothers. Miller suggests he tries using a context such as thinking of things they did together. (This scene is very similar to one in Episode 3 of the 1967 *Doctor Who* story *The Tomb of the Cybermen*, where Victoria Waterfield (Deborah Watling), reveals to Patrick Troughton's Doctor that she cannot visualize her dead father's face.)

This prompts Ryan to tell a story about how he once spied one of his brothers making out with an ugly girl in a barn back home. The story was ad-libbed by Matt Damon and isn't particularly interesting or funny, but Spielberg kept it in as he thought it was the sort of anecdote Ryan's character would relate.

As their conversation is coming to an end, Miller hears a loud, distorted, clanking and squeaking mechanical noise in the distance. German heavy armour is approaching the town. These weird and frightening sounds were created using the sound of metal scraping against the ground, and WW2 veterans who saw the movie commented that one thing that the filmmakers got right was the sound of the German tanks.

A soldier on watch in the church bell tower uses hand signals to tell Ryan what he has seen. Two Tiger tanks are approaching, plus two 'Panzer tanks' (sic) and supporting infantry. The term 'Panzer tank' is actually a tautology, since 'Panzer' is the German word for tank.

Miller disperses his men to face the attack while two soldiers set off in a German *Kettenrad* in an attempt to attract the German tanks and entice them down the narrow street where they can be attacked from all sides. The NSU *Kettenrad* was a unique vehicle, as it was a form of motorcycle in which the rear wheel was replaced by a set of tracks, making it effectively a 'motorcycle halftrack'.

The first Tiger doesn't take the bait but a second (with the number '232' painted on the turret side) stops and turns right to attack the Americans. Almost immediately the tank's supporting German troops are cut down by fire from the two Browning thirty-calibre machine guns. The first sticky bomb attack on the Tiger fails, and apparently kills the soldier attempting to plant it as the bomb explodes prematurely. But two more American soldiers attach a couple of sticky bombs to the Tiger's main road wheels. The bombs explode, causing the Tiger's left track to break and come off. The soldiers have achieved what is called a 'mobility kill' as the vehicle is now stationary, making it harder for it to defend itself.

Sticky bombs were developed by the British in 1940 when a German invasion seemed likely. The best-known device was the Grenade, Anti-tank number 74. The problem with such devices was that they often lacked sufficient stickiness to adhere to a tank, particularly if it was moving. There was also a risk that the device would stick to the clothing of the soldier attempting to place it, resulting in his death. I would also doubt whether a sock covered with grease would be sticky enough to adhere to the rotating roadwheel of a tank, particularly as centrifugal force would tend to throw the bomb off. And even if it worked as planned, it would damage the roadwheel rather than break the track as depicted in the movie. A more sensible military strategy would have been to hit the two Tigers from the sides and rear at close range using the two bazookas.

Meanwhile, Miller's men light two petrol bombs and throw them into the open compartment of one of the Marders, causing the crew to burn to death while Private Jackson – from his sniper position in the bell tower – kills several German soldiers while quoting from the Bible.

Miller's men move forward in an attempt to neutralise the Tiger. The Captain puts the muzzle of his Thompson submachine gun through the driver's vision slit in the front hull and sprays bullets inside the tank (actually an impossibility, since a real Tiger has several layers of armoured glass in this position). Other soldiers open the hatch on top of the turret and chuck grenades inside (again an unlikely occurrence as all tanks, including the Tiger, have a mechanism on the underside of the hatch to lock it during combat). The Americans appear to be winning the battle, but suddenly the Germans wheel forward a 20mm anti-aircraft cannon and spray the Tiger with shells, killing all the US troops.

From his position on the bell tower, Jackson continues to take a heavy toll of German soldiers with his sniper rifle while Miller attempts to eliminate the 20mm gun and its crew with bursts from his Thompson submachine gun but he is not successful. Other Germans set up a *Panzerschreck*, a German version of the American bazooka, which was larger and more powerful as it fired an 88mm rocket rather than the puny 2.36 inch missile of the US original.

Jackson continues to kill enemy soldiers with his sniper rifle, but his luck is about to run out as he has been spotted by the crew of the remaining self-propelled gun (the one based on a Swedish SAVM/43). The vehicle moves into position, elevates its main gun and blasts the bell tower with a single high-explosive round.

Miller realises they must knock out the 20m cannon, and the only way to do this is to outflank it. He breaks cover, firing his weapon. In a building nearby, two American soldiers – Private Mellish and Corporal Henderson – are in a first-floor room when they hear German soldiers coming up the stairs. Henderson fires his Thompson through the wall and kills one soldier with five rounds, as evidenced by an expanding puddle of blood, but others arrive and charge the Americans. Both Americans are killed, including Mellish who is stabbed with a bayonet by an SS trooper after a lengthy struggle. The SS trooper exits the room and on the way downstairs passes Corporal Upham, but both soldiers are too traumatized to attack each other.

Outside the building Horvath knocks out the remaining self-propelled gun with a bazooka round and then kills a German soldier with a pistol. The SS trooper who has killed Mellish manages to slip away.

By now the Americans have knocked out two self-propelled guns and one of the Tigers, but the second Tiger is unscathed. Miller is out of ammunition for his Thompson but Ryan hits on an idea to continue the battle. The soldiers have some mortar bombs but no tube to fire them, so Ryan suggests they hit the tail of each bomb on the ground to arm them and then throw them at the enemy. The tactic proves effective, and the two Americans kill several more German soldiers.

Suddenly the surviving Tiger arrives and chases the Americans out of the crater they have been sheltering in. The soldiers run for their lives, pursued by the Tiger and an Sd Kfz.251 halftrack. Miller grabs a bazooka, but Horvath takes it from him and suggests he confronts the Tiger while Miller retreats to a better position. Horvath fires a round at the Tiger, but it hits the thickly-armoured gun mantlet without achieving a penetration. Horvath falls back and reloads his weapon as Miller and Ryan cross the bridge and connect wires to a detonation plunger. He is hoping to blow the bridge.

From a new position, Horvath fires his bazooka again at the thick frontal armour of the Tiger, but the round bounces off. Horvath is then hit and killed as the Tiger rolls forward, blowing up buildings with its main gun, while Miller is stunned and deafened. He then crawls forward in an attempt to reach the detonator but is hit by a bullet fired by 'Steamboat Willie', the German he spared earlier, who can be easily identified as he lacks a helmet.

Badly wounded, Miller pulls out his Colt 0.45 pistol and fires repeatedly at the advancing Tiger in a futile gesture. Suddenly the Tiger explodes. This scene may have been inspired by a similar one in director Steven Spielberg's first big hit, *Jaws* (1975), in which Matt Hooper (Richard Dreyfuss) fires his rifle repeatedly at an oxygen cylinder in the mouth of the giant shark, causing it to explode (which is actually not scientifically possible).

However, it not Miller's bullet which has killed the Tiger but a P-51D Mustang, which Ryan describes as a 'tank-buster'. A single P-51D Mustang in natural metal finish with invasion stripes and chequered nose flies over, followed by two others. None of them carry any tank-busting ordnance such as bombs or rockets, so the Tiger would appear to have been destroyed by the 'Hollywood invisible bomb'! Two P-51D Mustangs were used in the production, namely G-HAEC of the Old Flying Machine Company at Duxford and N167F of the Scandinavian Historic Flight, and were flown by pilots Ray and Mark Hanna. Both these aircraft had taken part in the filming of *Memphis Belle* in 1989.

A moment later, a large force of American soldiers backed by vehicles, including a single Sherman tank, arrive at the bridge. A medic arrives to tend to Miller, but it is later revealed that he eventually died from his wounds.

A voiceover then announces that Private Ryan is on his way back to the USA, having done his duty. A close-up of Ryan's face then morphs to that of his older self, visiting the War Cemetery at Omaha Beach in 1998. This is one of the surprises of the film, as the old man is revealed to be Ryan and not Captain Miller. As Ryan kneels at the gravestone – which we can now see has Miller's name on it and the date of his death (13 June 1944) – the old man admits that he tried to live his life as best he could and always remembered the conversation he had with Miller on the bridge on that fateful day in 1944.

Saving Private Ryan was released on 24 July 1998, and was a critical and commercial success making $491.8 m at the box office with another $44m from various home entertainment releases. The film was nominated for eleven Academy Awards and won five for Best Cinematography, Best Sound Mixing, Best Sound Effects Editing, Best Film Editing and Best Director.

It was widely praised for the realism of its battle scenes, and many war veterans who saw it were quite shaken by the experience. The film influenced many subsequent war movies and also started the trend for 'washed out' colour which – in my personal opinion – has now become an over-used cliché. Would films such as *Goldfinger* (1964) and *You Only Live Twice* (1967) have made such an impact if they had been filmed in muted colour rather than Technicolor? Indeed, when *Saving Private Ryan* was first broadcast on satellite television in the USA, many viewers 'phoned in to say there was something wrong with the colour, resulting in the broadcasters turning up the colour saturation to produce a 'normal' looking picture.

In 2005, Channel 4 broadcast a documentary on the *100 Greatest War Films*, with *Saving Private Ryan* being at number 1. Would I agree with that assessment? Personally, my choice would be *A Bridge Too Far* (1977) as my Number 1 war film.

Apart from the muted colour and the technical and historical errors in *Saving Private Ryan*, it suffers (like most of Spielberg's films) from an excess of sentimentality and emotional manipulation of the audience. Indeed, one of the staunchest critics of the film has been respected Oscar-winning American screenwriter William Goldman, who you may recall wrote the script for *A Bridge Too Far* (1977). In his book *The Big Picture: Who Killed Hollywood?*, Goldman criticizes the film – particularly the last hour, which he describes as 'fifty plus minutes of phoney, manipulative shit'. Goldman also disliked the opening and closing scenes with the aged Ryan. How could this individual have a 'flashback' to the landings at Omaha Beach, given that he wasn't there? If you are interested in reading Goldman's views on the film, his essay has also been reproduced in full in a number of websites.

Quite apart from Goldman's concerns, the film also implies that D-Day (and the Second World War in general) was won by the Americans alone without any help from the British, as had been suggested before in Hollywood films like *Objective Burma* (1945) and *Patton* (1970).

Despite these qualms, *Saving Private Ryan* remains an impressive technical achievement and a landmark in the history of war movies. It is certainly one of the most realistic war movies ever made, though not necessarily the best ever. It also led to the HBO TV miniseries *Band of Brothers* (2001), which had a similar style to *Saving Private Ryan* including the use of faded colour. This series was followed by *The Pacific* (2010) about the exploits of a group of US Marines. A third HBO miniseries, *The Mighty Eighth* – about the US Eighth Air Force in Europe in WW2 – is planned for broadcast in 2019, so it seems the legacy of *Saving Private Ryan* is still with us.

Saving Private Ryan (1998)
Production Credits

Production Team
Director: Steven Spielberg
Screenplay: Robert Rodat

Cast
Captain Miller: Tom Hanks
T/Sgt Horvath: Tom Sizemore
Private Reiben: Edward Burns
Private Jackson: Barry Pepper
Private Mellish: Adam Goldberg
Private Caparzo: Vin Diesel
T/4 Medic Wade: Giovanni Ribisi
Corporal Upham: Jeremy Davies
Private Ryan: Matt Damon
Captain Hamill: Ted Danson
Sergeant Hill: Paul Giamatti
Lt. Colonel Anderson: Dennis Farina
Steamboat Willie: Joerg Stadler
Corporal Henderson: Max Martini
Toynbe: Dylan Bruno
Weller: Daniel Cerqueira
Parker: Demetri Goritsas
Trask: Ian Porter
Rice: Gary Sefton
Garrity: Julian Spencer
Wilson: Steve Griffin
Lyle: William Marsh
Fallon: Marc Cass
Major Hoess: Markus Napier
Ramelle Paratroopers: Neil Finnighan, Peter Miles
Field HQ Major: Paul Garcia
Field HQ Aide: Seamus McQuade
Coxswain: Ronald Longridge
Delancey: Adam Shaw
Lieutenant Briggs: Rolf Saxon
Radioman: Corey Johnson
Soldiers on Beach: Loclann Aiken, John Barnett, MacLean Burke, Victor Burke, Aiden Condron, Paschal Friel, Shane Hagan, Paul Hickey, Shane Johnson, Laird MacIntosh, Brian Maynard, Martin MacDougall, Mark Phillips, Lee Aaron Rosen, Andrew Scott, Matthew Sharp, Vincent Walsh, Grahame Wood
Corporal: John Sharian
Doyle: Glenn Wrage
Senior Medical Officer: Crofton Hardester
Czech Wehrmacht Soldier: Martin Hub
Goldman: Raph Taylor
Private Boyd: Nigel Whitmey
Private Hastings: Sam Ellis
Germans: Erich Redman, Tilo Keiner, Stephen Grothgar
Jean: Stephane Cornicard
Jean's Wife: Michelle Evans
Jean's Son: Martin Beaton
Jean's Daughter: Anna Maguire
Minnesota Ryan: Nathan Fillion
Lieutenant De Windt: Leland Orser

Paratrooper Lieutenant: Michael Mantas
Paratrooper Oliver: David Vegh
Paratrooper Mandelsohn: Ryan Hurst
Paratrooper Joe: Nick Brook
Paratrooper No.1: Sam Scudder
Old French Man: John Walters
Old French Woman: Dorothy Grumbar
MP Lieutenant: James Innes-Smith
General Marshall: Harve Presnell
War Department Colonel: Dale Dye
War Department Colonel: Bryan Cranston
War Department Captain: David Wohl
War Department Lieutenant: Eric Loren
War Department Clerk: Valerie Colgan
Mrs Margaret Ryan: Amanda Boxer
Ryan as Old Man: Harrison Young
Old Mrs Ryan: Kathleen Byron
Ryan's Son: Rob Freeman
Ryan's Grandson: Thomas Gizbert
French Villager: Sebastian J. Brook
Letter-Reader (voice): John De Lancie
German Paratrooper: James Embree
Soldier: Declan Geraghty
German SS Soldier: Frank Huseyin
Soldiers on Beach: Michael P. Jahoda, Joah Costa Menezes, Vincent Ventresca
A23 Platoon: Alan Joyce
Bangalore Assistant: Derek Lea
Sergeant Blaine: Taylor Murphy
Ryan's Granddaughter: Abbe Muschallik
Ryan's Grandaughter: Nina Muschallik
Soldier: Paul Sacks
Waffen SS Soldier: Mac Steinmeier
German Sniper: Leo Stansky
Paratrooper: Paul Woodadge

Production

Producers: Ian Bryce, Mark Gordon, Gary Levinson, Steven Spielberg
Co-producers: Bonnie Curtis, Allison Lyon Segan
Associate Producers: Kevin De La Noy, Mark Huffam
Music: John Williams
Film Editor: Michael Kahn
Casting: Denise Chamian
Production Design: Tom Sanders
Assistant Production Designer: Phil Zagajewski

Art Direction

Art Directors: Tom Brown, Ricky Eyres, Chris Seagers, Alan Tomkins, Mark Tanner
Supervising Art Director: Daniel T. Dorrance

Set Decorator: Lisa Dean
Costume Design: Joanna Johnston

Make-Up Department
Key Make-up Artist: Lois Burwell
Trainee Make-up: Polly Earnshaw
Chief Hairstylist: Jeanette Freeman
Hairstylists: Tapio Salmi, Elizabeth Yianni-Georgiou, Betty Glasow
Assistant Hairstylist: Hugh McAllister
Hairstylist (Ireland): Martina McCarthy
Makeup Artists: Sian Grigg, Jennifer Hegarty, Tina Phelan, Roisin O'Reilly, Andrea Finch, Catherine Heys, Fiona Hogan, Pauline Heys, Ailbhe Lemass
Mr Hanks' Make-up: Daniel C. Stiepeke
Special Make-up Effects: Michelle Freeborn, Rob Mayor
Make-up Dept Runner: Tara McNamee
Trainee Make-up Artist: Ailsing Nairn
Trainee Hairstylist: Joe Whelan

Production Management
Post-production Supervisor (Ireland): Erica Frauman
Production Manager: Mark Huffam
Production Manager (Ireland): Seamus McInerney

Second Unit Director or Assistant Director
Third Assistant Director (Ireland): Daisy Cummins
Second Assistant Director (Ireland): Catherine Dunne
Second Assistant Director: Adam Goodman
Third Assistant Director: Martin Krauka
First Assistant Director: Sergio Mimica-Gezzan
Third Assistant Directors (Ireland): Barbara Mulcahy, Hannah Quinn
Second Assistant Director: Karen Richards
Third Assistant Director: Andrew Ward
Assistant Director: Toby Hosking

Art Department
Construction Coordinator: Terry Apsey
Wood Machinist: Norman Baker
Supervising Plasterer: Peter Black
Chargehand Carpenter: Alan Booth
Art Department Assistant: Joanna Branch
Draughtsman: Stephen Bream
Webbing Props: Stephen Brown
Illustrator: Matt Codd

Construction Buyer: Hillery Cope
Junior Draughtsman: Robert Cowper
H.O.D. Plasterer: Allan Croucher
Construction Manager (Ireland): Michelle Deegan
Standby Stagehand: Gerry Delaney
Props (Ireland): William Draper, Cos Egan
Illustrator: Tim Flattery
Assistant Set Dresser: Veronique Fletcher
Props: John Fox
Standby Art Director: Gary Freeman
Props: Barry Gates
Welder Fabricator: Colin Gibbs
Webbing Props: Alan Hausmann
Draughtsman: William Hawkins
Property Storage: Robert Hill
Chargehand Dressing Props: John Hogan
Property Storage: Robert Hill
Chargehand Dressing Props: John Hogan
Junior Draughtsman: Mags Horwood
Head Sculptor: Any Hunt
Art Department Assistant: Peter James
Assistant Art Director: Kevin Kananaugh
Storesman: Louis King
Standby Carpenter: Micky Law
Construction Manager (Ireland): David Lowery
Production Buyer: David Lusby
Chargehand Props: Steven McDonald
Plant Engineer: Paul Maling
Assistant Welder: Mark McBarron
Standby Rigger: Ginger McCarthy
Props: Christian McDonald
Property Master: Maxie McDonald
Supervising Carpenter: John McGregor
Assistant Set Dresser: Phillipa McLellan
Supervising Plasterer: Malcolm Mister
Standby Painter: Joe Monks
Supervising Painter: Brian Morris
Carpenter: David Murphy
Props: Philip Murphy
Chargehand Carpenter: Fred Myatt
Assistant Construction Coordinator: John New
Chargehand Rigger: John Newvell
Head of Department Rigger: Ron Newvell
Graphic Artist: Lawrence O'Toole
Supervisor Rigger: Steven Pollecutt
Supervising Standby Props: Mickey Pugh
Welder: Christopher Rose

Chargehand Stagehand: Nigel Ross
Props: David Rossiter
Chargehand Plasterer: Keith Shannon
Props: Christian Short
Chargehand Plasterer Labourer: David Silverton
Standby Plasterer: Derek Smith
Chargehand Carpenter: Philip Smith
Wood Machinist: William Sower
Head of Department Stagehand: Kenneth Stachini
H.O.D. Painter: Adrian Start
Model Maker: Keith Stephen
Art Department Assistant: Eric Stewart
Plant Engineer: Steve Taylor
Art Department Coordinator: Lavinia Glynn-Jones
Draughtsman: Paul Westacott
Props (Ireland): Gary Wiffen
Props: Ben Wilkinson
Supervising Carpenter: Paul Williamson
Standby Props: Micky Woolfson
Supervising Carpenter: Tony Youd
Concept Model Maker: Greg Aronowitz
Plasterer: Mark Buck
Carpenter: Steve Furneaux
Storyboard Artist: John Greaves
Set Dresser: Jeff Hay
Illustrator: Kevin Hunter
Carpenter: Robert Jackson
Art Department Coordinator: Caitlin Maloney
Paint Foreman: Bruce G. Smith
Painter: Glenn Start
Painter: Matthew Start
Junior Draughtsman: Andy Thomson
Props Maker: Richard Walker
Research Specialist: Randall D. Wilkins
Painter: Ian Zawadzki
Foley Editor: Sandino Bailo-Lape
Machine Room Operator: Christopher Barrick
Dialogue Editor: Sara Bolder
Supervising Sound Assistant: Lisa Chino
Re-recordist: Matt Colleran
ADR Mixer: Dean Drabin
Foley Mixer: Tony Eckert
Effects Editor: Teresa Eckton
Assistant Effects Editor: Dan Engstrom
Effects Editor: Frank E. Eulner
Supervising Sound Assistant: Andre Fenley
Digital Transfer: Jonathan Greber
Sound Transfer Supervisor: Marni L. Hammett
Assistant Effects Editor: Larry Hoki
Supervising Sound Editor: Richard Hymns
Boom Operator: Robert Jackson
Sound Mixer: Ronald Judkins
ADR Assistant: Stephanie D. Krivacek
Foley Editor: Bruce Lacey

Engineer: Tom Lalley
Foley Recordist: Frank Merel
Assistant Sound Designer: Shannon Mills
Cable Operator: David Motta
Re-recording Mixer: Andy Nelson
Effects Editor: Larry Oatfield
Re-recordist: Rudy Pi
Assistant Foley Editor: Susan Popovic
Sound Intern: Gerard Roche
Machine Room Supervisor: Ronald G. Roumas
Re-recording Mixer: Gary Rydstrom
Digital Transfer: Dee Selby
Mix Technician: Tony Sereno
ADR Supervisor: Larry Singer
ADR Recordist: Cary Stratton
Re-recording Mixer: Gary Summers
Dialogue Editor: Ewa Sztompke Oatfield
Foley Artist: Dennie Thorpe
Effects Editor: Ethan Van Der Ryn
Foley Artist: Jana Vance
ADR Editor: Denise Whiting
ADR Editor: Thomas Whiting
Effects Editor: Karen G. Wilson
Assistant Dialogue Editor: Mary Works
Dialogue Editor: Gwendolyn Yates Whittle
Machine Room Operator: Chris Barron
Sound Effects Recordist: Christopher Boyes
ADR Mixer: Al Gomez
Sound Mix Technical Assistant: David P. Hart
Client Service: Mike Lane
Sound Effects Recordist: Shannon Mills
Re-recordist: Steve Romanko
Supervising Sound Editor: Gary Rydstrom
Sound Transfer: John Soukup
Mix Technician: Kent Sparling
ADR Technician: Gwendolyn Yates Whittle

Special Effects

Special Effects Technicians: Michael Bartlett, Gareth Wingrove, Alan Young, Mark Roberts, Bradley Barton, Daniel Bennett, Steve Borthwick, Caimin Bourne, Trevor Williams, Dave Williams, David Watkins, Steven Warner, Anne Marie Walters, Colin Umpelby, Paul Taylor, Timothy Stracey, Kevin Rogan, Grant Rogan, David Roddham, Lee Rider, Tony Richards, Melanie Rayski, Simon Quinn, Graham Povey, John Pilgrim, Kevin Nolan, Andrew Nolan, Dave Miller, Rob Malos, Michael Kearns, Adam Hillier, Joseph Geday, John Fontana, Raymond Ferguson, Michael Durkan, Paul Dimmer, Stuart Digby, Michael Curran, Cliff Corbould, Simon Cockren, Philip Clark, Alex Burdett,

Christopher Brennan, Caimin Bourne, Steve Borthwick
Senior Special Effects Technicians: Peter White, Terry Cox, Ray Lovell, Gerry Johnston, Peter Pickering, Melvyn Pearson, Mark Meddings
Special Effects Supervisor: Neil Corbould
Senior Special Effects Technicians: Kenneth Herd, Jeff Clifford, Ian Corbould
Special Corpse and Animal Effects: Neill Gorton
Lead Senior Special Effects Technicians: David Hunter, David Brighton, Paul Corbould, Kevin Herd, John Evans
Special Effects Coordinator: Carol McAulay
Special Effects Assistant Buyer: Katie Gabriel
Corpse and Animal Effects: Steven Painter
Senior Sculptors: Colin Ware, Stuart Bray, Paul Catling, Stuart Conran, Amy Garner, Duncan Jarman, Waldo Mason, Philip Matthews
Modelmaking Supervisor: John Schoonraad
Special Effects Floor Supervisor: Clive Beard
Special Effects Buyer: Krissi Williamson
Special Effects Workshop Supervisor: Trevor Wood
Prop Maker: Dave Chagouri
Stunt Weapons Constructor: Peter Hawkins
Special Effects Assistant Technician: Tara McDonald
Senior Sculptor: Ian Morse

Visual Effects

Visual Effects Production Coordinator ILM: Lori Arnold
Stage Technician ILM: Carl Assmus
Plate Restoration ILM: Trang Bach
CGI Artists ILM: Kathleen Beeler, Mary McCulloch, Jennifer McKnew, Christa Starr, Paul Theren, Terry Chostner, Gonzalo Escudero, Bridget Goodman, Joanne Hafner
Visual Effects Producer: Kim Bromley
Sabre Artists ILM: Caitlin Content, Chad Taylor
Digital Production ILM: Kathleen Davidson
Stage Technicians ILM: Berny Demolski, Rob Doherty
Visual Effects Supervisor: Stefen Fangmeier
Film Scanning Supervisor: George Gambetta
Negative Line-up ILM: Tim Geideman
Digital Production ILM: Jennifer Gonzalez, Garrick Meeker
Sabre Supervisor ILM: Pablo Helman
Digital Matte Artist ILM: Matthew Hendershott

Visual Effects Co-supervisor: Roger Guyett
Lead Effects Technician ILM: Geoff Heron
Visual Effects Camera Assistant ILM: Robert Hill
Visual Effects Editor ILM: Bill Kimberlin
CG Sequence Supervisor ILM : Gregor Lakner
Visual Effects Art Director ILM: Alexander Laurant
Digital Technologies ILM: Danny Lee
Visual Effects Production Assistant ILM: Amanda Montgomery
Effects Technician ILM: Dan Nelson
Scanning Supervisor ILM: Joshua Pines
Visual Effects Camera Operator ILM: Martin Rosenberg
Modelmaking Supervisor: John Schoonraad
Associate Visual Effects Producer ILM: Heather Smith
Colour Timing Supervisor ILM: Kenneth Smith
Digital Production ILM: Erin West
Digital Technologies ILM: Jeffrey Yost
Digital/Paint Rotoscope: Katharine Baird
Assistant Concept Artist: Beth D'Amato
Animatronics: Adam Howarth
Digital Paint & Roto Artist ILM: Jiri Jacknowitz
Prosthetics Sculptor: Brendan Lonergan
Technical Support: Kristen Millette
Digital Support: M. Zachary Sherman
Production Engineering Supervisor: Joe Takai
CG Resource Assistant ILM: Marc Wilhite

Stunt Department

Stunt Performers: Andy Bennett, Pavel Cajzl, Marc Cass, Steve Caswell, Viktor Cervenka, Stuart Clark, Aris Comminos, Laurie Crane, Ray De Haan, Jim Dowdall, Neil Finnighan, Steve Griffin, Paul Heasman, Lyndon Stuart Hellewell, Mark Henson, Paul Herbert, Dominick Hewitt, Jeff Hewitt-Davis, Ian Holicek, Martin Hub, Dusan Hyska, Ron Inch, Tiddler James, Jindrich Klaus, Pavel Kratky, Derek Lea, Dimo Lipitkovski, Guy List, David Listvan, Tony Lucken, Sean McCabe, Peter Miles, Ray Nicholas, Donal O'Farrell, Jaroslav Peterka, Gary Powell, Jaroslav Psenicka, Seon Rogers, Mac Steinmeier, Leo Stransky, Tom Struthers, Pavel Vokoun, Shaun Wallace, Bill Weston, Sebastian Foxx, Jurgen Klein, Michael Mohr, Adam Richards, Paul

Sacks, Blake Sporne, Steve Truglia, Matthias Werner
Aerial Stunts (P-51 Mustang Pilots): Ray Hanna, Mark Hanna
Stunt Coordinator: Simon Crane
Stunt Double (Matt Damon): Lyndon S. Hellewell
Stunt Double (Tom Hanks): Mark Henson

Camera and Electrical Department
Electrician (Ireland): Garret Baldwin
First Assistant Camera (Ireland): Ciaran Barry
Camera Operator: Seamus Corcoran
Camera Operator (Ireland): Cian de Buitlear
Chief Lighting Technician: David Devlin
Video Assist Operator: Noel Donellion
Camera Operator: Mitch Dubin
Clapper/Loader: Rosalyn Ellis
Key Grip: John Flemming
Video Assistant: Sarah Francis
First Assistant Camera (Ireland): Donald Gilligan
First Assistant Camera: Kenny Groom
Electricians: Marek Bojsza, Alan Grosch, Darren Grosch, Paul Kemp
Camera Operator: Chris Haarhoff
Camera Trainee: Alan Hall
Still Photographer: David James
Second Assistant Camera: Tom Jordan
Second Assistant Camera (Ireland): Declan King, Dochy J. Lowe
Key Grip: James Kwiatkowski
First Assistant Camera: Steven Meizler, Mark Milsome
Rigging Chief Lighting Technician: Ossa Mills
Camera Trainee: Angus Mitchell
Chief Lighting Technician (Ireland): Terry Mulligan
Electricians: Neil Munroe, Steve Pattenden
Grip (Ireland): Philip Murphy
Electrician (Ireland): Peter O'Toole
Second Assistant Camera: Robert Palmer
Best Boy: Ricky Pattenden
'B'-Camera Dolly Grip: David Rist
Best Boy Grip: Derek Russell
Best Boy: Richard Seal
Crane Grip: Ian Townsend
Electrician: Terry Townsend
Video Playback Intern: Tadhg Conway
2nd Unit Director of Photography: David Devlin
Additional Photographer: Dan Moore
Assistant Camera: David O'Brien
Libra Technician: Ian Speed

First Assistant Camera: Simon Starling
Electrician: Daniel Windels

Casting Department
Casting (UK): Priscilla John
Casting Assistants (LA): Kara Katsoulis, Jeff McNally
Casting Assistant (UK): Orla Maxwell
Casting (Austria/Germany): Fritz Fleischhacker

Costume and Wardrobe Department
Costume Assistant (Ireland): Fiona Belton
Wardrobe Master: Anthony Black
Costumer: Nigel Boyd
Military Costumer: David Crossman
Costumer : Peter Edmonds
Costume Supervisor (Ireland): Sheila Fahey
Key Costume Special Effects (Stunts): Philip Goldsworthy
Costume Coordinator: Sarah Hinch
Costume Special Effects (Stunts): Peter Hornbuckle
Costume Assistants (Ireland): Maeve Hunter, Colette Jackson
Costume Production Assistants: Helen Jerome, Natalie Rogers
Costume Assistants (Ireland): Louise Keating, Oona McFarkland, Ann Regan, Anne O'Halloran
Costume Breakdown: Thomas Lightfoot
Set Costumer: Marcus Love-McGuirk
Key Set Costumer: Tom McDonald
Set Costumer: Laura May, Adam Roach
Costume Breakdown: Nicola Rapley
Key Costume Breakdown: Timothy Shanahan
Costumer: Rupert Sheggle
Assistant Costume Designer: Sally Turner
Costume Breakdown: Emma Walker
Costume Department Key: Patrick Wheatley
Crowd Wardrobe Master: Dave Whiteing
Seamstress: Pat Williamson
Key Costumer (LA): Diana Wilson
Costume Supervisor : Pamela Wise
Wardrobe Buyer: Jon Timothy
Costume Props Maker: Peter K. Christopher
Costume Cutter: Lee Clayton
Costumer: Paul Colford
Costume Coordinator: Elvis Davies
Wardrobe Trainee (Ireland): Jill Graves Power
Daily Wardrobe Assistant: Tom Hornsby
Costume Assistant: Marcus Howard

Wardrobe: Steve O'Sullivan
Costume Special Effects: Chris Tulloch

Editorial Department
Negative Cutter: Gary Burritt
First Assistant Editor: Richard Byard
Post-production Executive (Ireland): Martin Cohen
First Assistant Editors: Simon Cozens, Patrick Crane
Post-production Associate: Mike Cuevas
Post-production Coordinator (Ireland): Sven E. Fahlgren
Assistant Editor: Alex Garcia
Colour Timer: Dale E. Grahn
Assistant Editors: Bradley Souber, Michael Trent
Apprentice Editor: Julie Zunder
Assistant Editor: Jens Baylis
Post-production Assistant: Kevin Du Toit
Assistant Editor: Kent Kreiger
Post-production Services: Chris Miller

Location Management
Assistant Location Manager: Simon Burgess
Assistant Location Manager (Ireland): James Cloney
Location Managers: Alex Gladstone, Robin Higgs
Location Manager (Ireland): Melanie Gore Grimes
Assistant Location Manager: Rebecca Jones
Assistant Location Manager (Ireland): David Morris
Assistant Location Manager: Katryna Samut Tagliaferro
Assistant Location Manager: Hugo Smith-Bingham
Location Manager: William Bowling
Location Manager: Steven Forrester
Location Coordinator: Nial Fulton
Location Assistant: Hugh Gourlay

Music Department
Scoring Consultant: Sandy De Crescent
Executive in Charge of Music: Todd Homme
Orchestra Personnel Manager: Lynn G. Larsen
Assistant Music Editor: Kelly Mahan Jaramillo
Solo (Trumpet): Tim Morrison
Music Mixer and Recordist: Shawn Murphy
Orchestrator: John Neufeld
Solo (Trumpet): Thomas Rolfs
Solo (French Horn): Gus Sebring
Music Editor: Ken Wannberg
Music Clearances: Julie Butchko
Musician (French Horn): James Thatcher
Conductor: John Williams

Transportation Department

Transportation Captain: Brian Baverstock
Unit Driver: Gary Birmingham
Unit Driver: Freddy Chiverton
Driver (Mr Spielberg): John Coleman
Driver (Mr Bryce): Mike Faulkner
Transportation Coordinator: Brian Hathaway
Unit Driver: Keith Horsley
Military Vehicle Coordinator: Steve Lamonby
Unit Driver: Barry Leonti
Unit Driver: Bruce Neighbour
Unit Driver: Sean O'Connor
Mr Hanks' Driver: David Rosenbaum
Unit Driver: Billy Turner
Unit Driver: Darren Helman
Location Transportation: Stephen McGillen
Unit Driver: Eamonn Murphy
Camera Car Driver: John Ott
Unit Driver: Michael Phelan
Driver (Action Vehicle): Paul Sacks

Other Crew

Assistant to Mr Hanks: Sharon Aiken
Head Chef: Colin Anderson
Chef: Ed Anderson
Landing Craft Crew (Ireland): Alan Armsby, Rupert Barnes, Colin Bates, Robert Brian
Assistant Armourer: Derek Atherton
Armourer: Simon Atherton
Military Advisor: John Barnett
Technician: Cath Blackett
Assistant Production Coordinator (Ireland): Clodagh Bowers
Marine Rigger (Ireland): Dan Britton
Production Assistant: Jane Burgess
Production Coordinator (Ireland): Elaine Burt
Production Office Assistant (Ireland): Maeve Butler
Technician: Chris Byrne
Fireman: Christopher Caullum
Catering Manager: Sara Chappell
Assistant Production Coordinator: Tania Clarke
Technician: Aron Collins
Technician: Lee Craik
Production Office Assistant (Ireland): Aileen Curtin
Unit Publicist: Sue D'Arcy
Assistant Production Accountant: Sophie Dasic
Marine Coordinator (Ireland): Robin Davies
Landing Craft Crew (Ireland): Stephen Dawson
Fire Safety Officer: David Deane
Post-production Accountant: Maria De Vane
Landing Craft Crew (Ireland): Patrick Devereux
Corpse and Animal Effects Coordinator: Lindy Diamond
Production Office Assistant (Ireland): Lisa Drayne

Assistant Armourer: Tommy Dunne
Senor Military Adviser: Capt Dale Dye USMC (Retired)
Workroom Head: David Evans
Prosthetics Crew: Martha Fein
Production Assistant: Carlos Fidel
Assistant Production Accountant (Ireland): Anne-Marie Fitzgerald
Webbing Supervisor: Andrew Fletcher
Landing Craft Crew (Ireland): Robert Foley
Mechanic: Andy Gray
Supervising Production Accountant: Carolyn Hall
Production Coordinator: Lil Heyman
Landing Craft Crew (Ireland): Donald Hind
Technician: Sam Ives
Prosthetics Crew: Emma Jackson
Nurse: Carrie Johnson
Landing Craft Crew (Ireland): David Kelly
Accounting Assistant: Claire Kenny
Technician: Veronique Keys
Landing Craft Crew (Ireland): James Kinella
Assistant Production Accountant: Lisa-Kim Ling Kuan
Mechanic: John Lehen
Marine Engineer (Ireland): Dave Leshore
Production Office Assistant (Ireland): Dickon Levinge
Assistant Chef: Sarah Linton
Financial Representative: James T. Linville
Prosthetics Crew: Brendan Lonergan
Technician: Suzie Owen
Landing Craft Crew (Ireland): Ronnie Longridge
Production Office Assistant (Ireland): Kathleen Lucking
Production Accountant: George Marshall
Accounting Assistant: Fry Martin
Technician: Rob Mayor
Landing Craft Crew (Ireland): David McDowall
ADR Group Coordinator: Mickie McGowan
Marine Rigger (Ireland): Roger McGowan
Landing Craft Crew (Ireland): Jason Mooney
Landing Craft Crew (Ireland): Lindsay Moore
Landing Craft Crew (Ireland): Peter Moore
Assistant Production Coordinator: Lulu Morgan
Production Assistant: Gail Munnelly
Landing Craft Coordinator (Ireland): Ken Murgatroyd
Production Accountant (Ireland): David Murphy
Landing Craft Crew (Ireland): John Murphy
Landing Craft Crew (Ireland): Noel Murphy

Landing Craft Crew (Ireland): David Need
Prosthetics Crew: Dan Nixon
Prosthetics Crew: Jackie Noble
Assistant to Mr Spielberg (LA): Elizabeth Nye
Landing Craft Crew (Ireland): Michael O'Leary
Prosthetics Supervisor: Conor O'Sullivan
Technician: Nicola O'Toole
Assistant Production Coordinator: Rick Osako
Technician: Anthony Parker
Technician: Will Petty
Fireman: Bob Pollard
Technician: Andrew Proctor
Accounting Assistant: Andrew Pyke
Script Supervisor: Ana Maria Quintana
Technician: Liz Ragland
Marine Engineer (Ireland): Geoff Raleigh
Assistant to Mr Spielberg (LA): Susan Ray
Catering Manager: David Reynolds
Landing Craft Crew (Ireland): Steve Richards
Production Associate: Jason Roberts
Technician: Graham Ross
Landing Craft Crew (Ireland): Gary Rowe
Marine Safety (Ireland): Alistair Rumball
Technician: Patrick Rushmere
Assistant to Mr Curtis: Mark Russell
Assistant Armourer: Karl Schmidt
Technician: Janine Schneider
Prosthetics Crew: Robin Schoonraad
Prosthetics Crew: Tristan Schoonrad
Landing Craft Crew (Ireland): Mick Sellen
Prosthetics Designer: Stuart Sewell
Technician: Rosie Shannon
Prosthetics Crew: Lawrence Simmons
Technician: Robert Simpson
Assistant to Mr Bryce: Carlyle Fairfax Smith
Head Chef: Sinjun Smith
Production Assistant: Aine Stacey
Prosthetics Crew: Katrina Strachan
Assistant Production Accountant (Ireland): Siobhan Sweeney
Landing Craft Crew (Ireland): Steve Sweet
Mechanic: John Symondsen
Technician: Annabel Tait
Landing Craft Crew (Ireland): Mick Thomas
Shipwright (Ireland): Paul Tingey
Mechanic: Michael Tombs
Mechanic: Peter Tombs
Video Services: John Torrijos
Landing Craft Crew (Ireland): Ray Tovey

Production Controller: Jim Turner
Video Services: Christia von Burkloo
Landing Craft Crew (Ireland): Gerald Wade
Landing Craft Crew (Ireland): Brian Walker
Landing Craft Crew (Ireland): Seamus Walsh
Technician: Tania Wanstall
Prosthetics Crew: Gavin Watton
Technician: Simon Webber
Technician: James Weston
Landing Craft Crew (Ireland): Stuart Weston
Assistant to Mr Spielberg: Keri Wilson
Landing Craft Crew (Ireland): David Winn
Assistant Chef: Becky Wiseman
Technician: Shell Woodall
Consultant: Stephen Ambrose (uncredited)
Additional ADR Voice: Scott Colomby
Script Doctor: Frank Darabont
Language Coach: Clifford De Spenser
Dialect Coach: Jessica Drake
Armourer: Dave Evans
Catering Assistant: Lydia Jay Finn
Special Make-up Effects Artist: Andy Garner
Studio Executive: Marc Haimes
Floor Runner: Nick Hopkins
Stand-in for Matt Damon/Barry Pepper: Jason Horwood
Production Assistant: Clare Keogh
Technician: Veronique Keys
Client Service: Mike Lane
Production Assistant: Jennifer Lew
Production Assistant: Mark Loughlin
Stand-in: Zack Milan
Armourer: John Nixon
Weapon Instructor: Joss Skottowe
Set Production Assistant: Rhys Summerhayes
Craft Service: Aurelia Thomas
Voice-over: Robin Thomas
Fire Officer: Derek Warman
Craft Service: Chris Winn
Aerial Coordinator: Mark Wolff
Production Assistant: Donald E. Wygal
Additional ADR Voice: Don Yesso

NEGLECTED WORLD WAR II CLASSICS

IN this book I have discussed some of the most famous war films of all time, but there are other less well-known movies that are often overlooked in any discussion of the genre. A good example would be *Sahara* (1943), which I would consider to be one of Humphrey Bogart's greatest pictures. Set in North Africa in June 1942 after the fall of Tobruk, it deals with the exploits of an American tank crew commanded by Sergeant Joe Gunn (Humphrey Bogart), part of a US Army detachment who have been sent to Egypt to gain experience of desert warfare under combat conditions.

The real star of the picture, though, is Gunn's vehicle – an air-cooled M3 Lee tank, *Lulu Belle*. The immediate predecessor of the famous M4 Sherman, the M3 had a highly unusual design as it had a very high profile and two main guns: a 37mm anti-tank gun in a small turret atop the hull, plus a 75mm cannon in a sponson on the right side of the main body (an idea which was very similar to the gun mountings on the early British tanks in WW1 and the French Char B, first produced in 1936). The version of the M3 used by the British (the Grant), was fitted with a larger turret and lacked the cupola fitted to the Lee. Hundreds of Grants were supplied to the British Army from May 1942 onwards, and they remained in service for less than a year as they were eventually replaced by the superior M4 Sherman. One Grant was used by General Montgomery as an observation and command tank, and was fitted with a dummy 37mm gun barrel. It is currently preserved in the Imperial War Museum in London.

Following the rout of Allied forces at Tobruk, Gunn and the crew of *Lulu Belle* escape east towards Egypt. On the way his men pick up a disparate squad of soldiers who hitch a ride on the back of the tank, and also acquire an Italian prisoner, Giuseppe (J. Carrol Naish), who is being guarded by the Sudanese Sergeant Major Tambul (Rex Ingram). The M3 is subsequently attacked by a German fighter (a North American P-51A Mustang, standing in for a Messerschmitt Me109), but Sergeant Gunn shoots it down using *Lulu Belle's* turret-mounted machine gun and 37mm cannon and the pilot – Captain von Schletow (Kurt Kreuger) – is captured.

Eventually Gunn's men end up at a deserted fort at Hassan Barani where there is a well. Unfortunately they only manage to extract a small amount of water before it dries up but, despite their perilous situation, Gunn elects to hold the position against superior German forces who are themselves very short of water. Gunn refuses an offer of a ceasefire in return for them abandoning their position, and tricks the Germans into believing that his men have plentiful supplies of water. Gunn even offers the Germans a deal: he will give them water in exchange for them surrendering their weapons.

The Germans refuse the offer and, in a series of battles, the Allied troops hold off the Germans – assisted by *Lulu Belle's* powerful armament. Eventually a shell explodes in the sand and opens up the well, causing water to gush everywhere. The Germans – who are being driven crazy by thirst –

throw away their weapons, run forward and drink the water. They all surrender just as Allied reinforcements arrive to relieve Gunn's men.

The film was based on *Patrol*, a story by Philip MacDonald which was itself inspired by a Soviet film *The Thirteen* (1936). Later, the basic plotline was used for the Western *Last of the Comanches* (1953), which starred Broderick Crawford. What is less well-known is that the British produced their own version of *Sahara* called *Nine Men* (1943). Most of the cast were serving British soldiers, but the film also included a performance by a young Gordon Jackson. The plot was similar to the Bogart film as it involved a group of British squaddies who were holed up in a fort in the Western Desert which they held against impossible odds. At one point they are strafed by a German Me109 but don't shoot it down. Eventually, one of the British troops knocks out an Italian armoured car using a Boys anti-tank rifle. The Boys fired a 0.55 inch bullet, which could penetrate about an inch of armour but was eventually declared obsolete as it was ineffective against the later German tanks.

In 1995 *Sahara* was itself remade as a made-for-television action movie shot in Australia with James Belushi playing Sergeant Joe Gunn. Once again, the plot featured an M3 Lee tank called *Lulu Belle*, though on this occasion the vehicle was a replica built over the body of an M4 Sherman tank. A genuine British Matilda II tank (known as the 'Queen of the Desert') can also be glimpsed briefly near the start of the movie.

This newer colour version of *Sahara* was virtually identical to the original, though one change was that the strafing Luftwaffe fighter was played by an Italian Fiat G.59 in German markings. The G.59 was a post-war development of the wartime G.55 fighter, and was powered by a British Rolls-Royce Merlin engine. Though it has never been released on DVD, the film crops up occasionally on satellite television and is worth catching.

Another excellent desert warfare film is *Sea of Sand* (1958), about the adventures of a Long Range Desert Group (LRDG) patrol just prior to the Battle of El Alamein. Coming out the same year as *Ice Cold in Alex* and filmed in the same locations in Libya with many of the same vehicles, this film is not as well-known as the John Mills picture but has a lot to commend it as it depicts the harshness of desert warfare. The plot concerns an LRDG patrol commanded by Captain Tim Cotton (Michael Craig), which sets off to destroy a German fuel dump in five Chevrolet trucks. They succeed in their mission but sustain several casualties. Eventually, the survivors head east towards the British lines in the sole remaining lorry. Some distance from the British lines, their transport runs out of petrol and they have to walk to safety, though they have to leave behind the injured 'Blanco' White (Percy Herbert) who volunteers to hold up the Germans with a dismounted Vickers machine gun in order to buy time for the others. Blanco is eventually killed, as is Captain Bill Williams (John Gregson) who sacrifices his life in order to save the other members of the patrol.

Another excellent film about desert warfare is *Tobruk* (1967), which starred Rock Hudson as Canadian Major Craig and George Peppard as Lieutenant Bergman and was directed by Arthur Hiller, who later helmed *Love Story* (1970). The plot involved a British attack on German fuel dumps and gun batteries in Tobruk, a few weeks before the Battle of El Alamein. In order to gain access to the port, the raiding British LRDG soldiers are pretending to be prisoners of war while their *Afrika Korps* guards are really members of the Special Intelligence Group (SIG), German Jews working for the British. On the way to their target the Allied convoy is strafed by an RAF Kittyhawk fighter and Craig's men are forced to shoot it down.

The main highlights of the film are a number of spectacular action sequences near the end where the commandos storm a gun battery and use a flamethrower to torch the inhabitants (rather like the scene near the beginning of *Saving Private Ryan*). German tanks arrive, but Lieutenant Bergman destroys some of them with satchel charges and a flamethrower before being killed while Major Craig and some colleagues steal a German tank and use its main gun to blow up the German fuel dump. The resulting sequence, with spectacular explosions, is a *tour de force* of miniature work and lead to *Tobruk* being nominated for a Visual Effects Oscar, though it lost to *Doctor Doolittle.*

Though the plot may seem far-fetched, it was actually based on a true incident – Operation Agreement, on 13 September 1942 – which did indeed involve members of the SIG infiltrating Tobruk while guarding commandos posing as POWs. The real operation was far less successful than the film depiction would suggest, as little damage was caused to Axis facilities and most of the raiding force was either killed or captured. In addition, three Royal Navy warships supporting the operation were sunk by coastal batteries.

Tobruk was filmed entirely in California and Arizona, with one of the locations being Buttercup Valley in Arizona which was also where *Flight of the Phoenix* (1965) had been filmed. The 'sea' which appears behind the gun bunker in some of the climactic scenes was actually a (man-made) lake near Los Angeles. Contrary to inaccurate reports on the internet, none of it was filmed in Almeria, Spain.

One of the halftracks in the film was subsequently used in several film and TV productions including *Midway* (1976) and *The Bionic Woman* (1976-78), and spent 30 years on the Universal backlot as part of the studio's tram tour. In 2007 it was rescued by collector Ron Leatherman and restored to original condition.

Four years after *Tobruk* premiered, much of the action footage from the film was re-used in a low-budget production *Raid on Rommel* (1971) which was filmed in New Mexico. Directed by Henry Hathaway and starring Richard Burton, this must rank as one of the worst films ever made. In order to use as much footage from the earlier film as possible, the plot was very similar as it involved an attack on gun batteries and fuel dumps in Tobruk by a group of Allied commandos posing as POWs. Rather strangely, *Raid on Rommel* has been released on DVD whereas *Tobruk* has not!

Another classic war movie which has never been released on any home entertainment format (at least in the UK) is *Operation Crossbow* (1965), which was directed by Michael Anderson and dealt with British efforts to counter the German V-weapon programme. In reality 'Operation Crossbow' was the name given to the RAF's own attempts to photograph and then bomb V-weapon sites, but the film implies this was the name for Allied espionage operations in this field.

With an all-star cast including George Peppard, Richard Johnson, Richard Todd, Trevor Howard, Tom Courtenay, Sylvia Sims, Patrick Wymark, John Mills, Jeremy Kemp, Anthony Quayle and Sophia Loren, and a magnificent score by Ron Goodwin, *Operation Crossbow* is a top-notch production. The special effects team included Tom Howard, who had won an effects Oscar for *Tom Thumb* in 1958 and later worked on *2001: A Space Odyssey* (1968). Howard had been responsible for the effects in *633 Squadron* (1964), but those in *Operation Crossbow* were noticeably better and included accurate depictions (both in miniature and using full size mockups) of V1 and V2 launches. To ensure accuracy, genuine surviving V1s and V2s were loaned to the film-makers and were used as patterns to produce detailed mockups of the weapons. One of the V2s which appears in the film was a real weapon loaned by the RAF Museum at Cosford. The same missile was also used as a background prop in *Light the Blue Touchpaper*, a 1979 episode of *Secret Army* (BBC, 1977-79). A reproduction V1 and launch ramp which was built for the film still exists and can be seen at the Imperial War Museum in Duxford, Cambridgeshire.

The first section of the film is unusual as it depicts the Germans' efforts to solve instability problems in the early V1s. Top German test pilot Hanna Reitsch (Barbara Rutter) asks for an enclosed cockpit to be fitted to the missile to enable her to fly it manually, in order to discover why V1s keep veering to the right. This is a goof. Towards the end of the war, cockpits and a set of manual controls were fitted to some V1s in an attempt to turn them into manned missiles, but the resulting craft were effectively suicide weapons and were never used in action.

This early part of the movie is almost like a documentary with the Germans as the 'heroes' and speaking in their native language with English subtitles. Reitsch subsequently survived the war, but was not such a nice person (or so glamorous) as the film suggested as she became a Holocaust denier and an apologist for the Nazi regime.

The middle part of the film deals with the Allies' efforts to get agents inside the Germans' secret underground factory and includes a cameo appearance by Sophia Loren, who was producer Carlo Ponti's wife.

One of the highlights of the film is a brief sequence in which a Spitfire chases a V1 in a vain attempt to shoot it down. I had always assumed this scene was achieved using a miniature, but in his book *Flying Film Stars* (2014) author Mark Ashley suggests that the sequence was shot from a camera helicopter using a modified radio-controlled Jindivik target drone, with a simple streamer attached to the tail being used to represent the flames emitting from the V1s engine.

The film ends with RAF Lancasters bombing the Germans' underground V-weapons plant, which was on the point of producing a long-range version of the V2 which could hit New York. This is a gross over-simplification of what happened, as the Germans had many underground factories all over Germany – not just one.

The Train (1964) is a less well-known action movie directed by John Frankenheimer, who was responsible for a number of highly innovative films in the sixties and seventies including *The Manchurian Candidate* (1962), *Seven Days in May* (1964), *Grand Prix* (1966) and *Seconds* (1966). The film is set in the summer of 1944. With the liberation of Paris and much of France imminent, the Germans plan to send French art treasures to Germany. Resistance leader Paul Labiche (Burt Lancaster) vows to do everything he can to stop this happening before the Allies arrive and liberate Paris. Eventually the film develops into a battle of wits between Labiche and German Officer Colonel Franz Von Waldheim (Paul Scofield). Shot in black and white, the film features several authentic train crashes which were filmed for real (rather than with miniatures) using some obsolete steam locomotives.

Another war film which features trains is *Von Ryan's Express* (1965), which might be described as a cross between *The Great Escape* (1963) and *The Train.* Based on the best-selling novel by David Westheimer, it deals with the story of USAAF Colonel Joseph Ryan whose P-38 Lightning fighter is shot down over Italy in the summer of 1943. Ryan is captured by Italian soldiers and taken to a POW camp full of British troops which is run by the evil Major Battaglia (Adolfo Celi) and the more humane Captain Oriani (Sergio Fantoni). He is soon at odds with the British commanding officer, Major Fincham (Trevor Howard), as Ryan declares that escape attempts are a waste of time because the Allies will surely arrive soon. His apparent cooperation with his captors leads to him being dubbed 'Von Ryan'. However, Ryan soon earns the respect of the other prisoners when he forces the Italians to give everyone new, clean uniforms simply by telling his men to burn the old ones.

Soon after this incident, the guards learn that Italy has surrendered following an Allied invasion and the guards set them free. Accompanied by Battaglia, the POWs walk out the camp and head south, hoping to reach the Allied lines. Unfortunately they are soon captured by the Germans and put on a train heading for Germany. But the POWs break free, take control of the train and hatch a scheme to use it to take them to Switzerland, and freedom.

The train nears Switzerland, but by now the Germans have learned what is happening and send forces to stop them, including a train loaded with troops and three Messerschmitt Me109s fitted with ground-to-air rockets (a weapon which the Germans never used). The German fighters were actually

Nord 1002 Pingouin IIs, a French-built version of the Messerschmitt Bf108, while some shots were achieved with miniatures.

The Messerschmitts carry out a rocket attack and manage to destroy a section of track in front of the train, stopping its progress, but Ryan suggests they remove undamaged rails from behind the last coach and use it to fix the track.

As some of the escaped POWs carry out these repairs, Ryan leads a squad of men to hold off the pursuing Germans as long as possible in a desperate rearguard action. Eventually the track is fixed and the train sets off towards the tunnel that leads to Switzerland... and safety. But as Ryan runs towards the rear of the slowly moving train he is cut down by a hail of bullets and dies. In David Westheimer's original book Ryan survives (and even reappears in a sequel novel, *Von Ryan's Return*, in 1980), but Frank Sinatra insisted that he should die at the end as it makes the film more poignant.

The movie was shot mainly in Italy with the final scenes being lensed in Spain. The prison camp was an outdoor set built on the back lot at the 20th Century Fox Studios in California, and was re-used in an episode of the TV series *Voyage to the Bottom of the Sea* (1964-68).

Another movie which is greatly under-appreciated is the 1965 classic *The Heroes of Telemark*. Produced by Benjamin Fisz and directed by Anthony Mann, the movie deals with Allied efforts to destroy German stocks of 'Heavy Water' (Deuterium) in Norway in 1942-43,thus thwarting their attempts to produce an atomic bomb.

Rather unusually, the movie was filmed in the actual locations where the real events took place, particularly the hydro-electric plant and factory at Vemork in Norway. Hollywood legend Kirk Douglas played the fictional role of scientist Rolf Pedersen while Irish actor Richard Harris was Knut Straud, who was based on Knut Haukelid – one of the actual saboteurs on the real mission, and whose book *Skis Against the Atom* was one of the reference sources for the film.

The first part of the film deals with the initial British attempts to destroy the heavy water stocks (Operation Freshman), which involved sending 50 commandos by glider to high ground some distance from the plant. In the film only one glider is used and it crashes, killing all the soldiers. In reality two gliders took part in the operation. Both crashed, and the surviving troops were killed by the Gestapo.

The Special Operations Executive (SOE) in London then orders an attack by a few saboteurs (including Knut Straud) which causes great damage to the plant and destroys the heavy water stocks. But the Germans eventually repair the facility, make more heavy water, and decide to move the heavy water stocks to Germany by train. There is a weak link in the plan though, as the train has to cross a fjord on a special railway ferry. Though the Germans are closely guarding the train, no-one has put soldiers on the ship. As a result, Pedersen and Straud manage to fit time bombs in the bilges of the vessel, timed to go off when the ferry is travelling through the deepest part of the fjord. The ferry subsequently sinks, putting an end to Germany's hopes of making an atomic bomb.

The scenes of the ferry sinking are particularly impressive, and were achieved using a 1/5 scale miniature which was sunk in the exact spot where the original ferry sank during the war. Some shots were also achieved using a full-scale mock-up of the stern of the ferry (including a locomotive) which was filmed in the huge water tank at Pinewood Studios near London.

The score was by respected film composer Malcolm Arnold. Rather oddly, the title theme appears to be recycled from the John Mills movie *Dunkirk* (1958) and was also used as incidental music for the 1954 BBC TV series *War in the Air.*

Another film which premiered in 1965 was *Is Paris Burning?*, which dealt with events leading up to the liberation of Paris on 25 August 1944. An entirely French production, it was mainly filmed on location and had an all-star cast which included many famous French actors from the period such as Jean-Paul Belmondo, Charles Boyer and Yves Montand. A few American actors such as Anthony Perkins, George Chakiris, Glenn Ford, Kirk Douglas and Orson Welles also appeared in cameo roles to give the movie international appeal. The key role of General Cholitz was played by German actor Gert Frobe, who had previously appeared in *The Longest Day* (1962) and *Goldfinger* (1964). Kirk Douglas was reportedly paid $50,000 for just one day's work on the film.

The plot was relatively simple. By August 1944 the Allied Forces had broken out of Normandy and were rapidly advancing through France. Their original plan was to bypass Paris and head for Germany, but the French Resistance and Free French leader General Charles De Gaulle eventually persuades them to send some forces to liberate Paris. Substantial forces head for the French capital, led by a Free French armoured column under the command of General LeClerc. After some street fighting, Paris is taken and General Cholitz is persuaded by Swedish consul Raoul Nordling (Orson Welles) that he should defy Hitler's orders and surrender without first setting fire to the city.

The highlight of the film is a tank battle between Free French M4 Sherman tanks and German Panthers. The French

Army supplied 75 armoured vehicles for use in the production, including M3 halftracks and M4 Shermans. The Shermans were all late-war 76mm gun variants with T23 turrets, and were probably the very same vehicles which appeared in *The Longest Day* (1962). The Panthers in the film were all modified M24 Chaffees. Though they looked the part, they were much smaller than the German originals. The memorable score was by French composer Maurice Jarre, who also provided the music for a number of British and Hollywood films including *Lawrence of Arabia* (1962), *Grand Prix* (1966), *Doctor Zhivago* (1965), *Ryan's Daughter* (1971) and *Firefox* (1982).

Another war film which was based on real events was *Operation Daybreak* (1975). Directed by Lewis Gilbert, just before he made *The Spy who Loved Me* (1977), it told the story of the events leading up to, and following, the assassination of SS Reichsprotektor Reinhard Heydrich in Prague in 1942.

Most of Czechoslovakia had been occupied by the Germans in March 1939, almost six months before the start of WW2. Three years later the exiled Czech Government in London gave orders that Reinhard Heydrich must be assassinated, even though they knew that this would result in horrific reprisals by the Nazis. Accordingly a team of former Czech soldiers trained by the British Special Operation Executive (SOE) is parachuted into Czechoslovakia to carry out the mission. After Sergeant Jan Kubis (Timothy Bottoms) fails to kill Heydrich with a sniper rifle, Sergeant Jozef Gabcek (Anthony Andrews) comes up with a different – and very risky – plan. He will shoot Heydrich in broad daylight with his Sten gun as his staff car slows to take a bend in the middle of Prague, even though his vehicle is usually escorted by an armoured car. As a back-up, Kubis has a grenade which he can chuck into the vehicle.

Despite the riskiness of the plan, it almost works. Gabcek steps out into the road as Heydrich's car slows down and tries to shoot him, but his Sten gun jams without firing a shot (probably due to it being covered with grass to hide it inside a bag, though this detail isn't revealed in the film). Gabcek runs away, hotly pursued by Heydrich's driver, and eventually steals a bicycle to make his escape. Meanwhile, Kubis sees his chance and chucks a grenade into the car. It explodes, badly wounding Heydrich.

Heydrich is taken to hospital. Although his wounds are not severe, on 4 June he eventually dies from septicaemia caused by horsehair (from the car's upholstery) getting into his wounds. He is given a state funeral and the Nazis exact their revenge on the Czechs by raising the towns of Lidice and Lezky to the ground, killing hundreds of innocent civilians and sending many others to concentration camps.

The team of saboteurs hide in a crypt in St Cyril and Methodius Cathedral, but they are eventually betrayed by a member of the Czech resistance – Sergeant Karel Kurda (Martin Shaw) – who has lost his nerve. A few hours before they are due to leave Czechoslovakia by plane, a large force of German soldiers arrive at the Cathedral and lay siege to it. The crypt has a tiny slit which looks out onto the road – making it like a pillbox – and only has one entrance through a trapdoor in the roof, making it easy to defend, but the Germans eventually use fire hoses to flood the room. Just before they drown, Kubis and Gabcik shoot each other in the head.

The film contains a few inaccuracies. The real-life assassination of Heydrich took place on 27 May 1942, whereas in the movie it clearly happens in mid-winter. Replica Tiger tanks are seen during the Lidice sequences set in summer 1942, but this type was not yet in service at that point in time and was never deployed to Czechoslovakia. Also, the bomb used to kill Heydrich was a special anti-tank grenade, not an ordinary Mills bomb as shown.

Overall though, the movie is very gritty and realistic and features a haunting electronic score by David Hentschel. One might think that an electronic score would seem out of place in a WW2 movie, but it works beautifully. For some reason electronic tonalities can sometimes evoke a mood better than conventional musical instruments, as evidenced by Louis and Bebe Barron's score for *Forbidden Planet* (1956) plus the successful use of 'special sound' produced by the BBC Radiophonic Workshop for *Doctor Who* stories such as *The Mind Robber* (1968), *The Wheel in Space* (1968), *The Krotons* (1968-9) and *Inferno* (1970).

In 2016 a new film about the events surrounding Heydrich's assassination premiered. *Anthropoid* – starring Cillian Murphy and Jamie Dornan – had a higher budget than *Operation Daybreak* and was supposedly more accurate, but in my opinion it was a far inferior film to the earlier production. It was also made in 'washed out' colour which, as I explained earlier, has now become a cliché. What was also annoying was that the makers of the new film implied that this was the first movie to be made about this 'little-known' incident, when in reality it was actually a remake. In fact, *Anthropoid* was the *fifth* film to be made about these historical events, as there had been three films about this topic which preceded *Operation Daybreak*: namely *Hangmen Also Die* (1943), *Hitler's Madman* (1943) and the Czech film *Atentat* (1964), plus several TV documentaries. But it is *Operation Daybreak* which to me is the most entertaining film to be made about this event, and therefore merits consideration as a forgotten classic. The film was based on the book *Seven Men at Daybreak* by Alan Burgess, and was filmed in and around Prague in 1975.

APPENDIX I

Military vehicles and artillery used in *A Bridge Too Far* (1977)

All vehicles supplied by Charles Mann, Bapty and Co. and the 1939-45 Group unless otherwise indicated

Type	Number Used	Supplied by
Willys MB Jeep	20	
Jeep Trailers	6	
Airborne trailer	1	
Para/cart trailer	1	
Willys MB Jeep (expendable)	3	
Dodge Command Car	1	
Dodge Weapons Carrier	3	
Dodge Ambulance	1	
GMC 6 x 6 truck	2	
Chevrolet 1.5 tonner	1	
Dodge Recovery vehicle	1	
Diamond T wrecker	1	
Clark Airfield tractor	1	
Plymouth Sedan Staff Car	2	
Harley Davidson motorcycles	2	
Bren Gun carrier	5	

Type	Number Used	Supplied by
T16 carrier	1	
M5 halftracks	7	
White Scout Car	1	
Humber Armoured Car	2	
Daimler Armoured Car	1	
Daimler Scout Car	4	
Scammell Recovery Vehicle	2	
Ford WOT 6 3-tonner	1	
Bedford QL Trooper	1	
Bedford QL GS Truck	2	
Bedford QL (expendable)	1	
Bedford MWD truck	1	
Morris 15 cwt CS 8	1	
Austin K2	1	
Austin K2 Ambulance	2	
Bedford OYC bowser	1	
Didge D15 water tanker	1	
Chevrolet C8 A/1C5	1	
Humber heavy utility	1	
Bedford OY NAAFI tea-van	1	
Humber Staff Car	1	
BSA M20 motorcycles	3	
Royal Enfield 350 motorbikes	2	
Matchless motorcycle	1	
Welbike motorcycle	1	
Battery of Dutch 25-pounders	?	
6 pounder anti-tank gun	3	
Bofors 40mm AA gun	2	
Sherman tank 105mm	1	Dutch Army (Converted to Firefly)

Type	Number Used	Supplied by
Sherman bulldozer	1	Dutch Army (Fitted with fibreglass Firefly turret)
Sherman tank towable hulk	1	Dutch Army
Sherman tank towable hulk	1	Dutch Army
Sherman Firefly	1	Ecole De Troupes
Sherman 105mm	1	Ecole De Troupes (Converted to Firefly)
Sherman Firefly	1	Royal Army Museum (Brussels)
Sherman 76mm	2	Belgian Army
Fibreglass Sherman replica	5	Charles Mann
M24 hulk	1	Dutch Army
M47 hulk	1	Dutch Army
M10 hulk	1	Dutch Army

German Vehicles

Horch Staff car	1	
Mercedes Staff Car	1	
Citroen staff car	1	

Type	Number Used	Supplied by
VW Schwimmwagen	2	
VW Kubelwagen	4	
VW Kubelwagen (replica)	5	
NSU Kettenrad	1	
BMW Motorbike/sidecar	3	
Zundapp Motorbike/sidecar	1	
BMW motorcycle	1	
Zundapp motorcycle	1	
Krauss Maffei halftrack	1	
Demag halftrack	1	
Skd.Kfz.251 replica halftrack	1	
Sd. Kfz.251 replica (expendable)	1	
Marder II replica	1	
6-wheeled armoured car	2 (replica)	
4-wheeled armoured cars	2 (replica)	
Bussing-NAG 5-ton truck	1	
German Ford 3-ton truck	1	
Auto-Union Personnel carrier	1	
Opel Blitz Ambulance	1	
PAK 35 anti-tank gun	1	
PAK 50 anti-tank gun	1	
80mm Field Gun	2	
80mm Field Gun	3	
Nebelwerfer rocket launcher	1	
Panther tank replicas	4	Dutch Army (modified Leopard Is)
AMX self-propelled guns	4	Dutch Army

APPENDIX II

Aircraft used in *A Bridge Too Far* (1977)

Type	Identity	Supplied by	Role	Status (2017)
Douglas C-47A	K-685	Royal Danish Air Force	Paradropper	Seco Aviation USA
Douglas C-47A	K-687	Royal Danish Air Force	Paradropper	Extant: Dansk
Douglas C-47A	K-688	Royal Danish Air Force	Paradropper	Stored: Soesterberg
Douglas C-47A	DO-4	Finnish Air Force	Paradropper	Extant: Keski-Soemen
Douglas C-47A	DO-7	Finnish Air Force	Paradropper	Crashed, 29/09/96
Douglas C-47A	DO-10	Finnish Air Force	Paradropper	Crashed, 07/10/78
Douglas C-47A	Do-12	Finnish Air Force	Paradropper	Saber Aviation, USA
Douglas C-47B	N9983Q	Vision Air Ex-Portuguese AF & Camera Ship	Paradropper	Derelict: Addis Adaba
Douglas C-47B	N9985Q	Vision Air Ex-Air Djibouti	Paradropper	Scrapped

Type	Identity	Supplied by	Role	Status (2017)
Douglas C-47B	N9986Q	Vision Air Ex-Air Djibouti	Paradropper	Scrapped
Douglas C-53D	N9984Q	Vision Air Ex-Portuguese AF	Paradropper	Stored: Ndjili
Supermarine Spitfire IX	MH434	Adrian Swire	PR Spitfire	Old Flying Machine Company, Duxford UK
Auster III	PH-NGK	Stichting Vliegsport	Light Transport	Extant: Gilze-Rijen, NL
N.A. Harvard IIb	B-64	Koninklijke Luchtmacht	Typhoon HF-J	Extant: Gilze-Rijen, NL
N.A. Harvard IIb	B-118	Koninklijke Luchtmacht HF-N	Typhoon	Extant: Gilze-Rijen, NL
N.A. Harvard IIb	B-135	Stichting Vliegsport	Typhoon HF-L	Crashed
N.A. Harvard IIb	B-59	Stichting Vliegsport	Typhoon HF-S	Extant: Gilze-Rijen, NL

Note: The Harvards appear as P-47 Thunderbolts and Hawker Typhoons in different scenes. Six replicas of Airspeed Horsa gliders were also constructed for the film, plus some two-dimensional painted cutouts.

APPENDIX III

Vehicles and artillery acquired for use in *Saving Private Ryan* (1998)

Type	Number acquired	Notes
American Equipment		
Harley-Davidson Motorcycles	5	None used
Willys MB Jeep	9	
Buick Staff car	1	
Dodge Command Cars	5	Only two used
Dodge Weapons Carriers	5	Only three used
Dodge Staff Cars	3	
GMC 6-wheeled 2.5 ton trucks	20	
Dodge Ambulance	2	
White M3 halftracks	2	
M4 Sherman	2	Only one appears in final cut

Type	Number acquired	Notes
German Equipment		
NSU Kettenrad motorcycle halftrack	5	Only one appears in final cut
BMW motorcycle/sidecar	12	Only three used
Opel Blitz Radio van	1	
Opel Blitz truck	1	
Horch Staff Car	1	
Mercedes Staff Car	1	
VW Kubelwagen	5	Only one used
Steyr troop carriers	2	
Mercedes L3000 troop carrier	1	
Praga 6-wheel truck	1	
Mercedes L4500 truck	1	
Sdd.Kfz 251 halftrack	2	Converted Czech OT-810
Marder III	2	Both based on Panzer 38(t) chassis; One converted SA/M 43, 105mm
Panzer VI (Tiger I) Replica	2	Based on T34/85 tanks
Skoda 105mm gun	1	Used in beach defences
Flak 38 20mm gun	1	Used in beach Defences & Ramalle
150mm gun	1	Used in beach defences

Type	Number acquired	Notes
Panzerschreck 88mm	1	Used in Ramelle scenes

Notes: One Marder III was constructed using a genuine Panzer 38(t) chassis found in Czechoslovakia. The other Marder III was a cosmetically altered Swedish SAVM/43.

All vehicles and artillery were supplied by Steve Lamonby of Plus Film Services. Some period civilian cars were also acquired for the film, though most do not appear in the final cut.

APPENDIX IV

Aircraft used in *Saving Private Ryan* (1998)

Aircraft Type	Fegistration	Supplied by	Current status
N.A. P-51D Mustang	G-HAEC	Rob Davies	Crashed, 2011 Woodchurch Warbirds
N.A. P-51D Mustang	N167F	Scandinavian Historic Flight	Now G- SHWN; Shaun Patrick, Sharkmouth Ltd.

REFERENCES

Wikipedia (*en.wikipedia.org*) and the Internet Movie Database (*www.imdb.com*) were used as basic reference sources for all the movies mentioned in the book. The Internet Movie Cars Database (*www.imcdb.org*) and the Internet Movie Firearms Database (*www.imfdb.org*) were also used for all films except *Sink the Bismarck!* In addition, the following sources of information were used:

Introduction

Planes on Film: Ten Favourite Aviation Films by Colin M. Barron. Extremis Publishing. 2016.
ISBN 978-0-9934932-6-3.

***Sink the Bismarck!* (1960)**

All My Flashbacks by Lewis Gilbert. Reynolds and Hearn. 2010. ISBN 978-1-904674-24-5.
Flying Film Stars by Mark Ashley. Red Kite Publishing. 2014. ISBN 978-1-906592-15-8.
Model Ships Movies from 1960, on:
www.modelshipsinthecinema.com

***The Guns of Navarone* (1961)**

The Guns of Navarone by Alistair MacLean. Harper Collins. 1957. ISBN 978-0006-172-475.
The Making of the Guns of Navarone by Brian Hannan. Baroliant Press. 2013. ISBN 978-1-873586-04-4.
Flying Film Stars by Mark Ashley. Red Kite Publishing. 2014. ISBN 978-1-906592-15-8.
Model Ship Movies from the 1960s, on:
www.modelshipsinthecinema.com
Movie Classics: World War II Movies of the Sixties. Cinema Retro Special Edition. Number 6. ISSN 1751-4606.

***The Longest Day* (1962)**
Movie Collector Magazine. Article on Making of *The Longest Day.* Vol 1. Issue 6. May/June 1994. ISSN 0969-5842.
After the Battle. Article on Making of *The Longest Day.* Number 4. ISSN 0306-154X.
Flying Film Stars by Mark Ashley. Red Kite Publishing .2014. ISBN 978-1-906592-15-8.
The Longest Day Revisited. Documentary on the making of the film on *The Longest Day* DVD release.

***Battle of the Bulge* (1965)**
Movie Classics: World War II Movies of the Sixties. Cinema Retro Special Edition. ISSN 1751-4606.
After the Battle. Number 4. 1974. Article on *Battle of the Bulge.* ISSN 0306-154X.
Battle of the Bulge. Warner Brothers Cinerama promotional brochure. 1965.
Battle of the Bulge. DVD. 'Making of Featurettes'.
Website on special effects: www.nzpetesmatteshot.blogspot.com

***Where Eagles Dare* (1968)**
Where Eagles Dare. Movie Classics Special Edition. *Cinema Retro.* ISSN 1751-4606.
Movie Collector. Feature on *Where Eagles Dare.* Volume 2. Issue 1. 1994.
Movie Collector. Feature on *Where Eagles Dare.* Volume 2. Issue 2. 1994.
De Agostini special release of *Where Eagles Dare* on DVD. 2004. Production Notes.
Where Eagles Dare. Soundtrack CD. Production notes.
Where Eagles Dare by Alistair MacLean. Harper Collins. 1967. ISBN 0-00-615804-8.

The Bridge at Remagen **(1969)**

Cinema Retro. Volume 11. Issue 33. Article on the making of *The Bridge at Remagen* by Steven Jay Rubin. Part 1. ISSN 1751-4606.
Cinema Retro. Volume 12. Issue 34. Article on Making of *The Bridge at Remagen* by Steven Jay Rubin. Part 2. ISSN 1751-4606.
A Fortunate Life by Robert Vaughn. Thomas Dunne Books. 2008. Chapter 11: *A Prague Summer.* ISBN-13: 978-0-312-37112-8. ISBN-10: 312-37112-8.

Kelly's Heroes **(1970)**

Cinema Retro Movie Classics Special Edition on *Kelly's Heroes.* Issue No.3. ISSN 1751-4606.
Classic Military Vehicle. Article on filming of *Fury.* Key Publishing. Issue 163. December 2014.
Myths of American Armor. Presentation by Nicholas Moran. Available to view on YouTube.

The Eagle Has Landed **(1976)**

Flying Film Stars by Mark Ashley. Red Kite Publishing. 2014. ISBN 978-1-906592-15-8.
Photoplay Film Monthly. May 1977. Article on making of *The Eagle Has Landed.*
Website on MTB 102: www.mtb102.com

A Bridge Too Far **(1977)**

Flying Film Stars by Mark Ashley. Red Kite Publishing. 2014. ISBN 978-1-906592-15-8.
The Arnhem Report. TV Documentary. ITV. 1977. Narrated by Iain Johnstone. Available on YouTube.
The Arnhem Report: The Story Behind A Bridge Too Far by Iain Johnstone. W.H. Allen & Co Ltd. 1977. ISBN 0-352-39775-6.
After the Battle Magazine. Article on the making of *A Bridge Too Far.* Number 17. 1977. ISSN 0306-154X.
Arnhem Airborne Assault 1944. Key Publishing Special Edition. 2014.

Story of A Bridge Too Far by William Goldman. Coronet Books. 1977. ISBN 978-034-022-3406.

Saving Private Ryan **(1998)**

After the Battle Magazine. Article on the making of *Saving Private Ryan*. Number 103. 1998.
Saving Private Ryan. Blu-Ray. Various featurettes on the making of the film.

Neglected World War II Classics

Flying Film Stars by Mark Ashley. Red Kite Publishing. 2014. ISBN 978-1-906592-15-8.
Movie Classics. Cinema Retro Special Edition. ISSN 1751-4606.

INDEX

#

A

B

C

D

E

F

G

H

I

J

K

L

M

N

O

P

Q

R

S

T

U

V

W

Y

Z

About the Author

Dr Colin M. Barron was born in Greenock, Scotland in 1956, and was educated at Greenock Academy (1961-74) and Glasgow University (1974-79) where he graduated in Medicine (M.B. Ch.B.) in 1979. He worked for the next five years in hospital medicine, eventually becoming a Registrar in Ophthalmology at Gartnavel General Hospital and Glasgow Eye Infirmary.

In December 1984 he left the National Health Service to set up Ashlea Nursing Home in Callander, which he established with his first wife Sandra and ran until 1999. He was the chairman of the Scottish branch of the British Federation of Care Home Proprietors (BFCHP) from 1985 to 1991, and then a founding member and chairman of the Scottish Association of Care Home Owners (SACHO) from 1991 to 1999.

Colin has a special interest in writing – his first non-fiction book *Running Your Own Private Residential and Nursing Home* was published by Jessica Kingsley Publishers in 1990. He has also written around 150 articles for various publications including *This Caring Business*, *The Glasgow Herald*, *Caring Times*, *Care Weekly*, *The British Medical Journal*, *The Hypnotherapist*, *The Thought Field* and many others. He was a regular columnist for *This Caring Business* between 1991 and 1999.

Colin has always had a special interest in hypnosis and alternative medicine. In 1999 he completed a one-year Diploma course in hypnotherapy and neuro-linguistic programming with the British Society of Clinical and Medical Ericksonian Hypnosis (BSCMEH), an organisation created by Stephen Brooks who was the first person in the UK to teach Ericksonian Hypnosis. He has also trained with the British Society of Medical and Dental Hypnosis (BSMDH) and with Valerie Austin, who is a top Harley Street hypnotherapist. Colin is also a licensed NLP practitioner. In 1992 he was made a Fellow of the Royal Society of Health (FRSH). He is a former member of various societies including the British Society of Medical and Dental Hypnosis - Scotland (BSMDH), the British Thought Field Therapy Association (BTFTA), the Association for Thought Field Therapy (ATFT), the British Complementary Medicine Association (BCMA), and the Hypnotherapy Association.

Colin has been using TFT since early in 2000, and in November 2001 he became the first British person to qualify as a Voice Technology TFT practitioner. He used to work from home in Dunblane and at the Glasgow Nuffield Hospital.

Colin has also had 40 years of experience in public speaking, and did some training with the John May School of Public Speaking in London in January 1990.

In May 2011 his wife Vivien, then 55, collapsed at home due to a massive stroke. Colin then became his wife's carer but continued to see a few hypnotherapy and TFT clients. In late July 2015 Colin suffered a very severe heart attack and was rushed to hospital. Investigation showed that he had suffered a rare and very serious complication of myocardial infarction known as a ventricular septal defect (VSD) - effectively a large hole between the two main pumping chambers of the heart.

Colin had open heart surgery to repair the defect in August 2015, but this first operation was unsuccessful and a second procedure had to be carried out three months later. On 30th November he was finally discharged home after spending four months in hospital.

As a result of his wife's care needs and his own health problems Colin closed down his hypnotherapy and TFT business in April 2016 to concentrate on writing books and looking after his wife.

Colin's books for Extremis Publishing include *The Craft of Public Speaking* (2016), *Planes on Film: Ten Favourite Aviation Films* (2016), and *Dying Harder: Action Movies of the 1980s* (2017).

His interests include walking, cycling, military history, aviation, plastic modelling, and reading.

For more details about Colin and his work, please visit his website at: **www.colinbarron.co.uk**

A German Sd.Kfz 251 'Hanomag' halftrack, photographed by the author at the Tank Museum, Bovingdon, in November 2009. These vehicles appeared in *The Bridge at Remagen* (1969), *A Bridge Too Far* (1977), and *Saving Private Ryan* (1998).

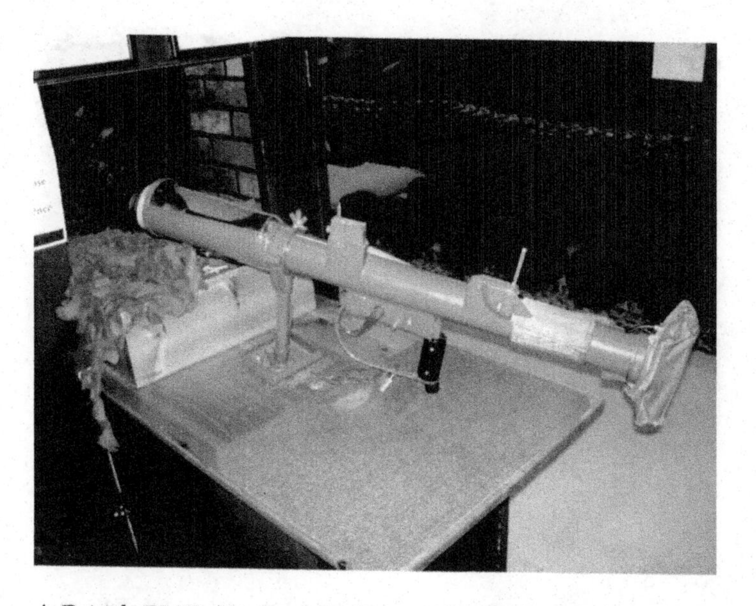

A British PIAT (Projector Infantry Anti Tank), photographed by the author at the Tank Museum at Bovingdon in November 2009. PIATs appeared in *The Longest Day* (1962) and *A Bridge Too Far* (1977).

The author standing in front of an M3 Grant tank at the Bovingdon Tank Museum in November 2009. The American version of this tank (the M3 Lee) appeared in *Sahara* (1943) and the 1995 remake.

Also Available from Extremis Publishing

Dying Harder

Action Movies of the 1980s

By Colin M. Barron

The 1980s were a golden age for action movies, with the genre proving popular at the box-office as never before. Across the world, stars such as Sylvester Stallone, Arnold Schwarzenegger and Bruce Willis were becoming household names as a result of their appearances in some of the best-known films of the decade.

But what were the stories which lay behind the making of these movies? Why were the eighties to bear witness to so many truly iconic action features? And who were the people who brought these legends of action cinema to life?

In *Dying Harder: Action Movies of the 1980s*, Colin M. Barron considers some of the most unforgettable movies of the decade, exploring the reasons behind their success and assessing the extent of their enduring acclaim amongst audiences which continues into the present day.

Also Available from Extremis Publishing

The Craft of Public Speaking

By Colin M. Barron

Public speaking is one of the most important skills in personal and professional life. Yet too often this key ability is neglected, leading to presentations which are dull, uninspired and poorly delivered.

The Craft of Public Speaking examines some of the crucial aptitudes which are fundamental to delivering an effective presentation for listeners. These include preparation, structure and rehearsal, in addition to some of the more overlooked aspects of oration such as the use of visual aids, adding humour, and dressing for success. As well as discussing how to deliver effective live addresses in public settings, the book also covers interview techniques for TV and radio along with how to organise seminars and conferences.

Dr Colin M. Barron has delivered hundreds of lectures and presentations to audiences during a long career, giving speeches on a wide variety of different subjects over many years. In *The Craft of Public Speaking*, he shares the essential knowledge that you will need to become a truly successful public speaker.

Also Available from Extremis Publishing

The Spectrum of Adventure

A Brief History of Interactive Fiction on the Sinclair ZX Spectrum

By Thomas A. Christie

The Sinclair ZX Spectrum was one of the most popular home computers in British history, selling over five million units in its 1980s heyday. Amongst the thousands of games released for the Spectrum during its lifetime, the text adventure game was to emerge as one of the most significant genres on the system.

The Spectrum of Adventure chronicles the evolution of the text adventure on the ZX Spectrum, exploring the work of landmark software houses such as Melbourne House Software, Level 9 Computing, Delta 4 Software, the CRL Group, Magnetic Scrolls, and many others besides.

Covering one hundred individual games in all, this book celebrates the Spectrum's thriving interactive fiction scene of the eighties, chronicling the achievements of major publishers as well as independent developers from the machine's launch in 1982 until the end of the decade in 1989.

Also Available from Extremis Publishing

A Righteously Awesome Eighties Christmas

Festive Cinema of the 1980s

By Thomas A. Christie

The cinema of the festive season has blazed a trail through the world of film-making for more than a century, ranging from silent movies to the latest CGI features. From the author of *The Christmas Movie Book*, this new text explores the different narrative themes which emerged in the genre over the course of the 1980s, considering the developments which have helped to make the Christmas films of that decade amongst the most fascinating and engaging motion pictures in the history of festive movie production.

Released against the backdrop of a turbulent and rapidly-changing world, the Christmas films of the 1980s celebrated traditions and challenged assumptions in equal measure. With warm nostalgia colliding with aggressive modernity as never before, the eighties saw the movies of the holiday season being deconstructed and reconfigured to remain relevant in an age of cynicism and innovation.

Whether exploring comedy, drama, horror or fantasy, Christmas cinema has an unparalleled capacity to attract and inspire audiences. With a discussion ranging from the best-known titles to some of the most obscure, *A Righteously Awesome Eighties Christmas* examines the ways in which the Christmas motion pictures of the 1980s fit into the wider context of this captivating and ever-evolving genre.

Lightning Source UK Ltd.
Milton Keynes UK
UKOW01f2137040118
315503UK00005BA/642/P